The Georgia Dutch

GEORGE FENWICK JONES

The Georgia Dutch
From the Rhine and Danube to the Savannah, 1733–1783

◆

THE UNIVERSITY OF GEORGIA PRESS
Athens and London

Paperback edition, 2012
© 1992 by the University of Georgia Press
Athens, Georgia 30602
www.ugapress.org
All rights reserved
Designed by Erin Kirk
Set in Janson Text by Tseng Information Systems, Inc.

Printed digitally in the United States of America

The Library of Congress has cataloged the hardcover
edition of this book as follows:

Jones, George Fenwick, 1916–
The Georgia Dutch : from the Rhine and Danube to the Savannah,
1733–1783 / George Fenwick Jones.
xi, 364 p. : ill., maps ; 24 cm.
Includes bibliographical references (p. 327–336) and index.
ISBN 0-8203-1393-9 (alk. paper)
1. German Americans—Georgia—History—18th century.
2. Salzburgers—Georgia—History—18th century. 3. Palatine
Americans—Georgia—History—18th century. 4. Georgia—History—
Colonial period, ca. 1600–1775. 5. Georgia—Emigration and
immigration—History—18th century. I. Title.
F295.G3J66 1992
975.8'00431—dc20   91-12878

Paperback ISBN-13: 978-0-8203-3941-2
ISBN-10: 0-8203-3941-5

British Library Cataloging-in-Publication Data available

Crown copyright material in the Public Record Office
is reproduced with the permission of the Controller of
Her Majesty's Stationary Office.

Contents

Preface .... *vii*

Acknowledgments .... *xiii*

One. The European Background *1*

Two. Arrival in Georgia *33*

Three. The Georgia Palatines *68*

Four. Acton and Vernonburg *86*

Five. Success at Ebenezer *114*

Six. Swabian and Later Immigrants *139*

Seven. Decline of Ebenezer *171*

Eight. Diaspora *193*

Summaries

One. Manna from Heaven and Earth *201*

Two. Health, Medicine, and Daily Life *231*

Three. Indians, Slaves, and Soldiers *258*

Notes *281*

Bibliography *327*

Index *337*

Preface

The term *Georgia Dutch* in the title of this work was chosen through analogy with the term *Pennsylvania Dutch*. Despite the windmills and wooden shoes with which some merchants in the heart of the "Dutch" country decorate their shops to attract tourists, better-informed people know that the term *Pennsylvania Dutch* designates the descendants of colonists from the South German linguistic area of the Palatinate, Württemberg, Alsace, German Switzerland, and adjacent areas. On the other hand, most Americans, even well-educated ones, are unaware that for a while the percentage of Germans in colonial Georgia was even greater than that in Pennsylvania.

Except for the religious exiles from Salzburg, the Germans of Georgia have received very little scholarly attention, mainly because the chief sources are locked away in German manuscripts not readily accessible to most Georgia historians. Also, the colonial records of Georgia were written mainly by men totally ignorant of the language and history of Germany, who normally anglicized German names, often beyond recognition.

This study is based primarily on the reports and letters sent back to Germany by the Lutheran pastors assigned to the Salzburgers at Ebenezer and now housed in the archives of the Francke Foundation, a charitable institution in Halle, Germany. Many of these were edited by Samuel Urlsperger of Augsburg in his *Ausführliche Nachrichten* and later in his *Americanisches Ackerwerck Gottes*. Other letters from the Ebenezer pastors, all in English, are preserved among the Colonial Office Papers in the British Public Record Office at Kew and in the Henry Newman Salzburger Letterbooks in the London archives of the Society for Promoting Christian Knowledge. Most of the pertinent items in the Colonial Office Papers have been published in *The Colonial Records of the State of Georgia*, and the Newman letters have been published by the University of Georgia Press. Still other information derives from contemporary diaries and letters such as those of Baron Philip Georg Friedrich von Reck, Henry Melchior Muhlenberg, Johann Christoph Bornemann, and Colonel Friedrich von Porbeck. Very little use has been made of secondary sources.

Many historians now champion "social history." That is to say, they wish to reconstruct the way that ordinary people lived rather than to commemorate only lofty individuals who performed great political and military deeds. This view is, of course, not new. It was expressed already, at least with regard to literature, by Adalbert Stifter, an Austrian author who was born in 1805 not very far from the Salzburgers' homeland. Stifter considered the growing of the grain and the twinkling of the stars to be more important than storms, volcanoes, and earthquakes. He concluded:

> Just as it is in external nature, so it is in the inner nature of mankind. A whole life of righteousness, simplicity, self-control, reasonableness, effectiveness in one's circles and admiration for beauty, combined with a serene and resigned death—these I consider great. Great passions, frightful thundering rage, craving for revenge, the inflamed spirit that strives for activity, tears down, changes, destroys, and often throws away its own life in its agitation—these I consider not greater, but rather smaller, since these things are merely the products of individual and one-sided forces, just like storms, fire-spewing mountains, and earthquakes.[1]

Judged by these criteria, the simple life of the German settlers in Georgia deserves to be recorded, however trivial their humdrum affairs may appear.

Johann Martin Boltzius, the first pastor of the Georgia Salzburgers, had expressed somewhat similar views, but only with regard to the priority of spiritual over secular matters. On 27 January 1742 he wrote that, while certain people were at first distressed by the behavior of some Salzburgers, they must be refreshed when they see what changes God has made in them, for "those are the true *magnalia dei* that God doeth in our days and to which we by rights should pay more attention than to other adventures and external worldly events in times of war and peace." This attitude explains Boltzius's choice of noteworthy subjects for inclusion in his journal. For example, he devotes far more space to the divine chastisement, repentance, and salvation of a sinner named Josef Ernst than to Oglethorpe's stirring victory over the Spaniards at Bloody Marsh.

A critic of one of my previous publications complained that I cited my sources too copiously, for it is "an historian's duty to summarize and interpret." With this I do not agree entirely: I consider it the historian's chief duty to discover, gather, verify, and consolidate the evidence, and let the reader draw his own conclusions. To learn about the eighteenth century, I prefer to read what a contemporary wrote, despite his quaint grammar and spelling, than to have a modern scholar give me his own twentieth-century interpretation. I hope the present reader will accept this view and read this work as a chronicle, not as an analysis. Perhaps I should apologize for the numerous and sometimes lengthy lists of names included in the text, which could just as well be relegated to the footnotes or appendixes; yet I find them more meaningful in the context of the narrative. An impatient reader who is not looking for an ancestor is free to skip over them and rely upon the extensive index.

My *Vorstudie* to this work, *Salzburger Saga*, was undocumented to keep it from resembling a dissertation. In this volume, every effort has been made to suppress footnotes, while retaining adequate documentation. Whenever the source is Boltzius's reports, I have replaced footnotes with dates. All statements clearly referring to Boltzius or the Salzburgers, if dated between 1734 and March 1751 but not documented, can be found under the pertinent date in the *Ausführliche Nachrichten* and also in the *Detailed Reports*, the English translation of the first sixteen volumes of those reports. Items dating from March 1751 through 1754 and from January 1759 through 1760 are documented in the *Americanisches Ackerwerck Gottes*, which is now being published as a continuation of the *Detailed Reports*. In the notes these three important sources appear as *AN*, *DR*, and *AG*, just as the *Colonial Records of the State of Georgia* appears as *CR*. Also informative, not only for the Moravians, is the Unitäets-Archiv (UA), or Moravian Archives, in Herrnhut, Germany. These and other sources can be found in the appended bibliography.

My endnotes deviate from those used by most historians and are closer to those favored by the Modern Language Association. In the case of letters, I do not give the names of the author and recipient and the date in the notes, since these, if significant, have already appeared in the text. Because there is a single alphabetical list of works cited, titles can be drastically shortened yet quickly found, far faster than in books that require the reader to look through pages of preceding notes or under several bibliographical headings to find the expanded form of an abbreviation. Successive documentations concerning a single person or event are sometimes consolidated in a single note. Nearly all events in the text are dated. Since the volume grew largely by interpolation, it was convenient to have every item dated so that new material could be inserted in the proper chronological sequence without constant research.

To give recognizable identity to the German settlers whose garbled names appear in the British records in varied spellings, their names are restored, as far as possible, to the correct German form. In many cases the spellings have been confirmed later from German sources. In those cases for which no confirmation has been found, the names have been reconstructed according to the philological principle of the *lectio difficilior*, or the more difficult (i.e., usually the more "German") reading. For example, if a man's name appears as Sliterman, Slyterman, Slighterman, and Schlechtermann, the last form is obviously the correct one, since no English scribe would have added the two *ch*'s and the unnecessary *n*. Likewise, of Ashperg, Aschperger, and Eischperger, the last is the most convincing, especially in view of the fact that many Georgia Germans were named Eischperger, but none was named Aschperger. (In both these cases, the correct forms of these examples were later confirmed by German documents.)

On some occasions the British authorities in Georgia translated family names, as in the case of Schmidt, Schneider, and Soeldner, which were rendered as Smith, Taylor, and Soldier; but that was exceptional. Christian names, on the other hand, were consistently translated, so that Heinrich, Friedrich, and Wilhelm became Henry, Frederick, and William. To remind the reader that we are dealing with German-speaking people, Christian names anglicized in the records have also been put back into their German forms. Most Germans in Georgia had two Christian names. If the first was Johann or Maria, as was often the case, the person was called by his or her second name, or *Rufname*; Johann Adam Treutlen and Maria Magdalena Gruber were called Adam and Magdalena, not Johann and Maria.

The English scribes generally wrote German names more or less phonetically, or else they just chose the closest English name. Sometimes there are so many different English renditions of a single name that it is impossible to ascertain the correct form, and in such cases the most frequent form has usually been chosen. For example, it is impossible to be sure what name is hiding behind the spellings Ubjer and Upshaw. A name like Nicholas Fisher would appear to be English, until it is noted that Fisher's will had to be translated from German; and a John Smith might appear to be English, until it is noted that he was a Lutheran and that his children were named Ulrich, Ruprecht, and Ursula.

Although this study treats only those Germans who settled in Georgia, it should have national historical and genealogical interest, for the descendants of these people are now spread throughout the fifty states of the Union.

Acknowledgments

I wish to thank the American Philosophical Society for several grants that allowed me to visit the Francke Foundation in Halle, Germany, to find and microfilm documents in the Missionsarchiv, on which I based the *Detailed Reports on the Salzburger Emigrants*, an edited translation of the reports sent back to Germany by the Lutheran ministers at Ebenezer. I am also indebted to the National Endowment for the Humanities for supporting my research at the British Public Record Office in Kew and at the Georgia Historical Society in Savannah and to the German Academic Exchange Service for supporting my research in the Hessian State Archives in Marburg. I especially wish to acknowledge the courteous and expert assistance given me by the officials and staffs of the above institutions, as well as by those of the Murhardsche Bibliothek in Kassel, the Moravian Archives in Herrnhut, and the archives of the Society for Promoting Christian Knowledge in London. I also wish to thank the many scholars in Germany and America who have kindly answered my inquiries. The University of Maryland, with which I have been associated for thirty years, has consistently encouraged my research.

The Georgia Dutch

◆ *Chapter One* ◆

The European Background

Nearly all of Georgia's colonial German immigrants came from areas which, like England, had once been parts of the Roman Empire. These areas had long been inhabited: both the Heidelberg man and the Neanderthal man had come from there, but of their lives we know very little. Archaeologists have learned something of the dwellings and artifacts of the various peoples occupying these areas in prehistoric times, but we know nothing of their languages and customs. Therefore we will concern ourselves only with the Indo-European tribes that occupied the region about a half millennium before our era. The earlier and little-known populations of these regions were subdued several centuries before Christ by Celtic tribes.

The Celts were one of the many peoples belonging to the Indo-European or Indo-Germanic family, which first occupied an area now belonging mostly to eastern Germany and Poland. About two millennia before our era, this language group began spreading out and breaking apart. Some fragments migrated to India and Iran, where they imposed their language on the native populations but finally blended with them racially. The same was true of those Indo-Europeans who later occupied Greece and Italy. One of the last groups to leave the old homeland was the Celts, who spread westward into what is now western Germany and Great Britain, southwestward into what is now southern Germany and France, and southward into Switzerland, Austria, and northern Italy. The center of their culture was Gaul, which included everything between the Rhine and the Pyrenees.

The Gauls were numerous, sturdy, and courageous but too independent and disorganized to resist the disciplined legions of Julius Caesar and his successors. As a result, within two centuries the Romans conquered all of

Gaul and extended their northern frontier to the Rhine and Danube. The old Celtic towns of Juvavum (Salzburg), Turicum (Zurich), and Mogontiacum (Mainz) became thriving Roman cities; and the Roman provinces along the Rhine and Danube were among the most prosperous and advanced of the empire.

For reasons still disputed by historians, the Romans gradually lost their pristine virtues. As in coastal Georgia a millennium and a half later, the yeoman farmers were largely replaced by slaves who had little interest in the republic's welfare. Besides that, the ruling classes became luxurious and entrusted their defense to mercenaries. Along the northern frontier, most mercenaries were Germanic barbarians from across the Rhine and Danube. The Germans were the last of the Indo-Europeans to leave the old homeland; but, while Rome was still a young republic, they too felt wanderlust and moved west and south, encroaching upon the Celts, until stopped by the Romans along the Rhine and Danube.

Rome's attempt to advance its northern frontier from the Rhine to the Elbe shattered in A.D. 9, when three Roman legions were destroyed by barbarians under a Romanized chieftain called Arminius, who, as a pretended ally, led them into an ambush in the Teutoburg Forest.[1] After that, except for minor face-saving skirmishes, the Romans retired to the Rhine and Danube, where they maintained their frontier for three more centuries. If we can believe the *Germania* of the Roman historian Cornelius Tacitus, while the Romans were growing soft, the Germans retained their barbaric courage and vigor. The Romans did succeed in extending their territory somewhat by occupying an almost depopulated area, called the Agri Decumates, reaching from the Rhine to the Danube, which they fortified with a wall and forts called the Limes, but even that they lost about two centuries later. The Agri Decumates happens to have been the area from which a large number of Georgia Germans emigrated.

Eventually the Romans degenerated to the point that they could no longer defend themselves even with the help of barbarian mercenaries. When the Goths threatened Rome in A.D. 410, the Romans withdrew their legions from Britain; soon thereafter Angles and Saxons from Denmark and northern Germany invaded and settled there, making England a Germanic country. Meanwhile, Franks had crossed the Rhine and occupied all the Rhineland, including the area later to become the Palatinate. The Alemanni occupied what was later to become Switzerland, Alsace, Baden, and

Württemberg, and the Bavarians occupied what was to become Bavaria and Austria, including Salzburg.

In occupying the old Roman Empire, the barbarians did not exterminate the native population but merely constituted a ruling class, whose language gradually displaced the Romance dialects in all areas close to the old homeland except in small enclaves such as Grisons in Switzerland and the Dolomite areas of South Tyrol. From the native population the invaders learned old Roman skills in agriculture and manufacture, and all but the warrior class eventually overcame their warlike scorn for labor. The Roman handicrafts inherited by the German invaders are reflected in many old Georgia names, such as Faber, Keller, Kessler, Kieffer, Kübler, Maurer, Metzger, Müller, Torkler, Weinkauf, and Ziegler.[2]

The Germanic invaders of Gaul also accepted Christianity, at least the outward forms of it, from the native Gallo-Romans. In A.D. 496 the Frankish chieftain Hlodowics, known to us as Clovis, converted to the Roman Catholic faith, and all his tribe followed suit. In the seventh and eighth centuries the German tribes that had settled in the old Roman provinces of Helvetia and Noricum were converted to Christianity by missionaries, first from Ireland and later from England. By A.D. 800 a Frankish chieftain, Charlemagne, united most of Western Europe into one Christian empire; but in 843 his grandsons divided it into three parts. The western area became France, which later absorbed much of the central section; the eastern part, along with the remainder of the central region, gradually developed into the Holy Roman Empire of the German Nation. It was from areas of the Holy Roman Empire, usually just called the Empire, that nearly all German-speaking settlers came to Georgia.

Among the pagans, religion had been a tribal matter. When Clovis was baptized, all his tribe were automatically Christian, and all dissidents were considered traitors. This religious policy was defined by the term *cuius regio, eius religio*, meaning that he who has the rule may determine the religion of his subjects. This law, reconfirmed in 1648 by the Treaty of Westphalia, had tragic results for Germany but benefited the colonization of North America. When Charlemagne was crowned emperor by the pope, the Frankish empire became closely bound to the Roman Catholic Church. Charlemagne considered the pope his chaplain; the pope, who needed protection from the Lombards in northern Italy, accepted his subordinate position. Subsequently, during periods in which the emperors were weak, the Church steadily increased its secular power until it wielded both the spiritual and the secular sword. Friction between pope and emperor was constant, culminating in confrontations like Emperor Henry IV's surrender in 1077 to Pope Gregory VII at Canossa. Throughout the Middle Ages, German rulers and poets alike ranted against the greed and secular aspirations of the papacy, which was draining good silver from the German lands.[3]

A break finally occurred in 1521, when Martin Luther took his stand at Worms. Luther's motivation was theological: he believed that the Roman Church had corrupted Christian dogma. Many of his backers, on the other hand, were more interested in freeing themselves from the inordinate financial burden caused by the avaricious popes, which was then being aggravated by the sale of indulgences. Luther's Reformation, which began as a popular national movement, was embraced by most of the northern states of the Empire and by most of the imperial free cities, those that had their charters directly from the emperor and were therefore practically independent. Naturally, it was opposed by the many church princes in southern Germany, such as the archbishop of Salzburg.

While the Treaty of Augsburg of 1555 recognized the Lutheran Church, it did not recognize Calvinism, the Protestant faith propagated at Geneva by the French reformer John Calvin. This new religious movement gained ground in France, Scotland, the Low Countries, and the western parts of the Empire, and it also spread into Bohemia and Hungary. Meanwhile, Huldrych Zwingli of Zurich had founded a similar faith that spread to most of German Switzerland, while the French Swiss became mostly Calvinists. Zwingli's dogma was so similar to Calvin's that the Reformed Swiss in Georgia considered themselves Calvinists. It is to be remembered that the word *Reformed* always referred to the Zwinglians or Calvinists, never to the Lutherans. Although Luther had initiated the Reformation, his movement was called Evangelical (*evangelisch*), or, in America, Lutheran.

Because of infighting among the Protestant princes, the Catholics, through the agency of Loyola's Jesuits, were able to mount a Counter-Reformation, which recovered much of southern Germany, as well as much of the lower Rhineland and Westphalia in the west. Fearing the well-organized Catholics, some of the northern rulers, along with the Rhinegrave of the Rhenish Palatinate, formed a Protestant Union as a defensive alliance; in turn the Catholic rulers formed a Catholic League. The cold war between these two hostile groups broke out into open warfare in 1618, when the Catholic party forced its religion on the Bohemians, who had introduced Calvinism and invited Frederick V, the son of the prince elector of the Palatinate, to be their king.

This young king of Bohemia, called the Winter Monarch, ruled with his English bride for only one hundred days. The Catholic army, mostly Bavarians, defeated the Bohemians at the White Mountain near Prague in 1620, and war raged almost continuously for twenty-eight more years until concluded by the Treaty of Westphalia of 1648. This treaty restored the old religious order, except that the Calvinists were now recognized along with the Roman Catholics and Lutherans. The various sectarians, such as the Baptists and Mennonites, were still outlawed and severely persecuted by all three recognized churches. After the Thirty Years' War all Germany lay prostrate, and the Holy Roman Empire was virtually defunct. As Voltaire later remarked, it was neither holy, nor Roman, nor an empire. France took what German territory it wished and dominated the remainder.

The Palatines

Although there were many Palatinates in Germany, the term *Palatinate* always referred to the Rhenish Palatinate (*Rheinpfalz*), a territory straddling the Upper Rhine, extending from its capital at Heidelberg in a southerly direction to Alsace and in a southwesterly direction to Saarbrücken.[4] Over the centuries, these boundaries, like all those in Germany, have shifted constantly as a result of battles, marriages, and treaties. For example, it will be seen later that eighteenth-century records place Weiher, the home of the Georgia Schubdreins, in Nassau-Saarbrücken in Germany, whereas Weyer is now in Bas Rhin in France. Sovereign states were considered the personal property of their rulers, who were free to dispose of them as they wished, regardless of the desires of their subjects.

During the Middle Ages the Palatinate was considered the wealthiest province of Germany, its proverbial wealth giving birth to the legend of the Rhinegold. The terrain and soil of the Palatinate are very similar to those of southeastern Pennsylvania and western Maryland, a fact that explains the attraction of those regions for eighteenth-century emigrants from the Palatinate. The flat valleys and gently rolling limestone hills of

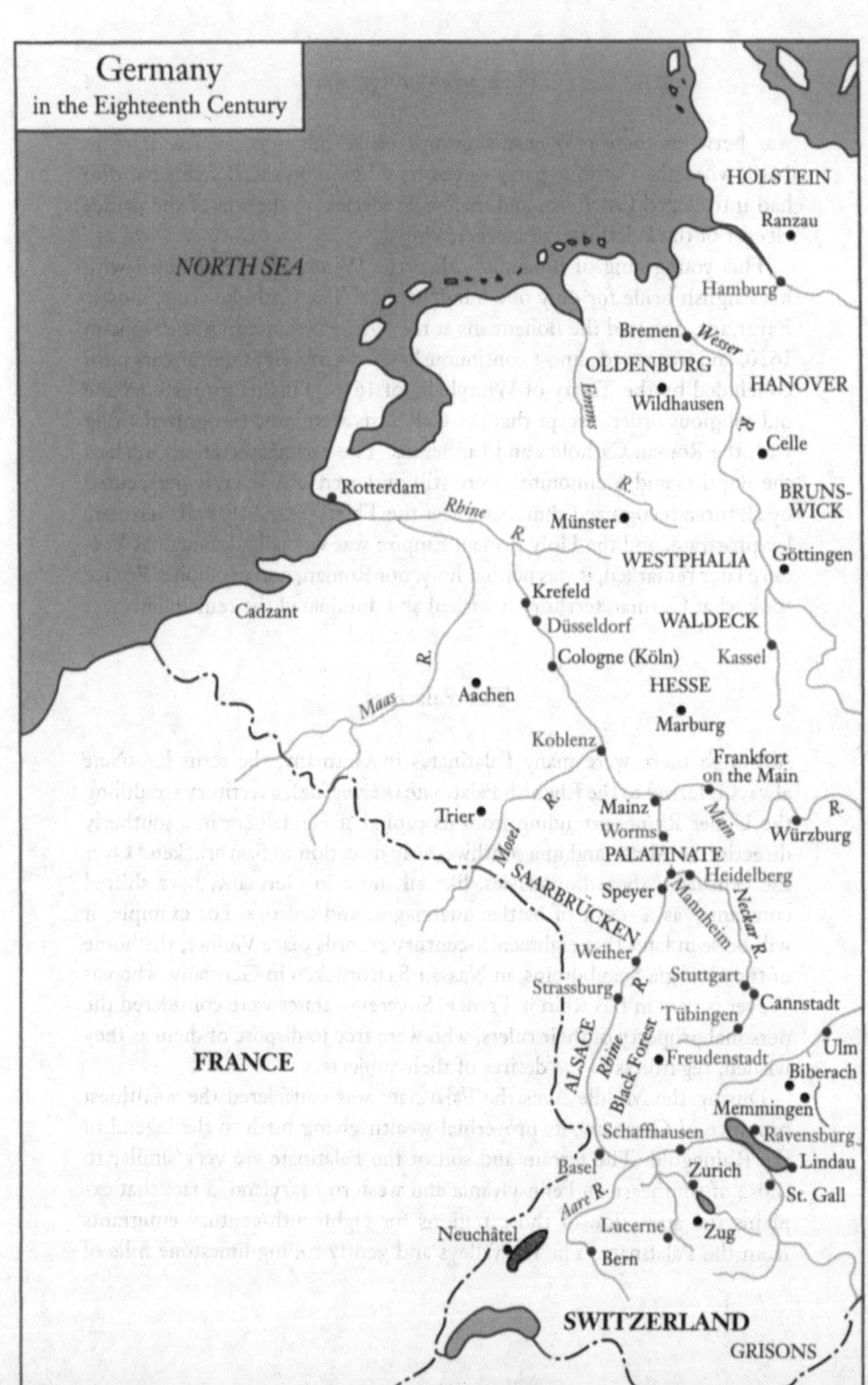

the Palatinate, now devoted almost exclusively to vineyards, were formerly planted largely in grain. Because the region is drained by the Rhine, its inhabitants were often designated as Rhinelanders.

The Palatinate's prosperity ended with the Thirty Years' War, in which the area was devastated by both sides. When the war ended, the land was so depopulated that its rulers invited emigrants from Switzerland, which had been spared by the war and had a surplus population. This mingling of Swiss and Palatines is one of the reasons why it is difficult to distinguish between the two groups in colonial Georgia. Many of the Palatines had Swiss names because their parents or grandparents had come from Switzerland. As we shall see, the Swiss and Palatines in Georgia felt a strong cohesion, due in no small part to their common Calvinist faith. French names were also very common in the Palatinate, because many Huguenots had found refuge there after the revocation of the Edict of Nantes in 1685.[5] This explains why some of the Georgia Palatines had French-sounding names such as Aingere, Belligut, Berrier, Dusseign (Tussing), Ferrier, Lion, Nobellet, Ragnous, Taissoux, and Tubear.[6] Huguenots from the Palatinate founded New Paltz on the Hudson, "Paltz" being the Palatine form of *Pfalz*. Like the Swiss and most of the Palatines in Georgia, the Huguenots were also Calvinists.

When Luther broke with Rome, the Palatinate supported him; but soon thereafter the count of the Rhine (*Rheingraf*) converted to Calvinism, and most of his subjects did likewise. As a result of French encroachment, his successors reverted to Catholicism for political expedience. While this did not result in any wholesale expulsion of Protestants, it does appear that life was sometimes made difficult for them, particularly for the professional classes.[7] On 12 March 1737 Johann Peter Hek, former *Stadtschreiber* (town scribe) at Pedersheim, wrote to Samuel Urlsperger, the senior Lutheran minister at Augsburg, to complain that he had lost his office after twenty-four years of faithful service because of his Protestant religion.[8] A *Stadtschreiber* was actually more than a municipal scribe and was sometimes equivalent to a mayor.

On 24 April 1737 some Palatines, having heard of the warm reception given to some Lutherans in Georgia, wrote to Samuel Urlsperger that they were being mistreated because of their Protestant faith. The forty-eight heads of family, representing some three hundred persons, saw no future in the Palatinate, where the Roman Church was expanding.[9] It is possible, of course, that some of these Palatines wished to emigrate primarily for

Mezzotint of Samuel Urlsperger, Senior of the Lutheran Ministry in Augsburg and Reverend Father of the Georgia Salzburgers (De Renne Collection, Hargrett Rare Book and Manuscript Library, University of Georgia)

secular reasons but thought this a good way to ingratiate themselves with the Georgia Trustees in London, who were known to champion distressed Protestants.[10]

Whether actually dispelled or not, the "Poor Protestants" of the Palatinate received much sympathy from the British: in 1733 Parliament allotted the Trustees ten thousand pounds "to be applied towards defraying the charges of carrying over and settling foreign and other Protestants." The Palatines in Georgia were even remembered in the will of Stephen (Etienne?) Lamolliere, a gentleman who died in Dublin on 11 May 1737 and left ten guineas to them.[11] From his surname, one might infer that he had once suffered as a Huguenot exile.

Even after the Thirty Years' War the Palatinate endured repeated undeclared wars waged by Louis XIV, whose strategy was to keep the area scorched to prevent its use as a staging area in case the emperor should try to regain Alsace, which the French had annexed illegally. The result was dreadful suffering on the part of the peasantry, who saw their barns and fields burned and their cattle driven off. Their misery reached its peak in the winter of 1708–9, the severest in Palatine history. Not only did much of the livestock perish, but spring came too late for any planting. With starvation staring them in the face, hordes of desperate farmers abandoned their farms and made their way down the Rhine and across to England, whose ruler, Good Queen Anne, was rumored ready to receive all distressed Protestants.[12] Because of such rumors, the British authorities in London were overwhelmed by some fourteen thousand unexpected guests. About three thousand Catholics were sent back home, and some Protestants were settled in Ireland, while many of the remainder were sent to New York and North Carolina. Those who went to North Carolina were settled there by a Swiss gentleman named Christoph de Graffenried, who founded a town that he named New Bern in honor of his native city. The town survived an Indian massacre; but, as soon as retaliatory expeditions had expelled the Indians from the surrounding area, many of the survivors moved inland because they found their land titles at New Bern to be questionable. De Graffenried had sold the grants to pay his debts.

The first group of Palatines in New York, under the guidance of Josua Kocherthal, prospered and founded the town of Newburgh on the Hudson. The larger party, some three thousand souls, lost more than a quarter of their number on the voyage over and were then ruthlessly exploited by the director of the naval stores industry for which they had been engaged. Some disgruntled Palatines moved up to the frontier at Schoharie, where the Indians gave them land; but there, too, they were cheated by the great landowners.[13] Consequently, some moved on to the Mohawk Valley, where they eventually flourished. Others, in the dead of winter, trekked to Pennsylvania, where they were kindly received by the Quakers. From then on, all German emigrants wished to go to the Island of Pinssel Fania, or Buensel Fani, as Werner Hacker has noted in his *Kurpfälzische Auswanderer*. Because so many of this first large German emigration had actually come from the Palatinate, all later working-class or indentured Germans were called Palatines, even if they were known to have hailed from Baden, Alsace, Württemberg, Nassau, Switzerland, or even from more distant areas.[14]

The Palatine exodus toward North America continued unabated despite gruesome reports of the hardships endured by the earlier emigrants both on shipboard and on land, and despite dreadful catastrophes suffered by many boatloads at sea. Two of the worst of these disasters, along with many minor ones, occurred in the year 1738. In July of that year more than three hundred Swiss and Palatines departed from England on the *Oliver*, which lost its captain and other officers and fifty passengers to typhus. The ship was battered by heavy seas and thrown off course; and, when it finally reached Virginia under the command of a common seaman, it went aground and was destroyed by the surf. Only a few of the passengers survived.[15]

Of 340 Palatines aboard the legendary *Palatine*,[16] which left Rotterdam in August 1738, nearly two hundred died of malignant fever and the bloody flux. Only 105 were still alive when the ship went aground on Block Island on 26 December, and fifteen of these soon died. Captain George Long died on the voyage, and his successor would not let the surviving passengers take their luggage ashore, which he held as payment for the passage of those who had died.[17] As we shall see, one of the Georgia Palatines lost his baggage on this ship; his luggage had gone aboard, but he and his family did not sail, since he was unable to pay their passage.

Two of the ships bringing Germans to Georgia fared badly: both the *Europa* in 1741 and the *Judith* in 1745 were afflicted by a fever that killed many of the passengers and crew. This was probably typhus, a disease so frequent on immigrant ships that it was called Palatine fever. Johann Martin Boltzius, pastor to the Salzburgers in Georgia, reported on 20 November 1749 that four hundred Germans had perished in a shipwreck off Port Royal.[18] Hardly more than two months later, on 2 February 1750, he reported that a ship full of sick Swiss had arrived at Charleston and that a Reformed minister named Johann Joachim Zubli had wished to visit them but was turned back by the stench of death.[19] Fortunately, not all tragic reports were true. The fourth and last party of Salzburgers reached America after a safe and healthy voyage, yet rumors spread throughout Germany that they had been reduced to cannibalism and that only a handful had survived.

Perhaps the best antidote to the craze for America was a little booklet published by Gottlieb Mittelberger, a Württemberger who journeyed to Pennsylvania in 1750 to serve as organist and schoolmaster. He returned to Europe in 1755 and wrote a treatise to dissuade others from making the trip.[20] Mittelberger gives a vivid account of the slow and difficult voyage down the Rhine, on which the poor emigrants are robbed not only by customs officials but also by all sorts of rascals, before being mistreated by the Dutch dealers in human flesh. Next comes the rough crossing to England, further delays, and then the long and perilous voyage across the Atlantic. The author spares no words in depicting "the pitiful signs of distress—smells, fumes, horrors, vomiting, various kinds of sea sickness, fever, dysentery, headaches, heat, constipation, boils, scurvy, cancer, mouth-rot, and similar afflictions," also "hunger, thirst, frost, heat, dampness, fear, misery, vexation, and lamentation," to say nothing of body lice and storms.

The disillusioned returnee particularly stresses the high mortality, especially among children, who must be thrown overboard to the sharks. He also relates the fate of many ships that arrive with few survivors, or do not arrive at all. He then describes the sufferings of those who are bought and of the even worse suffering of those who have to remain aboard because no one will buy them. He likewise tells of parents permanently separated from their children, whom they must sell to pay for their passage and who are often brought up without any Christian nurture and remain pagans. Even those who survive all these hardships and indignities are no better off than if they had remained at home in Europe, for they must do the heavy work of clearing forests for demanding masters.

Mittelberger is entirely convincing. It is clear that he is telling nothing but the truth, for most of the conditions he describes also appeared, in varying degrees, on the ships coming to Georgia and in the lives of the indentured servants there. He implies, however, that all these drastic conditions were typical rather than exceptional. This can hardly have been the case, or not many Germans would have reached Pennsylvania. Despite the widely publicized accounts of shipwrecks and of calms that led to death by thirst, starvation, and pestilence on shipboard, records show that the large majority of passengers arrived in America safe, if not always sound. When a German church register records that an individual or party left for the island of Pennsylvania in the West Indies, it is highly likely that the person or persons appear in later American records, often as successful and prosperous when judged by the economic conditions that they had left behind in Europe.

Mittelberger's bias can be explained by his purpose, which is suggested by the very title of his work: *Journey to Pennsylvania in the Year 1750 and Return to Germany in the Year 1755, Containing not only a Description of the Country in its Present Condition, but also a Detailed Account of the Sad and Unfortunate Circumstances of Most of the Germans who have Moved to that Country or are About to Do So.* The author dedicated this book to the duke of Württemberg and commended himself to the duke's continued high princely grace and favor. Since, as we shall see, the duke was then actively trying to prevent emigration from his realm, it was expedient, especially for someone who had had the audacity to go to America, to champion his cause.

It is ironic that, despite its stated purpose of warning against emigration to Pennsylvania, the book gives such a glowing account of the economic opportunities and civil liberties enjoyed there that all but the most timid would be tempted to risk the awful dangers. Mittelberger's only complaints against the country were the crudity and licentiousness of the inhabitants, who were free of clerical control. Such rough mores may have offended a sensitive organist and schoolmaster, to say nothing of the fact that an intellectual brought less on the redemptioner's block than did a muscular moron. Most prospective emigrants, on the other hand, would have welcomed the chance to live free of clerical restraint.

The Salzburgers

Salzburg, a small province lying in the eastern end of the Alps, is now in the Republic of Austria. It is drained by the Salzach, which flows north and northeast into the Danube. Like the Palatinate and Switzerland, Salzburg had likewise been part of the Roman Empire until conquered by Germanic tribesmen, in this case by the Bavarians. The pagans were converted by Irish missionaries, and later on Salzburg became an ecclesiastical state ruled by an archbishop. Because of the worldly nature of the Church at the time, most of the archbishops were as greedy and materialistic as any secular lords and devoted their major energies and wealth to erecting magnificent buildings to their own glory, all at the expense of their small peasant and miner population.

Luther's reform quickly reached Salzburg and gained many converts before being ruthlessly suppressed by the archbishops, who saw their secular authority threatened. While the new movement was successfully suppressed in the city of Salzburg and its environs, it survived in the remote valleys of the Pongau at the headwaters of the Salzach, where the peasants and miners maintained their Protestant beliefs secretly while outwardly conforming to Catholic practices. Most of the archbishops had been aware of the heresy in their realm but had preferred to ignore it, as long as the Protestants remained unobtrusive and productive.

In 1731, long after tolerance was becoming fashionable elsewhere in Europe, Salzburg's new ruler, Archbishop Anton Leopold Eleutherius, count of Firmian, resolved to rid his country of heretics once and for all. Urged on by the pope and by his own nefarious chancellor, von Rall, he signed on 31 October 1731 his notorious Edict of Expulsion, which required all unpropertied Protestants to leave within three weeks and for the remainder to leave within three months.[21] According to the stipulations of the Treaty of Westphalia, Firmian had the right to expel his nonconformist subjects; but he was obligated to give them three years in which to settle their affairs. He operated with such haste in order to give the Protestant princes no time to object or take action before he had rid his country of the heretics. He could also see that the Protestant sect was growing rapidly, and he wished to nip it in the bud. Later we shall see that some of the Salzburgers in Georgia were recent converts to Protestantism.

The unpropertied expellees had to depart in winter with insufficient clothing and supplies and with no destination, with the result that many perished. When the property owners followed a few months later, they at least had their wagons and some of their possessions, and they also had a destination; Frederick William, the Soldier King of Prussia, had meanwhile invited them to settle in his underpopulated provinces of Prussia and

Salzburger exile and son (Hargrett Rare Book and Manuscript Library, University of Georgia)

James Edward Oglethorpe, founder of Georgia (Hargrett Rare Book and Manuscript Library, University of Georgia)

Lithuania. Motivated by Christian charity and also by practical considerations, he arranged for the multitude of exiles to be led in small groups by parallel routes to his distant lands. The Salzburgers' property was not officially confiscated; they were allowed to sell it. The sudden dumping of so many farms on the market, however, depressed the prices so greatly that the sellers hardly covered their emigration tax and the costs of their armed guard and other expenses. Urlsperger tried to obtain some compensation for the Georgia Salzburgers, apparently without success.[22] A list of properties for sale was published in Salzburg in 1733.[23]

All Protestant Europe was thrilled by this manifestation of Christian fortitude. The Salzburger exiles were greeted enthusiastically all along their way, as recorded by many engravers.[24] As we shall see, an amazingly accurate account of their sufferings was already printed in London in 1732. A relatively small number of Salzburgers remained in the Protestant cities of southern Germany, and it is from this group that Georgia received its share. One group of Salzburgers, more specifically Dürrenbergers, found an unsatisfactory refuge in Holland; of these one family, that of Matthias Kurtz, eventually reached Georgia.

During the seventeenth and eighteenth centuries much English farmland had been converted into pasturage for sheep, with the consequence that many rural laborers found themselves without employment and without any commons on which to graze their cattle. This caused a migration to the cities, chiefly to London, where the rural folk lost their agricultural skills and where many joined the ranks of the depressed urban proletariat, useless to themselves and to the realm. Even the industrious and motivated of these displaced persons were often unable to find suitable employment.

Seeing the sad state of the urban underclass, a group of substantial and philanthropic gentlemen, among them James Edward Oglethorpe and John Percival, later earl of Egmont, resolved to found a colony south of South Carolina that would serve as a haven for these unhappy souls. Organizing themselves as the Trustees for Establishing a Colony in Georgia, they formulated grandiose and idealistic plans for their Utopian venture and set out to collect money. Receiving far fewer donations than expected, they turned to Parliament for assistance. Since not all members of Parliament were philanthropists, the Trustees stressed other aspects of their undertaking, especially the advantages Georgia would offer to the older colonies as a bastion against the Spaniards in Florida and to England as a source of raw materials for its home industries, as well as a way to rid England of its unemployable and burdensome poor.[25]

Unfortunately, these diverse purposes were somewhat contradictory. Unsuccessful city people were hardly fitted for clearing a wilderness, or even for defending it. The colony could, however, fill one of the goals of the Trustees, that of furnishing a "Comfortable Retreat for Persecuted Foreign Protestants and other Indigent Industrious Foreign Protestants."[26] By this time most Huguenots had already found refuge, and there were very few Waldensian exiles. Therefore the term *persecuted Protestants* most often referred to the Salzburgers and other Germans. Likewise, the term *industrious foreign Protestants* usually referred to Germans and German Swiss.

The first English colonists in Georgia, who arrived there on 12 February 1733, were unsuccessful folk from London, but not debtors as most history books would have us believe. The Georgia Trustees soon saw that these first inhabitants were not only too few but also too unsuitable for the strenuous physical effort required to clear the forests. The English in America had already learned that they could not depend on the native Indian population for labor, as the Spaniards could do in Central and South America only by brutal means. The Indians in Georgia were few in number, they were nomadic, and it was beneath the dignity of Indian men to work: if enslaved, they pined away, either from heartbreak or through susceptibility to European diseases. Besides that, slavery was to be prohibited in Georgia in order to protect the morals of the colonists. Since Protestant England feared Georgia's French and Spanish neighbors, who were Catholic, all immigrants would have to be Protestant. To be sure, some industrious rustic laborers were obtained from England, Scotland, and northern Ireland, but these proved insufficient. Meanwhile, word had come from New York and Pennsylvania that the Germans there were industrious and uncomplaining laborers. Many of them were used to the hoe and the plow and were more accustomed to physical drudgery than were the down-and-out populace of London.

One of the earliest entries in the journal of the Georgia Trustees gives a good overview of their whole Salzburger venture. At their meeting of 12 October 1732, Mr. James Vernon and Dr. Bundy advised the Trustees that the Society for Promoting Christian Knowledge wished an asylum to be provided in Georgia for the persecuted Salzburgers. The resulting resolutions are so informative and succinct that they deserve to be quoted in full:

Resolved
That the Trustees for establishing a Colony in Georgia in America do greatly approve the Proposal of the Society for Promoting Christian Knowledge for defraying the Expence of settling certain of the poor Saltzburghers in Georgia in America; And will readily join and concur in sending and settling so many of them, as by the Contributions which the said Society shall transmit to the Trustees, and What other Money the said Trustees shall for that purpose receive, they shall be enabled to send, and settle in the said Colony.
Resolved
That the said Society be desired to inquire by their Correspondents in Germany, in the Name of said Trustees, Whether any of the said Saltzburghers will be willing to become British Subjects, and to settle in the said Colony of Georgia, on the Terms to be offered by the said Trustees.
Resolved
That the said Society be desired to publish further Accounts of the deplorable State of the poor Saltzburghers, as they shall think proper; and at the same time to make publick the Design of the said Society, jointly with said Trustees, to supply such Contributions as shall be receiv'd for the Relief of the said Poor Saltzburgers, to the settling as many of them as they shall be able as British Subjects in Georgia in America.[27]

After thanking Vernon and Bundy for the pains they had taken, the Trustees agreed to the following articles for the Salzburgers:

1st. The Trustees will defray, so far as their Contributions will enable them, the Charges of Passage and Provisions for the Voyage to Georgia in America of such Emigrants, Tirnberghers, or Exiles from Bertoldsgoden, as are persecuted for the Protestant Religion.
2dly To all those Who want it some Allowance will be made for Tools.
3rdly On their arrival in Georgia Each Family will have Provision given them Gratis till they can take in their Harvest, and also Seed will be there given them sufficient to sow all the Land they shall in the first Year make ready for sowing.
4thly Each man shall be intitled to three Lots; Viz a Lot for a House and Yards within the Town, a Lot for Garden Plots near the Town, and a Lot for Tillage at a Small distance from the Town; Sufficient in the Whole to give a comfortable Maintenance to themselves and Families; And that they shall have the said Lands Freehold and their Heirs Male forever.
5thly They shall obey such Orders and Regulations for the maintenance of Property, Peace, and good Government as the Trustees shall think necessary from time to time to Establish; And on their Arrival shall assist Each Other in

clearing their lands, building Houses, and other Works as shall be necessary for their mutual Safety, in common with His Majesty's Other Subjects there.
6thly   That They upon their settling in Georgia shall become Denizens, and have all the Rights and Priviledges of Englishmen.
7thly   That They shall be protected in the free Exercise of their Religion, and in the full enjoyment of all the Civil and Religious Rights of Free Subjects of Great Britain.[28]

The Trustees then issued commissions for taking subscriptions for this worthy project. Unlike so many individuals and commercial agencies that contracted with German emigrants, the Trustees loyally fulfilled all promises to the best of their ability, which is not surprising in view of their being philanthropic gentlemen of means who had no intention of gaining personal advantage from the Georgia venture. On 24 January 1733 Benjamin Martyn, the Trustees' secretary, wrote to Oglethorpe that an invitation had already been sent "to Germany for the sending over Fifty Saltzburger Families, to be transplanted at the Charges of the particular Collection for those People."[29]

As indicated in their journal, the Trustees were collaborating with the Society for Promoting Christian Knowledge, a missionary society in London to which several of the Trustees belonged. Although this society had been founded to bring the gospel to the poor of England and of the overseas "plantations," as the colonies were then called, it had already played a large role in bringing the plight of the Salzburger exiles to the attention of the British public.[30] In this the group had been aided by the nationality of their king, George II, who was also the duke of Hannover and a loyal Lutheran, even though officially the head of the Anglican Church.

The SPCK, as the society was called, immediately made contact with Samuel Urlsperger, who was one of its corresponding members. Once engaged, the members of the SPCK were just as vigorous in their propaganda as any professional recruiters, as one can see in their letters of 18 May 1733 to Urlsperger.[31] By 25 April 1733 they collected between three and four thousand pounds for the Salzburgers.[32] Meanwhile, Urlsperger had published an invitation to the Salzburgers to come to Georgia, the title of which constitutes a long paragraph in true baroque style, beginning with the words *Georgia; or, A Short Report of the Christian Plans of the Royal English Trustees.*[33] The pamphlet was published in 1733 at Frankfurt am Main. The SPCK was blessed with a capable and competent secretary, a New Englander named Henry Newman, who served the Salzburgers loyally and kept a file of all their correspondence with the SPCK.

By 1733 the main expulsion had already ended, but there were still a few stragglers as well as small groups of Salzburgers remaining behind in southern German cities after the great mass of exiles had gone northward to Prussia. Urlsperger began recruiting immediately, and by August 1733 he had persuaded some seventy-eight individuals to go to Georgia; but some of these backed down despite much pressure, leaving only fifty-seven still willing to go.[34] These were housed in the Evangelical poorhouse in Augsburg until sent on their way on 31 October 1733 under the conduct of Baron Philip Georg Friedrich von Reck, a charming, but still inexperienced, young nobleman from Hannover.[35]

Von Reck, in a chaise, led his pedestrian charges along what is now known as the Romantic Way to the Main River, on which the party proceeded by boat into the Rhine and on to Rotterdam, being feted at every Protestant city through which they passed. In Rotterdam the Salzburgers met their new pastors, Johann Martin Boltzius and Israel Christian Gronau, two young Pietist instructors from the Francke Foundation, a charitable institution in Halle.[36] Boltzius was to be the Salzburgers' guiding light for the next thirty years in matters both religious and secular.[37] From Rotterdam the Salzburgers crossed over to Dover on the *Purysburg*, with Captain Tobias Fry. After a short sojourn in Dover they continued to Charleston and then on to Savannah, where they arrived on 12 March 1734 and were warmly welcomed by the local populace. Their passage from Augsburg to Rotterdam had been paid by the SPCK, while the cost of the remaining voyage was paid by the Trustees.[38] Before describing the Salzburgers' arrival in Georgia, it might be best to tell something about the background of other immigrants who were to join them there.

The Swiss

Like the Palatinate, the German part of Switzerland is drained almost entirely by the Rhine and two of its tributaries, the Reuss and the Aare. The Rhine arises near the St. Gotthard Pass and then flows northward along the eastern edge of the country, before bending westward into Lake Constance. The Reuss flows into the Aare just before the latter empties into the Rhine below Lake Constance and not far above Basel. The south of Switzerland is covered by the Alps, which, until recently, were scarcely populated. Consequently, there was little arable land in Switzerland, and the Swiss, like the Scots, had to be industrious and frugal merely to survive.

During the Germanic migrations Switzerland was occupied by the Alemanni, who moved in among the Romanized Celtic population and gradually forced their language and customs upon them, except in remote areas where Romansh, an old Latin dialect, still survives. Even though Switzerland marked the extreme southern limits of the German-speaking realm and was far removed from the original Germanic homeland, many old words and customs survived there long after being discarded elsewhere. For example, the old word *Ziesdig*, related to English "Tuesday," lingers there although replaced by *Dienstag* in most other German areas. Likewise, in half of Switzerland the word for pasture is *Matt* (cognate with English "mead" and "meadow"), whereas the standard word is *Wiese*. Johann Ulrich Giessendanner, a Swiss pastor in Orangeburg County, South Carolina, used the English words "Haymonth" for July, "Fall Month" for September, "Summer Month" for October, and "Winter Month" for November. These were his translations of German terms coined by Charlemagne to render their Latin equivalents.[39] Charlemagne's terms had long since been forgotten outside of Switzerland.

The Swiss were first converted by the Irish missionary Gallus, whose hermitage in northeastern Switzerland later developed into the city of St. Gall, which provided colonial Georgia with one of its foremost ministers. Like the Palatinate, Switzerland was at first part of the Holy Roman Empire, to which it still acknowledged nominal allegiance even after the peasants of the four Forest Cantons defeated the heavily armed knights sent against them by the Austrian Habsburgs at Morgarten in 1315 and at Sempach in 1381. Through alliance and conquest, the four Forest Cantons spread their confederacy steadily until it was free of the Hapsburgs and all other outside lords.[40]

Unfortunately, the Reformation divided the Swiss into two camps. Zwingli's movement won the cities of Basel, Zurich, Bern, and St. Gall and their rural territories but failed to win the original cantons and some other areas, which remained Catholic. Because of English policy, all the Swiss in colonial Georgia were, or claimed to be, Protestants.[41] At that time, the Protestants dominated the intellectual and economic life of Switzerland.

During the eighteenth century there was almost no social mobility in

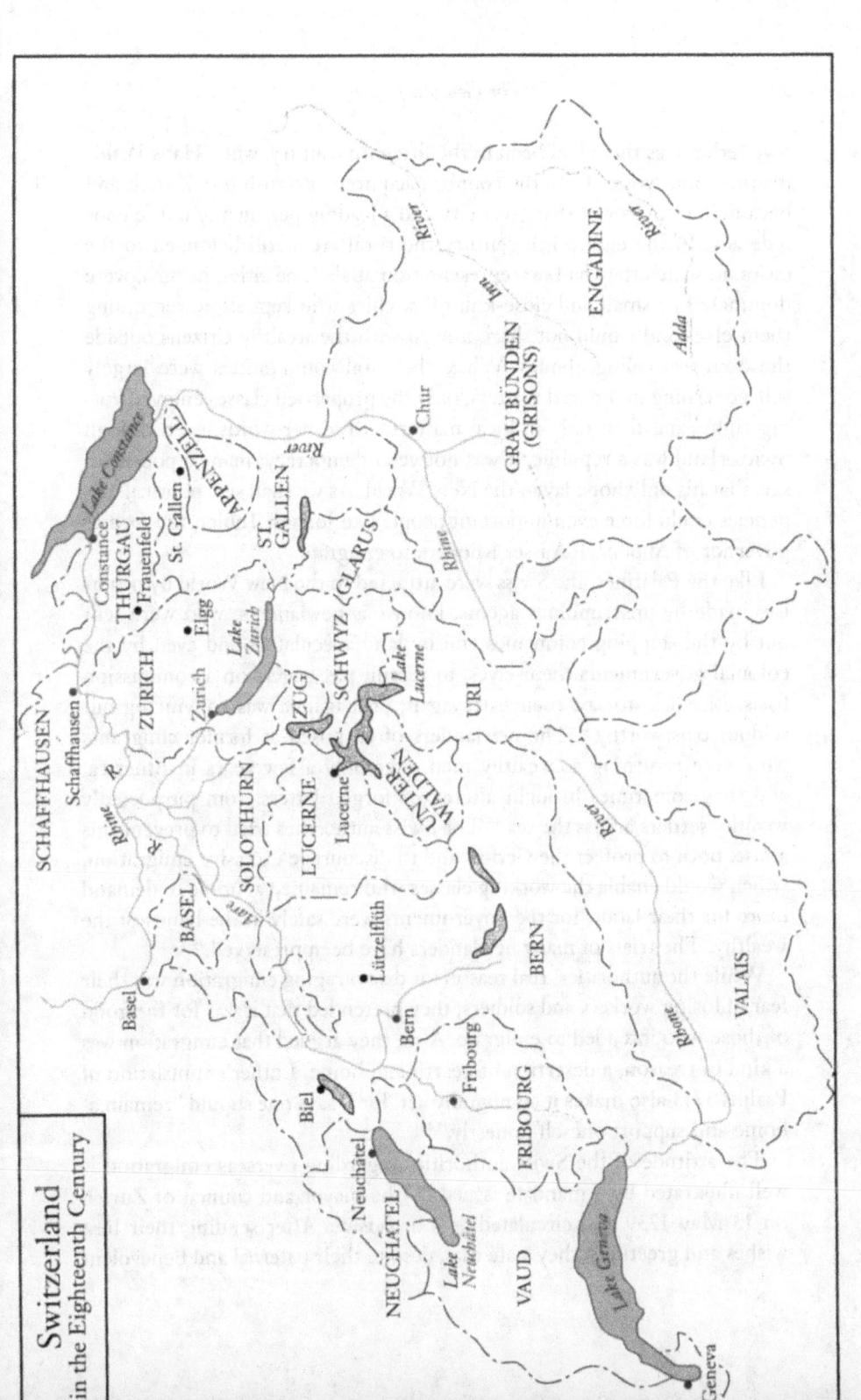

Switzerland, as there had been in the fifteenth century, when Hans Waldmann, a poor youth from the country, acquired citizenship in Zurich and became lord mayor of that great city and a leading personality in the confederacy. In the eighteenth century the rural areas still belonged to the cities, in which they had no representation at all. The cities, in turn, were dominated by small and close-knit oligarchies who kept all power among themselves and would not share it even with the wealthy citizens outside the exclusive ruling cliques. While the rural communities were largely self-governing in internal matters, only the propertied classes enjoyed voting rights and then only in local matters.[42] In other words, even though Switzerland was a republic, it was not yet a democracy; many a poor man saw that his only hope lay in the New World. As we shall see, political exigencies could force even important people like Johann Tobler, the former governor of Appenzell Ausser Rhoden, to emigrate.

Like the Palatines, the Swiss were attracted to the New World by promises made by unscrupulous agents, known as newlanders, who were sent out by the shipping companies and by land speculators and even by the colonial governments themselves, to recruit passengers on a commission basis. Needless to say, their extravagant propaganda was convincing but seldom trustworthy.[43] The newlanders often posed as former emigrants who were returning as wealthy men after only a few years in America, and they sometimes brought altered or forged letters from purportedly wealthy settlers across the sea.[44] The Swiss authorities tried to prevent this abuse, both to protect the victims and to discourage excessive emigration, which would enable the working classes who remained at home to demand more for their labor, for the governments were safely in the hands of the wealthy. The trials of many newlanders have been preserved.[45]

While the authorities' real reason for discouraging emigration was their fear of losing workers and soldiers, they pretended that it was for the good of those who intended to emigrate. Also, they argued that emigration was a kind of treason, a desertion of hearth and home. Luther's translation of Psalms 37:3 also makes it an ungodly act, for it says one should "remain at home and support oneself honestly."[46]

The attitude of the Swiss authorities regarding overseas emigration is well illustrated by a mandate issued by the mayor and council of Zurich on 13 May 1739 and circulated as a broadside. After sending their best wishes and greetings, they state that, despite their paternal and benevolent warnings, many inhabitants have persisted in immigrating to Pennsylvania, South Carolina, and Georgia, only to discover to their misfortune that the land there is poor and unsuitable for them. Many, especially among the children, have died on the way, others have been victimized by unscrupulous people, and still others have been carried away by sickness. Some survivors roam about the country as beggars, without even the comfort of organized religion and often exposed to sectarians. Some have returned home impoverished and have become a great burden to their communities. The authorities are therefore enjoined to repeat the mandates of 1724, 1735, and 1736, to warn against the dangers of emigration, and to forbid anyone from leaving without official permission. All emigration is entirely forbidden to anyone with young children, elderly parents, or sick spouses. Such people may not sell their property; if they do, it can be seized from the buyer. If they leave any property, it will be confiscated to help support any indigent kinsmen, and they will lose their right of domicile forever. Anyone recruiting emigrants is to be arrested and punished.[47]

The repeated issuance of these mandates suggests that the authorities had been unable to eradicate the *rabies Carolinae*, as the Carolina madness was called.[48] The Swiss continued to emigrate in droves. According to a letter of 30 November 1734 from Horace Walpole, the British ambassador at the Hague,

> There are fifty Familys of Protestant Swizzers come to Rotterdam out of the Canton of Zurich, with a design to go over to England and to be from thence transported to the English Plantations, and I dont hear that they have had any particular Invitation, or made any agreement with any body for that Voyage, and they are destitute of all Subsistance and Means, besides their own Craft and Industry, to get their Living, or to carry them forward. I have been spoken to about them, but as I have no Orders upon this head, I have absolutely refused to concern my self any ways in the Affair. In the mean time I find, they are at present supported by the Charity of the Magistrats and Burghers of Rotterdam, and as they are determined not to continue here, but by a sort of Enthusiasm seem resolved to proceed to ye West Indies, and as they have since their Arrival very much ingratiated themselves into the Good Will of this People, I am told, that a Collection will privately be made for them, to enable them to transport themselves into England, with which I thought fit to acquaint Your Lordship, that it may be considered what is to be done with them upon their Arrival there.[49]

The feelings and hopes of such Swiss emigrants are well expressed in a short memorial addressed to Lord Harrington, "one of his Majesty's Principal Secretaries of State in London":

> May it please your Excellency. We have been informed by a little Book printed in Bern that the King of England wants Maun that are brought up to country Buissiness and know to improve Land and make Butter and Cheese, in the Royal Province of Carolina wich as wee heard is a land flowing with milck and Honey, wee think ourselves happy to bekome the Subjects of so great and generous a King and usefull to the most charitable Nations under Heaven. We have sold our small Substance in our native country and meight have paid our expences But as wee were instead of fourteen days, fourteen Weeks upon the Rhine where the Armees have made all things scarce wee have laid out all our money and must now beg your Excellency to recommend us and our wives and children to the Kings bounty that he may send us to that blessed Country in the Two Boathes commandet by Captain Thomson, who has been so good to the Salzburgers while our Captain has been so hard to us and wee shall for ever pray that God may bless the King and his good people.[50]

Like so many of the emigrants, these were detained on the Rhine. We shall hear about Captain Thomson later.

It appears that not only the downtrodden and dispossessed caught the *rabies Carolinae*, if we can trust a letter of 30 August 1735 sent by Urlsperger to a Huguenot merchant of London, either Peter or J. C. Simonds, who forwarded it to Oglethorpe on 30 August 1735.[51] This letter stated that a Swiss gentleman, lord of a large territory, wished to move to South Carolina with a thousand families to found a Swiss colony there, for which purpose he would require three hundred thousand acres of land. Needless to say, nothing came of this fantasy.

In 1732 the government of South Carolina had commissioned Jean-Pierre Pury of Neuchâtel in Switzerland to found a Swiss colony on the left bank of the Savannah River some forty miles from its mouth at the highest point that the tides reach. An old hand at colonial promotion, Pury had little difficulty persuading enough settlers to accompany him.[52] These were not only French Swiss but also German Swiss and Palatines, as will be illustrated by a group of transients whom the Trustees met in London. Incidentally, most settlers from Neuchâtel could speak German,[53] because the city, which was also called Neuenburg, lay near the French-German linguistic boundary. Surprisingly, Neuchâtel was then the private property of the king of Prussia, although surrounded by the Swiss confederacy.

For his venture, Pury circulated a great deal of promotional literature.[54] Robert L. Meriwether states that among the Purysburg settlers were forty Protestants from Piedmont and twenty-five Salzburgers, but this is obviously an error, since Boltzius would surely have mentioned it if there had been any Salzburgers there.[55] Von Reck tried to obtain Waldensians for Georgia, but nothing came of his efforts.

On 25 March 1735 a Captain Quinche of Neuchâtel wrote to his nephew, Jean-Pierre Pury's son Charles, in London, that, even though the gentlemen of Bern and Schaffhausen would not allow the good reports from South Carolina to be printed in their gazettes, three hundred people had departed to go down the Rhine.[56] The senate had held a session to see whether it had the authority to stop them; but it merely resolved that they should be persuaded not to go but be allowed to go if they persisted. When asked why they were leaving, the emigrants said it was "the bad treatment of the bailiffs for the great part, but principally on account of the lack of fertility of their land."[57]

Captain Quinche goes on to say that it has occurred to him that a certain Stricker "had treated for their transportation with Messers Arnaud and Isaac Hoop of Rotterdam, not knowing whether it would take place. The desire to go to Carolina was so strong among our Swiss, if the king or some lord would be willing to advance their transportation, I am persuaded that in ten years all these uncultivated lands of this country would be inhabited. Mr. Laphart of St. Gall writes me often and asks me many explanations, apparently that he wishes to engage in some enterprise."[58]

One group of Swiss emigrants received and ignored a last warning against going to America. In 1735 a Swiss minister named Hieronymus Annoni journeyed to Rotterdam and met a boatload of his countrymen headed for America. As a member of the establishment, he tried to dissuade them from emigrating, but in vain.[59] Three years later, after John Wesley's disastrous sojourn in Georgia, Wesley met a group of Swiss at Neuss on their joyful way to make their fortunes in Georgia. Believing that God had put them into his hands, he "plainly told them what manner of place it was." If they were to leap into the fire with open eyes, then their blood was on their own heads.[60] Albert B. Faust has published a document excellently illustrating the efforts of the Bernese authorities to discourage a large group of emigrants and the reasons its members gave for refusing the good advice.⁶¹

Von Reck was one of the best propagandists for Georgia. Having left the first Salzburger transport in Georgia soon after arriving, he was so thoroughly convinced that they had settled in a fertile and promising area that he hurried back to Europe to get a grant for five hundred acres for himself and enough farmhands to cultivate them. The glowing reports he gave in Augsburg came to the ears of Johann Heinrich Labhart, a rather gullible merchant of St. Gall, who had delusions about developing trade with the British colonies. Labhart wrote to Urlsperger for further information and asked him whether he could send thirty Swiss settlers to join the Salzburgers; Peter Simonds forwarded the letter to Oglethorpe on 30 April 1735.⁶² Labhart's letter explained that some citizens of St. Gall had paid the way for three men of that town to go to Purysburg to see whether it would be a suitable place for them to send three hundred of the "poorer sort" of their inhabitants, both to give them a better opportunity and to spare the municipality the burden of supporting them. When Urlsperger read Labhart's proposal, he tried to dampen his enthusiasm.⁶³ Although the city of St. Gall had long belonged to its bishop, it had embraced Zwingli's reformation and become a free city and an important textile center.

Nothing was heard from the three scouts, who may have preferred to go to Pennsylvania and to forget those who had paid their passage, so now Labhart wished to send the people to Georgia because of the purported success of the Salzburgers. His naïveté is shown by his reasoning that Ebenezer was better than South Carolina because one did not have to clear away any trees: he was apparently unaware that the absence of trees in some areas where the Salzburgers lived betrayed barren soil. Believing von Reck's fanciful descriptions, he had calculated that his laborers could harvest two hundred bushels of corn per acre within five months after arriving and would need only one twentieth of this for their subsistence. Thus they would be able to sell the remainder northward. As soon as the advance party proved successful, the magistrates of St. Gall would send the remainder of the three hundred "warlike, laborious, peaceable, and experienced Men, provided with Pastors and prudent Leaders." Labhart did not realize that the indigent of his city were probably no closer to that ideal type than was the unsuccessful populace of London.

A far more mature suggestion was made by Johann Tobler of St. Gall, who wished to send thirty to forty Swiss with the Salzburgers.⁶⁴ Nothing came of this scheme, but perhaps some of Tobler's group were among the large party of Swiss that spent the night at the Salzburgers' settlement on 8 May 1737 on their way up the Savannah River to establish the colony of New Windsor.[65] A Swiss named Zuberbiller had tried to interest the Trustees in such a transport, but without success.[66] The travelers, who proceeded without the Trustees' help, were angry at their young conductor, Sebastian Zuberbiller, because he had written overly laudatory letters from South Carolina. They also complained that one of the Salzburgers, Ruprecht Steiner, had likewise sent an inaccurate letter that had been published and had persuaded some of them to undertake the calamitous journey. Boltzius, the Salzburgers' pastor, denied that Steiner's description was excessively favorable.[67]

A member of the Swiss party, Hans Wernhard Trachsler of Elgg in Canton Zurich, returned home some years later and gave a gloomy picture of the voyage to and the life in South Carolina. His account is detailed, accurate, and convincing; but he may have stressed the negative aspects to please the Bernese authorities, who were trying to discourage emigration.[68] Johann Tobler, the leader of the New Windsor settlers, remained in South Carolina and prospered.[69] Sixteen years later he wrote a positive, even though objective, account of the colony, in which he listed both its advantages and disadvantages.[70] Two years earlier Boltzius had written a factual and generally commendatory description of South Carolina and Georgia, yet he advised people not to come if they were well situated in Europe.[71] A group of discontented members of the New Windsor party broke off from the others in Purysburg under the leadership of an old engraver, Johann Ulrich Giessendanner of Toggenburg, whom they elected as their minister, and settled at Orangeburg in South Carolina.

Purysburg survived for almost a century, but it never prospered.[72] A certain John Rudolph Ochs wrote an undated memorial to the Trustees' successors, the Right Honourable the Lords Commissioners for Trade and Plantations, wisely suggesting that in the future Swiss settlers not be taken to the Savannah River but be settled in the mountains of North Carolina and Virginia.[73] This indicated either compassion on Ochs's part or an interest in directing future migration further north, in an area that he himself was trying to colonize.

The Württembergers

Swabia, the area immediately north of German Switzerland and across the Rhine and Lake Constance, had also been settled by the Alemanni. Therefore the respective dialects of German Switzerland and Swabia, Swiss German and Swabian (*Schwyzerdütsch* and *Schwäbisch*), were closely related. It was a Swabian dynasty, the Hohenstauffens, who brought the Holy Roman Empire to its greatest glory under Frederick I (Barbarossa) and Frederick II (Stupor Mundi). In the Middle Ages the strongest realm in Swabia was Württemberg, which became an important duchy.[74]

Württemberg supported Luther during the Reformation and played a leading role in that struggle. Therefore, although the Swiss and Württembergers shared a common tribal origin, they differed henceforth in religion, for the Protestant Swiss were Reformed, or Calvinists, while the Württembergers were Lutherans. Württemberg, as a political entity, had unstable frontiers, whereas Swabia was a tribal territory, whose boundaries have remained almost intact. All Württembergers were Swabians, but not all Swabians were Württembergers. At the time Urlsperger was aiding the Salzburgers, Augsburg was a free Swabian city. It is still Swabian ethnically and linguistically, even though it now belongs to Bavaria. The Lutheran church of Württemberg kept its independence. Being almost totally surrounded by Catholic lands, the Württembergers fought hard to defend their Protestant faith.

The legal and economic status of most peasants in Württemberg, even of those in the territories of the free imperial cities like Ulm, was similar to that of the peasants in the Palatinate. The result was that they, too, welcomed news about the unpopulated lands across the seas and responded enthusiastically. Many of them lived near the Neckar River and therefore had access to the Rhine and thus to the Atlantic and to America. The Georgia Salzburgers' triumphal march through Württemberg in 1733 must have sparked an even keener desire among restless people along the way to follow them to America. For some reason, true or otherwise, the Swabians have been thought to suffer from wanderlust more than all other Germans, and their emigration rate would seem to bear this out.[75] In any case, the rulers of Württemberg issued numerous rescripts against emigration and even persuaded the emperor of the Holy Roman Empire, Joseph II, to do likewise in 1768.[76]

Despite these efforts, Württemberg gave America more immigrants

The Imperial City of Ulm (© Stadtarchiv Ulm)

than any other German territory. According to an Austrian gentleman who visited Ebenezer in 1880, the German language of Effingham County had a touch of Swabian accent. He noticed this in the speech of the last surviving speaker of German at Ebenezer, an eighty-year-old Mr. Niess, who had been born in 1800 while German was still the language of Ebenezer Church.[77] Since the Niess family had come from Swabia, their pronunciation would not prove that all the people of Ebenezer in its last days had spoken with a bit of a Swabian accent; yet there are other indications that most of them did. The Swabian dialect is reflected in rhymes such as "Bei mir bist du schön, please let me explain" (which may have been of Yiddish origin) and probably by the spelling of the Georgia name Shanbacker (from Schönbacher).[78]

There were some Swabians among the Salzburgers and so-called Palatines who arrived in Georgia, examples being Leonhard Rauner of Hirnstein by Ulm, who arrived with the first Salzburger transport, and Hieronimus Salomo Ade or Adde, a shoemaker from Tübingen, who arrived with a Palatine transport in 1738. The great bulk of Swabian immigrants to Georgia arrived with the three Swabian transports of 1750, 1751, and 1752. Other boatloads of Württembergers landed in Georgia of whom we know less. On 7 October 1752 Boltzius heard that a ship full of indentured Württembergers was in Savannah, where the captain had landed because he knew that two other ships full of redemptioners had landed in Charleston and might have spoiled his sales. This was confirmed two days later.[79] There is no record of how many sales the captain made in Savannah.

◆ *Chapter Two* ◆

Arrival in Georgia

Even before the first Salzburger transport was recruited in Augsburg, the Trustees had become acquainted with German-speaking immigrants: the entry in their journal for 24 May 1733 states that "Jacob Winckler, Theobald Kuffer, Ludwig Koel, Henric Croneberger, George Mengersdorff, Andereas Winckler, & Nicolas Riger, German Swiss, being Labourers & Vine Dressers; Attended, and Received from Lord Carpenter, Mr. Vernon & Mr. Oglethorpe, Three Guineas towards furnishing them with Working Tools; They with their families being the first Germans that are to Establish the Town of Purisburg."[1] Here the people are first correctly termed German Swiss but then called Germans. As we shall see, the Trustees' donation to these settlers paid off in good public relations, for several of them later moved to Georgia. Elsewhere this gift is recorded as having been made to "Jacob Vinckler, and Six other families of German, Swiss, and Palatines."[2]

Such distinction between nationalities was unusual: the Trustees tended to give the name of the dominant element of a transport to all its members and to make no allowance for the minority groups. Most of the transports were designated as Palatine, even though many of the members were Swiss, while the passengers on the *Europa* were all listed as Swiss, even though a good proportion of them were actually from the Palatinate or Württemberg. Once some indentured servants were even designated as "Swiss Palatines."[3] Eventually the word *Palatine* could denote any working-class Continental emigrant: on 14 March 1765 Robert Nettleton petitioned Lord Halifax to assist some Palatine families consisting of sixty-two persons, all of whom had French names.[4]

As mentioned previously, many German Swiss had settled in the Palatinate after the Thirty Years' War and had intermarried with the native inhabitants. For this reason it is often hard to distinguish between them; for example, it would be difficult to classify two children of Swiss immigrants to the Palatinate, one of whom was born in Switzerland but the other in the new homeland. Even now it is often hard to distinguish between the Swiss and the Palatines mentioned in colonial records of Georgia. As we shall see, the eighteenth-century German Swiss allowed themselves to be called Germans. Today that is no longer the case, especially since the enormities perpetrated by Hitler. There are German Swiss (*Deutschschweizer*); but there is no such thing as a Swiss German, for which there is not even a German word. My apologies are therefore offered to Swiss sensibilities for the few times that this book subsumes Swiss under the term *German* in its broader sense of "German-speaking person."

Many of the so-called Palatines in Georgia had names with a distinctly Swiss flavor. For example, Christian and Margaretha Lewenberger, two Palatines assigned as servants to the Salzburger schoolmaster Christoph Ortmann, had the same last name as Niklaus Leuenberger, the famous leader of the Swiss peasants' revolt of 1653, who signed his name as Louwenberger.[5] Gregorius Stierle, who married Maria Rosina Hammer at Ebenezer in 1759 and was classified as a Palatine, was surely the Gregorius Stierlin, born in 1722 at Birmenstorff in Canton Zurich, who migrated to South Carolina.[6] Although Theobald Kieffer of Purysburg associated mostly with Swiss, he was a Lutheran and therefore very probably a Palatine or Württemberger. He was the Kuffer who received a gift from the Trustees.[7]

The British authorities in Georgia, like those in the other colonies, made little effort to distinguish between the various German-speaking nationalities but merely lumped all of them together as Palatines, Germans, or Dutch. The word *Dutch*, an anglicization of the German word *Deutsch*, was used of all German-speaking people. The term *High Dutch* was sometimes used to render *Hochdeutsch* in designating the High German language, the language of South Germany, which had become the standard. The Pennsylvania Germans were regularly called "Dutch," and even today some proprietors in Lancaster County decorate their shops and restaurants with windmills and wooden shoes, through either ignorance or the desire to capitalize on the ignorance of the tourists.

Because no Netherlanders are mentioned in this volume, the word *Dutch* will be used as in its sources, namely, to designate speakers of German, regardless of nationality, especially when it is not clear whether the reference is to Germans, Swiss, Austrians, or Alsatians. In such cases the word is, etymologically speaking, correctly used, because the word *Deutsch* originally referred to a language, not to a nation. While the English, French, Lombards, Andalusians, and Burgundians acquired their names from Germanic tribes, the Germans composed their term *deutsche Sprache* (German language) as a loan-translation of the Latin term *lingua vulgaris*, the "language of the people," which was first translated as *diutisca zunga*. Originally it meant any national language as opposed to Latin; but, being used only in German areas, it eventually came to designate the language of the tribes of North Central Europe. It is to be remembered that, generally speaking, a "Dutchman" was not a man who could speak German, but one who could not speak English. Once he had mastered English, he was no longer "Dutch."

When the first Salzburger transport arrived in Savannah on 12 March 1734, the immigrants were greeted by Benjamin Sheftall, a Jew from Frankfurt on the Oder, a city east of Berlin. Boltzius commented that Sheftall spoke "good German" (*gut Teutsch*), by which he meant that he spoke standard German, not Yiddish or the German-Jewish dialect. Sheftall and his wife, Perla, invited the entire Salzburger party to a breakfast of rice soup. Later, he came to the Salzburgers' tent to return some money, for he did not wish any "unjust property" to be in his possession. A Salzburger woman had made a purchase at his shop, and Perla, unfamiliar with the coin she received, had given too little change.[8] A year later a Jew, no doubt Sheftall, gave the Salzburgers some cakes and assured them of his continued help.[9]

During their brief stay in Savannah, most of the Salzburger men found employment in the forests and fields or on the waterfront, while an advance party, led by Oglethorpe, set out to find a fitting place for them to settle. Theoretically, the Salzburgers had complete freedom to settle anywhere they wished; but Oglethorpe led them to a general area strategic for a military post and then let them choose the precise spot. The site chosen was on a sluggish stream, later named Ebenezer Creek, which was assumed to be navigable to the Savannah River. Because of its rank vegetation, the surrounding land appeared fertile. Giving thanks to God, the Salzburgers named their town Ebenezer, meaning "the Lord hath helped so far." The word *Ebenezer* was sometimes translated as "the Stone of Help," which gave birth to the legend that the Salzburgers erected a stone to the glory

Map of coastal Georgia and lower South Carolina, circa 1741 (De Renne Collection, Hargrett Rare Book and Manuscript Library, University of Georgia)

of God. That would, of course, have been impossible on the coastal plain of Georgia, where there are no stones. As soon as the Salzburgers had set to work clearing the forest and building huts, Baron von Reck returned to Europe via New England, convinced that Ebenezer was a true paradise and eager to apply for a grant for five hundred acres in Georgia.[10]

Von Reck's faith in the future of Georgia was enhanced when he saw what astounding progress had been made in such a short time in Pennsylvania and the other northern colonies. His great enthusiasm caused him to travel about recruiting emigrants everywhere in Germany, including Bohemians, until the Trustees sent him stern orders to desist, since they had no money to support any more transports.[11] Von Reck then tried to associate himself with the Moravians, but they rejected him because of difficulties with Urlsperger.[12]

Aided by English sawyers, as well as by African slaves lent by Paul Jenys, South Carolina's speaker of the House, the Salzburgers made rapid progress in felling trees and building huts and bridges. They also attempted to grow a crop; but it did not take them long to agree with certain "ill-designing people," as Thomas Causton called them, who had warned them that the soil around Ebenezer was sterile sand, covered by only a thin layer of humus which would blow away as soon as the land was cultivated. Causton, a former wigmaker, was the "keeper of the stores" in Savannah, a position that gave him so much power that Boltzius thought him the mayor.

Ebenezer Creek proved unnavigable, being merely the outlet of local swamps and being blocked in places by impenetrable cypress knees before emptying into the Savannah River. Von Reck and Oglethorpe's factotum, Noble Jones, spent days trying to cut their way up Ebenezer Creek to the Salzburger settlement, but without success. An Englishman named Marmour succeeded in bringing a boat to within two miles of Ebenezer by 30 May.[13] Walter Augustine, another Englishman, finally reached Ebenezer by water, but he could not make Ebenezer Creek navigable for loaded boats.[14]

To make matters worse, most of the Salzburgers quickly sickened, and many died after contracting dysentery in the village of Abercorn on their way from Savannah to Ebenezer. The first death was that of Tobias Lackner, who died of dysentery in Abercorn.[15] The settlers had been promised immediate ownership of fifty acres as soon as they settled; but Noble Jones, in his capacity of surveyor, failed to measure out their lots, possibly because

Oglethorpe wished them to work the land communally. Since Ebenezer Creek had proved unnavigable, the Salzburgers had to drag all their supplies some eight miles from Abercorn, the nearest landing. Luckily, they had received the use of ten horses and could improvise sledges, but to use them they first had to clear a trail and build seven bridges.[16] Sledges, still used in the Georgia mountains in the 1920s, seem to have been introduced by the Swiss and Austrians.

Despite the Salzburgers' difficulties, Oglethorpe, who had delayed his return to England for their sake, had only positive things to say about them. On 2 April 1734 he wrote from Charleston that "the Ministers are very devout and the eldest is a very wise Man; the whole are a religious, industrious and cheerful People and in all probability will succeed very well."[17] Soon thereafter, in a letter of 27 June 1734 from St. Helen's near the Isle of Wight, he wrote similarly: "I gladly report that, on departing from Georgia, I left Baron von Reck, the two pastors, and the entire community of Saltzburgers in excellent health. They are a modest, industrious, cheerful and devout people." He then says that they plan to erect a stone to commemorate God's aid, this being perhaps the earliest record of that pious myth, which was surely suggested by 1 Samuel 7:12.[18] Captain George Dunbar, the Scots mariner who brought the first transport to Georgia and visited the immigrants at the end of the same year, agreed that the "Salsburgers particularly [are] still cheerful and are a pyus Sobir laborious people."[19]

Because the first news from Ebenezer had been so favorable, Urlsperger continued organizing a second transport even after distressing reports began to trickle in. A member of the first transport, a Bavarian distiller named Georg Bartholomäus Roth, or Rott, had the effrontery to cause another Bavarian, Matthias Braumberger, to write a damaging letter, which happily fell into Urlsperger's hands and was promptly suppressed.[20] The second transport departed Augsburg on 23 September 1734, approximately a year after the first. It consisted of Salzburgers who had found refuge in Memmingen, Lindau, Leutkirch, and Leipheim, and it was conducted by Jean Vat, a Swiss from the city of Biel who had been engaged by Stephen Hales on 1 June 1733. Vat was a mature and realistic man who sent informative letters along the way while in Europe and then from Georgia.[21] The captain of the ship, George Dunbar, praised both Vat and Gordon, the leader of the Highlanders on board his ship: "Messrs Gordon and Vat manage their people with so much prudence and good sense that everything is as orderly as could be expected and I think myself extremely happy on both."[22]

This second transport followed the same route as the first, except that it stopped off in London rather than Dover and was thus exhibited to a far larger number of spectators and donors. A brief account of the journey to London and the sojourn there is given by Urlsperger in his preface to the first volume of the *Ausführliche Nachrichten*. When the party reached Ebenezer, they found everything in a shambles. Many of the earlier settlers had died, and most of the remainder were sick. Vat did his best, but, although officially in charge of secular affairs, he had no control over the settlers from the first transport, who continued to take all their troubles to Boltzius.

While Boltzius and Vat were wrangling individually against each other and jointly against Oglethorpe, von Reck arrived with a third Salzburger transport. This transport contained few actual Salzburgers, but there were a number of Protestants who had been expelled from Upper Austria and Carinthia and had remained in Regensburg, the seat of the Imperial Diet, in hope of recovering their minor children who had been held back by the Catholic authorities.[23] Without permission, von Reck also picked up people in Frankfurt, London, and even Savannah.

The third transport arrived in Georgia on the *London Merchant*, with Captain John Thomas, having occupied what appeared to be the best quarters.[24] The *London Merchant* sailed in a convoy with the *Symonds*, on which were Oglethorpe, John Wesley, and a party of Moravians. The two passenger ships were guarded by a warship named the *Hawk*. On board the *London Merchant* the Salzburgers were entrusted to John Terry, a Frenchman actually named Jean Thierry, who took his responsibility most seriously and was later appointed recorder at Frederica, a city Oglethorpe was establishing on St. Simons Island just north of the Spaniards in Florida.[25] When the convoy arrived off Tybee Island at the mouth of the Savannah River on 17 February 1736, the Salzburgers' supplies were unintentionally sent to Frederica, where Oglethorpe had wished to settle them. The third transport was taken up to the Red Bluff, where they found everything in confusion. The Salzburgers had discovered the Red Bluff on the Savannah River at the mouth of Ebenezer Creek while gathering acorns for their pigs. Because of the presence of oak trees, they knew that the soil was richer than in the pine barrens where they had been placed.

As a good Lutheran, Boltzius first agreed with the authorities that the

Drawing of the first shelters on Red Bluff, from the folio of Philip Georg Friedrich von Reck, a young Hanoverian nobleman placed in charge of the first and third Salzburger transports. The original, of uncertain authorship, is in color. (Det Kongelige Bibliotek, København)

Salzburgers should remain where God had placed them; yet in time he realized that Vat, von Reck, and the Salzburgers were right in saying the settlement ought to be moved. In a secret confrontation with Oglethorpe, Boltzius demanded a removal; Oglethorpe was compelled to accede. Boltzius had already complained to Oglethorpe on 9 February 1736 about Ebenezer's poor soil and inaccessibility.[26] The two earlier transports removed to the Red Bluff, leaving all their improvements intact at Ebenezer. To maintain an appearance of continuity, the name Ebenezer was taken along to the Red Bluff, and the older location was henceforth called Old Ebenezer.

Oglethorpe had intended to settle the third transport at Frederica, the city he was building on St. Simons Island as a fortress against the Spaniards in Florida; but the immigrants refused to go there, having been promised they might settle with their coreligionists at Ebenezer. In a letter of 16 March 1736 to the Trustees, Oglethorpe wrote, "The last transport under Mr. von Reck was destined to strengthen me here, yet at their desire I suffered them to settle on ye River Savannah, tho' by that Means we lost the assistance of 50 Men able to bear arms."[27]

Because the third transport's supplies had been inadvertently sent by boat from Tybee to Frederica, the travelers arrived at Ebenezer empty-handed. In addition, most of them were sick with scurvy, which Boltzius described in lurid detail. Boltzius succeeded in playing Vat off against von Reck and thus gradually regained his former authority. He also complained to the Trustees about Vat's tyranny,[28] a charge previously leveled by Dietzius, the second transport's German shipmate. During this time von Reck annoyed Oglethorpe with ceaseless complaints against Vat, Thomas Jones, who would succeed Causton as keeper of the stores, and others.[29] The friction between Vat and von Reck became so bitter that Oglethorpe tried, but failed, to reconcile them.[30]

When things were at their very worst for the third transport, von Reck sent a letter in French to Oglethorpe, dated 7 March 1736, requesting land across Ebenezer Creek and complaining that Causton, as keeper of the stores in Savannah, had refused to pay the two soldiers who helped Noble Jones with the surveying and that he was demanding five shillings each from the Salzburgers to pay for the surveying. He also complained that the poor people had received no cauldrons or other utensils.[31] He sent another letter, also in French, to James Vernon, one of the Trustees, explaining the sad situation and complaining that the Salzburgers' supplies had not yet arrived and that they had to bring up provisions from Savannah in a clumsy boat designed by Causton, which required nine to eleven men from eight to fifteen days to make a single trip.[32] Von Reck also enclosed a drawing of this boat, contrasting it with the type of boats generally used on the Savannah River.[33] The squabbling and name-calling between Vat and von Reck became so intense that Oglethorpe had to ask John Wesley to investigate the situation. Since the two commissioners could not agree about the stores in Ebenezer, Oglethorpe requested Boltzius to resume charge of them.[34]

Oglethorpe naturally blamed the third transport for their lack of supplies, which they would have received if they had accepted his invitation to settle at Frederica; and Harman Verelst, the Trustees' accountant, seems to have been in agreement.[35] When Vat abandoned Ebenezer for some

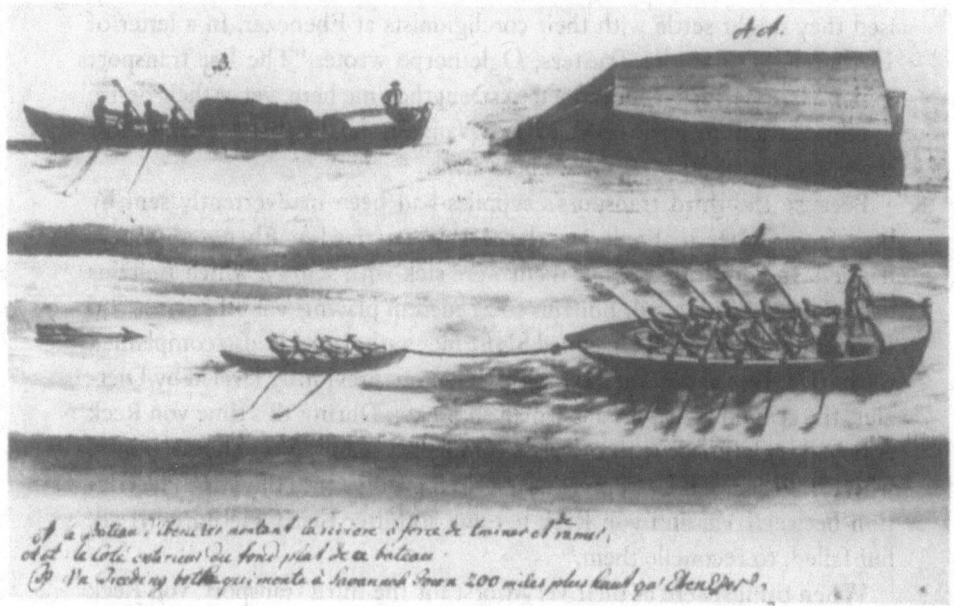

Bottom: Thomas Causton's unwieldy barge (with supporting rowboat), by which supplies were brought up to Ebenezer from Savannah; *top right:* view of the bottom of the barge; *top left:* more efficient type of boat favored by Indian traders.
(Crown Copyright, PRO CO 5/638 [p 304])

time and left the storehouse locked during his absence, von Reck broke into it and distributed some of the goods. Resenting such treatment from "Schoolmasters and School Boys," Vat sent Oglethorpe his resignation on 10 March 1736.[36] Having met with so little success at Ebenezer, von Reck followed Oglethorpe to St. Simons with various petitions; but he succeeded only in annoying Oglethorpe, even though he had brought a much-needed work detail with him. Von Reck claimed to have brought thirty men, but that seems to have been an exaggeration.[37]

From his journey to America von Reck brought back an interesting travelogue and a folio of priceless drawings of the flora, fauna, and Indians of Georgia.[38] Depressed by the heat, fever, and lack of respect and success, von Reck seems to have suffered a breakdown, which would explain his rage when a Salzburger woman insisted on buying some honey from an Indian even though he, a baron, wished to buy it. Because of such impudence on the part of a commoner, inconceivable in class-conscious Europe, von Reck drew his sword and drove the woman and her husband away.[39] Such behavior may help explain why Benjamin Martyn wrote that he hoped that, because of von Reck's restless disposition, he would be settled away from the Salzburgers.[40] Discredited before his people, von Reck gave up the fight and left Ebenezer. Before returning to Europe, he and his brother, Ernst Ludwig, both grievously sick, were nursed back to health in Savannah by John Wesley.[41]

The most important task in 1736 was the distribution of the long-promised land. As mentioned, von Reck reported to Oglethorpe that Causton had refused to pay the two soldiers who were to help Jonas (Noble Jones) survey and that he expected each Salzburger to pay Jonas five shillings.[42] It seems that, at this time, a Hugh Ross (or Rose) of Purysburg was also serving as surveyor, when he did not have more lucrative business in Purysburg.[43] Jones was accused of laying out the lots in the sterile pine barrens, which were easy to survey, instead of in the overgrown and fertile canebrakes.[44] As Jones's successor, Ross also laid out the Salzburgers' lots in pine barrens, giving Oglethorpe's orders as his excuse.[45] Despite all the confusion, the new settlement prospered, especially after the land was distributed. A year and a half later, in 1737, Boltzius wrote to a friend in Berlin to report that things were faring well. He justified the removal to the Red Bluff on the grounds that, although the soil at Old Ebenezer had been good for cattle raising, it was infertile for crops and too inaccessible.[46]

Fortunately for the Salzburgers, they had a champion in London in the person of Court Chaplain Friedrich Michael Ziegenhagen, who had the ear of his Lutheran king, George II, and therefore wielded considerable influence. Ziegenhagen's complaint of 22 February 1737, apparently to the earl of Egmont, surely alleviated some of the Salzburgers' grievances; a letter from Boltzius to the trustee James Vernon dated 28 June of that year suggests that Ziegenhagen had been very successful in his intercession with the Trustees.[47] Along with Gotthilf August Francke and Samuel Urlsperger, Ziegenhagen was one of the "Reverend Fathers" of the Salzburgers. The winter of 1737–38 marked a turning point in the progress of Ebenezer.

The Trustees' Servants

For the public works in Savannah, the Trustees needed dependable labor, and this they could not find among the British settlers, who demanded

Earliest sketch of New Ebenezer, from von Reck's folio. Original in color. (Det Kongelige Bibliotek, København)

Arrival in Georgia

more for their service than their work was worth. Nor were the Trustees able to find enough English redemptioners for their needs. In March 1735 a party of Swiss arrived in Savannah and signed a testimonial commending the humanitarian treatment given them by Captain William Thomson and the crew of the little 150-ton frigate *Two Brothers*.[48] A few of the passengers signed with an *X*, but most of them signed their own names, which is regrettable, since many signatures are crabbed and scarcely legible. They would appear to have been Johann Abraham Brauniger, Heinrich Enderli, Johann Mugg, Heinrich Fritschi, Joseph Volker, Hans Cunrad Brandenberger, Hans Stumli, Heinrich Meierhoffer, Benjamin Heinrich Fahan, Jacob Mohr, Jacob Verlii, Friedrich Pauli, Hans Pral, Johannes Ohnfeld, Ulrich Stageritz, Caspar Meier, Heinrich Johannes, Jacob Meier, Zich(?) Heinrich Engller, Heinrich Dübendorfer, Jacob Ösler, Heinrich Meyerhoffer, Hans Heinrich Meier, Hans Dudwiller, and Hans Seuti. Despite the difference in spelling, Meierhoffer and Meyerhoffer may have been father and son, or at least kinsmen.

In 1756 Henry Myerhoffer, a German subject of the king of England and resident of Georgia, was captured along with another British subject aboard a Spanish vessel off the coast of Cuba by a New York freebooter, who claimed that the ship was French. England and Spain were then allies against France in the War of the Spanish Succession.[49] It is not clear whether this Henry Myerhoffer was one of Thomson's passengers by that name, or possibly a son of one of them.

Thomson's passengers were destined for South Carolina. The *South Carolina Gazette* for 19–26 April 1735 stated that Thomson put 110 of the Swiss ashore in Georgia and that the king was to pay their passage, but only if they settled in Purysburg. The ones who signed Captain Thomson's testimonial, however, are listed above because some of them subsequently moved to Georgia. In the index to the *Colonial Records of the State of Georgia* several of the people on the above list have three or even four names: Ulrich Stagerisz Zufrieden, Caspar Meier Wol Zufrieden, and Heinrich Johannes Wol Zufrieden. Anyone acquainted with the German language will realize that these were not names, but merely statements that the individuals were "content" or "well content" with the treatment they received on board.

These contented passengers seem to have been a part of a group of one hundred "Swiss, Grison, and Germans" who had been examined to see whether they were really Protestants. Although only twenty-three passengers signed the testimonial, Thomson must have carried all hundred of these Swiss, Grisons, and Germans, since the Trustees paid him six hundred pounds on 26 February 1736.⁵⁰ In this context the "Germans" must have been Moravians, since they were also aboard the *Two Brothers*.

On 1 May 1735 Benjamin Martyn, the Trustees' secretary, wrote to Samuel Eveleigh, a Charleston merchant, advising him to get German servants rather than Negro slaves because the Germans "are a sober, strong, laborious people; and since at the Expiration of their Service they will be fit to become Tenants, they will make your lands of much more value."⁵¹ He then gives good reasons for not importing slaves. The Trustees' faith in German workers may have been confirmed by the reports coming back of the industrious and uncomplaining Salzburgers. Unable to attract enough Salzburgers for the colony's needs, the Trustees began recruiting actively among the German and Swiss emigrants then in England.

Already on 10 May 1735, when the colony was little more than a year old, the Trustees bound a number of Palatines as indentured servants. These were:

> Gaspar Schumacher and Christian his Wife for five Years from the Date of the Indenture, Agatha Bandley, Hans Frederick Christer and Maria Magdalena his Wife, Thomas Meyer and Ursula his Wife and Andreas Michel and Margaret his Wife, all for the same term, Henry Meyer, Son of Thomas Meyer for ten Years, Margaret Maddis, Widow of Peter Phizzel for five Years, Margaret Phizzel, Daughter of Peter Phizzel for two Years, Barbara Phizzel Daughter of said Peter for Eleven Years, Nicolas Carpenter for the same term, and John Robinson for nine Years from the Date of the Indenture.⁵²

It will later appear that most of these "Palatines" were actually Swiss. The last two passengers named were English lads who were sent as servants to Boltzius but turned out badly.

On 14 May 1735 Captain John Yoakley of the *James* departed from England with eight British servants and twenty-two foreign ones specifically for Georgia. Since the widow Phizzel was aboard, Yoakley must have been carrying the servants indentured on 10 May. Also on board was Adelhait Hoffmann, who had been indentured to the Trustees for ten years.⁵³ After leaving his passengers in Georgia, Captain Yoakley sailed to Philadelphia to load supplies for Georgia and then returned to chart the channels to Frederica. Yoakley's ship must have been the one mentioned by Boltzius as arriving about 31 July 1735 with Swiss servants for Savannah. On

3 September 1735 it was decided that some of these servants were to work on the Trust's lands under the supervision of William Bradley.[54]

On 18 July 1735 Harman Verelst wrote to Causton that "In 14 Days time Capt. Daubuz will sail with Servants &c. Passengers for Georgia which Servants are for the Acct. of the Trust; to be employed for them to raise Provisions for the Store."[55] Daubuz's ship, the *Georgia Pink*, carried ten British and seventeen foreign servants, whose nationalities were not listed.[56] Two families, Anton and Catherina Salice (or Salis) and one other couple, were from Grisons, or Graubünden, a canton in southeastern Switzerland where Romansh, a Latin dialect, is still spoken.[57] Grisons was dominated by the German-speaking cantons, so most educated people there could speak German, albeit of a Swiss variety. Although the earl of Egmont states that Salice and his family were Grisons, he also calls him a German.[58]

The *Georgia Pink* also carried a couple named Giovanni and Maria Giovanoli, who would appear to have been Italians or Piedmontese but could possibly have been the second couple designated as Grisons.[59] Most of the remainder must have been German Swiss and Palatines, including a man named Daniel Taissoux, who was German despite his French name.[60] A man named Heinrich Meyer, of whom we shall hear later, was bringing his large family over at his own expense. On 9 August 1735 Verelst wrote to Causton that Meyer was coming to Frederica as a free man, not to be "Imployed to labour for the Trust."[61] Germans were needed at Frederica for labor on the fortifications and for raising crops for the garrison; it was not long before there were enough of them there to have their own German Village.

On 7 December 1735 Causton wrote to the Trustees that Captain Yoakley had just returned from Philadelphia and that "Capt. Daubuz arrived on the 27th November with all the Passengers in good health, and they all praise the Tenderness and Humanity towards them, he had ten Children, which had the Small Pox in the Passage; every One of them recovered. One of the Grizon's wife had a Daughter born, which was this day Baptized."[62] According to the earl of Egmont this happy group left England on 1 August and arrived in Georgia on 27 November, thus having a relatively slow voyage.[63] We do not know which Grison's wife had the daughter.

After serving out their indentures, the Salice and Schumacher families returned to London in 1740.[64] Salice, who had been a gardener at the

Trustees' Garden, complained of harsh treatment by Thomas Jones, the new keeper of the stores, who had replaced Causton. Mrs. Schumacher claimed she and her husband had been cheated out of their clothing, and Mr. Schumacher said he had not taken up his own land because he had no means of support. Even though the Trustees promised them a cow, a calf, and a hog if they would return to Georgia, they refused; Schumacher was not heard of again. Salice, on the other hand, reappeared before the Trustees on 5 October 1741 and agreed to return with his two children, Anthony and Catherine, and to resume the post of gardener. He was ordered aboard the ship "wherein the other Germans are to go falling down this day to Gravesend."[65] This ship would appear to have been the ill-fated *Europa*, yet Egmont says Salice arrived in Georgia on 2 December 1741, whereas the *Europa* arrived on 4 December. It should be remembered, however, that ships sometimes anchored at Tybee Island, at the mouth of the Savannah River, two or more days before disembarking their passengers at the city, so both dates could be correct.[66] When Salice had first arrived in 1735, Verelst warned Causton to keep an eye on him lest he correspond with the Spaniards and French; this would suggest that he was, or was suspected of being, a Catholic. Unfortunately, Salice died soon after arriving in Georgia the second time, along with so many of the passengers of the ill-starred *Europa*.[67]

The Moravians

Roman Catholicism was forced on the Bohemians after their defeat at White Mountain in 1620. While most of the population submitted, many kept their Protestant faith, which, for some sects, went all the way back to the movement under Jan Huss in the fifteenth century. Among the persecuted Protestants was a denomination calling itself the Unitas Fratrum, or the Unity of Brothers.[68] Whereas the Treaty of Westphalia of 1648 recognized the Calvinists as well as the Lutherans, it did not recognize the Unitas Fratrum, which had no lobby at the negotiations. Consequently, the group was looked upon as an illegal sect with no more rights than the Anabaptists or Mennonites.

While the Hapsburgs were suppressing the Protestants in their Crown lands of Upper Austria and Carinthia and thereby indirectly causing some to immigrate to Georgia with the third Salzburger transport, they were also putting great pressure on the Unitas Fratrum in Bohemia. As a result, many of these nonconformists slipped across the border to Saxony, a state that was still principally Protestant even though the royal family had reverted to Catholicism for reasons of state.[69] Because most of these religious refugees came from the province of Moravia (*Mähren*), they are known in America as Moravians.

Reaching Saxony, the Moravian exiles found refuge at Herrnhut, an estate belonging to a Saxon nobleman named Nikolaus Ludwig von Zinzendorf, as a result of which they henceforth called themselves *Herrnhuter* rather than Moravians. Also, this small church was embraced by so many people from elsewhere in the Empire that the original refugees from Moravia were only a small minority. We shall see that, in Georgia, they actually called themselves "the Germans." They did not have to proselytize because more candidates came to them than they cared to accept.

On 7 January 1735 the Trustees resolved to give five hundred acres of land to Nikolaus Ludowicus, count of Zinzendorf and Pottendorf, and also to give twenty acres of land contiguous to his to each of his ten male servants upon expiration of their service.[70] Three months later, on 2 April, David Nitschmann, Zinzendorf's "Master of the Household," brought the Trustees a proposal from the count to send over fifty-five heads to Georgia, for which the Trustees would lend £450. Here Nitschmann's name is correctly written, whereas nearly all other English records call him Nitchman. On 9 January 1735 Nitschmann had been granted a house lot in Savannah.[71]

The minutes of the Trustees' common council for 26 September 1735 state that a benefaction of two hundred pounds had been given to Nitschmann and the fifteen people he had brought with him, and the same page stated that he and the twenty-five persons lately arrived from Germany under his conduct would be sent to Georgia under the same terms agreed to by the count on 2 April 1735.[72] Although the members of the Unitas Fratrum were all brothers in Christ, Count Zinzendorf kept his social prerogatives in this world. This had a major advantage. By coming as his servants, the others would not have to perform military service, which was required only of freeholders.

Gottlieb Spangenberg, the Moravians' leader in Savannah, sailed on 6 April 1735 with nine colleagues on the *Two Brothers*, having been furnished with complete powers of attorney to act for Zinzendorf.[73] Every day Spangenberg wrote a list of victuals and nailed it to the mast so the German-speaking passengers could know what to expect. Although transport conductors usually ate at the captain's table, the captain, James Horner, reported that Mr. Spangenberg preferred to eat with his nine friends, where they could be alone and undisturbed.[74] Later on, Horner composed a remarkable ecumenical letter defending Spangenberg from some Lutheran detractors.[75]

Causton wrote on 7 July 1735 that "Mr. Spangenberg had his Town Lott set out immediately after his Arrival, they are very Industrious, have planted three Acres of Corn & Peas which thrive well."[76] Oglethorpe advanced Spangenberg twenty pounds of his own money to help him settle in Savannah.[77] The Trustees were also generous with cows, hogs, and poultry.[78]

Another party of Moravians followed the next year in the "Great Embarkation" on the *Symonds*, along with Oglethorpe and the religious leader John Wesley and his younger brother, Charles.[79] (Since Charles was seldom concerned with the Germans, the name Wesley, unless otherwise indicated, will always refer to John.) On the voyage a storm terrified most of the passengers, while the Moravians remained calm and sang God's praise. Their devout faith greatly impressed Wesley, who remained their close friend in Savannah. There he considered joining the brotherhood, but they did not encourage him, and the matter was protracted. Impressed by their hymns, he translated some of them into English. Boltzius's journal entry for 19 July 1737, which was suppressed by Urlsperger, mentions the "good German songs" that Wesley had translated, but it fails to mention that they were from the Moravians. The story of the Moravians' fortitude under stress during the storm is often attributed to the Salzburgers, but that cannot be the case, because the third transport was on the *London Merchant*, while Wesley and the Moravians were on the *Symonds*.[80]

The economic condition of the Savannah Moravians could be minutely reconstructed from the voluminous records kept at Herrnhut.[81] Very interesting is Abraham Minis's record of the money earned by the Moravians, mostly for carpentry and carting.[82] For the Moravians, these physical accomplishments were far less important than spreading the gospel among the heathens, which they tried to do by conducting a school for the Yamacraw Indians at Irene on the bank of the Savannah.[83]

The Trustees had granted Zinzendorf five hundred acres of land on 10 January 1735; yet, even though Noble Jones took Spangenberg up the Great Ogeechee River to inspect the land,[84] the Moravians never moved there but preferred to remain in Savannah, where they plied many trades and were of immense benefit to the town.[85] Wesley wrote to the Trustees that "the Moravians are the most laborious, cheapest workers and best Subjects in the whole Province, and have among them the best carpenters."[86] This explains why many English laborers resented them.

As an orthodox Lutheran minister, Boltzius feared the Moravians as dangerous innovators and tried to protect his parishioners from any contact with them. That proved impossible, since the Moravians were both hospitable and helpful to the Salzburgers who visited Savannah. A Salzburger woman apprenticed her son to the Moravians' shoemaker, Tannenberger, to the great peril of the lad's soul. The Salzburgers also made use of the Moravians' doctor, Jean François Regnier, even though Boltzius denigrated his skill. Boltzius refused to recognize the Moravians as bona fide Lutherans, believing that they rejected the sacraments as well as ordained ministers like himself, as he explained in a journal entry on 10 March 1736 and again on 2 October 1738.

In August 1739 the Moravians disgraced themselves in the eyes of many people, including Colonel William Stephens, the Trustees' newly arrived secretary for Georgia. Upon leaving for London, a widowed father named Howe had put his two children in the care of the Moravians for a stricter Christian nurture. One of them died. When the grandmother heard that the other one was sick, she tried to visit the child and gained admission only with great difficulty. The child had been severely flogged for bedwetting. To make matters more inexcusable, the stripes had been laid on by a man; it did not help the girl that the man was required to post bail that he would appear at the next court.

Boltzius reported a similar example of Moravian punishment in Purysburg, where Simon Harper, an English boy in the service of the Moravian missionaries there, had been similarly whipped.[87] It is of course possible that Boltzius's informant exaggerated the incident, well aware of the pastor's dislike of the Moravians. The two missionaries in question, Peter Böhler and Georg Schulius, were supported by the Associates of Dr. Bray to convert the blacks in Purysburg and to catechize any white children who would submit to instruction.[88] On 21 February 1737 Zinzendorf had acknowledged receipt of thirty pounds via Vernon from the Associates.[89] According to a letter of 9 March 1738 from Zinzendorf to Oglethorpe, the latter seems to have been behind this missionary undertaking.[90]

David Zeisberger, Jr., wishing to find his father, arrived on the *King*

George, captained by Jacob Ayres, which departed from England sometime after 5 November 1737. He brought with him another lad named Johann Michael Schober, who is listed as John Michael Schaub.[91] The younger David Zeisberger later became a famous missionary to the Indians in Ohio.[92] In Georgia the Moravians had no success in converting the Indians, which had been one of their major purposes in coming.[93]

The Trustees mistakenly thought that all the Germans accompanying Bishop Spangenberg were Moravians, including such diverse people as the carpenter Michael Volmar and the warrior Adolf von Hermsdorf, who, as a professional soldier, obviously could not have been a Moravian. Likewise, although the Swiss laborer Abraham Grüning arrived with the Moravians, he cannot have been one of them, since he, too, served as a soldier. According to Boltzius's entry for 18 June 1736, Grüning's passage had been paid by the SPCK, whereas Volmar's had been advanced by the Moravians, whom he refunded by 9 October of that year. Even though the seventy-three year old had paid back his debt, he absconded from Ebenezer surreptitiously with the aid of the schoolmaster Ortmann, as Boltzius reported on 20 November 1736. Boltzius called Volmar a shoemaker in that entry, but he corrected it to carpenter on 5 December.

As servants to Zinzendorf and Spangenberg, the pacifistic Moravians were to be exempted from military service, but they would have to support two soldiers to represent their freeholding masters, and these did not have to be Moravians.[94] Even this they did not wish to do, since it would contribute to violence. Instead, they preferred to do any kind of nonmilitary service. Unfortunately, the populace of Savannah was incited by rumors of impending war against Spain and objected to their exemption, even though the Trustees upheld their rights as pacifists.[95] On 21 February 1737 the Moravians signed a petition asking permission to leave Georgia on the grounds that their faith forbade them to bear arms, as they had explained in London before proceeding to Georgia.[96] In a letter of 3 August 1737 to Causton, the Trustees sided wholeheartedly with the Moravians.[97]

The Moravians signed their petition of 21 February 1737 as "the Germans," which was carelessly written as "the Gormans"; thus the name appears in the records.[98] On 30 April 1737 Spangenberg, writing from Philadelphia, requested permission for the group to leave Georgia, asking only that they be paid some little consideration for the improvements they had made.[99] Already on 23 September 1737 the Trustees gave them leave to depart as soon as they had paid back the £260 advanced them.

This they did on 28 June 1738.¹⁰⁰ Most of them moved to Pennsylvania, but their doctor, Jean François Regnier, returned to Europe. He will re-enter our story later. In 1741 Josef Hagen was back in Savannah trying to collect some money for the Moravians, but Boltzius assumed that he was proselytizing among the English there.¹⁰¹ As we shall see, in 1765 another Moravian, Johann Ettwein, traveled from Wachovia in North Carolina to Savannah to try to sell the Moravians' remaining lots.

Thomas Christie, the recorder in Savannah, reported that all Moravians had left before the year 1742.¹⁰² This seems to be in error, since Colonel Stephens reported that the last German Moravian family left Savannah on 16 March 1745. Even after the Moravians had left Georgia, Oglethorpe continued to take an interest in them; on 14 October 1746 he offered them five hundred acres of land in South Carolina opposite Augusta so that they could preach to the Indians.¹⁰³ When the Moravians attempted to sell their holdings in Georgia in 1761, James Habersham, the president of the Council, advised them that, because their land had been abandoned, it had been granted to someone else. If they would send proper powers of attorney in time, he might be able to secure their two town lots.¹⁰⁴ Two years later, in November 1763, he brought the money for the lots in person to Philadelphia.¹⁰⁵

The German Moravians must have been joined by non-German inhabitants of Savannah, because, after their departure, some Moravians, all of whom had English names, were ridiculed by Colonel Stephens. On 3 July 1744 Stephens complained that the English Moravians were refusing to participate in the military muster, even though only two of them would have to attend, and that this caused great murmuring among the other citizens.¹⁰⁶ Here he must have been referring to the English converts. As we shall see, other Moravians were later called to Georgia to convert the African slaves of William Knox and James Habersham.

Because the Moravians always spoke kindly of the Salzburgers, the British were surprised that Boltzius spoke so disparagingly of the Moravians. Urlsperger expurgated almost all reference to them in his edition of Boltzius's reports, replacing their name with *N.N.* He did this even when the Moravians were the donors of gifts, such as a barrel of dried apples from Pennsylvania that the Salzburgers received on 7 February 1738. The Lutherans' aversion to the Moravians can be explained by their fear that the Moravians might proselytize good and loyal Lutherans to what they considered a rather questionable faith. When Zinzendorf had visited Halle, considerable dissension followed, as was later the case among the Lutherans of Philadelphia when he visited there.[107]

German Settlements Around Savannah

Ten of the first German-speaking families to arrive in Savannah were settled in an area just southwest of Savannah named Hampstead, which the new inhabitants at once germanized into Heimstatt. In July 1738 an observer named William Bird reported that many people had left the colony and added the footnote: "N. B. Burgholder, Holtstaller, Houlster, and Dester are all industrious and Laborious Men: The Rest of little Account."[108] A short-term denizen of Hampstead was Samuel Wagner, who had intended to alienate his lot at Hampstead on 20 December 1738 but died first. His heirs asked that his property be disposed of, and this request was granted.[109] For a short time the people of Hampstead received religious instruction, which they could not understand, from the minister William Norris.[110]

The most important inhabitant of Hampstead was Michael Burckhalter, usually called Burgholder, who had absconded secretly from Lützelflüh in Canton Bern to avoid an emigration tax.[111] In 1737 Daniel Phyfer, a Swiss settler at Hampstead, wrote his will acknowledging his debt to Michael Burckhalter, who had paid his passage from Bern via Calais and London to Georgia.[112] Partly because he had five sons for labor, Burckhalter prospered, and on 7 August 1742 the Trustees recommended that a grant of five hundred acres of land be given to him to divide among his sons as he saw fit.[113] Some of these "sons" were actually sons-in-law.

A short distance east of Hampstead was Highgate, a hamlet for French-speaking people, mostly Swiss. Foremost among these was Pierre Rodolf Morel, who had paid for his and his family's passage in 1733.[114] The people of Highgate, like those of Hampstead, were mainly Reformed and collaborated well with their German neighbors. Perhaps the leading man in Highgate was Morel, who, according to Stephens, was "Born a Swiss, and Bred a Soldier, and looked on by us as a Man of Resolution."[115] Since he spoke both French and German, he was the logical man to command the local militia.

When Oglethorpe allowed the Salzburgers to move from Old Ebenezer to the Red Bluff, he required them to leave all their buildings and lumber behind for the Trustees, who had decided to use the area for a cowpen, or cattle ranch. The managers of the cowpen were English and Irish, mostly unsavory and dishonest characters, if we can trust Boltzius; but the actual work was done largely by German and Swiss redemptioners. Two of the redemptioners, Christian Rump and Henry Miers (Meyer), corroborated Boltzius's negative view by testifying that the manager, Barker, had diverted the grain from the Trustees' horses to his own livestock and poultry and had even falsely branded the Trustees' horses. Like the German redemptioners in Savannah, those at the cowpen were disorderly and offensive, again in the eyes of Pastor Boltzius, who judged them by his well-disciplined flock.[116]

According to Benjamin Martyn, the Trustees' secretary in London, in 1741 some of the German families at the cowpen maintained plantations.[117] It must be kept in mind, however, that in those days the word *plantation* could connote any cultivated field, even a patch of an acre or two, just as a "ranch" in California need not be larger than that. A Palatine family named Schwarzwälder eventually moved from the cowpen to Ebenezer and became substantial citizens. Some of their descendants, understanding only the first half of their name, changed it to Blackwelder, or else they gave up on the first syllable and became Welders. The name had, of course, designated an inhabitant of the Schwarzwald, or Black Forest.

Boltzius was highly annoyed by two of the cowpen servants, Martin Dasher (Taescher) and the previously mentioned Henry Miers (Meyer), who came to Ebenezer while drunk and disturbed the divine services by parodying the Salzburgers' hymns and cursing and defying the pastor. When Boltzius sent the constable, Thomas Bichler, to arrest them, Meyer escaped and fled up the Savannah River, where he soon killed an Indian in a drunken brawl.[118] Dasher was sent down to Savannah at great expense and trouble on 14 September 1744, but the tolerant authorities there only reprimanded him, put him on probation, and told him not to bother Boltzius again.[119] With his German ideas of authority, Boltzius could not see why Dasher could not be severely punished at the pastor's request. Dasher also debauched a "Swish" girl named Magdalena Meyer under her mother's roof in Ebenezer while everyone else was at church.[120] She was the daughter of the Thomas and Ursula Meyer who had been indentured in London on 10 May 1735.

Among the forts radiating out from Savannah was Fort Argyle on the Great Ogeechee River some miles southwest of Ebenezer. Various Germans worked at the fort, among whom was the Bavarian distiller Georg Bartholomäus Roth. In less than a year after reaching Ebenezer, Roth, like his accomplice Braunberger, had to be ejected for refusing to conform to good order and for threatening someone's life and even defying Boltzius.[121] This was the first of the very few times that Boltzius had to call upon the civil authority in Savannah to enforce God's will. When Roth died not long afterward still unrepentant, he furnished the Salzburgers a frightening example of a lost sinner. His wife, Maria Barbara, went into exile with him but soon disappeared from the records, through death, departure, or possibly marriage. In the official records Roth is listed as Roht and Rolf. The George Lewis Roth who later served in the military and died in Ebenezer in 1767 was probably unrelated because, as the *Ebenezer Church Records* state, "He was a Catholic."[122]

Another recalcitrant from Ebenezer was Gabriel Bach, a Swabian who had joined the second Salzburger transport. When Boltzius traveled down to Savannah to dissolve a common law marriage between two Palatine servants, Bach accompanied him and fell in love with the sinful woman, Margaretha Stout.[123] With so many women in Ebenezer named Maria Magdalena, the Salzburgers must have thought sinful women worthy of salvation if truly penitent, so Boltzius could hardly refuse Bach's desire to marry Margaretha Stout. She would, however, have to submit to a most degrading church penance, in which she would acknowledge her sin of whoredom.

Unwilling to see his bride humiliated before the entire congregation, Bach determined to take her away. He therefore went to Fort Argyle and enlisted in the Rangers, the mounted scouts who patrolled the frontier. Margaretha endured the disgrace of church penance and was forgiven, and her guilt was relegated to oblivion and attributed to anyone who ever mentioned it again.[124] The enlistment, however, was binding, and the young couple moved to Fort Argyle. Soon thereafter hostilities broke out with Spain. Bach distinguished himself as a Ranger, but he was the first casualty. The Indians scalped him, and Oglethorpe is reported to have sent his head to the governor at St. Augustine with a threat that any more such acts would be paid in kind. The British, of course, also rewarded their Indian allies for taking scalps. In 1757 the new governor, Henry Ellis, promised some Creeks twenty shillings "for every scalp of our Enemies."[125] In his entry for 16 October 1760 in the *Americanisches Ackerwerck Gottes* Boltzius mentions that an Indian had just been paid a reward for two scalps taken from French Indians. The widow Bach returned to Ebenezer, where she married the Salzburger Christian Leimberger a year later.

We have seen that Count Zinzendorf had obtained a grant for five hundred acres near Fort Argyle. Noble Jones took the count's deputy, Bishop Spangenberg, up the Ogeechee River in his patrol boat to view the area, but nothing came of the plan to settle the Moravians there. Like the Salzburgers, the Moravians called Jones "Jonas," that being the German name of the biblical man swallowed by the whale. When Captain Thomson brought his Palatine transport to Georgia in 1738, a large family named Schlechtermann was sent to Fort Argyle to work on the fortifications or to supply food for the garrison. Both parents and several of the children died very shortly, and the surviving children asked Boltzius for refuge, but he could not help.[126] Two of the boys, Jeremias and Peter, eventually became slave-owning planters, known by such names as Sliterman, Slyterman, and Slighterman. According to the Malcontents, a disaffected group in Savannah, by 1741 the garrison at Fort Argyle had been reduced to one officer, his Dutch servant, and a woman. The servant and the woman were murdered by two escaped prisoners from Savannah.[127] The two murderers, a Spanish doctor and an Irish soldier, were hanged for their crime.[128]

Frederica

Some of the first Swiss and Germans to arrive in Georgia had settled at Frederica to work on the fortifications. Already in 1736 Oglethorpe had sent a "Detachment of Germans, English & Americans" to build a fort on St. George's Point. Unfortunately, this fort was soon abandoned, without Oglethorpe's permission, by Captain Adolf von Hermsdorf, who had recently come over with the Moravians.[129] Lacking trust in the men under his command, he deserted the fort and fled, sick, back to the Moravians in Savannah to escape Oglethorpe's wrath. Abraham Grüning, the Swiss laborer from Burgstein in Canton Bern, also served for a year at Frederica and married a Scots lass there. Boltzius was sure that this marriage was not for Grüning's spiritual good, because the girl received too much attention from the other soldiers and would not return with Grüning to Ebenezer, where he had planned to settle.[130]

Having a regiment to feed and forts to build, Oglethorpe needed reliable labor, which was best obtained from German workers. As previously

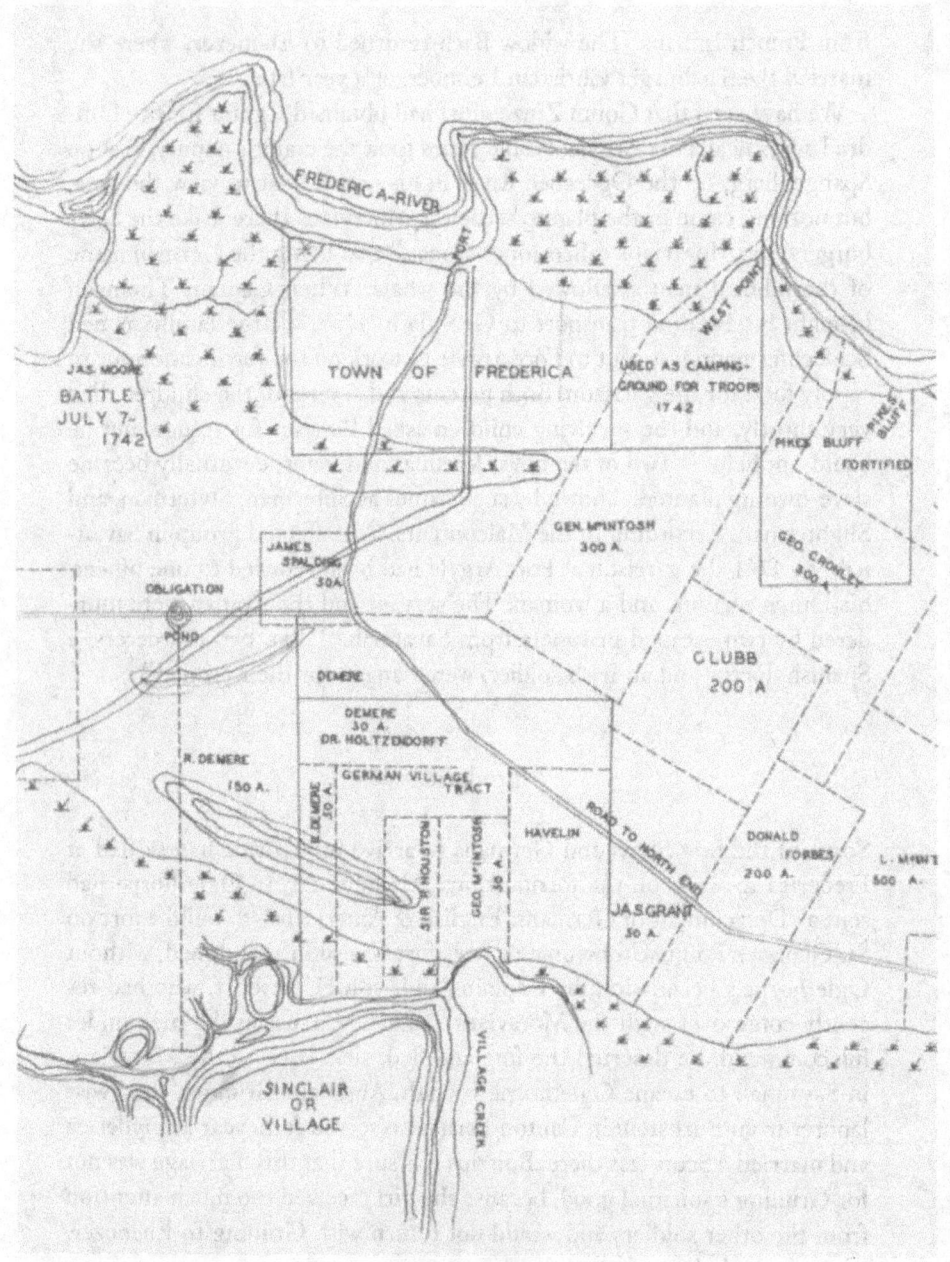

Map of Frederica. Note L-shaped German Village tract, bottom center. (Margaret Davis Cate Collection, Fort Frederica National Monument, Georgia Historical Society)

related, he pressured the third Salzburger transport to settle at Frederica instead of joining their countrymen at Ebenezer, but they flatly refused and settled at Ebenezer, while all their supplies and equipment were erroneously sent from Savannah to Frederica. The work detail that Baron von Reck took to Frederica to ingratiate himself with Oglethorpe did not remain long, so the inhabitants of German Village should not be called Salzburgers, as is sometimes done.

Even without the Salzburgers, the German Village on St. Simons continued to grow through gradual accretion, not only of the indentured servants but also of individuals who arrived at their own expense. Oglethorpe had redeemed Thomson's Palatines at his own risk, assured that the Trustees would approve on humanitarian as well as practical grounds.[131] In his letter of 29 December 1739 he gave the names of the people who received these servants, but not the names of the servants.[132] Among Thomson's redemptioners delivered to Frederica were Jacob Ruf, his son, Jacob, and his daughter, Margaretha; Elisabeth Cluer; Johann Friedrich Bineker, his daughter, Christiana, and his son, Johann Ulrich; the widow Victor, her daughters, Anna and Annalies, and her sons, Peter, Jacob, and Sule; Andreas Waldhauer (Volthoward!), his wife, Anna, his sons, Tobias and Hans Georg; the widow Shanbacker, her sons, Hans Michael and Hans Georg, and her daughter, Magdalena; the widow Clements; Philip Gephart, his wife, Martha, his daughter, Maria Catherina, and his sons, Philip and Hans Georg; the widow Derick, her daughters, Elisabeth and Margaretha, and her sons, Melchior and Jacob; Christopher Kensler, his wife, Agnes Christiana, his daughter, Anna Margaretha, and his son, Bastian; Jacob Ichinger, his wife, Catherina, his daughters, Sophia and Annalies, and his sons, Hans Michael and Jacob.[133] In addition there was a Joseph Upshaw, who also appears under the name Ubjer. Because his name was so completely anglicized, it is not possible to ascertain the correct German spelling, but Egmont clearly attests that he was a German.[134]

Among the freeholders of Frederica on 29 September 1738 were Samuel Augspurger; Christian Gampert and his wife; Ernst Ambrosius Detzner and his wife, Martha; Heinrich Meyer and his wife, Catherina, and their children, Anna (married to Henney), Donald, Peter, Margaretha, Johann, Catherina, and Thomas; Heinrich Meyerhoffer; Andreas Walser and his wife, Barbara, and their children, Johann and Anna; Christian Bere(?) and his wife, Maria, and their daughter, Elisabeth; and Ri(chard?) Kirchner and his wife, Elisabetha.[135]

Between September 1741 and September 1742 the best crops at German Village were grown by Johann Ragnous, Walther Denny, and J. Michael Aingere.[136] In the same year Heinrich Meyer, a freeholder, invented a new way to manufacture tabby, a building material made of clay and oyster shells; and Heinrich Michel, a "Duch Servant," and Heinrich Meyer, the "Duch" freeholder, built houses of squared timbers.[137] Andreas Walser was a German freeholder of whom Oglethorpe wrote on 29 December 1739: "Walset is a good Planter, has a large family, came at his own Expense from Germany."[138] Walser received two of the servants brought over by Captain Thomson in 1738, one of whom was Bineker. People like Ragnous, Denny, Aingere, and Walser caused Oglethorpe to write that "the Germans seem to take more to Planting than the English do."[139] It is of note that both Meyer and Walser had residences in the town of Frederica itself.[140] Oglethorpe's satisfaction with Palatine redemptioners is reflected in a letter of 20 April 1741 to the Trustees, in which he states that the second best service for Frederica (after sending married recruits with industrious wives) would be "to get the Messrs Hope to send the Germans from Rotterdam hither as they do to Pensylvania."[141]

The indentured servants at Frederica enjoyed considerable privileges, if we can believe the complaints of disgruntled Englishmen. On 16 May 1739 the widow Germain, who had returned to England to inherit some money, reported to the Trustees that only Germans were employed in building the new storehouse in Frederica, "the English not being allowed that favour."[142] On 28 April 1740 a Samuel Davison complained to Harman Verelst that, although he had been appointed as overseer of the Trustees' servants, he found the position filled by one "Shats, a German Trust Servant who came over in Decemb. 1738 & who hardly knows one word of English."[143] The situation was similar in Darien, where the Highlanders spoke only Gaelic, or "Irish," as it was then called. On 22 March 1740 Oglethorpe wrote to the Trustees that "those Servants cannot be put under the Direction of any body at Frederica, nor any one that does not understand the Highland Language."[144]

The Germans at Frederica retained their reputation as farmers. On 11 February 1744 Colonel Heron returned to London and reported to the Trustees that "the Palatines on the German Village on St Simon's (being six or seven Families) have no other Dependence but the Produce of their Lands. That They raise sufficient for their Support, That he has often bought of their Peas, Sallading, Fowls and Other Things. That Widows among these Palatines have supported themselves and Families on their Plantations, but that he do's not know any except them Who support themselves only by Planting."[145]

Like most Germans in America, the inhabitants of German Village soon requested a clergyman, and Oglethorpe wrote to Boltzius for help in finding a suitable person. Boltzius's first letter in this regard seems to have gone astray, as suggested by Oglethorpe's answer to a follow-up. Oglethorpe's letter, although long, deserves to be reproduced here both because it has been overlooked so far and because it reveals Oglethorpe's sincere concern for the Salzburgers.[146]

Frederica July 17 1741

Rev. Sir

I received the Pleasure of Yours the Copy of one dated 24th March the original of which I do not remember to have received, otherwise should certainly have ordered Corn from Augusta to be ground at Ebenezer.

I desire to know whether Mr. Jones has paid for the Indian Corn Flour you sent down which if he has not I desire he would. I should also have given you the Assistance which I now send for Erecting the Mill.

I am still more concerned at the not receiving your Letter, since it has so long Deprived the People here of a Minister. At the same time I spoke to you of a Minister for here, I wrote to Mr. Verelst to defray the Passage et other Expences from Germany to England, et from England hither, of the Minister, Mr. Professor Francke should recommend; by the Trustees answer it seems that, that letter had miscarried; I am afraid wicked people often stop Letters besides the accidents of War. I send you a Letter to Mr. Verelst which I desire you would inclose to him. I send it to you open that you may see how this office must be managed.

I desire you would make my Respects acceptable to the Revd. Mr. Urlsperger at Augsburg. I rejoice much in hearing of the health of so devote a Man, et worthy a Pillar of the Church of Christ.

I wrote to Mr. Jones to Pay all the Bounty on Corn that is allowed by the Trustees.

This is the Answer to the first Letter (of which you sent me the copy) which I should have answered long ago.

With respect to your second. I am very glad to find that your Congregation is able et willing to Plow in case they had Horses et Oxen, also that you intend to go upon silk, Mulberry Trees et Vines. I therefore send you enclosed a Bill of Exchange for One Hundred Pound, which the Trustees will Lend without interest to such Persons, or in such manner, as you shall think proper to enable the building of the Mill, the buying Horses et Cattle for Plowing et the Planting of Vines and raising of silk by the Saltzburghers. The said Mill et Cattle bought to be security for the repayment of said sum after the Expiration of 5 years.

I am sorry that the Accounts you heard of my Health are not so true as I could wish since I have not been thoroughly well since the seige of S. Augustine, though thank God I am better now than I have been.

I desire you would make my service acceptable to etc. Pray also. Let me know how the young Man Bishop does. I am Revd. Sir
      your very humble serv.
      James Oglethorpe

The Mr. Jones mentioned in the letter was Thomas Jones, the new keeper of the stores in Savannah; and the young Mr. Bishop was Henry Bishop, the son of a London grocer, who was indentured to Boltzius as a servant.[147] All Oglethorpe's other points will become clear as our story unfolds.

When passing through Ebenezer on 19 July 1739, Oglethorpe expressed a desire for a German pastor for his German workers at Frederica, a request he repeated on 3 November of that year in a very flattering letter to Boltzius.[148] Although Boltzius sent many letters to Halle to obtain a minister for Frederica, no candidate was found for a considerable time, until finally a Württemberg pastor named Johann Ulrich Driessler volunteered. He was recommended by Francke, whose student he had been at Halle. Driessler, born on 14 August 1692, had served as minister at Gröningen near Crailsheim in Württemberg until being ejected from office, despite his parishioners' attempt to resist the duke's soldiers.[149]

Even after Driessler offered his services, red tape caused a delay of almost two years between Oglethorpe's first letter and Driessler's arrival in Georgia. Driessler landed at Frederica on the *Georgia Packet* with his wife and niece on 22 December 1743 and, according to Boltzius, was very well received by Major William Horton in the absence of Oglethorpe. At Frederica he found a congregation of sixty-two souls awaiting him.[150] Soon after arriving in America, Driessler visited Boltzius at Ebenezer, where he preached and where the Salzburgers gave him a Communion chalice for his Frederica congregation. He also preached to the Germans in Savannah on 26 February 1744, at which time almost everyone in the outlying German settlements flocked to Savannah and made the largest congregation seen there in a long while.[151] Driessler maintained a cordial correspondence with Boltzius and also sent voluminous letters to Francke, sometimes of as many as a thousand lines, about conditions in Frederica.¹⁵²

On 23 May 1745 the Trustees resolved "That Mr. John Ulrick Driezler be appointed School Master at Frederica with a Salary of ten Pounds Sterling per Ann. And that the Revd Mr. Burton be desired to appoint the said Mr. Driezler to Officiate for him as Chaplain to Genl Oglethorpe's Regiment." This resolution was put into effect on 1 June 1745.¹⁵³ John Terry, the recorder, soon wrote that Driessler "is extreamly well Liked by Every body here and Acknouledged to be a Worthey Pastor, but more particularly By the Germans, He takes a Great deal of pains Not only In instructing all their Children in Reading, Writing & in The foundamantal Articles of their faith And keeps an Evening School for all Men and women Who Are Not So."¹⁵⁴ Terry had been very kind to the third Salzburger transport when it was under his charge on the voyage from London to Savannah.

While at Frederica, Driessler translated the Lord's Prayer and certain Bible verses into the Cherokee language, no doubt with the aid of Christian Pricber, of whom we shall hear shortly. He also performed the marriage ceremony for his shipmate Thomas Bosomworth, the new Anglican minister, and the recently widowed Mary Musgrove, the Indian "princess." Coming into possession of Mary's lucrative trading house and cowpen, Bosomworth retired from the ministry and left Driessler to minister not only to the Germans but also to any English or Scots who made any claim to religion.

On 20 September 1746 Major Horton wrote to Verelst praising Driessler: "We have amongst us one Mr. Driessler, a Clergyman of most exemplary Piety and is by all sorts of people here held in the greatest Esteem perticularly on account of the indefatigable pains he takes every day in the week in teaching the English as well as the German children to read and instructing them in Matters of Religion yet this injurious miscreant Terry has in a most infamous manner scandalized this poor Gentleman's Character both in Savannah and Charles Town but what will not a Villain do to save his Neck from the Halter." Patrick Graham, a neighbor of the Salzburgers, also complained to the Trustees that Terry had "scandalized the Name and Character" of the Reverend Mr. Driessler by saying that Driessler had caused a woman to accuse him, Terry, of rape.¹⁵⁵

It was a pity that Driessler became involved in this sordid affair, because it soon became obvious that Horton was in the wrong. Terry had objected to the rapes committed by the officers against the German women. Abraham Bosomworth, the brother of the new Anglican pastor, forced himself on Christina Penniker, daughter of one of Samuel Augspurger's Palatine servants, who was being sent to Driessler for religious instruction; but she was saved by her brother. Margaret Myers, "a freeholder's Daughter, one of the Most Modest & verteous young Woman of the Place," accused a soldier of climbing into her window and bed at midnight; but the court believed that she had invited him in.[156] To repay Terry for his complaints, Horton suborned a Dutch woman named Elisabetha Suitor to bring charges of the same sort against him. Elsewhere she is called Luttor and Yutire, probably mistakes for Sutor.[157] Unfortunately, Stephens believed the charges at first. Yet the trial, which was held in Savannah, made it evident that the woman's testimony was being dictated to her by her husband: the eighteen jurors, five of whom were French, exonerated Terry.[158] Terry believed that Driessler had been drawn into the case by trickery and was then saddled with it after the conspiracy was revealed. Elsewhere Terry wrote well of Driessler.[159]

The officers were not the only offenders, for the Anglican pastor, William Norris, seduced a Dutch maid named Elisabetha Penner. When a scandalmonger in Savannah gossiped about this affair, she had to retract to avoid a hundred lashes; Stephens, a good Anglican, continued to trust the pastor.[160] Nevertheless, time was to prove that the girl was pregnant. Norris's friends attempted to pin the blame on a Palatine named Jacob Ruf, and the girl reluctantly accused him.[161] When Norris tried to send her to Charleston, she lost her way and ended up at Ebenezer, where Boltzius persuaded her to divulge the whole ugly story. Her child, who was eventually attributed to Norris, died a few years thereafter. But serving girls were not safe even in the celestial city of Ebenezer, as we have seen in the case of Magdalena Meyer.[162]

The Palatines were not the only German-speaking denizens of St. Simons Island. There were also two gentlemen, one from Brandenburg and one from Switzerland. According to a letter of 3 May 1745 from Terry to the Trustees, Friedrich Holtzendorf, an army surgeon, owned one of the few improved plantations at Frederica.[163] Holtzendorf, from a well-known Brandenburg family, had settled at Purysburg before Oglethorpe sent him to Switzerland to recruit laborers.[164]

Not far from Holtzendorf's property was an island developed by Samuel Augspurger, a gentleman from Bern, who had also settled in Purysburg in 1734 and moved two years later to Frederica, where he served as a surveyor at three shillings per day. On 18 July 1739 Augspurger returned to Switzerland to recruit ten servants.[165] On 14 November he visited the Trustees, gave them a map of Frederica, and requested a grant of five hundred acres and permission to use slave labor.[166] The grant was approved, but Augspurger was denied permission to keep slaves. Augspurger then made several more demands, for example, that he not have to fence in his land, which was an island, and that his servants each be granted fifty acres.[167] On 16 January 1740 he received a gratuity of five guineas for his map of St. Simons Island. On 10 February 1741 he wrote from Bern that his family affairs were in disorder and that he wished a leave of absence until 1744; this was granted.[168] Later, on 3 December 1760, long after slavery was permitted in Georgia, Augspurger sold his estate, Little St. Simons, for £280 to Gabriel Manigault, a Huguenot planter from South Carolina.[169]

Perhaps the most interesting figure at Frederica, although resident there only a short time, was Christian Gottlieb Prieber (or Pryber), a Saxon visionary who had tried to found an Indian commonwealth to protect the Indians from white encroachment.[170] On 18 June 1735 he had asked the Trustees to send him to Georgia; they approved, but he seems not to have waited.[171] Arriving in South Carolina as an officer in the British army, Prieber sold all his belongings, dressed himself as an Indian, and went up to the Cherokees, where he learned their language and won their admiration.[172] When the British authorities in Charleston heard of this subversive character, they sent an emissary to the Cherokees to demand his extradition; yet the Cherokees refused despite their treaties with the English. Thereupon the captain at Augusta bribed some Creek Indians to kidnap Prieber on one of his diplomatic missions, and he was delivered to Frederica and imprisoned in the guardhouse. Because of his mastery of Indian languages, we can safely assume that he was behind the translation made by Driessler, who had just arrived and had never lived among the Indians.

It is not clear what charges the British authorities leveled against Prieber. In a letter of 22 April 1743 to the Duke of Newcastle, the secretary of state, Oglethorpe enclosed a report of the proceedings that is so detailed that it deserves to be reproduced here in full:

> Christian Pryber, who came over to Carolina and was naturalized there, went amongst the Indians, learnt their Language, has proposed to them many

things to alienate them from their Subjection to his Majesty. He is accused for attempting to incite them to begin a War with the English, by killing all those who traded amongst them. In his Journal wrote with his own hand, and taken upon him, is the following paragraph. "Hercules, an Indian, promised at my demand, to assist upon occasion against the English Government in settling my designed Town & Society about Cusaten. Jama (the Negroe) is to be free after our return from the French, on a good Expedition there, and if the English should hurt us amongst the Cusas, they were to kill all the English and make War upon that Nation."

This like many other things in the Journal is a little difficult to understand, the whole being wrote like dark hints for his own Memory only. He proposed to make a Town or Settlement in that Part of Georgia which lies within the Cherokee Nation, & to settle a Town there of fugitive English, French, Germans & Negroes, & they were to take particularly under protection, the runaway Negroes of the English. He has been between Six & Seven years striving to bring this Project to bear.

His Journal mentions several Partakers & Correspondents in Virginia and Carolina. All criminals were to be sheltered, their Provisions were to be first purchased from the Indians, or Herds of Cattle & Hogs drove up by Persons who fled for Shelter, & some they already have. They were as soon as might be, to raise their own corn. Where they were to receive the funds by which they were to purchase the Provisions from the Indians, does not plainly appear, but he mentions a private Treasurer in Charles Town, also that he expected many things from the French, & from another Nation wh he leaves blank. He was going to demand of the French Protection for those Bands of Outlaws, when our Indians apprehending that he would occasion a War, took him & brought him to me with all his Papers, amongst which are some which seem to be Letters from the French or Spanish Governors, but neither sealed nor signed, their Contents demanding Protection & referring for Particulars to the bearer Mr. Pryber.

His Scheme seems to have been chiefly in imitation of the Paulists at Brazil, that is to say, to make an Asylum for all Fugitives, & the Cattel and Effects they might bring with them, & he hoped for the protection of the Cherokee Indians & the French. He expected a great Resort for the benefit of the Asylum from the number of debtors, Transport Felons, Servants, & Negro Slaves in the two Carolinas & Virginia. Amongst his Papers are the articles of a Government regularly drawn out, all Crimes & Licentiousness were to be tolerated except Murder & Idleness.[173]

By "Paulists" Oglethorpe meant the Jesuits, who maintained large settlements in Brazil and Paraguay to protect the Indians. This gave historians the idea that Prieber was a Jesuit, whereas he was most likely a free thinker. As a Saxon, he had probably been Lutheran. In any case, he was not a Jesuit.[174] Oglethorpe does not tell who translated the journal from French, or how competent the translator was. It was lost, possibly destroyed because it would have proved that Prieber was not a Jesuit as charged. From reports made by people who had seen him among the Indians, it appears that he intended his Kingdom of Paradise to be a communistic haven for all oppressed people.

While Prieber was incarcerated in Frederica, his cell became a salon for the local intelligentsia, and all were impressed by his learning and philosophical equanimity. When the arsenal next door exploded and shells rained down, everyone fled in terror except Prieber, who sat calmly among the falling grenades. Before he could be convicted, a fever relieved the British of the need to prefer charges.[175]

The German Village on St. Simons lasted only as long as Oglethorpe's regiment remained there: it began to fade away as the garrison diminished. Actually, the settlement seems to have been abandoned rather abruptly in 1746 when a Captain Davis brought sixty-four "German Servants" and their baggage from Frederica to Savannah.[176] It will be remembered that, on his arrival in Frederica, Driessler had found sixty-two souls awaiting him. On 24 May 1747 Boltzius received a letter from the widow Driessler; she wrote, "Our Germans are moving away, one by one, because we have no pastor here." We see that she was mistaken about both the reason and the manner of the departures, since the greater bulk had left on a single day. On 20 December 1747 Terry wrote to Verelst that all the Germans had left Frederica except for two families.[177]

♦ *Chapter Three* ♦

The Georgia Palatines

𝓕inding few Palatines in England willing to go to Georgia, the Trustees decided to do their own recruiting in Germany. On 7 May 1735 they commissioned Georg Ludwig Wentz of Seckingheim in the Palatinate to engage one hundred Germans at twenty shillings a head to go to Georgia as indentured servants.[1] Wentz agreed but demanded twenty pounds before starting, with twenty more pounds to be paid upon his reaching Worms, twenty more at Cologne, and twenty more at Rotterdam.[2] When Wentz finally arrived in London a year later, the Trustees told him it was too late and that they had no money.[3]

A year later, on 29 April 1737, the Trustees read a proposal from Zinzendorf's secretary, Johann Matthias Krämer, "to translate some Part of the Book call'd *Reasons for Establishing the Colony of Georgia*[4] into High Dutch [*Hochdeutsch*, or standard German] at the Trust's Expence;[5] And to engage a Number of Persons in High Germany to go over to Georgia and to conduct them from Worms to Rotterdam at the said Persons Expence." The Trustees resolved to consider the matter and "to contract with Messrs Hope for the Passage of Sixty Heads of twelve Years of Age and upwards to be repaid to the Trust in six weeks after their Arrival in Georgia, or they to be indentured to the Trust for servants." On 11 May 1737 Krämer received ten pounds for carrying out the Trustees' instructions.[6]

Zachary Hope and his brothers, English merchants in Rotterdam, were notorious exporters of human cargoes who cornered the Palatine market. There were many complaints that they deliberately detained the poor Palatine emigrants on their way to or in Rotterdam until they were desperate enough to accept whatever terms it pleased the Hopes to offer them. On 24 May 1736 a group of three hundred Palatines complained to Azenheim, the British resident at Frankfurt, that they had been held up at the Dutch border at the Hopes' command.[7] Azenheim forwarded the letter to Walpole at the Hague, who in turn passed it on to Lord Harrington.[8]

By 1739 the Hopes' machinations had become so insidious that a Mr. Robert Trevor advised having an agent in Rotterdam to assist and protect the emigrants.[9] When the fourth Salzburger transport reached the Dutch frontier in 1740, barges full of distressed Palatines were being held up at the Dutch customs office while the people were rapidly running out of money and supplies. It is very probable that the Hopes had contrived this situation through properly placed bribes.[10]

While praising the kind treatment accorded a later transport by Captain MacClellan, Pastor Boltzius quoted a letter from a friend in Charleston to contrast MacClellan's behavior with that of "the Merchants Hoops at Rotterdam (very famous Men for having ruined large Numbers of Protestant Germans, being sent by them to Pennsylvania)." He then cites some particulars from the Charlestonian's letter: "I may not omit acquainting you of a very melancholy scene, that daily presents itself in our Streets. It is a Number of poor Germans brought over by George Austin, and sent I think by 2 Merchants of Rotterdam named Hoppe. These poor creatures are reduced to the Depths of Distress, Mothers begging about the Streets and exposing their dying Infants in their Arms. Old Men & Maidens pityously begging from Door to Door. I did not 'till now know that dutch Servants sent here, must be so miserable!"[11]

Boltzius could assure Martyn that such ill treatment never occurred under "the wise & Courteous Management of our Excellent Governours the Honble Trustees."[12] In view of the Hopes' reputation, it is surprising that the Trustees would consider using their services. On 26 June 1737 Krämer wrote that he had not yet succeeded in engaging sixty reliable servants for Georgia because all the fellows desired to go to Pennsylvania and hoped the captains would take them without demanding any fare. Perhaps not all aspirants would be taken, however, and those who were left might possibly be persuaded to go to Georgia. Since Mr. Hope could not afford to send only sixty passengers, Krämer requested authority to recruit more in order to increase the number to at least 140 or 150, in which case he would require an immediate advance to defray expenses.[13] Here we see that the Trustees did not scruple against Hope's practice of packing his ships as tightly as possible with his human cargoes.

While awaiting the Trustees' answer, Krämer went to nearby Krefeld, where he received a letter from the Trustees dated 1 July asking how many people he could recruit. On 23 July 1737 he answered that, at his departure from Rotterdam, the ships for Philadelphia had not yet sailed and therefore he did not know how many Palatines were available. It seems that the Hopes' policy was to wait until the Delaware River froze and no more ships would head for Philadelphia, at which time the poor emigrants still remaining in Rotterdam would be forced to accept passage for less desirable destinations such as Georgia. For a consideration, Krämer agreed to return to Rotterdam and see how many Palatines he could find.[14]

On 20 December 1737 a large Palatine transport arrived off Savannah aboard the *Three Sisters*, with Captain Hewitt.[15] The passengers, who had been mistreated by the Hopes in Rotterdam, were suspicious of Hewitt and refused to go back aboard the ship at Cowes, a port of clearance on the southern coast of England, until better provisions were provided. Theobald Kieffer, Valentin Intzig, Caspar Schneider, and Johann Georg Keller took a well-written petition to London and asked the Trustees to send a deputy to look into their grievances. A Mr. John Godfrey of Southampton investigated the matter and found many of the grievances fully justified, even though Hewitt and his mate made proper excuses for the provisions. They also insisted that the leg irons taken aboard, which had disquieted the Palatines, were only for the crew in case of mutiny. Godfrey suspected that the interpreter, Anna Maria, the only one of the Palatines who could speak English, had been bribed or threatened by the captain. The unpublished correspondence concerning this affair, housed in the British Public Record Office, reveals not only the skulduggery of Hope and his henchmen, but also the sincere solicitude of the Trustees for their protégés.[16]

Later on, in 1738, some merchants, including the Charleston shipper Samuel Wragg, objected to a letter the Duke of Newcastle had written concerning the mistreatment at Cowes; on 28 January Oglethorpe asked that some words be deleted.[17] Wragg seems to have billed the Trustees for expenses incurred by the delay at Cowes and the detour in going to Savannah instead of directly to Charleston, to say nothing of demanding £154.17.6 for twenty-nine and one-half heads who deserted before departure.[18] Wragg must have been very active in the Palatine trade to South Carolina, for on 7 October 1736 he had been expecting "every day an account of the arrival of some Germans in Holland in order to be transported to that Province."[19] According to Kieffer, there were seventy-three families on the *Three Sisters*, totaling some three hundred persons. On

17 September 1737 Vernon instructed Captain Hewitt to take not less than ninety nor more than one hundred passengers, and the sex, name, and age of all of them were to be recorded. Infants were not counted, and children from four to fourteen counted as one-half freight.[20]

On 21 December 1737 Colonel Stephens reported that "Capt. Hewett in the *Three Sisters* arrived here, leaving his Ship full of Palatines at Tybee," where they had to remain aboard for ten days for want of a pilot.[21] Without authorization, Causton let nine and a half heads indenture themselves to him, while the remainder were retained by the Trustees and put under the supervision of William Bradley, who misapplied some of their labor for his own purpose.[22] Besides that, as Colonel Stephens reported, Bradley used "some severity towards a woman, whom he caused to be corrected, (very justly for ought I know) a general Discontent spread soon among all of 'em; and it being industriously (I think) at the same time propagated, that any who within 6 weeks could either pay or find Friends to pay £6:5:0 for 'em, as the Cost whch the Trustees were at for their Passage, might claim their discharge." Stephens went on to say that many bought their freedom, while others turned themselves to private hands, sometimes with later regret.[23]

One of Hewitt's passengers, John Stout (Johann Staude) of Kirckel in Saarbrücken, the father of Gabriel Bach's wife, Margaretha, was given to the seventeen-year-old orphan John Milledge, who had become head of his household soon after his arrival on the *Ann* at the age of twelve.[24] With his indentured servant's help, Milledge was able to take his two sisters away from Bethesda, George Whitefield's orphanage, not wishing them to be objects of charity. Oglethorpe approved, and perhaps instigated, this abduction.[25] Milledge later became the captain of the local militia unit, in which many Germans served.[26]

Stephens reported that Causton had chosen twelve of Hewitt's passengers to serve the Trust at the store, the crane, and the public garden, as occasion might require; and he voiced the opinion that, if a true judgment could be formed of them as a whole, "a more lazy, obstinate, & dissatisfyd people" could scarcely be found.[27] These Palatines still harbored suspicions and grievances because of the treatment they had received from the Hopes. At Cowes they had been frightened not only by the handcuffs and leg irons they saw being loaded on the ship but also by rumors that they were to be sold as slaves in the West Indies.

Boltzius first met Hewitt's passengers when he preached to some of them on 29 December 1737. He found them a very rough group and predicted trouble for the Trustees; yet he ministered to them anyway and married two couples, at which time some Englishmen and Jews attended through curiosity. Boltzius maintained that Hewitt's whole transport was a disorderly lot.[28] On the other hand, on 10 June 1738 he sympathized with two of the Trustees' servants at Old Ebenezer, who wished to substitute a Saturday for Ascension Day so that they could celebrate the latter at Ebenezer. Stephens soon saw that Boltzius had been right in his unfavorable judgments and predictions: on 2 April 1738 the keeper of the stores advised Stephens that some of the Germans employed at the public works, the crane, and elsewhere would not work, considering the day a holiday. Stephens well knew that they were a "slothful and mutinous Crew, always complaining of too much Work, and too little Victuals, and that they were daily growing more and more troublesome."[29]

Stephens concluded he had been too lenient, yet he also realized it was too late to round up the strikers on that day. Fortunately, the German servants on the plantations, including his own Bewlie, had not struck. On 2 January of the next year there was another strike by Germans who said they would not work until justice was done to them. Finding their complaints frivolous, Stephens and his colleagues made the strikers work on three Saturdays to make up for lost time and threatened to punish the next mutineers with the whipping post. Some ten weeks later some of them wrote a letter to Oglethorpe claiming that they had not received their rations and clothing properly; but an enquiry showed that they had received provisions yet had done no work. Stephens had four of the ringleaders jailed; but three of them showed penitence and were released.[30]

On 7 March 1739 Boltzius concurred in the view that the Germans of Hewitt's transport were "disobedient loiterers, violators of the Sabbath, and drunkards," and that "they live in all sorts of disorder." On 2 October of the same year he wrote in his journal that the German servants were so useless that their masters wished they could recover their passage money. Stephens particularly feared the use that might "be made of the Arms so frequently carried by the Dutch, German, and other Servants." As a consequence, a law was passed authorizing the constable and tithingmen to take away the arms of any servants lacking a special one-day license from their masters.[31]

People were displeased with the Dutch servants for other reasons. Some complained that Hewitt's disobedient passengers sat around fires at night in the woods, surely to shoot other people's cattle. Also, a Dutch woman was accused of fencing property stolen by an Indian, but punishment was deferred.[32] One of Causton's servants, who had asked to be assigned to him, left his work at Ockstead to go hunting. Seeing the man with his gun on his shoulder, Causton called the constable, John Fallowfield, to apprehend him. Fallowfield could do this only by clubbing the servant on the head with his leather riding crop. The next day the culprit was found dead in jail with his face in a pool of vomit. The English coroner determined that the man had not died of the beating but had smothered in the vomit; and Christian Ernst Thilo, the Salzburgers' physician, agreed with the verdict. The widow and the rest of the Germans strenuously disagreed, and Boltzius was summoned to handle the delicate public relations.[33]

As a good Lutheran, Boltzius endorsed St. Paul's advice to the Romans: "Let every soul be subject to the higher powers. For there is no power but of God: the powers that be are ordained of God" (13:1). Even more to the point at this time was St. Peter's admonition on the same subject: "Submit yourselves to every ordinance of man for the Lord's sake: whether it be to the king, as supreme, Or unto governors, as unto them that are sent by him for the punishment of evildoers, and for the praise of them that do well" (1 Peter 2:13–14). Despite his disappointment in the Palatines' lack of faith and morals, Boltzius resolved on 31 July 1739 to serve as their defender, because he saw that they were receiving little food from their masters. About a week later, on 5 August, however, he heard that the indentured Germans in Savannah were causing the authorities and their masters much trouble and that they were disobedient, defiant, extravagant with supplies, and lazy.[34] Finding his preaching of so little avail, Boltzius wrote to Urlsperger on 30 October to say that there was little profit in preaching to the Germans in Savannah and that he thanked God for putting them so far out of the Salzburgers' reach.[35]

Whereas Hewitt had sailed in the employ of the Charleston merchant Wragg, Thomson's success in transporting the Swiss in 1735 had emboldened him to go into business for himself and "at his own Risque," as Verelst informed Oglethorpe. On 7 October 1738 Thomson arrived in Savannah with a human cargo he had loaded at London.[36] This was a party of from 180 to 200 Palatines who had crossed over from Rotterdam to London in July on the *Adventure*.[37] Thomson took the group the rest of the way on the *Two Brothers*.[38] When he reached Savannah, his passengers were in a rather deplorable condition, some being so sick and swollen that they had to be carried ashore. A few were disposed of in Savannah, for example, on 11 June 1740 Andrew Duchee, the potter, was charged £14 for two servants, and Noble Jones was charged £23.6.8 for three and one-third heads. Larger numbers were retained for work on the Trustees' garden and the glebe lands.[39]

Unlike the indentured passengers brought by Daubuz and Hewitt and previously by Thomson, these immigrants were redemptioners: they had not yet engaged themselves to an employer but had merely obligated themselves to the ship's captain to pay for their passage, or the part not yet paid, with money to be advanced by an employer in America. If the market for labor was good, they could choose their own employer and make their own terms. This system of redemption, recently developed by Zachary Hope, was first recorded in 1728. It was the method favored by most German immigrants, especially by those traveling in family or village groups. Since many had paid a part of their passage, they tended to be more substantial than the run-of-the-mill indentured servants.[40] If a redemptioner found a friend who would reimburse the captain, then he was free. Since the redemptioner could negotiate with his future employer, several members of a family might indenture themselves to the same employer, or to others, for different periods or types of labor.

At Boltzius's request, the Trustees bought eleven and five-sixths heads of Thomson's passengers as servants for the Salzburgers, for which Thomson was eventually paid £82.16.8.[41] These newcomers were Salomo Ade, or Adde, a shoemaker from Tübingen, his wife, Margaretha, and son, Johann; Hans Michael Schneider and his wife and two children; Conrad Held and his wife, Elisabetha, his daughter, Elisabetha, and his sons, Georg and (Hans) Michael; Barbara Waldhauer; Magdalena and Elisabetha Gephart; Peter and Juliana Heinrich and their daughters, Catherina, Eva Barbara, and Margaretha; and also a woman named Catherina Custobader.[42] As we shall see, two other Heinrich children were sold to a trader at Augusta.

The young girls redeemed by Boltzius were to serve as domestics until becoming proficient in housekeeping and in their Christianity and thus fitting mates for the single Salzburger men. Three of these girls found husbands within two years. Schneider became the community's cowherd for the outlying herds, which required him to put his six-year-old child, Johann, in the orphanage.[43] The Schneiders had intended to cross over on the ill-fated *Palatine*, as Whittier named it, which foundered on Block Island; but they had been unable to pay the half fare demanded. Their luggage, however, had gone aboard in the care of friends and was lost, as Boltzius recorded on 30 December 1740.

Because the inhabitants of Savannah had no money with which to buy the remaining passengers on the *Two Brothers*, they, including the parents of the Gephart girls at Ebenezer, had to go back on ship even though some were so sick and swollen that they had to be carried aboard on wheelbarrows, as Boltzius wrote on 29 November 1738. They were taken to Frederica, where Oglethorpe redeemed them at his own risk, for both humanitarian and practical reasons. He did not wish to turn the poor people "astarving into other Provinces" or to deprive the colony of so many "able bodied industrious People."[44] On 20 June 1739 Captain Thomson billed the Trustees for £826.2.11 for the 116 heads of German servants delivered to Oglethorpe.[45] It is not known how many of these "Palatines" actually came from the Palatinate, and it is to be noted that Boltzius stated that Thomson's transport consisted of "Palatines and Württembergers."[46] The Ade family, being from Tübingen, were among the Württembergers.

Stephens tells the unhappy story of two Württemberg children who came over with Captain Thomson in 1738 and were sold to a trader near Augusta, thus being separated from their parents in Ebenezer. The trader put them out on a remote plantation to work under two slaves, whom he encouraged to molest the children. When one of the slaves tried to rape the girl, she cried out, thus angering her master, who had her stripped and whipped. When the governor at Augusta heard about such cruelty, he had the slaves sent down to Savannah for punishment.[47] Although heavily chained, the slaves broke out of jail and escaped to South Carolina, from which the authorities would not extradite them. Apparently, the trader was not punished. Boltzius was personally interested in this case because the children's father, Peter Heinrich, had been his faithful and productive servant until his death one year earlier.[48]

Most German redemptioners in Georgia remained practically anonymous, hidden behind garbled and fluctuating anglicizations of their names. An exception was Christian Steinhübel, whom Thomas Jones praised as the competent, industrious, and loyal foreman of the German workers on the Trustees' farm, whose thirty cultivated acres were the best anywhere around.[49] Since Jones wrote the foreman's name as Steinhevel, we may safely assume that he was a true Palatine, for the Palatines pronounced *b* as *v* (as in the case of Hoover instead of Huber).

Only a small number of German immigrants wrote letters home that have been preserved. One of these was Conrad Held, who came with Captain Thomson in 1738. Upon arriving in Georgia, he and his family were sold to an Englishman; but not long afterward they were transferred to Ebenezer to help the Salzburgers. Conrad and his son Hans Michael served the orphanage as farmhands and herdsmen, while his wife, Elisabetha, and his daughter, Elisabetha, served Salzburger families. After a year elapsed, he wrote to another son, a weaver apprentice in Durlach, to tell him about the journey to America and to give information about his shipmates the Gebhards, or Gepharts, who were among those taken on to Frederica after leaving their daughters at Ebenezer. This would suggest that the Helds and Gebhards were probably from the area of Durlach, a fact not suggested elsewhere.[50] Durlach was a small principality on the right bank of the Rhine, then a part of Baden-Durlach but now a part of the Palatinate.

Praise of Private Enterprise and German Labor

We have seen that already in 1736 Boltzius had concluded that the Salzburgers worked better individually than collectively, and it was not long before the same fact was discovered with regard to the Palatines. On 21 November 1739 Stephens wrote to Egmont that "the Palatin servants sent over from Holland on board Capt. Hewet are the most lazy of all, but those which went with Capt Thomson are good, and would have done well, if immediately upon their arrival they had been made free, a little land given them, and a tolerable support in the beginning."[51] Stephens remained firm in his belief that the indentured servants would work better as free men. On 23 February 1741 he wrote to Verelst to complain of how little was being accomplished with the Trustees' servants:

> As for their own servants (the Germans) 'tis ashame to see how little is done by 'em, to answer the great expence they have stood them in; whether 'tis mostly to their not being so closely look'd after by their Overseers as they ought (which I fear may be one cause) or rather to their Stubborn slothfull dispositions under Servitude; is hard to determine: but this I repeat as a certain Truth, that what time they have to follow their own business; no people living employ themselves more diligently: and they are withal so parsimonious, that many of them have saved Money to purchase several Head of Cattle. From whence I have been induced to be of the Opinion (as yet I am) that if a certain Number of such as had Familys, were made choice of to

form a Village, & settle upon it: they would soon shew their Freedom to be not ill bestowed on them whereas in the way they now are, they are a certain dead weight on the Trust, with very little benefit accruing by their Labour, to Ballance it.[52]

A few years later, in discussing some newcomers to Ebenezer, Boltzius wrote to Martyn, "The difference in Labour of such free Persons & of the Servants is surprisingly great, the latter rackoning it hard & unjust to serve for their Passage some years, therefore are very burthensome to their masters, tho' used [i.e., treated] almost like children."[53] Here we have further evidence concerning the relative value of free labor and servitude, a lesson now being learned by the Soviet and Polish governments. On 23 July 1750 Boltzius was still deploring the uselessness of German servants, but this time in favor of slaves!

Stephens was not the only one to see the advantage of importing Germans. A number of leading citizens of Georgia signed a document entitled "State of the Province of Georgia in the year 1740," which praised the colony and, among other things, gave arguments for bringing over more Germans.[54] This document deserves to be quoted as a good depiction of the redemptioner business:

> It ought not here to be passed over, how ready the Country is to receive a Number of German Familys, accustomed to Husbandry, such as usually come once a Year down the Rhine to Holland, and Embark thence for America, or the East Indies some of these we have already had experience of, in so much that the People here, would take off a Good Number of them: and 'twould be of great Service (as we apprehend) to this Colony at present, to send a ship over loaden with Germans, on the same Terms Mr. Hope does to Philadelphia, only taking care that Provisions for 'em on their passage be more Plentifull, and that they are less crowded than on board his Ships, The Terms are; they pay half their Passage themselves on Embarking; and Six Weeks after their Arrival, to pay the other half; which they generally do, with Private Contracts to People; but in Case they do not; then they may be bound by the Ship Master for 4 or 5 Years if they are above 21 Years of Age; But if under, they may be bound until the Age of 21 if Men, and 18 if Girls. It must be at this time confessed, that divers of these Foreigners have, during the time of their Servitude, shown themselves of a dogged Disposition, surly and obstinate, discovering an Aversness to their Masters Orders; Which proceeds (as we imagine) from a Dislike of their being subject to Strangers, Whilst others again, have behaved well: But it may be alledged with Truth that when, or

wheresoever among Us any of them have worked for their own Benefit, they are indefatigable and outdone by None; which joined with great Parsimony, fits them for excellent Settlers when Free.

While this may have been the conclusion of the leading lights in Georgia, it seems to reflect Stephens's earlier ideas and was surely composed by him. The document suggests that the Palatines should have better food and less crowded quarters than on Hope's ships; but it does not indicate whether this is motivated by Christian compassion or by the realization that Hope's passengers often arrived too debilitated to be of much use.

The document concludes with the observation that it was not sufficient for the laborers to be free; they should labor individually rather than communally. Oglethorpe had at first ordered the Salzburgers to work jointly, but Boltzius finally convinced him that communal work was ineffective. Already on 29 May 1736 Boltzius reported in his journal that "less industry, supervision, and care are applied in communal work than each householder expends on what belongs to him." On 5 June of the same year he wrote that the Salzburgers had found it necessary to divide up the communal lands so that each could take proper care of the land that fell to him and plant what he wished, because in communal work everyone depends on the other and the lazy stay away. One of Boltzius's parishioners backed him up in this view by saying, "It is indeed hard work, but we are working for ourselves because the land belongs to us and we have true freedom."[55]

The *Europa*

Persuaded that still more laborers were needed, the Trustees commissioned the Swiss recruiters Hans Jacob Riemensperger and Hans Caspar Galliser on 26 February 1741 to fetch a hundred Germans and Swiss, who were to be mainly silk workers. On 9 March of that year the Trustees resolved to reimburse Riemensperger and Galliser for their preparations, and they sent them very precise terms and conditions.[56] Riemensperger, who hailed from Toggenburg in northeastern Switzerland, had recently returned to Europe from Saxe Gotha in South Carolina to recruit colonists in Switzerland and Germany, even though that was a dangerous profession because of the stringent laws against newlanders, or "soul catchers," as they were familiarly called.[57]

Riemensperger's party, which originated in Bern, was detained at Aarau and Frauenfeld by the authorities, who thought the passport a forgery. The leader had to slip back to Bern to procure better identification.[58] This gives us an idea of the city fathers' continuing concern with the *rabies Carolinae*. The bulk of this transport was destined for Saxe Gotha, but Riemensperger picked up an additional twenty-six persons along the way for the Trustees, who agreed to pay their fare if they would go to Georgia. The entire party consisted of 172 Swiss and Germans, whose badly recorded names are still preserved.[59]

To the credit of the Trustees, they had made careful arrangements for the safety and comfort of this large transport, which sailed on the *Europa*, with John Wadham as captain. The contract between Wadham and the Trustees insured generous fare for the passengers. The Trustees also loaded three half hogsheads of "Rape/Eager" for sprinkling between decks and forty-eight gallons of English brandy for mixing with water after the supply of beer gave out.[60] Nevertheless, despite such precautions, Palatine fever broke out among crew and passengers. The fever, attributed to contaminated drinking water, felled so many people that not enough remained well to tend the sick or even to throw the corpses overboard. John Terry wrote that forty died en route and forty later in Savannah. As noted, Antonio Salice, from Grisons, appears to have made his second voyage to Georgia on this pestilential vessel along with his son and daughter, and this may explain his death soon after arriving.[61]

Johannes Vigera, the commissary of a fourth Salzburger transport that crossed at the same time, reported that the *Europa* entered the Savannah River on 4 December 1741 and that on 7 December he went aboard with Thomas Jones and Dr. Ludwig Mayer, the Salzburgers' new physician, to examine the sick. Stephens was deeply impressed by the way that Mayer treated the sick despite the stench of death.[62] Because of the infectious fever, the Georgia authorities at first refused to let the miserable survivors go ashore and kept them quarantined for several days on the contaminated ship, with the result that many more died on it. Even after the survivors had been taken up to Savannah, still more died despite the loving care of compassionate "Dutch Wives," as Stephens called the brave women who nursed them. Apparently, Boltzius had chosen well in recruiting the nurses.[63] When Riemensperger finally resumed his journey to Saxe Gotha, he had only a small party with him. Boltzius wrote to Verelst on 15 January 1742 that "a Party of them are carried by their Conductor Riemsperger to Saxe Gotha in South Caroline, & the rest, that hope to recover from their dangerous sickness, design to settle with their Countrymen about Savannah."[64] Those who settled around Savannah received £264.2.6 support for six months to help them cultivate their lands.[65]

Stephens relates that the Anglican minister Christopher Orton married four German Swiss couples on 27 January 1742, and the Reformed minister Henri François Chiffelle of Purysburg married three more on 22 April.[66] These numerous marriages resulted from the large number of widows, widowers, and semi-orphans among the survivors of the *Europa*. Some of these Swiss, seeing that they were not strong enough to clear land for themselves, contracted to plant fields that had been cultivated but later abandoned. Others hired themselves out to the Trustees' farm, where they worked very well. Stephens seemed rather annoyed when Friedrich Holtzendorf came up from Frederica to hire the Swiss survivors, who were so greatly needed in Savannah.[67]

The Trustees soon learned to recognize the value of the much-maligned Palatine and Swiss servants, as we may infer from their alacrity on 13 February 1742 in granting petitions of Johann Hennery, Heinrich Meyerhoffer, Abraham Grüning, and Christian Gampert for back pay. It is surprising what large sums were owed to some of the Swiss, and the records do not explain why. It is possible, of course, that they were collecting for work gangs they had supervised. On 18 April 1743 the Trustees owed £35.11.3 to Meyerhoffer, £30.12.1 to Gampert, and smaller sums to Grüning, Michael Hart, Christian Steinhebel, Conrad Densler, and Theobald Kieffer.[68] Meyerhoffer appears to have been one of the two Meyerhoffers who signed Captain Thomson's testimonial in 1735 rather than the one at Frederica, unless possibly the three names referred to only two people.[69] Theobald Kieffer was one of the men who composed, or at least signed, the eloquent complaint at Cowes. He, being Reformed and living near Savannah, is not to be confused with Theobald Kieffer of Purysburg and Ebenezer, who was Lutheran. Not only the Trustees but even the private inhabitants were indebted to the Swiss. On 25 October 1743 "one Burgomaster (one of the last Imbarcation) made a Complaint against Mr. Houston for Wages due."[70] The actual name was Burgemeister.

Lutherans and Reformed in Savannah

On Sunday, 15 January 1738, Boltzius preached to the newly arrived Palatines in Savannah "in the regular church," taking as his text the gospel for the Second Sunday after Epiphany, John 2:1 ff. Therefore this date could well be given for the founding of the Lutheran Church of the Ascension, although the year 1741 is usually given. During the next few years the Ebenezer pastors, most often Israel Christian Gronau, preached to the Savannah Lutherans every four weeks.[71]

On Sunday, 11 September 1743, Stephens wrote that, for want of an Anglican minister, the schoolmaster John Dobell had read the service in English and had divided "the time with Mr. Boltzius, who preached to those that understood the German language and were Lutherans, whereof he got a pretty full Congregation out of this and the Adjacent parts."[72] Dobell had come over as a servant to Charles Wesley and had served in the storehouse before becoming a schoolmaster. It would appear that, when no minister came from Ebenezer, the Savannah Lutherans had to make do with a schoolmaster, just as the Anglicans did.[73] The German schoolmaster could not have had many older children in his classes, because indentured children over twelve years of age had to work a long day like the adults, as Boltzius mentioned.[74] It was through the generosity of Michael Burckhalter that little Johann Adam Treutlen, of whom we shall hear more, was lucky enough to go to school in Ebenezer even though indentured. Unfortunately, neither Boltzius nor Stephens gives the German schoolmaster's name or explains who supported him. Boltzius likewise failed to mention the name of the schoolmaster at Purysburg, even though he praised him highly.[75] Only later do we discover that his name was Schönmannsgruber.

Even though the Germans who had come over with Hewitt made a bad impression at first, Captain Thomson reported to the Trustees on 5 October 1741 that, whereas the other inhabitants of Savannah were a vile and unruly crew, the foreigners there were quiet and industrious people and that it was a great misfortune that the Trustees had sent any others over. To be sure, Thomson may have been biased, being, as he was, in the business of importing German immigrants. When Boltzius railed against the ungodly eating and drinking of the Savannah Germans at weddings and baptisms, he was merely comparing them with his dour and docile congregation.[76] This does not mean that the Savannah Germans were any more worldly than the other inhabitants of the city. Despite the general poverty in Savannah, in 1743 the Lutherans there, like those in Ebenezer, contributed money toward the building of a church in Philadelphia, as Boltzius reported on 21 July of that year.

Not all the Palatines fared well, for there was no Boltzius in Savannah to organize charities for the sick and orphans. In 1740 George Whitefield, the English evangelist, wrote: "Tuesday, Jan. 9. Took in three German orphans, the most pitiful objects, I think, I ever saw. No new negroes could look more despicable, or require more pains to instruct them. They have been used to exceedingly hard labour, and though supplied with provisions from the Trustees, were treated in a manner unbecoming even heathens. Were all the money I have collected, to be spent in freeing these three children from slavery, it would be well laid out."[77] As we shall see, the authorities in Savannah were responsible for the destitute Germans there, whereas the Salzburgers had to rely on their own poor box.

Boltzius heard constant complaints from his German congregation in Savannah, yet these complainers asked him on 29 May 1741 to forward letters in which they were urging their kinsmen in Germany to come and join them in Georgia. Boltzius described their work as easy and stressed the fact that they could work for themselves in their free time and also gather grass for their cattle.[78] In general, Boltzius considered the Palatine servants ungrateful for the exceptionally kind treatment they received from the Trustees.[79] He was much chagrined when they broke laws, by, for example, shooting cattle or fencing stolen property. Only one German is recorded as committing a serious crime: Boltzius reported on 20 October 1749 that a locksmith from Württemberg had passed through various degrees of sin and ended up on the gallows in 1748.

Receiving visits from the Ebenezer pastors every month, the Savannah Germans were better cared for spiritually than the British, who had no ordained minister at all much of the time. On Sunday, 18 October 1741 Stephens recorded that in the courthouse, which served as the church, Boltzius spoke first to the "Dutch Servants and other Lutherans: A Minister from Purysburgh preached to the French and Swiss, who liv'd amongst us, the Doctorine of Calvin; and Mr. Barber from Bethesda taught the same to a Number of Britons."[80] The Purysburg minister was Henri François Chiffelle, while Jonathan Barber was the chaplain at Whitefield's orphanage at Bethesda.

While the Lutherans in Savannah were being ministered to by the pastors from Ebenezer, the Swiss and German Reformed received occasional visits from Chiffelle. Boltzius disliked Chiffelle, whom he considered greedy and grasping; perhaps that is why he sent Gronau in his stead when the Swiss minister asked him on 4 February 1738 to perform his marriage. Such an attitude may help explain why Stephens believed that, if the Lutherans and Calvinists would be "less rigid towards each other Charity would more abound."[81] Despite his antipathy, Boltzius let Chiffelle preach first on 4 April 1741.

Because of opinions like those expressed by Boltzius, the Calvinists of Savannah had to counter the "Calomnie" uttered against the "Sieur Chiffelle Ministre" in their petition to Oglethorpe to compensate the Swiss minister for travel from Purysburg to Savannah during the preceding five years.[82] Although many people wished to blacken Chiffelle's reputation, the Calvinists said he was really a good and respectable character who had given fine sermons and services in Savannah. This eulogy, which was forwarded by Oglethorpe to the Trustees on 10 June 1743, may well have been composed by the good minister himself. It was signed by the following:

Matthieu Mauve	Peter Baillou
Jaque Papot	Peter Joubert
Nicholas Rigbye	Anne Emery
Jacob Truan	Michel Germain
Jean Pierre Breton	J: O: Valloton
David Truan	Abram Bugnon
Peter Morel	Michel Burkhalter au nom
Isab: MacRai	de tous les Allemans
John Scillie	Jean Altherr
David Gunter	Jacob theiss
Gile Becu	Jean f: Ritter
Simon Rouviere	Michel Swizer
Jaque Chaussac	J: George Uhlant
Christian Steinhübel	J: Jagz Berker

The Gile Becu in this list is the Gilbert Beque who came from Rotterdam to Georgia with the first Salzburger transport.[83] It is surprising to find David Gunther and Christian Steinhübel listed with the French, unless they just happened to be with the French and French Swiss when they signed the petition, whereas the other German and German Swiss names were added by Burckhalter. "Jean f: Ritter" must be Charles John Fredrick Ritter, who will appear later. The names Schweitzer and Uhland are recognizable, and "J: Jagz Berker" may be the Johann Berger who bought a lot in Vernonburg in 1749 and a lot in Savannah in 1758.[84] The name Theiss, regularly anglicized as Dice, was a derivative of Matthis (Matthew). In the spring of 1745 Christoph Ortmann collected names and penned another petition, this time requesting Zubly, as Boltzius reported.[85]

The German Jews

The Jewish community of Savannah had arrived a half year ahead of the Salzburgers and consisted of many Sephardim, or Iberian Jews, and a few Ashkenazim, or German Jews. Of the German-speaking contingent in Savannah the leading families were the Sheftalls, who had treated the first Salzburgers to a breakfast of rice soup, and the Minises, who were from either Germany or Poland. Misled by the Sheftalls' kindness to the Christian exiles, Boltzius thought them ripe for conversion; he even gave them Christian propaganda published in Yiddish by Johann Heinrich Callenberg, a missionary to the Jews in Germany. Newman seems to have shared Boltzius's hope.[86] Samuel Quincy, the Anglican minister in Savannah, however, disagreed. When Newman wrote to Quincy to ask whether the Jews wished to embrace Christianity, Quincy answered that the Portuguese Jews were lax in their ways but that "the German Jews, who are thought the better sort of them, are a great deal more strict in their way, and rigid Observers of their Laws. Their kindness shewed to Mr. Bolzius and the Saltzburgers, was owing to the good temper and humanity of the people, and not to any Inclination to change their Religion."[87] The Iberian Jews had become "lax in their ways" in order to survive as crypto-Jews or Marranos in Spain, where "New Christians" were burned at the stake if they lapsed back into Judaism. Like Quincy, Spangenberg also noticed that the German Jews were stricter than the Spanish and Portuguese Jews, who would even eat pork.[88]

Because of their blind obstinacy, Boltzius gradually took a dislike to the Sheftalls. Perla Sheftall died in 1738. In the same year Benjamin married Hanna, whom he had imported from London. Being fluent in both English and German, Benjamin served as a sort of advocate and interpreter for the Germans in Savannah. For example, on 1 October 1738, Boltzius noted that Mrs. Rheinländer, one of his unruly parishioners who was in jail there, sent a Jew to ask him to get her out. The following year a Catholic girl fled to St. Augustine, after leaving a baby on a Jew's doorstep. Boltzius believed in the Jew's paternity, as he noted on 18 May 1739. The accused may have been Sheftall, since the German girl would have most likely chosen a German-speaking victim, and Sheftall was the one most able to support an infant.

The other successful German-speaking, or at least Yiddish-speaking, family in Savannah was that of Abraham Minis, who first farmed at Hampstead but soon built up a trading company. Already in 1736 Causton wrote a letter empowering Jacob Franks of New York to send Minis "200 barrils of Beef 50 barrils of Pork and 30 firkins of Butter."[89] The name Franks reveals the British tendency to add an *s* to German names. Because the German Jews in Savannah were "rigid Observers of their Law," we are safe in assuming that the pork was for their Christian customers. By 1740 Minis was a purveyor to the British troop at Frederica.[90] In a letter of 20 June 1743 to Thomas Jones, Boltzius implied that "the Jew Minis" was receiving the Salzburgers' produce and livestock.[91]

On 3 July 1739 Boltzius wrote to Mr. R., a friend in Berlin, that the German Jews in Savannah wished to build a synagogue and share it with the Spanish Jews but that nothing came of the plan because the latter insisted upon having precedence.[92] This seems amazing in view of the fact that the Sheftalls and Minises and an individual named Yowel (Joel) were the only German Jews recorded in Savannah at that time. The Sheftalls and the Minises remained in Savannah and prospered. When the Spaniards in Florida threatened to overrun Georgia in 1742, the Sephardic Jews fled northward. As lapsed "New Christians," they rightfully feared the tender mercies of the Inquisition, which at least one of them, Samuel Nunes, had experienced first-hand.[93] According to Boltzius, in November 1752 there were still only two Jewish families in Savannah, both of them German.[94]

On 7 May 1759 Boltzius reported that there were still a few Jews in Savannah, but he does not distinguish between Sephardim and Ashkenazim. Because of their prosperity and civil liberties, the Jews were even accepted by the Free Masons, and Boltzius predicted that more would join them. Two were serving as Indian traders and had married squaws, one family kept a tavern, and one was in business with a German butcher. Boltzius's greatest displeasure seems to have been the vanity and elegance of the Jewish girls, who even wore hoopskirts. He was not impressed by a sermon, written by a prominent rabbi, which the Salzburgers' old friend Benjamin Sheftall showed him.

♦ *Chapter Four* ♦

Acton and Vernonburg

Stephens's remarks about the industriousness of self-employed Germans heralded the settling of more German-speaking workers in the vicinity of Hampstead. The Trustees wished the colony to profit from the energy of laborers working for themselves, being now convinced of the value of free enterprise. On 28 December 1741 President Stephens and his assistants granted fifty-acre lots just south of Hampstead to some of Hewitt's passengers, who had now served their time, and to some of the survivors of the *Europa*. Among these were "Gaspar Herbach and his wife who had servd their time with Tho. Causton, Jacob Herbach and his wife who servd their time with Abm De Leon, Christopher Burgemeister, Hans Joachim Schad, Rudolf Burgie & his sister, Hans Stutz, and Nicolas Haner."[1] All these appear to have been Swiss. Three days later the president and his assistants resolved that "Hans Ulrick Peltz and Ezekiel Stoll, being German Switzers lately arrived, petitioned that they might have lands near Herback and others of their Countrymen before mentioned the same is allowed." Stephens had recently been named president of the Council of the County of Savannah, comprising the northern half of the colony.[2]

The crop report for the year from Christmas 1741 to Christmas 1742 for the Northern District of Georgia lists the names of several inhabitants of the Hampstead area, including "Michael Bourghalter, Ulrick Peltz, Ulrick John Haltz, Jacob Herback, Gaspar Herback, John Erinxman, and Samuel Lyon."[3] Of these, Burckhalter had by far the greatest yield. Dobell reported that Michael Burckhalter "was the best planter in the colony."[4] Word of these farmers' good work must have reached London quickly, because on 7 August 1742, even before their harvest was in, the Board of

Trustees resolved that "it be recommended to the Common Council that the grant of Lotts of 50 acres each to Jacob Harbeck, Harbecks brothers Samuel Lyon, John Erixman, and John Ample Dutch servants, whose time of service is lately expired, made by the President and Court of Assistance for the Northern part of the Province should be approved of." It is to be remembered that the word *brother* could also designate a brother-in-law. On 18 April 1743 the Trustees confirmed all the above grants as well as grants to Leonard Rigler, Jacob Danner, Henry Curraudi, Johannes Torgler, and Joseph Wachster.[5] The name Torgler, which appears in many forms, was probably a corruption of Torkler, meaning "wine-presser."

On 1 July 1741 Thomas Jones had written to Verelst that

> The Trusts German servants in generall behave well, and are industrious (tho' I found them quite otherwise for some time after I came to the Colony, being then very Stubborn & unwilling to work but when obliged thereto, and under One's Eye—They had (as they have since complained) been treated with great Severity on their first Arrival, (especially those with Wm Bradley) and debarred from the allowances of Provisions & Clothing promised them by the Trust. Of those German Servants, eight or ten Families are remarkably industrious, quiet & frugal, And have this last Year purchased a good Stock of Cattle; Some having six Cows—the least two; And each having a Garden where they raise some Corn, Pease, Pompions, Potatoes, &c. which with the Milk of their Cows is the chief part of their Food: They are at little Expence in Cloathing; but this exposes them to the Envy and hatred of Our Negroe-mongers, & such who seek the Extirpation of the Colony, as well as of the Drunken, Idle Sort amongst us.
>
> I am informed by Francis Harris & William Russel (who are very conversant with them and can talk the German Tongue) That they have lately joynd in a Letter writ and sent to their Friends and acquaintances in Germany, persuading them to come to Georgia where they may, by their Industry, live in greater Plenty and more Comfortably than they can elsewhere.
>
> These Servants are very Desirous That (when the Time of their Service is expired) they may have Lands allotted to them within twelve or fifteen Miles of Savannah, (where they may bring Things by Land-Carriage) in a Vicinage, and that they may make one Common Fence (as the People of Ebenezer have done,) and be assisting to one another.[6]

According to Stephens's journal entry for 27 January 1742, all the Trustees' Dutch servants had long had their eyes on a piece of land between Hampstead and the Vernon River, a saltwater tidal stream situated some ten miles south of Savannah.[7] At a meeting of the president and his assistants on 29 September 1742, the following was recorded:

> The Body of Dutch Servants (some of them now free and the Rest being so at Christmas next) applying to the Board that they might have lands granted to them at a Place now called the White Bluff on Vernon River, were told that the Person lately employ'd in running out Lands, was ill, but that as soon as he was able, or some other Person could be found, a Town on the said White Bluff should be immediately laid out and each Man should take out his equal Chance by Lott, And the Farm Lotts or Lands thereunto belonging should also as soon as possible be laid out, wherein Care should be taken of their having good Land, and that if any Quantity of barren Land should intervene, the same should be set by for future Purpose.[8]

During the first years of the colony land was often measured out according to maps that in no way indicated the quality of the soil. Consequently, some settlers received entirely, or mainly, sterile pine barrens. The surveyor mentioned by Stephens, Joseph Avery, must have recovered quickly; for on 27 October 1742 he wrote that forty Dutch servants out of their time wished contiguous plantations, and he proposed a place at the head of the Vernon River about nine miles from Savannah.[9] The Vernon River was probably named for Admiral Vernon, who then commanded the British navy's West Indian fleet that was backing up Oglethorpe, rather than for the Trustees' James Vernon. Stephens decided to name the new town Vernonburg from the name of the river and the "Dutch Termination 'burgh.'"[10]

By 14 November, while Avery was busy running out the land, the Dutch servants had already cleared much land and built "neat Commodious Hutts to live in."[11] Nearly two months later, on 24 December 1742, a lottery was held for thirty lots, twenty-six of the winners being Leonhard Radner, Daniel Deigler, Conrad Ferrier, Jacob Plessi, Johann Nobellet, the widow Häfner, Johann Belligut, Conrad Densler, the widow Kühler, David Kieffer, Theobald Kieffer, the widow Fritz(ler), Adam Ordner, the widow Maria Barbel Jung, Heinrich Steinhübel, Heinrich Nungasser, Christoph Schiefer, Carl Reiter, Valentin Blume, Jacob Dice (Theiss), Jacob Nungasser, Johannes Berrier, Caspar Schneider, Christian Steinhübel, Peter Diehle, and Adam Rheinstettler. These names are horribly mangled in the list. All of these except Nobellet, Belligut, Steinhübel, Schiefer, and Blume were among Hewitt's maligned crew, as were also Johann Ampel, Johann Erinxmann, Samuel Lion, and Caspar and Jacob Herbach,[12] who received

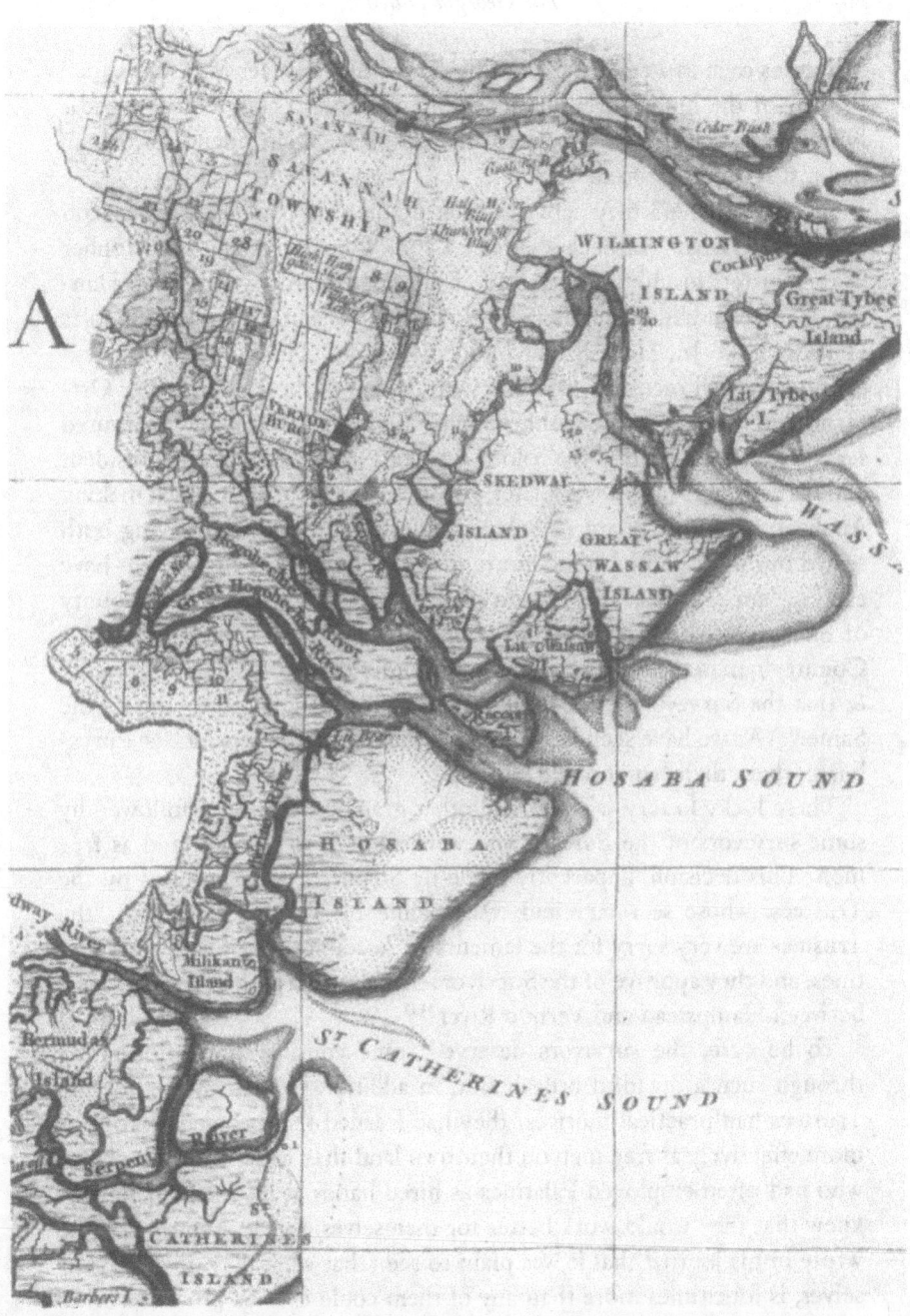

Christ Church Parish, detail from Stuart's map of South Carolina, 1780, adapted from original by Wilhelm Gerhard de Brahm (De Renne Collection, Hargrett Rare Book and Manuscript Library, University of Georgia)

fifty acres each as a reward for having served the Trustees for four years.[13] In view of the high mortality and the temptation to abscond, it is gratifying to see that so many had actually served out their indentures, which had just recently expired.

On 18 April 1743 fifty-acre grants at Acton were confirmed for "Jacob Harbeck, Gaspar Harbeck, Samuel Lyon, John Erixman, Christopher Burgemeister, Joachim Schad, Rudolf Burgi, Leonard Rigler, Jacob Danner, Henry Kuradi, Ulrich Betz, Ezekiel Stoll, Johannes Torgler, Nicholas Hanner Sr. & Jr., Hans Stutz, Joseph Wachter." These names were exceptionally well recorded, possibly with the aid of the schoolteacher Ortmann.[14] Because of the favorable conditions offered, even some indentured servants who had quitted the colony returned, as reported by the president and his assistants only a week later, on 26 April 1743: "John Rinck making Application to this Board in Behalf of himself & Son, (who having both serv'd out their Time by Indenture in this Colony) that they might have each of 'em a Lott granted them of fifty Acres each within the County of Savannah, & more especially being desirous to be settled near their Countrymen in the Village of Acton It is order'd that the same be granted, & that the Surveyor be acquainted therewith for the Running out of the Same."[15] As we have seen, Ring and his son had tried their luck at Purysburg, where their land proved bad.[16]

These lucky lottery winners and other grantees were soon followed by some survivors of the *Europa*, who were allowed to take up land as free men. This decision, apparently made by Stephens, was approved by the Trustees, whose secretary had written him on 11 June 1742 that "the Trustees are very sorry for the lamentable Account of the Swiss and Palatines, and they approve of the Survivors being settled at their own Request between Hampstead and Vernon River."[17]

To be sure, the survivors deserved some consideration after going through such a dreadful ordeal. But, in addition to their sympathy, the Trustees had practical motives: they had learned that people work much more effectively as free men on their own land than as servants. Stephens, who had often employed Palatines as hired hands at his estate at Bewlie, knew that they would work better for themselves. On 12 August 1743 he wrote in his journal that it was plain to see "that what they do for themselves, is four times more than any of them could ever be prevailed on to do for the Trust."[18]

As mentioned, Riemensperger's original group had been destined for

Saxe Gotha in South Carolina, and only the twenty-six extras had been engaged by the Trustees; yet it would appear that the Trustees, through their humane treatment, had won over some of the original party who had remained behind sick in Savannah. Among these later Swiss arrivals were Christoph Burgemeister, Hans Joachim Schad, Rudolf Burgi, Leonhard Riegler, Ezekiel Stoll, Johannes Torgler, Nikolaus Häner, Sr., Nikolaus Häner, Jr., Hans Stutz, and Josef Wachster, some with sizable families. It will be noticed that some of these had already received grants at Hampstead. They were soon joined by Jacob Danner, Heinrich Kuradi, and Ulrich Beltz.[19]

The close ties between these settlers is suggested by Egmont's reference to Samuel Lyon, Johann Erinxmann, and Johann Ampel as Jacob Herbach's "brothers," by which he must have meant brothers-in-law. As a redemptioner who had served the Trustees, Erinxmann received a cow, whereas his friend Lyon, who requested one at the same time, did not, because he had served a private master.[20] We know nothing certain about the nationality of Jacob Kurtz, who came over with Hewitt in 1737, or of Christian Lewenberger and Simon Guring, who came over with Thomson in 1738 and settled soon thereafter in Acton or Vernonburg.

When Joseph Avery began to survey the lots, the settlers insisted that he lay out "long Lots" like those at Ebenezer. Such long lots date from the Middle Ages. In their history of Württemberg, Karl Weller and Arnold Weller describe those in medieval Swabia, which fit the description of those in Vernonburg: "Between Enz and Nagold, as in other forest regions of Germany, one finds the arrangement of row villages or forest farm villages, in which the individual farmyards are placed in a row at equal intervals along the village street so that closed properties directly adjoin each farmyard and continue in long parallel strips back to the forest."[21]

Long lots assured everyone some good and some bad soil; in Georgia they had the further advantage of enabling close-knit families to live near together at the same end of their properties, thereby making the boundary along the short sides of their lots into a *Strassendorf*, or "Street Village," in which each family could live on its own land yet be no more than a hundred yards from the next neighbor.[22] Also, twelve property owners of adjoining plots could fence in the whole square mile with a single fence.

Already by 16 January 1744 Avery could report that the Vernonburgers had opened up the land on both sides of the road and built their houses on it for a distance of two miles. Avery acceded to the demand for long lots only after the future Vernonburgers had threatened him with bodily harm, as they did again later when he tried to alter their boundaries.[23] The long lots were one of the first things Boltzius observed in visiting Vernonburg on 7 February 1743. On 6 November 1745 Stephens had to send out a surveyor to determine the boundaries, which were being disputed by the inhabitants of Vernonburg, Acton, and Abercorn.[24]

Like the Pennsylvania Germans described by Benjamin Rush, the Vernonburgers distinguished themselves by their excellent fences, especially their "common fences" enclosing several individual farms.[25] Their practice of surrounding a number of farms with a single fence may also have been suggested, or at least justified, by the Salzburgers, who also erected "common fences." These fences were constructed to keep the cattle out, since "fencing out" was the law in Georgia, rather than "fencing in."

The Salzburgers had been diligent in making communal fences, as Boltzius noted on 23 March 1737 and at other times. The adjoining vertical planks of which these fences were made had to be close enough together to keep a rabbit from going through them, high enough to keep a deer from jumping over them, and strong enough to keep a bear from knocking them down. Unfortunately, they often burned when brush fires got out of control. In addition to the plank fences, the Salzburgers also made split-rail fences, which only served to keep the livestock in or out. One of these, built for the orphanage cattle, required four thousand rails.[26] Unlike the Salzburgers, the Moravians wove a fence around their garden within eight days of their landing, a work that greatly impressed the English.[27] Such "hurdles" were well known in England, but perhaps not by the Londoners. Whereas New Englanders thought that good fences made good neighbors, the Georgia Dutch proved that good neighbors made good fences.

Vernonburg Progress

On 1 November 1742 the earl of Egmont wrote that "the families of the German Swiss are about 19 and have made surprising Improvements." In this case he actually seems to have tried to distinguish between the Swiss and the thirty-eight German families for whom lands had also been run out after they had served their time. Although the lots had been officially assigned, the president and his assistants were liberal in allowing exchanges. For example, on 12 November 1742 Leonhart Riegler and Jacob Kurtz were allowed to exchange their lots.²⁸ By 31 January 1743 Avery could write to the Trustees that whenever they wished "to send over a ship with Duch (or German) familys there is a Town and land lay'd out ready to receive them, with some of their Own Country people at it, who will Instruct and supply them with what they are Able, for they are Undoubtedly very kind to one another, but not much so to Strangers."²⁹

By 26 February 1743 Stephens could note that the "Progress which the New Settlers made at Vernonburgh and Acton, was so remarkable, that many of our Freeholders at Savannah took occasion often to visit them, and gratify their Curiosity in so doing, having rarely seen the like Instance of Labour in Cultivation of Land." One year later, on 29 February 1744, Stephens wrote to Verelst that, because there are no hired hands to be had, "those Dutch, Swiss, &c, that have settled among Us within two Years past, make the best appearance as they are all labouring Men, & work for themselves."³⁰

Somewhat later the settlers at Vernonburg were joined by the Salzburgers' schoolmaster Christoph Ortmann and his wife, Juliana, who had been evicted from Ebenezer, and also by Johann Ring and his son Johann, indentured Swiss who, as we have seen, had left Georgia after serving their time and had settled in Purysburg, only to change their minds and take up grants at Acton on 26 April 1743. Another Swiss settler of Purysburg, Johann Linder, was offered a grant at Vernonburg on 27 July 1743 after having been refused one in Savannah, where he was known as a troublesome man.³¹

About two months later, on 13 September, a Joseph Faulker (Josef Falcker?, Folcker?)³² petitioned for a lot in Vernonburg, as did Heinrich Enderli on 7 October.³³ Enderli, being Swiss, pronounced the first vowel of his name so flatly that the British thought his name to be Anderly, just as they heard the names Densler and Bentli as Danzler and Bandley. The following men applied for lots at Acton: "Christian Levenburger, Conrade Hauver, Joseph Waxter & George Derrick. . . . One lot to be in the Stead of Joachim S. Chad, deced."³⁴ Here we see typical murdering of the names Lewenberger, Häfner, Wachter, and Schad.

On 10 May 1743 Benjamin Martyn wrote to Colonel Stephens to advise him that the Trustees "have granted Petition of Christian Steinhavell, Theobald Kiefer, and Johannes Berrier, in behalf of themselves and the rest of the German Servants; And have resolved, that at the Expiration of their Service, their Children likewise should be free, that they may be better able to proceed in the Cultivation of their Lands, notwithstanding the children were bound by Indenture to serve, the Males till the age of twenty-five, and the Females till the Age of Eighteen."[35]

It is strange that Martyn waited so long to send this news, for the Trustees had made the decision on 26 July of the previous year. Here again, the Trustees no doubt realized that the parents would get more work from their children than strange and resented masters would. At Boltzius's request, the favor was extended to Ebenezer, where the indentured Palatine herdsman Michael Schneider also regained the services of his children.[36]

On 16 December 1743 Stephens wrote that it was "some Satisfaction, that the Rate of our New Settlers at Vernonburgh and Acton are going on. I promise myself there will be more land planted this Spring than has been in any one year yet known by me." Nine months later, on 13 September 1744, Stephens reported that the best harvests were those in Vernonburg and Acton.[37] This was not especially high praise, since the surveyor Avery had written on 31 January 1743 that the area around Savannah was almost deserted and that "there will be little or no clearing or planting this Year unless it be what is done by the Duch and Saltzburgers."[38]

John Dobell seems to have shared Avery's high regard for the settlers of Acton and Vernonburgh. To discredit a proslavery petition written to the Trustees by Colonel Stephens's son Thomas, Dobell wrote them that Thomas Stephens's friends think that

> the Dutch folk, the Inhabitants of Vernonburgh &c, as soon as they cease to be Supported, will become more Clamourous than themselves are. But I hope to see them disappointed also in this, because the People are a Harmless and Industrious Set of people, Easy to be Influenced by those they respect, of whom there are two in this Town: Francis Harris, who came over with Mr. Thomas Jones, and William Russell, Your Honours Clerk in the Store: Both these are such, whose Behaviour begets Respect from their very enimies, and can speak the German Tongue, and are faithfully attach'd to Your Honours Interest.[39]

He then suggests that such a person should reside among them, for then they would continue to respect the Trustees. Dobell believed "the People to be as good a Set of people as them of Ebenezer are, and that they will become as prosperous as them, if they are so well managed as the said people of Ebenezer are." Unfortunately, having no Boltzius, they were never so well managed.

On 21 October 1743 Dobell, then the schoolmaster at Savannah, wrote to the Trustees that he was sending them lists of the inhabitants of Savannah, Vernonburg, Acton, Hampstead, and Ebenezer, which were made possible "Oweing to the great Assistance I have received from Mr. Thomas Causton, and Capt. Noble Jones, which they favoured me with, with much readiness And did not spare to Assist me by night as well as by Day."[40] On 16 January 1744 the Trustees received "A Plan of Mr. Avery's Survey of the Towns of Vernonburgh and Acton."[41] Dobell's list and Avery's map have been lost or, let us hope, lost sight of. The list seems to have reached Egmont, who appears to have made use of it.[42] Oglethorpe had recently commissioned Jones as a captain, after which Boltzius and even Stephens referred to him as "Mr. Jones."

On one occasion the Vernonburgers were less passive than usual, for they tried to circumvent the local authorities and go straight to the Trustees with their petitions. Stephens reported that they were reviling the local authorities and claiming that soon they would be ruled by their "own Country Laws." He did make allowance for "those of Acton of a mixed Sort of Germans and Swiss" who "go on quietly with diligence and Contentment."[43]

In any case, the Trustees continued to support the "Germans at Acton and Vernonburg" in various ways, for example, by sending them a cask of plows, hoes, and other things on 28 May 1748.[44] In his letter of 31 January 1743, which the Trustees received on 7 July, Avery informed them that there were still only thirty families, or a total of about a hundred people, in Vernonburg, whereas there was room for eighty or a hundred families. After describing the new settlement, he tells of the "missarable State" of Georgia, which has been almost deserted. He then praises the chief inhabitant of the new town:

> Michael Burkholder of Hampstead has a Tract of Land of 500 Acres Adjoining to those Dutch Settlements; and very soon he intends to leave Hampstead and settle thereon: This Man of all others in the whole Colony is the best Planter, and if any man in the Colony may be said to live by Planting 'tis this Man: He of all others has made the greatest Proof of his Skill and Industry, an Honest Man & a regular liver, is Master of several handycraft Trades, such as a Millwright, a Wheelwright a Cooper, and a Carpenter: His Eldest Son is a Shoemaker and Carpenter; his Son in law the same: His Eldest Daughter supplies the place of a Taylor, and his Five other younger Children are daily train'd in those Trades. In all moderate weather they work in the Lands, and

when it becomes immoderate, or in the Heat of the day, they come home and within doors work at their respective Trades: Neither is this Man less careful of observing the Lords day and performing continually Religious duties in his Family.[45]

On 13 January 1744 Stephens seconded Avery's favorable judgment: "Michael Bourghalter, with his Sons upon his 500 Acres, had exceeded imagination, and within 2 years cleared a very large Tract, part of which he planted last year, and more than twice as much will he get done this Season, besides making a Mill of his own contriving, on a little Brook that runs thro his Land, which turns a wheel, that with several Coggs upon it lifts up, and lets fall a number of heavy Pestles, wherewith he pounds rice and fits it for sale." Since the Vernonburg terrain is very flat, sandy, and not much above sea level, the "little Brook" must have been a tidal creek. A week later Stephens repeated his praise of Burckhalter as "the principal man in these parts."[46]

On 11 November 1742 Boltzius had written in his journal:

The Lord Trustees have freed all the children of the German servants in Savannah who still have some years to serve after their parents have achieved their freedom so that they can move with their families at Christmas to the plantations that are now being surveyed for them along a large river in the neighborhood of the orphanage. Together they should found a large town. These servants have cause never in their lives to forget what the Lord Trustees have done for them. Their work is negligible, and at the same time they and their families have received better provisions than they will have on their own land. But they have mostly sinned against the Lord Trustees through disloyalty and unrighteous behavior, and because of that they have already felt the heavy hand of God through the cattle disease but have not yet become any better. Divine truth is freely dispensed to them when we visit them because of our office; but they just listen to it, there is no true repentance or withdrawal from unrighteousness.[47]

When Boltzius visited Vernonburg on 9 July 1743, he was not impressed: "In this first year the German people on their land on the White Bluff have not made a good beginning, for their cattle are still perishing from the cattle disease. Because their corn is growing so poorly and they have little hope for their harvest, some of them are again working for daily wages."[48]

Only a month later, on his next visit on 11 August, Boltzius discovered that he had been too pessimistic. This time he wrote:

The German people have already expended much work in this first year on their new land, which they call Vernonburg, because it will be built on the Vernon River, and they will get more crops than they recently expected. They have very good land, and their city can be situated very advantageously. The souls who heard God's word were very pleased at my visit and would have shown me much love if I had allowed them to. I had come, however, only to serve them with my office through Christian encouragement and prayer. They greatly wished to hear something for their edification and gathered together for that purpose in a hut, where we prayed together and took cordial leave from one another. I hope in the near future to remain a couple of days with them and to edify myself longer with them.[49]

Five months later, on 13 January 1744, Stephens spent an agreeable day at Acton and Vernonburg

in looking over those Improvements they had made. At Vernonburgh there were 30 Families, among whom I did not find one but had been well employ'd, so that the whole Opening was entire, without any Interruption on the Front Line upward of a Mile and a half, and generally good Hutts built facing the Road, which gave a fair View, and their Several Improvements in clearing and Cultivating were backwards, more or less, according to the proportion of Strength they had, few under 4 or 5 Acres, and some near double. At Acton 22 Families had been placed, among whom 2 failed, one of them dying without any Family, and the other at present absent. These Lots were run out in Oblong Squares, 12 of which every way make a Mile, and these people (who are a mixture of Germans, Swiss, &c,) have most of them distinguished themselves by their Industry, and open'd the land about them to a great degree.[50]

Here we see that Stephens describes Vernonburg much as Weller and Weller described the "forest villages" of medieval Württemberg. A few weeks later Stephens's son Newdigate persuaded two or three of these Dutch settlers to work at Bewlie, and Stephens had to pay them thirty shillings per acre to clear out the underbrush, fell the trees, burn the branches, and leave only the logs for later use.[51]

Despite the good beginning, Avery remarked on 10 August 1743 that, notwithstanding the encouragement they had received, the Vernonburgers were not as industrious as had been expected, whereas the eighteen families at Acton had cleared a good deal of land and looked forward to a good crop. In contrast with Avery's pessimistic view about Vernonburg, Stephens reported on 16 December of the same year: "On this Occasion however, it is some Satisfaction, that at the Rate our New Settlers at Vernonburgh and Acton are going on, I promise my Self there will be more Land planted this Spring than has been in any one year yet known to me; to which, if we could add, what might be reasonably expected, from such as hold other Tracts of Lands, and depend mostly on their hiring men to labour (which I well know several that wish to do) the Increase would be far greater."[52]

Vernonburg Cattle, Crops, and Silk

Among the owners of cattle brands in the neighborhood of Vernonburg we find Michael Burckhalter, Heinrich Densler, David Fischer, Johann Grien, Jr., Nikolaus Häner, Michael Radick, Carl Johann Friedrich Ritter, all, of course, with anglicized names.[53] Because a cattle disease killed some of their cattle (a punishment for their sins, according to Boltzius), the Trustees saw fit on 5 March 1743 to give them forty cows, ten of them with calves. Sadly, half of these replacements died too, and Stephens estimated that three fourths of the cows donated by the Trustees had died.[54] This disease, which was called "black water" by the English, killed the afflicted cows with great speed.[55] Again, on 11 February 1744, Martyn ordered Stephens to give cattle from the Trustees' cowpen to the Vernonburgers who had lost theirs to the distemper. Luckily, the Trustees' cattle at the cowpen had been spared.[56]

By 1748 the wild cattle in the neighborhood of Abercorn and Joseph's Town had so increased that they were drawing off domestic cattle from the surrounding areas, so the Trustees sent orders to destroy the said cattle and divide them "among those in the first Place, who may have a Right in them, and afterwards among the most necessitous, especially the People of Acton and Vernonburgh." Although the cattle belonged chiefly to the Salzburgers, they renounced their claims.[57] The Council gave Boltzius plenipotentiary powers to exterminate the wild cattle, as he reported on 21 March 1749.

Second only to raising cattle, the Vernonburgers wished to raise grain, mostly wheat, rye, and barley, because bread was then the staff of life for Central Europeans. The list of crops raised by the inhabitants of the Northern District of the colony for 1742 shows that the Vernonburgers did exceedingly well, even though it was their first crop.[58] They did, of course, also raise vegetables for their own consumption and for sale in Savannah. On 27 August 1744 one of the "New Settlers" of Acton, despite having recently broken his leg, offered the Savannah storehouse one hundred bushels of new corn, but at such a high price that Stephens declined the offer.[59]

Unlike the Salzburgers, the Vernonburgers never succeeded in silk culture, probably because they lacked a good organizer like Pastor Boltzius. On 16 February 1741 Verelst wrote to Stephens asking him to help the Vernonburgers because Mary Camuse (Maria Camuso), the Italian tyrant of the filature in Savannah, was making outrageous demands.[60] Christoph Burgemeister and his wife and three sons came over on the ill-starred *Europa* later that year expressly to wind silk, but there is no evidence that they ever did so.

On 18 January 1743 Stephens gave the planters of Vernonburg twelve hundred young mulberry plants, which were taken there in Burckhalter's cart. The trees grew well and produced a quantity of leaves, but these had to be hauled with great difficulty to Savannah and to Mrs. Camuse's tyranny. Therefore, on 31 May 1748 Martyn wrote to Stephens and his assistants to urge the Vernonburgers to raise their own worms and wind their own silk. Somehow they do not appear to have done so, even though they could have obtained seed at that time near at hand from Noble Jones's daughter, who was raising worms at Wormsloe, the Jones plantation on the Isle of Hope.[61] On 16 February 1747 the Trustees resolved to send some copies of Boreman's *Compendious Account of the Art of Breeding, Nursing, and Right Ordering of the Silk Worms* to the people of Acton and Vernonburg, but this seems to have helped but little.[62] In 1760, however, Boltzius mentioned that a family at Acton was occupied with making silk.[63]

On 21 October 1743 Beltz of Acton sent a sample of cotton to the Trustees.[64] It is ironic that cotton, which received no encouragement, was one day to dominate Georgia's economy, but only after Eli Whitney devised a means to separate the lint from the seeds. As we shall see, the small amount of cotton grown by colonial Georgia's Germans was for domestic use. It must be remembered that all manufacturing was discouraged in Georgia, which was to remain a market for, not a source of, manufactured goods. Stephens belittled some weaving done at Acton and assured Martyn that it would not be hurtful to the manufactures of the mother country.[65] The Salzburgers had made some progress in spinning cotton by 16 July 1740. On 5 November 1743 Boltzius reported that a woman had sold his family a pound of cotton ready for spinning at a price of two shillings. On 17 October 1754 Boltzius reported that a nine-year-old child had separated twenty-five pounds of lint from the seed in one winter. Later we shall see that the widow of one of the Salzburger pastors raised cotton for making clothes for her Negroes.

Vernonburg Church and School

As soon as they had enough food for their bodies, the people of Vernonburg, 240 in number, hungered for the word of God. On 6 February 1743 they sent the Trustees a petition requesting a pastor, "a Man fearing God and hating Coveteousness; One that is well Grounded & Settled in the Calvinistical principles of Religion those being them we were brought up in, and which we stedfastly Adhere unto."[66] They then proposed Johann Joachim Zübli of St. Gall in Switzerland, son of David Züblin, or Zubli, of Purysburg, as a truly pious, prudent, learned, and conscientious man who was orthodox in their religion. The petitioners added that "the granting of this Request will Sweeten all our Comforts." It is more than probable that this encomium was written by the young man's father, who was not far away.[67]

This petition was signed by Michel Burckhalter, Hans(?) Berchoffer, Johannes Altherr, Carl Johann Friedrich Ritter, Diebald (Theobald) Kieffer, Christian Steinhübel, Michel Swizer, and Johann Joerg Uhland.[68] Unfortunately, the English scribe who wrote the petition transcribed the names from German script into English, thus introducing many errors which still appear in the colonial records.[69] Ritter, a planter of Acton who wrote a will under the name Charles John Fredrick Ritter,[70] was among the very few German planters in Georgia who affected three Christian names, a custom practiced mainly by noblemen like Philip Georg Friedrich von Reck and Johann Wilhelm Gerhard von Brahm (later de Brahm).[71] We have seen that Ritter was more modest when he signed the petition for a Calvinist minister as "Jean f: Ritter." He appears elsewhere as John Riter and as John Retter.[72] On the petition for a clergyman, Ritter's first name, Carl, was rendered as Earl because the capital letters E and C sometimes appeared almost identical in German script.[73]

On 8 March, even before the Trustees received this petition, Egmont had moved, and the board had agreed, to send the Reformed Germans and

Mr. Joachim Zubli being Recommended to their Appointment, who is their Country man newly come over, and abundantly well qualified.[80]

Stephens approved the request and, suggesting changes in wording, forwarded it to the Trustees. Meanwhile, Zubly preached to the Germans at Frederica for a few months after the death of Pastor Driessler.[81]

Zubly continued to preach regularly all that season, even though not licensed to do so. Savannah was often without an Anglican minister; yet even when Bosomworth deigned to come to town to hold services, he had far fewer hearers than Zubly, who, according to Stephens, was "in great Esteem for his Volubility of Speech and manner of Preaching among them."[82] On 26 February 1745 the inhabitants of Vernonburg and Acton again requested Zubly's services; but the Trustees had already appointed Bartholomäus Zouberbuhler, of whom we shall hear shortly.

On 3 August 1745 the Trustees granted a lot for a church in Acton, where some sort of a shelter must have been improvised. On 2 October 1759 a one-hundred-acre lot in Vernonburg, formerly used as a school, was granted to Michael Burckhalter, J.J. Zubly, Simon Gering, Georg Torig, Jacob Theiss, Thomas Frazer, and Georg Uhland.[83] Since the names Acton and Vernonburg were often used loosely for the German Swiss area, these could have been the same lot; but this time the plan was successful. In just over six months, on 27 April 1760, Boltzius and Zubly consecrated a church built with money collected by Joseph Ottolenghe, an Italian Jew converted to the Anglican faith, who was then managing the silk filature in Savannah.[84] For their church, the inhabitants of Acton and Vernonburg collected seven pounds to have a German silversmith in Savannah make a Communion chalice.[85]

As we have seen, the children of Acton and Vernonburg received a schoolmaster when Christoph Ortmann of Ebenezer was expelled from that celestial city. Boltzius had never been happy with Ortmann or his wife, Juliana, a worldly woman who enjoyed the company of itinerant Englishmen and had once even run away to Charleston to enjoy a festive Christmas instead of a dreary one like those celebrated at Ebenezer, as Boltzius related on 4 December 1736. Ortmann, previously a marine in the royal service, had conducted a charity school for the Reverend Henry Walter Gerdes of the Swedish Church in London, which was actually the German Lutheran Church. On 11 September 1733 Gerdes wrote to Henry Newman that he recommended

Swiss a Calvinist minister, who would receive the forty pounds allowed for the missionary to the Indians; for by now Wesley and Boltzius had convinced the Trustees that it was impossible to convert the nomadic savages, who simply would not learn English. The Trustees' resolution was to allow forty pounds per annum to a Calvinist minister for the "Swiss Palatines and others of the Calvinist Persuasion in the Northern District of the Province of Georgia."[74]

For administrative purposes Georgia had recently been divided into a Northern District with Savannah as its seat and a Southern District with Frederica as its seat. It is worthy of note that, even though the Presbyterian Church of the Northern District was establish by Lowland Scots, its first minister was Reformed. According to Stephens, there were only two or three families at Vernonburg who adhered to Luther.[75] This can be explained by the fact that the Lutheran servants out of their time preferred to settle with their coreligionists at Ebenezer.

As mentioned, the Vernonburgers' choice as minister was Johann Joachim Züblin, or Zubly as he later called himself,[76] who had been born in St. Gall on 27 August 1724 and educated at the gymnasium there.[77] His father, David Züblin of Purysburg, was the "wealthy" brother of Ambrosius and Johann Jacob Zübli of Ebenezer, who are mentioned often in the *Detailed Reports*.[78] David's son was still a nineteen-year-old student in Switzerland when the Vernonburgers requested his services.

On 16 January 1744 Zubly presented himself to the Trustees in London and offered to go to Georgia if they would give him fifty pounds per year and his expenses from Switzerland, a right presumptuous demand from an unordained youth. The Trustees refused on 23 January 1744; yet Zubly proceeded to Georgia anyway, after being ordained in the German Church in London on 19 August of that year.[79] Traveling overland from Charleston via Purysburg, he arrived in Savannah on 23 February 1745 and preached to the German Reformed on the same day. Three days later, on Shrove Tuesday, Stephens wrote in his journal:

> Several of our German and Swiss Settlers at Vernonburgh, Acton, &c, coming to Town, brought with them a Petition to the Honble. Trustees Setting forth the great want they were in of a Minister to Instruct them in their duty, that they were more than 240 in number, Men Women and Children, all agreeing in the same Protestant Confession of Faith and Doctrine, according to the Institution of Calvin, two or three familys only excepted, who adher'd to Luther; and humbly Praying that their Honrs. will be pleased to accept of

Christopher Ortman, who has kept here for these many years a Charity School under my own inspection and has always in his Office behaved to my entire Satisfaction. The man is about 50 Years of Age and is married to a Woman about 40. They have no Children. The Woman is likewise able to instruct Children in all manner of needlework, so she may keep a School for Girls for that purpose and has done so before now. Here they find it a difficult matter to Subsist and are therefore mighty desirous to go to Georgia.[86]

On 30 October 1733 the Trustees paid nineteen pounds to discharge Ortmann's debts and buy necessaries for him and his wife for the voyage.[87]

Ortmann had joined the first Salzburger transport at Rotterdam to serve as interpreter and teacher of English; but Boltzius found his English unacceptable, which is not surprising in view of his having learned it as a marine.[88] Because of his poor command of English, Ortmann taught only German and helped maintain himself by running a small retail trade, mention of which is all but suppressed in the *Detailed Reports*.[89] Boltzius's opinion of Ortmann fluctuated greatly. In a letter of 2 April 1735 to Newman he wrote: "Mr. Ortman our Schoolmaster and his Wife go in the path of Christian Virtue, and he is more and more serviceable to the Children of our School. We pray therefore the Society would forgive them their former Offences, for they repent heartily of the same."[90] In 1739, however, Boltzius was again complaining against both the schoolmaster and his scandalous wife.[91]

The final break came when Ortmann signed a petition circulated in Ebenezer by Colonel Stephens's undutiful son Thomas, requesting the Trustees to permit slavery.[92] Boltzius at once dismissed the disobedient pedagogue; but the Council decided that Boltzius had mistreated the schoolmaster. Colonel Stephens promised Ortmann twelve pounds per year to teach the Vernonburg children, but the Trustees disapproved this decision, apparently at Boltzius's insistence.[93] Nevertheless the old teacher did get the Vernonburg position. On 10 December 1743 John Pye wrote that Hamilton had told him that "the Council had given Mr. Ortmann (Thomas Stephen's assistant) . . . £50 Sterling."[94] Both the position and the sum sound questionable, but at least the teacher was again employed.

Ortmann's new position did not last long, either because there were not enough children in Vernonburg or because the inhabitants did not choose to send their children to him, so he had to appeal to Boltzius for help. Once the schoolmaster humbled himself enough, Boltzius had a change of heart. He closed his letter of 3 September 1747 to the Trustees with the request that they give Ortmann a subsistence because he was aged and infirm and because he, Boltzius, had forgiven him "all injuries to me & our Settlements."[95] Boltzius's change of heart enabled Stephens and his assistants to write to the Trustees on 2 October 1747 a very clear and compassionate letter on Ortmann's behalf telling them the whole story of the break between the pastor and the schoolmaster. They even decided to pay Ortmann twenty shillings per month to continue teaching the children at Vernonburg until the Trustees would assume the responsibility.[96] Stephens was much concerned about the old man and argued in his favor; after much hesitation, the Trustees finally agreed on 31 May 1748 to confirm Ortmann's modest stipend because he was "old and infirm."[97] They probably knew he had renounced a veteran's pension in London in order to go to Georgia. Being literate and understanding English, Ortmann often served the Vernonburgers as a witness in their business transactions and in writing their wills. Only two and a half years later, on 3 January 1751, he asked Boltzius to procure him a position at Abercorn because there were so few children at Vernonburg.

The *Judith*

On 27 May 1745 a group of 173 Protestants, through their spokesmen Matthias Wüst and Wendel Brakefield (Brachfeld?), petitioned the Trustees to take them to Georgia.[98] These unfortunate people had sailed a year earlier at their own expense for Philadelphia on the *Two Sisters*, with Captain Charles Stedman; but they had hardly left the English coast before being captured by two Spanish privateers and taken to Bilbao, where they lost all their belongings and were subjected to Dominican zeal to convert them to the True Faith. Ransomed by the British and brought to Gosport on the southern coast of England by the cartel ship *Drake*, most of those who could afford to do so returned to Germany. The remainder were lodged in Mr. John Carver's storehouse and supported by the charity of the townspeople. When the Trustees granted their petition, one hundred of them were still ready to go, of whom seventy-three signed the articles. Vernon's letter of 19 August shows the great concern the Trustees felt for the welfare of these emigrants.[99]

The voyage of the *Judith* came close to being as tragic as that of the *Europa*. Although the Trustees had allowed a liberal quantity of vinegar for disinfecting the decks, many of the passengers and crew caught Palatine fever, which killed the captain, Walter Quarme, and also Thomas Causton, who was returning to Savannah after being summoned to London to have his books audited. Another fatality was a Mr. James Bull of South Carolina, who had been put in charge of the Germans on board and had been promised the service of one of them when he settled in Savannah.[100]

The German passengers on the *Judith* fared somewhat better than the British; and Hermann Heinrich Lemke, the replacement for the late Gronau, and Bartholomäus Zouberbuhler, the new "English" minister, both survived.[101] It was fortunate that the latter remained well; with the captain dead and the mate grievously sick, there would have been no one else to plot the ship's course. Although a landlubber from Canton Appenzell, Zouberbuhler knew enough geometry to plot the course successfully with the aid of an illiterate seaman. He brought the ship directly into Frederica with the help of six German passengers serving as crew. If only a degree or two off course, he could have landed on the hostile shore of Florida, in which case the German passengers might have repeated the same ordeal they had suffered on the *Two Sisters*.[102]

Aboard the *Judith*, in addition to Wüst and Brachfeld, were passengers named Bormann, Foltz, Hermann, Ihle, Jäckli, Knippling, Kusmaul, Leinbacher, Litola, Mick, Müller, Betz (Pett), Portz, Raag, Ratien, Richard (Reichard?, Ritschard?), Schaaf, Stäheli, Treutlen, Ulman, Volz, Walthauer, Weissenbacher, Weisengert (Wyssengert), and Zorn, most of whom ended up at Ebenezer. All of these names were German or German-Swiss except for that of Litola, who may have been Piedmontese or Grisons; Boltzius reports that most of the passengers were Württembergers.[103]

In a letter of 10 March 1746 to the Trustees, John Pye wrote of the surviving passengers on the *Judith*: "Indeed Gentlemen it made my Heart Ach, to see some of them Begg on their Knees to Choose their own Masters, & Cry on the Refusal, they were soon Chose and put Out. The President & Assistants had 13 or 14 of them and the Clerk of the Council a Boy, and the first Choice of the Rest was given to such of the Town People, that made any Pretence of Planting."[104]

Some of the *Judith*'s passengers were assigned to Boltzius at Ebenezer for distribution as servants for his flock; others were assigned to Burckhalter for distribution among the residents of Acton and Vernonburg. Among Burckhalter's share was a Palatine woman named Maria Clara Treutlen and her sons, Friedrich and Johann Adam. Because Maria Clara's last name was garbled into Frideling on the ship's manifest, historians have failed to recognize the name.[105] Burckhalter signed a letter, obviously composed and penned by an Englishman, in which he thanked the Trustees for the Palatine woman and her three children and for the other kindnesses to "us Germains."[106] The third child may have been an orphan adopted by Mrs. Treutlen. Because Mrs. Treutlen soon remarried and assumed her second husband's name, she is unrecognizable in later records.

Zouberbuhler versus Zubly

It has been mentioned that the Trustees had refused Zubly's request for fifty pounds per year, possibly because of his youth. Since the new Anglican minister, Zouberbuhler, could speak German, the Trustees decided to let him minister to the people of Vernonburg as well as to those in Savannah, even though the people there preferred Zubly. Zouberbuhler was the brother of Sebastian Zuberbiller who had founded New Windsor.[107] Their old father had left the Swiss of New Windsor, with whom he had come to South Carolina; he soon died in Purysburg. On 19 February 1736 Boltzius sent his diary and some letters to young Zouberbuhler to take with him to Europe; but Oglethorpe detained the cleric to help him with some Swiss he hoped to bring to his barony at Palachocolas, as Boltzius reported on 19 February 1736. In July 1738 Zouberbuhler was with his sick father in Purysburg, where he preached on Sundays. He was ill much of the time and lost his father, mother, sister, and brother-in-law to sickness.[108]

On 3 December 1739, accompanied by a German captain and judge named Linder, Zouberbuhler came from Purysburg to Ebenezer to ask Boltzius for a recommendation to Oglethorpe for the position as preacher to some Swiss who had come from New Windsor to work on Oglethorpe's barony. Not liking the company the young man was keeping, Boltzius also refused to recommend him as pastor for the German Reformed around Savannah, whereupon the disappointed candidate sought a commission as a military officer at Frederica, as Boltzius recorded on 9 November 1741. Next he tried, by unfair means, to arrogate the post of Johann Giessendanner, the nephew and heir of the old minister in Orangeburg; but his effort was foiled by that pastor's grateful congregation, both German and English.

Failing to win a commission and finding no lucrative position for a Reformed minister in South Carolina, Zouberbuhler went to Charleston to study with the Anglican commissary Alexander Gardner, and there he converted to the Anglican faith. Gardner recommended him to the bishop of London, and he was ordained as an Anglican minister on 22 September 1745 in the Chapel Royal at Whitehall.[109] He was then appointed to replace the Anglican minister Thomas Bosomworth, who had quit his ministry in Savannah for the more remunerative post of Indian trader, his wife being the Indian "princess" Mary Musgrove.[110] As Anglican minister and schoolmaster in Savannah, Zouberbuhler was promised a salary of fifty pounds per year, plus two indentured servants to cultivate his three hundred acres of land. Because he could speak their languages, he was to preach to the French and the Germans in both Savannah and Vernonburg.[111]

While Zouberbuhler was having himself ordained in England, Zubly was preaching occasionally in Hampstead to the people of Acton and Vernonburg, who had requested his services as a regular minister.[112] Even after Zouberbuhler arrived and was officially installed, the Reformed people continued to stand by Zubly, who was still loyal to their Calvinist faith. Zouberbuhler wrote to Verelst on 14 August 1746 that not more than twenty Germans attended his services, the others preferring to stay with Zubly, who continued not only to preach but also to marry and administer the sacraments. Somehow neither Zouberbuhler nor the Trustees understood that, by deserting their "Calvinistical principles," Zouberbuhler had alienated himself from his Swiss and German flock, despite his native ability to speak their language.

Realizing that Vernonburg was too distant to be ministered from Savannah yet lacking funds to employ a second minister for that village, the Trustees decided on 14 March 1746 to employ Zubly as an assistant to Zouberbuhler at ten pounds per year, which was to be deducted from Zouberbuhler's salary of fifty pounds, and to give Zouberbuhler a third servant as compensation. Needless to say, Zouberbuhler was not pleased with this decision. In reporting on his ministry on 29 September of that year, he complained of difficulty in maintaining himself on his current salary, since his two indentured servants were unable to feed him.[113] Two years later, he was still unable to make a living on his glebe land, especially after one of his servants ran away; and the president and assistants recognized the truth of his convincing letter of explanation.[114] Knowing it impossible to subsist on ten pounds a year, Zubly declined the Trustees' offer and went to South Carolina to find "something better to his Liking."[115]

On 12 November 1746 Zubly married Anna Tobler at Ebenezer. Anna was the daughter of Johann Tobler of New Windsor, the former governor of Appenzell Ausser Rhoden.[116] Zubly next served in Orangeburg until the winter of 1748–49, at which time he became pastor at Wappetaw Congregational Church, about fourteen miles from Mount Pleasant, South Carolina. At about this time a contemporary wrote of him, "Mr. Zubly is a person of no mean parts and education; yea, he is a faithful, zealous, and laborious minister of the gospel." John Adams called him a warm and zealous spirit.[117] Zubly did not return permanently to Georgia until 1758. After his return it did not take him long to establish an extensive estate near Savannah, which he named St. Gall in honor of his native city.[118]

Zouberbuhler himself must have been unhappy with the Trustees' treatment, for on 2 January 1747 the Trustees informed Stephens that they were "concern'd to find that you have any Apprehensions of Mr. Zouberbuhler's being dissatisfied, and looking out for Preferment in any other Place. He has perform'd his Duty so well hither to, and so much better than any of his Predecessors, that the Loss of him could not easily be repair'd."[119] This was certainly true with regard to the previous Anglican ministers, all of whom quickly died, left, or misbehaved. Perhaps the Trustees' fear of losing Zouberbuhler caused them to cater to him, for on 7 July 1749 Martyn wrote to Stephens that "the Trustees have resolv'd to grant to Mr. Zouberbuhler 500 Acres of Land; And also to his two Brothers Mr. Sebastian Zouberbuhler of New England, and Mr. Melchior Liekenstaiger of South Carolina, a Grant of 500 Acres each, as near adjoining to his as possible, if it shall appear to you that they may have Abilities to cultivate the same."[120]

Sebastian Zuberbiller had been only about eighteen years of age when he brought the Swiss party to New Windsor; later he took another party to Maine, where he became a public figure. Melchior Lichtenstaiger must have been a brother-in-law rather than a brother, but as we have seen, such bonds were much stronger then than now. It does not appear that Lichtenstaiger, obviously a Swiss, ever tried to develop his grant.

Bartholomäus Zouberbuhler was to survive for many years as head of the Anglican Church, which became the established church when the colony reverted from the Trustees to the Crown.[121] As such he was opposed by Zubly, the champion of the Dissidents; thus the religious friction in Georgia became a matter of St. Galler versus Appenzeller. After Zouberbuhler's death in 1766, Zubly opposed his successor, Samuel Frink, at whom Zubly leveled a biting diatribe.[122] By the time Zouberbuhler died, he had amassed enough of a fortune to leave a legacy to support a missionary to teach his slaves Christianity. Zubly also amassed much property. According to the Lutheran patriarch Muhlenberg, Zubly's estate, St. Gall, was very extensive.[123] As we shall see, many people also praised his library.

Vernonburg's Prosperity and Signs of Decline

The British expressed marked admiration for the Vernonburgers' industry. On 14 March 1746 Benjamin Martyn wrote to William Stephens that

> the Trustees are pleas'd to see by the Journal August 15th 1745, the great Improvement made in Cultivation by the Germans and Swiss, the Neatness in which their Plantations lye contiguous to each other for such an Extent with proper Habitations, the Comfort and Tranquility in which they live at present, and the Foundation which they have laid for their future Plenty and Happiness. Surely such a Sight of the Country must be an Incitement to the English at Savannah and other Places to be industrious likewise, or it will be a perpetual Reproach to them. Can they be content to have it thought that Britons have less Strength, less Resolution, and less Virtue than every other People? Can they be content to see those, who were lately many of them their Servants, are now in a better Condition than they are, with Plantations still improving, whilst their Masters are in a manner totally neglected, or running into Ruins.[124]

It did not take Stephens long to observe, as he did on 11 December 1746, that scarcely a man at Ebenezer, Acton, Vernonburg, and Abercorn had not been brought up to hard work, in contrast with the earlier settlers in Savannah. On 29 December 1744 the Germans and Swiss at Vernonburg, Acton, and adjacent places numbered 240, just a little fewer than the 279 souls at Ebenezer in 1743.[125]

Vernonburg's prosperity would appear to have lasted little longer than that of German Village on St. Simons Island, if we can believe a letter Colonel Stephens wrote to Martyn on 2 October 1747:

> We were mightily glad to hear the Trustees were pleased with the Account of the great Improvements made in Cultivation of Lands by the Germans and Swiss at Vernonburgh and Acton in the Year 1745; which at that Time were two compleat Settlements; and it would be a great Pleasure to Us now

if We could acquaint them, that those Settlements still deserve the same Encomiums; But the Contrary is so Apparent, that our Duty oblidges Us to acquaint the Trustees with the several Degrees by which they rose and the means of their falling from that Appearance of Industry They first made (Viz) That most of those People were Servants to the Trustees, and in lieu of their Provisions, we paid in Cash Eight Pence a Day to each Man, six Pence to each Woman, and four Pence and three Pence to their Children according to their several Ages; besides Saturdays which was mostly spent in working for Hire in and about Savannah: By these Means they accumulated considerable Sums of Money, which enabled them to begin their Plantations with Vigour; And farther to encourage them, the same Allowance to Man and Woman was continued for one whole Year; besides the Allowance of working Tools, a Cow and Calf, Sow, Fowls &c.; all which enabled them to go on well for the first two Years of their Settlements; but during the second Year some of the Men found it more easy and beneficial being in the King's Forts, than cultivating Lands; The Sweets of which induced many of their Neighbors to follow their Example the succeeding Years during which Time they prevailed on their Officers to sufer them frequently to go to their Homes, sometimes a Month and sometimes two, to prepare their Plantations and to assist their Families in planting, which were left to their Wives and Children to take Care of in their Absence. These were the Methods used by those People, whereby they found a pretty good Subsistance, until such Times as the extra Troops were discharged, which has reduced them to a miserable State, even to the Want of common Necessaries of Life, and has so farr impaired their Healths that several of them have been driven to the Necessity of applying to this Board for Relief; The Expence of which will be too apparent in the Accounts both of Medicines and Provisions: We are well assured Sir that had you been fully informed, You would have hardly recommended them as an Example to the Inhabitants of Savannah or others to follow: It is true the People of Savannah are not so industrious in Cultivating their Lands as We could wish them to be; but as Most of Them are Trades People, They have found it much easier and more to their Benefit to gain their Living by their Trades.[126]

Stephens seems to have forgotten that he himself had contributed to the Vernonburgers' delinquency by having his son Newdigate hire some of them for work at Bewlie.

On 6 October 1744 Stephens had noted that some of the Vernonburgers who missed the military muster did so because they were rowing on Daniel Demaitre's and Noble Jones's scout boats. Among these were Hans Joachim Schad and also Georg and Johann Fretz, who received £9.15 for rowing six months and fifteen days.[127] Four years later, on 28 May 1748, the Trustees complained that the Rangers, as the mounted militia were called, were recruiting among the Vernonburgers, whom the Trustees had brought to Georgia at such great expense.[128] On the Rangers' rolls we find eleven residents of the Acton-Vernonburg area: Walter Denney, James and Peter Gunther, George Haisler, Nikolaus Häner, Jacob Kurtz, David Nungasser, Adam and Heinrich Ordner, and Matthias and Michael Salfner. All in all, there are some seventy-four German names on the muster rolls, most of which can be confirmed by land grants or other documents. Some of these names are written in almost as many anglicized forms as there are muster rolls.

Determined to keep the Germans and Swiss at Vernonburg, the Trustees sent much help. For example, on 19 March 1748 they resolved to allow a sum of twenty pounds for "Plows, Scythes, &c" for the people of Acton and Vernonburg, which paid for a cask of plows and other things that were sent on 28 May.[129] On 5 November of the same year Stephens wrote to Martyn that the "Charitable Presents of Working Tools &c to the poor Inhabitants of Vernonburgh and Acton for the better encouragement of Industry were distributed equally Amongst the Families and were received with a great deal of Thankfullness to the Honorable Trustees for their kindness towards them."[130] Such presents did not, of course, take the place of the cash support the settlers had enjoyed during their first year. At this time Boltzius and Gronau were providing the Vernonburgers with divine services every two months, as Boltzius recorded on 20 December 1749.

John Dobell, ever a champion of the Trustees and an enemy of the fault-finding Malcontents in Savannah, argued on 27 April 1748 that the Swiss of Acton were not leaving because of the heat or the lack of Negroes, but because of want of impartial justice.[131] He offered no examples, nor is there any evidence of discrimination. To be sure, disadvantages are suffered by foreigners who have not yet learned the language or laws of their new homeland. In any case, it was not long before the Vernonburgers were partially governing themselves. On 28 July 1757 Rudolf Burckhalter was appointed collector and assessor for Vernonburg and Acton, and on 6 March 1766 Henry Nungasser and David Kieffer were appointed surveyors of roads for the same area.[132]

Like Stephens, other people also noted Vernonburg's decline. On 2 January 1752 the old schoolmaster Ortmann wrote from there that the place was being deserted and requested a position in Abercorn; on 4 March of the same year Boltzius reported that settlers were leaving Vernonburg and Acton and taking their families to Augusta and into spiritual perdition. John Dobell wrote to the Trustees that the Malcontents were "unpeopling Georgia very swiftly discouraging the Young Mr. Zubly and driving away the Worthy Dutch planters."[133] Nevertheless, this emigration from Vernonburg did not foretell any immediate demise, because new settlers often replaced the old.

Despite Stephens's lugubrious description of Vernonburg and despite Ortmann's and Boltzius's predictions of its imminent fall, people still requested lots there. For example, when Johann Jacob Blasse sold his lot on 14 March 1748, it was bought by a newcomer named Hans Jacob Macher, who was probably the same as Johann Jacob Metzger of Purysburg.[134] In 1759 the Vernonburgers still felt permanently rooted, for they presented a petition on 10 August for a tract of land for their minister, Zubly.[135] At about this time a new German settlement appeared, a small hamlet just northwest of Acton that received the name Dutchtown. Until a short time ago it was remembered by the name Dutchtown Road, which has recently been changed to Netherlands Avenue by unknowing realtors.

On 4 December 1759 his Excellency the governor signed grants at Vernonburg for Sigismund Beltz, Walter Denny,[136] Henry Densler, Peter Dowle (Diehle), Henry Fritsee (Heinrich Fritschi), Christian Gampert, Caspar Garbet, Mathias Gugel, Samuel Hammer, Nikolas Hanner (Nikolaus Häner), Elisabeth Heinrich (Hendrick), Frederic Herb, Theobald Keiffer (Kieffer), John Lang (Lange), Jacob Nongezer (Nonngasser), Adam Ortner, David Rionstettler (Rheinstettler), Matthias Salfner, Gaspar Sneider (Caspar Schneider), George Uland (Uhland), and Peter Young (Jung). On 5 February 1760 he signed grants for David Kieffer, Jacob Theiss, and David Tubear.[137] On 25 September 1760 he signed additional grants for Uhland and Burckhalter, and on 3 December of that year he granted lots to Jacob Waldburger and Johann Scheraus.[138] Since many of these people already had lots in Vernonburg, the governor may have merely been confirming them. Although many people predicted an early death for Vernonburg and Acton, the towns remained populous enough until the Revolution to send one representative each to the royal council in Savannah in 1779 during the British occupation.[139]

The real reason for Vernonburg's failure was economic, caused in part by the British mercantilist policy, which had been an economic hinderance from the very beginning. Henry Newman had already made this clear to von Reck on 3 December 1734: "Your proposal of bringing over to Georgia Manufactures in Glass and Earthen Ware has been laid before the Trustees who do not think it proper to encourage Manufactures in Georgia which may interfere with those of Great Britain." Urlsperger seems to have gotten the word very quickly. On 2 May 1735 he warned Labhart, the eager merchant of St. Gall who had asked him about the feasibility of establishing a Swiss settlement at Ebenezer, that "only such fabriques and Manufactures would be allowed to erect in Georgia which don't hinder those in Great Britain." Benjamin Martyn gave similar advice to Samuel Wragg on 1 May 1735.[140] While the Trustees subsidized the production of silk, an unprofitable undertaking, they discouraged the weaving of flax and cotton, in which the Vernonburgers had made a successful start. On 19 July 1750 the president and his assistants wrote to Martyn that, whereas two of the inhabitants of Acton had woven a little cloth for their own use, it would be in no way "hurtful to the Manufactures of our Mother Country."[141]

Vernonburg had almost no market for perishable goods such as dairy products and vegetables, because Savannah was a small village in which many people had their own cows and gardens and had little money to buy anything anyway. While they could feed themselves easily, the Vernonburgers could not obtain cash with which to buy clothes, tools, and other necessities. That is the reason they continued to hire themselves out even after being established at Vernonburg. The same had been true at Ebenezer. As we shall see, many residents of that settlement also sought work elsewhere.

• *Chapter Five* •

Success at Ebenezer

At this point it might be well to backtrack to see what had been happening at Ebenezer. After much confusion and friction at the Red Bluff, the two squabbling commissioners von Reck and Vat departed in defeat and shame, leaving Boltzius in unquestioned command. The land was finally distributed on 3 December 1737, as had been promised three years earlier. After that, progress was phenomenal. Within a year after the removal to the Red Bluff, John Wesley wrote: "In the evening we came to . . . New Ebenezer, where the poor Saltzburghers are settled. . . . The industry of this people is quite surprising. Their sixty huts are neatly and regularly built, and all the little spots of ground between them, improved to the best advantage. On one side of the town is a field of Indian corn; on the other are the plantations of several private persons; all of which together one would scarce think possible for a handful of people to have done in one year."[1]

The Salzburgers also impressed George Whitefield, the great evangelist, when he visited Ebenezer on 11 July 1738: "Returned this evening from Ebenezer (whither I went yesterday) the place where the Saltzburghers are settled; and was wonderfully pleased with their Order and Industry. Their lands are improved surprisingly for the Time they have been there, and I believe they have far the best Crops of any in the Colony."[2]

By 23 September 1738 the Salzburgers received four square miles of land across Abercorn Creek on Abercorn Island. Because the land was flooded by the Savannah River every winter, the planters had to build their houses and keep their cattle on the high land on the Ebenezer side of the creek, but this inconvenience was well repaid by the fertility caused by the annual inundation. Francis Moore, the recorder at Frederica, visited his old

Salzburger shipmates at Ebenezer somewhat later and made the following observations:

> Besides the Indigent from England, many foreign Protestants and Highlanders were sent to the Colony; these being accustom'd to Hardship and Labour, were not afraid of it in Georgia, and they live by it very comfortably. . . . In the Town of Ebenezer, situated in the Northern Part of the Province, the Saltzburghers are planted. They are a sober and industrious People, and do at present reap the Fruits of their Industry. They have great Herds of Cattle which are increasing; their Land lies very neat, and is well cultivated. They raise large Quantities of Corn, Peas, Potatoes, Pompkins, Cabbages, and other Garden Stuff. They not only raise sufficient for their own Consumption, but are enabled to sell at the Town of Savannah. They are so contented with their Settlement, and so sensible of their Happiness, that they are frequently sending to their own Country Invitations to their Friends to go over to them, and have applied to the Trustees to send more Transports of their Countrymen to be settled with them.[3]

This passage was repeated later verbatim in Benjamin Martyn's response to the Malcontents.[4] Moore had visited Ebenezer with Thomas Jones and Colonel Stephens on 1 September 1739.

The request for another transport had been written on 13 March 1739 and signed by all adult males in the community. In this long letter, obviously composed by Boltzius, the Salzburgers assured the Trustees that the climate and soil of Georgia were good and that Germans could prosper there if given only a little support at first. They contended that white people could produce even rice, and they requested that no blacks be permitted in the country. They also asked that no one but their friends and countrymen be allowed to settle near them. Unlike most colonial lists of German names, this one spelled the names of the forty-nine signatories correctly, having been penned by Boltzius.

Benjamin Martyn, the Trustees' secretary, who visited Ebenezer on 24 June 1738, joined the laudatory chorus the following year with similar personal observations:

> Fifteen miles from Purysburg on the Georgia side is Ebenezer, where the Salzburgers are situated. Their houses are neat and regularly set out in streets, and the whole economy of their town, under the influence of their ministers, Mess. Bolzius and Gronau, is very exemplary. For the benefit of their milk cattle, a herdsman is appointed to attend them in the woods all the day, and

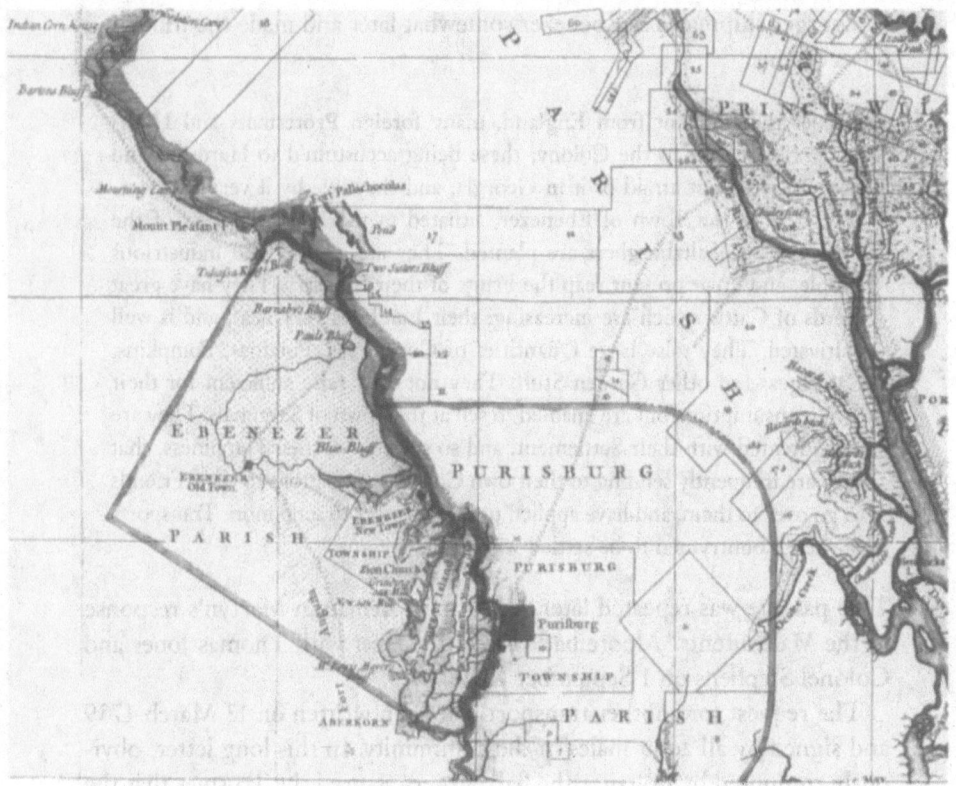

St. Matthews Parish, detail from Stuart's map of South Carolina, 1780, adapted from original by Wilhelm Gerhard de Brahm (De Renne Collection, Hargrett Rare Book and Manuscript Library, University of Georgia)

bring them home in the evening. Their stock of out-lying cattle is also under the care of two other herdsmen, who attend them in their feeding in the day, and drive them into cow-pens at night. This secures the owners from any loss, and the herdsmen are paid by a small contribution among the people. These are very industrious, and subsist comfortably by their labor.

Though there is no court of justice, as they live in sobriety, they maintain great order and decency. In case of any differences, the minister calls three or four of the most prudent elders together, who in a summary way hear and determine as they think just, and the parties always acquiesce with content in their judgement. They are very regular in their public worship, which is on week-days in the evening after their work; and in the forenoon and evening on Sundays. They have built a large and convenient house for the reception of orphans and other poor children, who are maintained by benefactions among the people, and are well taken care of and taught to work according as their age and ability will permit. The number computed by Mr. Bolzius in June, 1738, whereof his congregation consisted, was one hundred and forty-six, and some more have since been settled among them. They are all in general so well pleased with their condition, that not one of their people has abandoned the settlement.[5]

From the foregoing eulogies, we see that the Salzburgers were making great advances in their agriculture and cattle raising, further details of which are given in the appended Summary 2.

The Ebenezer Orphanage

The year 1738 marks the founding of the Salzburgers' most renowned institution, an orphanage modeled on that of the Francke Foundation in Halle.[6] Since both Boltzius and Gronau had taught at Francke's famous orphanage, it is understandable that they wished to build a replica of it at Ebenezer. For this purpose, money was contributed by benefactors in Germany; but most of the actual work was done *pro bono* by the Salzburgers themselves. Boltzius gives a detailed account of the occupants and management of the orphanage in his journal entry for 10 January 1738, the day the institution was consecrated. It had six structures: the orphan house proper, which was thirty by forty-five feet; a kitchen with a pantry; a cow barn; a pig sty with chicken coop; a utility shed for grinding, baking, and washing; and a privy. Naturally, no time was left in the children's rigid schedule for any play. David Copperfield and Jane Eyre could have felt very much at home there.

When George Whitefield visited Ebenezer on 11 July 1738, he was deeply impressed not only by the advances in farming and the piety of the two ministers but also by the orphanage, which he mentioned in his journal: "They have likewise an Orphan House, in which are seventeen Children and one Widow, and I was much delighted to see the Regularity wherewith it is managed. Oh that GOD may stir up the Hearts of His Servants to contribute towards that and another which we hope to have erected at Savannah."[7] He then goes on to say that he donated some gifts to Boltzius for the orphanage and that there was a little ceremony of gratitude, at which the children sang a hymn and kissed the donor's hand.

Whitefield next made the pious wish that God would raise up instruments to assist them, a wish that he himself was to fulfill two years later.

In August 1738 the orphanage acquired a barn, which Boltzius described on the thirteenth of that month. When the barn was destroyed by fire, a larger one, thirty-six feet square, was built with a threshing floor and storage bins in the attic, as Boltzius reported on 19 July 1740. It was fortunate that a selfless young couple, Ruprecht and Margaretha Kalcher, were willing to undertake the management of this enterprise, for they were industrious as well as competent. Because the first orphanage proved too small by 1743, the Salzburgers resolved to build a larger one with lumber from Old Ebenezer and to turn the old building into a silk house and infirmary.[8]

The orphanage was far more than just a home for orphaned children. Like its model in Halle, it was actually the economic nerve center of the settlement. It was the individual's insurance against adversity, serving as hospital and refuge for the down and out. As a result, the Salzburgers contributed generously of their time and effort whenever needed. The children and widows living there did their part: the girls shared in the housekeeping, and the boys helped Ruprecht Kalcher in the fields, for the orphanage was largely self-supporting with regard to foodstuffs.

The orphanage was particularly successful in cattle raising. Already by 19 June 1741 Kalcher could slaughter enough steers to make it unnecessary to buy meat, and he could also send four calves to Savannah for sale. At that time, however, the orphanage cows had to be grazed further from Ebenezer to make room for the town's growing herd. Later on Kalcher was helped by a Salzburger named Martin Hertzog and by various other Salzburgers, and still later by Palatine servants. On 8 November 1738 Boltzius had requested two families of Palatine servants as herdsmen for the orphanage cattle.[9] The orphanage rendered valuable service for several years, during which time it inspired Whitefield to found his own orphanage at Bethesda, some ten miles south of Savannah.

Nevertheless, by 1744 the orphanage was found no longer necessary, as Boltzius explained in a letter of 4 June to Francke. The last two widows could be provided for by relatives, and the children could be more useful if placed with families who needed them because they had lost their own. Boltzius suggested that Kalcher continue to live in the building and maintain the farming and silk manufacture.[10] The orphanage had become the center of the Salzburgers' rapidly expanding silk business. Later the orphanage building was used as an inn for out-of-town customers who lodged overnight while having their grain ground at Ebenezer.

According to Boltzius's journal entry for 13 January 1738, the year also brought the Salzburgers their long-desired physician, Christian Ernst Thilo, who had been born in 1708 in Lauchstedt in eastern Germany.[11] After the apothecary Andreas Zwiffler left Ebenezer in March 1737, Urlsperger and Francke, the Salzburgers' "Reverend Fathers" in Germany, tried to find a replacement, but this was difficult because the Trustees refused to grant a salary and expected the candidate to be content with three years' provisions. The only volunteer under these conditions was Thilo, who had studied for three years under Dr. Johann Juncker and Dr. Christian Friedrich Richter, celebrated professors of medicine at the University of Halle, then one of the most advanced medical centers in Europe. Thilo had also managed the orphanage clinic at Halle. Thilo, who arrived at Ebenezer on 13 January 1738, was hardly more effective than Zwiffler. In addition, he annoyed Boltzius by concerning himself with his patients' souls as well as their bodies and thus trespassing in Boltzius's territory.

Swiss and Palatine Additions

A Swiss named Bartholomäus Zant had come over with the second Salzburger transport. Although Zant was not one of them, the Salzburgers pitched in and maintained his plantation when he lost his sight for an extended period in 1738.[12] This may have encouraged other Swiss to cross over the river from Purysburg; for it was proof that the Salzburgers were not as exclusive as Avery found the Vernonburg Swiss to be. Even before this act of kindness, by the end of 1737 the Salzburgers had been joined by two unmarried Swiss named Ambrosius and Johann Jacob Züblin of Purysburg, whose wealthy brother David, the father of the Reformed minister Johann Joachim Zubly, had tired of helping them. Causton allowed them to settle in Ebenezer and even granted a year's provisions, but the plantation they tried to develop was remote and subject to depredations by wild animals and also by a jailbreaker from Savannah.[13] They started out to Boltzius's satisfaction, being much concerned with their salvation, but only as long as they were sick. Eventually they broke with Boltzius by seeking employment elsewhere, for example, as laborers at Bethesda and as rowers on Noble Jones's scout boat, as Boltzius recorded on 15 August 1741.[14]

Another addition to Ebenezer from Purysburg was an old Swiss carpenter named Hans Krüsy from Speicher, who brought a young son, Adrian, with him and was joined by a widowed kinswoman, Engel Koller, and her daughter. Krüsy was a good worker, but he argued theological matters with Boltzius and would not bow to the pastor's views. Both Krüsy and his son died in a few years. Writing in 1752, Johann Tobler reported that Krüsy was earning good wages and was able to send support to his eight children still remaining in Switzerland, but Boltzius reported that Krüsy had died sometime before April 1748.[15]

As has been previously mentioned, Ebenezer received various Palatines at this time, including the shoemaker Ade, the herdsmen Schneider and the Helds, and the young serving girls. Schneider was the man who had lost his baggage on the ill-fated Palatine ship that foundered on Block Island. Ebenezer also received some Palatine additions from Purysburg, including brides such as three Unselt girls, daughters of a deceased schoolmaster. The oldest of these married the Hungarian-German tailor Hernberger and departed with him a few years later for Pennsylvania. Eva (or Ephrosina) Regula married Georg Schweiger, and (Sibilla) Friederica married Heinrich Bischoff (Boltzius's servant Henry Bishop). The Kieffers of Purysburg, who gradually moved to Ebenezer, were "Palatines" in the general sense of the term, but their staunch Lutheran faith suggests that they may have been Württembergers.

In 1739 a minitransport arrived with the carpenter Georg Sanftleben of the second Salzburger transport, who had returned the previous year to his home in Silesia to fetch his sister and to recruit some tradesmen and some unmarried women to be wives of the single Salzburger men.[16] Among the five women he recruited was Ursula Wassermann's sister, Elisabetha, who promptly married the Austrian Johann Pletter. The most eagerly awaited member of the group was the shoemaker Johann Caspar Ulich, because the Salzburgers urgently needed his services. Unfortunately, he immediately sickened and lived only long enough to marry his shipmate Margaretha Egger.[17] Luckily for her, she was allowed to keep the leather provided him by the Trustees. Sanftleben's sister, Elisabetha, married the community's herdsman, Hans Michael Schneider, as Boltzius reported on 30 December 1740. By 10 August 1739 Gertraut Lackner was dead, and the rest of the party was down with fever. The Sanftleben correspondence with the Trustees, which was copious, generally maltreated the names of the voyagers. For example, Sanftleben appeared as Sanftle Ben and St. Leaver.[18]

Praise of Ebenezer

While Francis Moore had observed much progress in Ebenezer by 1738, the next two years were a period of even more rapid advance in cattle raising and agriculture, and also in house building. Many of the Salzburgers were replacing their crude huts with more comfortable cottages. By the beginning of 1740 Boltzius could inform Newman that the Salzburgers were faring well both temporally and spiritually, and on 4 June of that year a Mr. William Seward wrote to the Trustees that the Salzburgers were succeeding through help from Germany, while the rest of the province was abandoned except for those who "depended on the Regiment, or were in the Trustees' pay."[19]

After returning to Ebenezer on 25 June 1740, Whitefield wrote in his journal:

> Went on Monday to, and returned this evening from Ebenezer, which I have seen with no small satisfaction. Surely there is a difference, even in this life, between those that serve the Lord, and those that serve Him not. All other places of the colony seem to be like Egypt, where was darkness, but Ebenezer, like the land of Goshen, wherein was great light. For near four miles did I walk in almost one continued field, with a most plentiful crop of corn, pease, potatoes, etc., growing upon it — all the product of a few months' labour. But God blesses the labourers; they are unanimous; the strong help the weak, and all seem hearty for the common good. In a few years, the Saltzburghers, I believe, will be a flourishing people. Their land is good and lies very near the river. They already provide food, and before long, will be capable of providing raiment for themselves. I shall send them up cotton, etc., spinning wheels, and a loom to begin a manufactory for themselves; and next year they hope their own land will produce enough flax, cotton, etc, to carry it on. I had communications with their ministers. Our sister Orphan House there, is blessed by their means. Yesterday was set apart as a day of thanksgiving for assistance sent from Germany and Savannah. The people seemed very grateful. They willingly received me into their clean, but little huts, and seemed proud when I accepted any thing from their hands. As I said formerly, so I hope the Saltzburgers will do a good work. They want assistance. Lord, raise them up benefactors.[20]

Whitefield modestly suppressed the fact that the Lord had recently raised up many benefactors for the Salzburgers through his own efforts on a collection tour in England and the northern colonies, which had brought them seventy-six pounds and a quantity of hardware as well as a large bell for a church.[21] But in this case the Lord had to take second place to Mammon, because the Salzburgers needed a gristmill even more than a church. A power-driven mill would not only save the Salzburgers much physical effort; it would also encourage the growing of hard grains such as wheat, rye, and barley, which were of little value without a real mill.

Some three months later, in a letter of 18 September to a Mr. James Lyde of London, Thomas Jones expressed regard for Ebenezer like that of Whitefield. After describing the Highland settlement at Darien, he wrote:

> I know of no other settlement in this Colony more desirable, except Ebenezer, a town on the river Savannah at 35 miles distance from hence (Savannah), inhabited by Saltzburghers and other Germans, under the Pastoral care of Mr. Bolzius and Mr. Gronau, who are discreet worthy men. The town is neatly built, the situation exceeding pleasant; they consist of 60 families or upwards. They live in the greatest harmony with their ministers, and with one another as one family. They have no idle, drunken, or profligate people among them, but are industrious, many grown wealthy, and their industry has been blessed with remarkable and uncommon success, to the envy of their Carolina neighbours, having great plenty of all the necessary conveniences of life (except clothing) within themselves, and supply this town and other neighbouring places, with bread kind, as also beef, pork, veal, poultry, etc.[22]

Fourth Salzburger Transport

As Francis Moore mentioned, by 1738 the Salzburgers at Ebenezer felt secure enough to invite their kith and kin living in the South German cities to join them.[23] The following year they signed a letter requesting that another transport be sent, and the Trustees agreed to defray the cost of passage.[24] Samuel Urlsperger immediately began recruiting among the Salzburgers still residing in Swabian cities such as Augsburg, Memmingen, Lindau, Biberach, Stuttgart, and Ulm, in which he circulated a brochure reprinting the Salzburgers' letters of thanks of 26 and 29 October 1739 and certain favorable passages from the Ebenezer pastors' reports. The letter of 26 October was signed by only Boltzius and Gronau, whereas that of 29 October was signed by all adult male Salzburgers, with a postscript signed by both male and female inhabitants of Ebenezer.[25] Urlsperger wrote on 3 November 1739, apparently to Martyn, urging the sending of another transport.²⁶ The Trustees aided with the publicity for the next transport by paying for the printing of five hundred copies of letters from the Salzburgers in Georgia.²⁷

During the next two years things continued to go well, and the Salzburgers expressed general contentment. This is reflected in a letter they wrote on 6 June 1741 to their countrymen in East Prussia, whose pastor, Johann Friedrich Breuer, had written to them two years earlier. In this letter the Salzburgers told of their voyages across the Atlantic and then praised the good land they were in, especially the rich soil, the lack of taxes, and their right to hunt and fish at will. Then, in order to make contact with their kinsmen, they gave their domiciles in Salzburg.²⁸ Some of the disappointingly uninformative correspondence has survived.

Unlike the earlier three transports, this one went west from Augsburg to Cannstadt on the Neckar, from which it continued by boat to Rotterdam, then by ship to London and on to Georgia. Its first conductor, Johann Gottfried von Müllern, led it as far as London; from there on it was led by Johannes Vigera, a member of a prominent Strassburg family.²⁹ Both these gentlemen wrote careful and detailed accounts of their rather uneventful voyages.³⁰ Von Müllern scarcely mentioned the drowning of three Salzburger men who swam in the Rhine, against his expressed command to be sure.³¹

In his journal entry for 15 September 1741 Egmont wrote that "the Saltzburghers embark'd on board the *Loyal Judith*, Capt. John Lemon, and were 22 Men, 25 Women, 9 boys and 6 girls: in all 62." Fortunately, the ship manifest, giving names, professions, ages, and relationships, was clearly written and has been preserved.³² The Trustees' warm concern for this transport is reflected in the expenses they willingly incurred for its comfort.³³ The fourth transport had a remarkably good crossing: one child was born, and it and another infant died. There was only one adult death, that of Conrad Künlin (or Konej), which occurred after the ship reached Georgia on 2 December 1741. This was a far cry from the horrendous voyage of the *Europa*, which arrived almost simultaneously.

Instead of receiving rations from the storehouse in Savannah, as the earlier Salzburgers had, the fourth transport received a cash allowance of eight pence for males over twelve years of age, six for women over twelve, and four for children over six. This money was a great stimulus to the Ebenezer economy because, whereas the inhabitants had plenty of food to sell to the newcomers, they had little cash to spend in Savannah for necessities. The newcomers also received a generous supply of cattle from the Trustees.³⁴ According to Boltzius's letter of 31 August 1744 to Martyn, the Salzburgers had received twenty-one cows and twenty-one calves on the previous 14 May.³⁵ The new inhabitants were all still in good health at the beginning of the following year.³⁶ Despite the food and shelter provided for them, however, most of them sickened with malaria the next summer, and many of them died, including Andreas Piltz, Matthias Bacher, and the wives of Bernhard Glocker, Peter Kohleisen, Simon Rieser, Veit Lechner, and Johann Scheffler.³⁷ Vigera remained for a while at Ebenezer, but on 24 August 1750 Boltzius received a letter from him saying that he was in Philadelphia and had married an English woman.

After the fourth transport, only one more family of true Salzburgers arrived, that of Matthias Kurtz, which had undergone years of privation in Holland and England before being sent to Ebenezer in 1742. The father of the family died soon after reaching Ebenezer and was soon followed in death by his wife and one of his daughters.³⁸ He lived, however, long enough to write a letter to his friends and relatives in Cadzant. It must have praised Ebenezer, because Boltzius feared that it might make people think the Salzburgers were trying to lure away foreign subjects.³⁹

This ill-starred family was brought to Georgia by Heinrich Melchior Muhlenberg, a young clergyman who had been chosen to organize the Lutherans scattered in Pennsylvania and to guard them from the enticements of Count Zinzendorf and his fellow Moravians. Like Boltzius, Gronau, and the later Ebenezer pastors, Muhlenberg had been trained at the Francke Foundation in Halle. He had made the detour via Ebenezer to meet Boltzius and learn something about life in America; but, having been delayed en route, he could remain there for only a week. With him he brought a silver chalice as a gift for the Ebenezer parish. Boltzius was supposed to accompany the newcomer to Philadelphia, but they were delayed so long in Charleston by lack of passage that Boltzius found it necessary to return to his congregation at Ebenezer rather than risk being icebound for the winter in Pennsylvania. Both clerics wrote informative accounts of their journey from Ebenezer to Charleston,⁴⁰ and Muhlenberg later wrote many interesting facts about Ebenezer and its inhabitants.⁴¹

Death of Gronau and Arrival of Lemke

Boltzius's first great sorrow in America was the death of his "dear colleague," Israel Christian Gronau. The two had been friends in Halle, where they both taught at the orphanage school, and the tall and diffident Gronau not only loved but also admired his smaller but older and more domineering comrade. In America they sealed their friendship by marrying sisters, Catherina and Gertraut Kroehr, the daughters of a Salzburger woman named Barbara Rohrmoser. She had emigrated with her two older children while leaving her younger ones behind with her Catholic second husband. The two pastors acted as one man. Gronau never asserted himself against his more forceful colleague, and it is difficult to differentiate between their entries in their common journal, except that Gronau restricted himself almost entirely to religious matters. Gronau scarcely complained of his poor health, which never improved after his first bout with malaria; and he continued to perform his arduous chores, including many tiring journeys to preach to the Germans in Savannah.

On 21 October 1743 Boltzius recorded in his journal, "It is truly a great blessing to have a loyal colleague." Unfortunately, this blessing was to last only a little more than one more year. By 1744 Gronau was failing fast, and he was not helped by a rest at Bethesda, where the salt air was thought more wholesome than the miasmic vapors arising from the swamps surrounding Ebenezer. He passed away on 11 January 1745, leaving a widow and two daughters, Friederica Maria and Hanna Elisabetha.[42] Zubly gave Gronau's funeral oration, which is often listed among his publications but was actually never printed. Gronau was replaced as both pastor and husband by Hermann Heinrich Lemke; but he was never entirely replaced as Boltzius's dearest friend, even though Lemke, too, became Boltzius's brother-in-law.

Lemke, or Lemcke, as he sometimes spelled his name, was born in 1720 as the son of a teacher in Fischbeck in County Schaumburg in northwest Germany. After receiving his elementary and secondary education at the orphanage in Halle, he began his theological training in 1742 at the University of Halle, where he supported himself by teaching in the boys' school of the Francke Foundation. Although only average in his studies, he won approval through his fear of the Lord and his skill in teaching and maintaining order.[43]

As soon as word reached Germany that Gronau had died, Lemke was chosen as his successor. Setting out immediately, he stopped off at Wernigerode to be ordained by the court chaplain Samuel Lau, as Boltzius and Gronau had been. Then he passed through Fischbeck to see his parents before proceeding via Amsterdam, Rotterdam, and London to Gosport in order to sail on the *Judith*.[44] Landing first at Frederica, Lemke proceeded at once to Ebenezer, which he reached on 7 February 1746. One year later he visited Driessler, the pastor at Frederica.[45] Being an unassuming man, Lemke stood very much in Boltzius's shadow. In Ebenezer he married Gronau's widow, Catherina, thus sparing the SPCK the burden of supporting her.[46] In addition to Catherina's two children by Gronau, the Lemkes had two more daughters, Johanna Christina and Salome, and a son, Timotheus, who survived his father by only eight years. Timotheus was a teacher at Ebenezer in 1771 and died in 1776.[47]

Boltzius's Spiritual Problems

Boltzius was often annoyed by parishioners who wished to argue theological matters with him. This was particularly true of Dorothea Helfenstein, the widow of a tanner whom von Reck had picked up along the way on his second voyage. This woman seems to have had a mind of her own and dared to dispute with Boltzius on ministerial matters. She was Swiss and of the Reformed faith.[48] Worse than that, she had been contaminated by "the Inspired" (*die Inspirierten*), a sect with whom she had consorted in Heidelberg, as Boltzius mentioned on 14 July 1738. Helfenstein was not the only woman to dabble in matters of faith. On 17 January 1736, because Boltzius could not arrive in time to baptize a premature baby before its death, a layman performed the duty, and Boltzius commended him for the act. Even though Boltzius tried to assure the grieving mother that the child had been saved, Mrs. Rheinländer argued against the efficacy of lay baptism. As mentioned, Krüsy from Purysburg also disagreed with Boltzius on some points, which was a presumptuous thing in view of Boltzius's superior theological training. The physician Thilo often trespassed into Boltzius's theological garden, too. On one occasion Boltzius had to correct the German schoolmaster in Savannah on a fine technical point. Strangely, like Stephens, Boltzius never names this worthy man.

Boltzius was also plagued by independent wives who refused to render

Christian obedience to their husbands. The worst of these was Juliana Ortmann, the wife and master of the schoolmaster, who would not accept being the weaker vessel. The same was true of Magdalena Arnsdorf, a Palatine who had completed her indenture in South Carolina before coming to Ebenezer and marrying the Silesian carpenter Sanftleben. Even Eva Regina Unselt, who married the rough and ready Georg Schweiger, and Elisabeth Catherina Kieffer, who married the shoemaker Matthias Zettler, likewise failed to show proper deference to their lawful masters despite Boltzius's admonitions. Apparently "English freedoms" had gone to their heads.[49]

We have seen that Boltzius feuded, in a one-sided way, against the Moravians as long as they were in Georgia, suspecting them of trying to steal away his parishioners. He was particularly worried about the influence they had on Wesley, who had absorbed many of their errors.[50] He feared that patrons in Germany might think his flock had been similarly tainted. Wesley even translated some of the Moravians' hymns and had them published in Charleston.

Even more insidious than the Moravians' questionable tenets was the belief in predestination that Whitefield suddenly embraced even though he was an Anglican.[51] This belief, which he seems to have acquired from his chaplain, Jonathan Barber, ran exactly counter to that of the Lutherans, particularly of those of Pietist leanings like Boltzius, who thought that Jesus, through His death, had merited salvation for all true believers.[52] On 21 June 1742, to strengthen his arguments against this ungodly dogma, Boltzius requested a copy of Dr. Joachim Lange's *De Gratia universali wider Electionem ex Absoluto Decreto*.[53] With the help of Dr. Lange's book, Boltzius also convinced Johann Tobler, the Swiss almanac writer of New Windsor, to reject predestination; he quotes Tobler's revised views in his journal entry for 14 April 1748.

Stephens, a firm Anglican, shared Boltzius's revulsion at predestination. He tells with great glee how Barber and James Habersham, the manager of Bethesda, were jailed for annoying Pastor Orton with their unsolicited argumentation on this score. Thus the Anglican minister Orton found a kindred spirit when he lodged in Boltzius's house at Ebenezer during the threatened Spanish invasion of 1742.[54] Orton had crossed the Atlantic with the fourth Salzburger transport.[55] Except during the short period in which the Moravians sojourned in Georgia, Boltzius was never plagued by sectarians, as most orthodox ministers in America were. The few sectarians who came to the area came mostly as individuals, and they caused no trouble. For example, on 11 July 1747 Boltzius was visited by an Anabaptist from Pennsylvania, and on 8 April 1765 he was visited by the Moravian Johann Ettwein.[56] Boltzius was also largely spared from wolves in sheep's clothing, and few false prophets stalked his area. He refused to endorse a Swede named Falck, who claimed to be an ordained Lutheran minister who had lost his credentials on his voyage to America; yet this man posed no threat because the predominantly South German "Dutch" could not understand the Low German dialect that he, like many other Scandinavians, used as a lingua franca.[57] As we will see later, an imposter claiming to be both a royal prince and an ordained Lutheran minister caused a disturbance in Vernonburg.

Boltzius's Secular Problems

Like the Vernonburgers, many Salzburgers wished to earn cash by working elsewhere as laborers or rowers. This was much against Boltzius's will, because the pastor knew that association with the English would corrupt his pious flock and cause them to question the values he was so assiduously instilling. Although far too diplomatic to say so, Boltzius no doubt agreed with other colonial German pastors that German was the language of God and heaven, while English was the language of the devil and the world. Among the first to seek outside employment were Leonhard Rauner, Stephan Riedelsperger, Michael Rieser, and Josef Leitner, who worked in Savannah, rowed on the Savannah River, or served at a fort above Savannah Town.[58] Hans Michael Muggitzer and Leonhard Rauner were the first to desert the celestial city permanently; Muggitzer worked on Causton's estate, Ockstead, and Rauner rowed on the Savannah River.[59] Ironically, when Boltzius suggested on 10 October 1739 that some Salzburgers go to help Habersham at Bethesda, they declined, giving him the same spiritual reasons he had previously given them. Since the first Salzburgers had now fulfilled their promise to remain three years in Georgia, Boltzius could no longer detain them.

Boltzius tended to minimize these absences, and Urlsperger deleted many references to them in his edition of the pastor's journal; yet we still learn that on 28 April 1737 Simon Reiter went to work for Mary Musgrove at her nearby cowpen but soon left her to accompany the Appenzellers on their way up the Savannah River to New Windsor. Unlike some of the other wayward parishioners, Reiter tired of such an unstable life and returned to Ebenezer in time to sign the letter of 25 November 1738. He remained there as a valuable inhabitant until his early death. In 1741 Josef Ernst and both Züblins worked in Savannah; what was worse, Ernst worked for the Moravians, from whom, as he later confessed, he stole some tools. In the same year Michael Rieser worked on Whitefield's slave-operated plantation in South Carolina; later he worked in Abercorn and Savannah, while Mrs. Rauner worked in Savannah.[60] As mentioned, the two Züblins also rowed on Noble Jones's scout boat.

When Ebenezer finally received a large shipment of Palatine servants in 1749, some of them ran away to South Carolina, including one of their spokesmen, Balthasar Zoller. On 21 April 1750 Stephens wrote to the governor of South Carolina urging him to extradite the renegades, and some seem to have been captured.[61] By 3 December of that year there were further deserters, including Lorentz, Michael, and Peter Richard; Christoph Conrad Waldhauer and his brother; Johann Martin Voltz; Balthasar Kuhn; and Johann Friedrich Scheffer.[62] To facilitate arrest and extradition, Boltzius suggested that the indentures should be written individually rather than collectively. The runaways who were retaken were corrected "a good deal less than they deserved," and some of them reformed their ways and settled around Ebenezer. With this Palatine shipment came an English wigmaker named Henry Hamilton and his Silesian wife, Regina Charlotta, both thorns in Boltzius's flesh until they were finally returned to the Trustees, who had paid twenty pounds for them. Hamilton later served as a schoolmaster in Savannah.

For a short while Boltzius was saddled with a physician named Johann Christian Seelmann, or Soelmann, who came over with same transport. Unable to develop a practice in Ebenezer, he requested permission to depart for Philadelphia, from where he was to repay the cost of his passage.[63] We never learn whether Seelmann ever refunded his passage money.

Despite Francis Moore's claim that no Salzburgers had deserted Ebenezer, some had actually done so, and others would soon follow. The first of these was the Silesian apothecary Andreas Zwiffler, who left Ebenezer in 1737, having remained in Georgia the requisite time. He had been discredited for his inability to cure the Salzburgers of their fevers, and even Boltzius had caustically remarked that he was curing their flock to death. Also, Zwiffler had soon lost the bride who had followed him to Georgia.

He repaired to Philadelphia in order to earn money to return to Germany, but he seems to have remained in that city. The next defector was Franz Sigismund Hernberger, the Hungarian-German tailor, who departed in 1740 with his wife, Anna Justina Unselt of Purysburg.[64] Much later, Henry Bishop, Boltzius's former servant, was prevailed upon to leave Ebenezer and settle on a South Carolina plantation, the owner of which was trying to persuade other Ebenezer artisans to defect.[65]

Thomas Bichler planned to leave Ebenezer at the urging of his wife, who intuited that she would not live long at Ebenezer. When she proved her point by dying, Bichler could not leave because he had a very small and very sickly child. Stephan Riedelsperger, who had conspired with him, actually made the move and later sent letters to his friends that life in Pennsylvania was much better than that in Georgia. Among these friends were Michael Rieser, Veit Landfelder, and Johann Spielbiegler and his mother, Rosina. All these had resided for some time in Memmingen, and this suggests that they must have been kinsmen or neighbors back in Salzburg. Whenever Boltzius stated in his journal that certain Salzburgers were from Memmingen, Lindau, or some other Swabian city, he meant that they resided there after their expulsion from Salzburg. He mentioned their place of exile because he knew that their friends and benefactors there would be pleased to receive news of them.

Correspondence and Other Chores

Like all other missionaries from Halle, Boltzius was required to send frequent, one might say regular, reports to Halle. He also had to report to the SPCK in London. In addition, he had to send the Trustees statistics on crops harvested. This put him in a dilemma, since he wished to praise the Salzburgers' success without denying their need for help. Knowing that his letters were always liable to publication for propaganda purposes (his letter of 18 December 1742 met this fate), Boltzius had to be very careful of what he wrote.[66] As soon as he saw a copy of Urlsperger's bowdlerized edition of his reports, he knew what was unwanted and imposed his own censorship on unpleasant or controversial matters. Even then Urlsperger continued to delete individual passages and even entire entries, often combining several mutilated entries into one. Urlsperger had expressed his editorial policy frankly in 1734. When Boltzius and von Reck both complained of the treatment they received from Captain Tobias Fry on the *Purysburg* between Rotterdam and Dover, Urlsperger assured Newman, "I will suppress every Complaint thereof, That the main undertaking may not come under an Evil Report."[67]

Some of Boltzius's correspondence wished to take no end. This was true of his letters requesting compensation for a Swiss merchant named Schlatter, who had sent some unsolicited linen to Georgia for sale. Because it was of too fine a quality for the Salzburgers, Causton sold it at the store in Savannah but made no payment to Schlatter. As a conscientious Prussian, Boltzius would not drop the matter but wrote a score of reminders until, on 12 January 1741, the Trustees finally agreed to remit the money to Schlatter's London agents.[68] The same was true of Boltzius's attempt to persuade the Trustees to pay the Salzburgers their corn-shilling, or crop subsidy, for the year 1739, which the Trustees finally did on 10 May 1743.[69] All this heavy correspondence had to be kept in duplicate in case of loss, although no packet of mail was lost until 1744, when a Spanish corsair finally captured a ship carrying the Salzburgers' mail.[70] Later, in 1748, a Savannah merchant named Woodruf was taken by the Spaniards while carrying Boltzius's correspondence and reports.[71] Meanwhile, some cloth that Whitefield had sent from Philadelphia for the Salzburgers was captured by the Spaniards before the ship reached Charleston, as Boltzius recorded on 10 December 1747.

As the best-educated person in Ebenezer, Boltzius had to perform many secular duties not usually demanded of clerics. Among other things, he had to study English directives on agriculture, such as Jethro Tull's *The Horse Hoeing Husbandry*, books on sericulture, such as Thomas Boreman's *Compendious Account*, and books on curing distempers of cattle, winnowing corn, and keeping corn sweet in sacks.[72] Like many Protestant pastors of his day, Boltzius felt responsible for his parishioners' bodies as well as for their souls, with the result that he read everything he could get on colonial medicine, such as the works of the Virginian physician John Tennent, the author of *Every Man His Own Doctor*.[73]

To lessen his burdens and to avoid reproach in Savannah, Boltzius wrote to Martyn on 29 August 1747 asking him to request the Trustees to let Ludwig Mayer assume the responsibility for secular affairs.[74] Boltzius's secular chores were somewhat lessened in 1748 when Ludwig Mayer agreed to serve with him as conservator of the peace and Thomas Bichler was reappointed constable. Mayer was also granted a travel allowance for tending to the Salzburgers' business in Savannah.[75] An entry in Boltzius's diary for 31 December 1751 lists all his many ministerial chores and indicates that Mayer had not yet relieved him of many secular ones.

While in Halle, Boltzius must have studied more than just theology, for, upon reaching Georgia, he had, or quickly acquired, an amazing insight into economic theory. Today he could be classified as a "supply-sider." We have seen that he championed private enterprise as better than communal work, and he opposed unnecessary regulations. Above all, he denounced greedy or un-Christian wages, such as those demanded by Rauner to row the poor Appenzellers to New Windsor. On 4 August 1743 Boltzius wrote: "It is a major harm for this so blessed country that no one can keep men or women servants, as in Germany. Everyone can acquire his own land free or earns as wages more than one could pay a hired hand in three years. The excessive wages are the ruination of the inhabitants."

To be sure, some people claimed that Boltzius interfered too much in secular matters, but no one could deny that Ebenezer's prosperity was due in a large part to his leadership. Robert Williamson, the leader of the Malcontents, was not entirely wrong when he declared before Parliament that Boltzius was the Salzburgers' "God, priest, and king."[76] Johann Tobler, former governor of Appenzell Ausser Rhoden and then a resident of New Windsor in South Carolina, wrote in 1753 that there were two ministers in Ebenezer: "One of them, who is my esteemed friend, is named Martin Boltzius. He spares no pains to make the people there happy both in this world and in the next. There are, to be sure, people who claim that he meddles too much in secular matters, but who can please everybody?"[77] Tobler, like many others, was the recipient of edifying books forwarded by Boltzius.[78] He was highly educated and the author of an almanac printed in Switzerland and also of popular almanacs published in Savannah and Philadelphia.[79]

Law, Order, and Calumny

It has been seen that Boltzius was responsible for law and order at Ebenezer, even though he had little more than the spiritual sword with which to enforce it, chiefly by church penance.[80] Boltzius rarely called upon the civil authorities in Savannah for help, as he did in the cases of Georg Bartholomäus Roth and Martin Dasher; even then he received little co-operation. On 23 February 1743 Thomas Jones wrote to Vernon that a warrant had been sworn out against "Reaser & two Zublies Inhabitants of Ebenezer." He does not explain what the three men, Michael Rieser and Ambrosius and Johann Jacob Züblin, had done. Thomas Ellis was sent to arrest the men on Easter, a very holy day for the Lutherans. Boltzius promised to send them down on any weekday; but Ellis insisted, and Boltzius had to fetch the men from their plantations. He also had to supply his large boat and rowers, despite God's express command about keeping the Sabbath holy. When the boat finally reached Savannah, the men were put in custody but then released without bail and merely told to report on the third of May. When they appeared as ordered, no plaintiff appeared, and the case was dropped. Yet Boltzius still had to bear all costs.[81]

Boltzius remained on constant alert to protect his good name and that of the Salzburgers. When Thomas Stephens, Colonel Stephens's rebellious son, visited Ebenezer to solicit signatures for his proslavery petition, he could persuade only Ortmann, Spielbiegler, and Michael Rieser to sign.[82] He then accused Boltzius of dominating the remainder, and he may have been behind Spielbiegler when the latter, working as a brick mason in Charleston, swore out an affidavit that Boltzius was a tyrant who had robbed him of his property.[83] As a true German, Boltzius was deeply concerned with such calumny. Eighteenth-century men treasured their "characters" more than we do today, one's "character" being one's public image. In Boltzius's case it was particularly important to have a blameless reputation, for any smear on his escutcheon might well decrease the charities the Salzburgers enjoyed.

The earl of Egmont was likewise indignant when the Malcontents complained that Boltzius had been deceitful in refusing to sign their petition to permit slavery: "It is an outrage scarcely to be paraleled thus to defame the character of Mr. Boltzius. There is not a person in the Colony more eminent and more esteemed for piety, integrity and prudence than this clergyman: his letters and journals wrote in the German language for the use of his Countrymen, and his letters to his friends in England are constantly full of praises to God and thanks to the Trustees for the happy condition the Saltzburghers are in, and all who come from the Province and have seen them, declare the same."[84] Boltzius's indignation at Thomas Stephens's accusations was equally great, as expressed in his letters of 18 December 1742 and 20 June 1743.[85]

Boltzius also had to protect the good name of his parishioners. When

Mrs. Rheinländer maligned Theobald Kieffer in 1744, Boltzius sent her down to Savannah for punishment. The jury absolved her, however, and the magistrates Henry Parker and Joseph Watson ridiculed the church penance practiced at Ebenezer. To Boltzius's satisfaction, Watson at least made the gossip apologize to Kieffer.[86] It was probably because of disciplinary problems such as those with Mrs. Rheinländer and the previously mentioned Roth and Dasher that Boltzius and Gronau let themselves be appointed conservators of the peace on 13 September 1744.[87] By this time Boltzius had even thought it advisable to have "a Constable under me, and have built a Work House for a terror of disorderly people."[88]

Ebenezer's Dependencies

All this time the Salzburger plantations were spreading out toward the east. The first major acquisition of land was the Mill District, a large rectangle of land reaching from Ebenezer down to the mill on Abercorn Creek. Since this district abutted Ebenezer proper, some residents of the Mill District, like Michael Rieser, lived close to Ebenezer and at quite some distance from the mill. A map of this district, with the names of the property owners as of 1772, is still extant.[89]

Abercorn, the settlement down Abercorn Creek from Ebenezer, had been English when the first Salzburger transport stopped there en route from Savannah to Old Ebenezer, but it had been depopulated by sickness and desertion by the time the Salzburgers' plantations extended that far. Boltzius wrote a most informative letter to the board in Savannah requesting grants for various parishioners. As a result the Salzburgers had no difficulty in getting land grants there, one of the first of these being to Christian Dasher, which was dated 22 November 1745.[90]

Ebenezer gradually obtained another dependency when some of its inhabitants were granted land south of Abercorn in an area called Goshen because of the supposed fertility of its soil. It will be remembered that Whitefield had likened Ebenezer to the biblical land of Goshen, while the rest of Georgia was Egypt. The settlers at Goshen had a great advantage over earlier settlers: whereas previous surveyors had laid out the farms arbitrarily according to a map, Boltzius could require the surveyor to measure out only fertile land, leaving swamps and pine barrens unsurveyed, as Boltzius recorded on 29 June 1751.

Other Germans moved into the nearby area of the defunct Joseph's Town, once a Scots settlement. On 24 June 1752 thirty people took Holy Communion at Goshen, and by 1755 the inhabitants of Abercorn, Goshen, and Joseph's Town were numerous enough to build a church on Boltzius's plantation, which lay between them.[91] On 6 September 1760 the German Protestants of Goshen advised the Council that they had purchased fifty acres from Matthias West (Wüst) for the use and benefit of a school but had failed to take possession of it. The Council then allowed a grant to be issued to John Sheraus and Michael Bohrmann. According to Muhlenberg, by 1774 the church building was worth £130, some of it having been contributed by English neighbors.[92]

When the Salzburgers abandoned Old Ebenezer for their new location on the Red Bluff, the Trustees used the former site as a cowpen, or cattle ranch. The cowpen, with its obnoxious English and Irish managers and ill-behaved German servants, was a constant annoyance to Boltzius, who had no control over it. He complained to the Council in Savannah in 1743 against the manager, Hopkins, but he had to wait two years for satisfaction.[93] The Trustees' cattle frequently lured the Salzburgers' cows away, and the cowpen managers demanded outrageous sums for "finding" the unlost cattle.

Sensing that the Trustees were tiring of the great expense of maintaining their cowpen, especially after the costly sawmill there was destroyed by floods, Boltzius offered to buy it. The Trustees first asked £400, but on 18 July 1750 they lowered the price to £350.[94] The Salzburgers began paying in installments. On 2 January 1751, however, Habersham reported that the Salzburgers had paid only about forty pounds on their debt for the cowpen, and this they had earned by hunting down the Trustees' horses, mares, and colts and bringing them to Savannah.[95] By 8 August 1751 the people of Ebenezer had paid 150 pounds of their bond.[96] Boltzius could report by 1748 that the Salzburgers were receiving great advantage from "Our Common Cowpen."[97]

The next major dependency for which Boltzius became responsible was Bethany, which was founded on the Blue Bluff some five miles above Ebenezer in 1751. After acquiring the cowpen, Boltzius requested land along the Little Ogeechee River, a small freshwater stream southeast of Abercorn.[98] It is not clear whether the request was ever granted. On 18 July 1746 the land around Parker's Mill downstream from Ebenezer was promised to the Salzburgers; on 25 July 1749 Ludwig Mayer received a grant at its site to use as he wished.[99] This mill had been built some years earlier but was closed down because the owner insisted on using slave labor, which Causton, Noble Jones, and Captain Dunbar would not allow him to do.[100] Although no records indicate that Parker was not British, Boltzius reported very clearly on 22 June 1738 that he was actually a native Swede named Purker. While eighteenth-century spelling was a subjective matter, the spelling in one of Parker's letters was unlike any Englishman's.[101] The grant to the Salzburgers would appear to have been a reward to them for their stand against slavery.

Palatine Servants

Meanwhile, agriculture at Ebenezer was flourishing now that most of the husbandmen were at last supplied with horses and plows. Although the harvest in South Carolina was poor in 1747, Boltzius could report that it was good at Ebenezer and that all the Salzburgers needed were servants. For a long time Boltzius had been concerned about the older Salzburgers who had lost most or all of their children, for children were still the only staff of old age. On 25 July 1748 Martyn had asked Urlsperger to procure some servants for Ebenezer.[102] Nearly a year later, on 29 May 1749, a group of German Protestants in London asked the Trustees to send them to Georgia. They had been deserted by the unreliable Riemensperger, who had promised to take them to South Carolina at their own expense. Because of the delay, they were running out of money, and many were no longer able to pay the six pounds required for passage. The spokesman of this group was Balthasar Zoller, who had some seventy people in his party. The Trustees resolved to send all of them over.[103]

On 7 July 1749 Martyn wrote Stephens that eighty-two Germans were on their way to Ebenezer on the *Charles Town Galley*, with Peter Bogg as master. Sixty-three were to be indentured to the Salzburgers; the remaining nineteen, who had paid for their own passage at six pounds per freight, were to join them as free men and immediately receive fifty acres each.[104] Since the South Carolina government offered them a year's provisions but Georgia would not, all the free men went to South Carolina except for Jacob Kübler, who settled at the German Village on River Ness.[105] Also to settle there were Georg Philip Portz, half-brother of Michael Bohrmann; John Gabel, who had been indentured to Captain David Cutter Bradlock;

and John Staley, Jr., who took the grant previously given to the renegade Thomas Richard.[106] A few of these servants settled later above Ebenezer on the Blue Bluff.[107]

The elaborate contract between Bogg and the Trustees is a typical example of such contracts, stipulating the exact quarters and menu to be enjoyed by the passengers, who were to receive beef on two days, pork one day, fish one day, burgoo two days, flour and butter every day in generous quantity, and a quart of beer and two quarts of water per day.[108] Such fare, stipulated in most contracts, does not seem to have been realized, if we can trust the complaints of most eighteenth-century voyagers. Bogg's passengers arrived exceptionally healthy, as Boltzius twice mentioned; but on 4 September of the following year Boltzius had to report that some were down with fever.[109]

These immigrants had the best of two worlds. Being indentured to the Trustees, they were sure of employment, yet their contract stipulated that they had a three months' period of grace to redeem themselves by engaging themselves to anyone they wished. Some of them availed themselves of this stipulation, as Boltzius complained on 12 October 1749, when the sickly Salzburger Brandner lost his servant to a higher bidder. When some of the disgruntled servants threatened to run away on 20 October, Boltzius preached against violation of the Fifth Commandment, the words "father and mother" being extended to include the clerical and secular authorities. He also appealed to the immigrants' sense of honor to keep their promises, and he likewise warned of dire punishments that would follow them, even if they returned to Germany, where the king of England was also the influential duke of Hannover.

Martyn wisely suggested that the Lutheran servants be sent to Ebenezer, but he was mistaken in suggesting that Stephens retain the Reformed as being more proper for Zouberbuhler's church. In actuality, once Zouberbuhler left the Reformed Church to become an Anglican, he lost the loyalty of the Reformed, who preferred Zubly and his "Calvinistical principles." Boltzius submitted a careful report on the distribution of Bogg's Palatine servants, which also included the misfit physician Seelmann, who was a Dippelianer.[110] Seelmann soon departed, and Boltzius was glad to see him go, for he was a "great enemy to the Evangelical religion."[111]

Three of the best of these servants, the Schubdrein brothers, had been picked out in Savannah by Zouberbuhler, who had crossed over with them and therefore knew them well, yet Boltzius was able to redeem them at six pounds per head on 19 February 1750.¹¹² He praised these godly and pious carpenters highly on 28 March and again on 15 August of the same year. When their father, Daniel Schubdrein, Sr., died on 2 July 1752, Boltzius praised him lavishly. Apparently (Johann) Peter Schubdrein, Jr., had brought his father along when he returned from his visit to Nassau-Saarbrücken.¹¹³

In his letter of 17 October 1749 to Martyn, Boltzius extolled the kind treatment given to the Palatines by Captain Bogg and the resulting good health of the passengers. The only sick member was the wife of Andreas Seckinger, whose family had lost all their clothes to thieving fellow passengers. Boltzius took on this family for his own use and at his own risk, but eventually the Trustees paid Bogg eighteen pounds.¹¹⁴ Although this was nominally a "Palatine" transport, when Boltzius wrote a letter on 10 December 1749 for some of the contented servants, who had been farmhands and wished for some rural workers to follow them, he addressed the letter to a governor (*Vogt*) in Württemberg.

During the late summer of 1750 Boltzius was expecting the arrival of a large transport of Swiss Protestants from Lucerne, and he was seriously concerned about their safety during a period of severe storms.¹¹⁵ No more was heard of the exiles, however, and our records do not tell whether they ever left Switzerland.

◆ *Chapter Six* ◆

Swabian and Later Immigrants

Despite the good treatment Bogg's passengers received, some of them ran away without fulfilling their contracts, much to Boltzius's indignation.[1] Among these were Balthasar Zoller, one of their spokesmen, and the young Richard brothers, as well as Balthasar Kuhn and Johann Friedrich Scheffer.[2] Most of the party, however, served faithfully and became Salzburgers in good standing, one of them winning the hand of his master's daughter. The Trustees were also disappointed by the ingratitude of the unfaithful servants, some of whom they had found reduced to begging around the streets of London.[3] A complete list of these servants and their distribution appears in the *Colonial Records* and the *Detailed Reports*.[4]

Even after the Palatines arrived aboard the *Charles Town Galley*, the Salzburgers at Ebenezer still needed servants, since even more of them had lost all or most of their children to disease and were now growing weak with age. Boltzius again came to their aid by asking Urlsperger to recruit new emigrants. Urlsperger then turned to Chrétien de Münch, an Augsburg banker and benefactor of the Salzburgers, who seems to have had commercial ambitions in Ebenezer. The recruiting took place in the Territory of Ulm, the rural region subject to the free Imperial City of Ulm on the Danube in Württemberg, a prosperous center of trade graced by one of Europe's tallest cathedrals.[5] Since many people were emigrating to America anyway, Urlsperger could convince the Lutheran clergy there that it was better to direct the emigrants to a part of America where they could enjoy orthodox religion and thus be saved from the many sects abounding in America. Johann August Urlsperger, Samuel Urlsperger's son and later

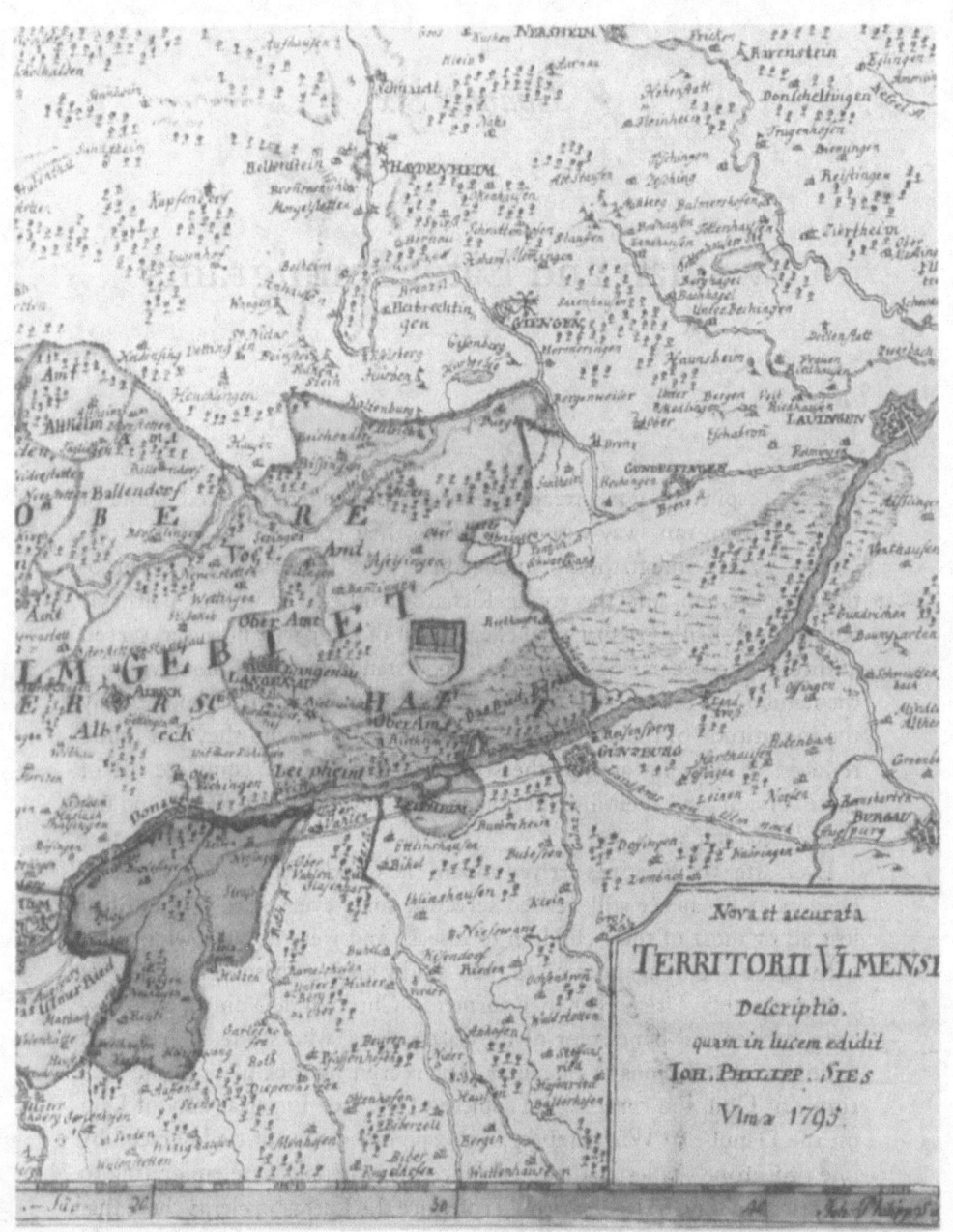

The Territory of Ulm, from which many of the Georgia Swabians emigrated
(© Stadtarchiv Ulm)

successor,⁶ wrote a promotional pamphlet which must have been aimed at the clergy, since it was in Latin.⁷ Nevertheless, when Pastor Conrad Daniel Kleinknecht, Urlsperger's collaborator at Leipheim in the Territory of Ulm, asked permission to recruit, his consistorium refused on the grounds that it was a secular matter, one more suitable for a politician than a theologian.⁸ Obviously, they did not wish to antagonize the municipal government or the duke of the surrounding duchy of Württemberg.

To carry this Swabian transport to America, the Trustees again engaged Captain William Thomson, who had already brought so many Germans to America; but this time they were able to beat him down to four pounds and ten shillings from the six pounds he had previously demanded and received. By 1750 Thomson had become a London merchant. His ship, the *Charming Martha*, was under the command of Captain John Lesslie, with whom the Trustees had to dicker at length.⁹ According to Habersham, the *Charming Martha* arrived at Cockspur Island at the mouth of the Savannah River on 29 October 1750.¹⁰ Lesslie's contract with the Trustees resembled Bogg's and stipulated that the mess was to be "to the liking of Philip Paulitsch and John Neidlinger." Thirty-seven of the passengers were to serve the Salzburgers, and twenty-four, having paid their passage, were to be free people; at the time of gaining freedom, every adult German was to receive fifty acres of land.¹¹ Four members of the party—two young men, an old carpenter, and a young woman—died on the journey or in Savannah, as Boltzius reported on 17 November 1750.¹²

Johann Heinle and his wife served at the sawmill, while their son Johann served Georg Glaner and their son Jacob served Johann Schmidt. Boltzius's letter of 1 May 1751 to Martyn lists all the servants and their masters.¹³ It should be remembered that a majority of these Swabians, such as the Heinles and Helmes, had been substantial people who had left Germany with what would have been sufficient passage money had it not been for rogues like the Hopes of Rotterdam. Nevertheless, most of them submitted cheerfully to their servitude, worked off their passage, and soon became solid members of their new community.

It has been mentioned that later accretions to the Salzburger community were also designated as Salzburgers. This was true of the Swabians even before they reached Georgia: Martyn had already referred to them as "Saltzburghers." Unfortunately, although these newcomers found far better living conditions than their predecessors had found, they, too, were "visited with the same intermitting Feaver" that had afflicted the earlier

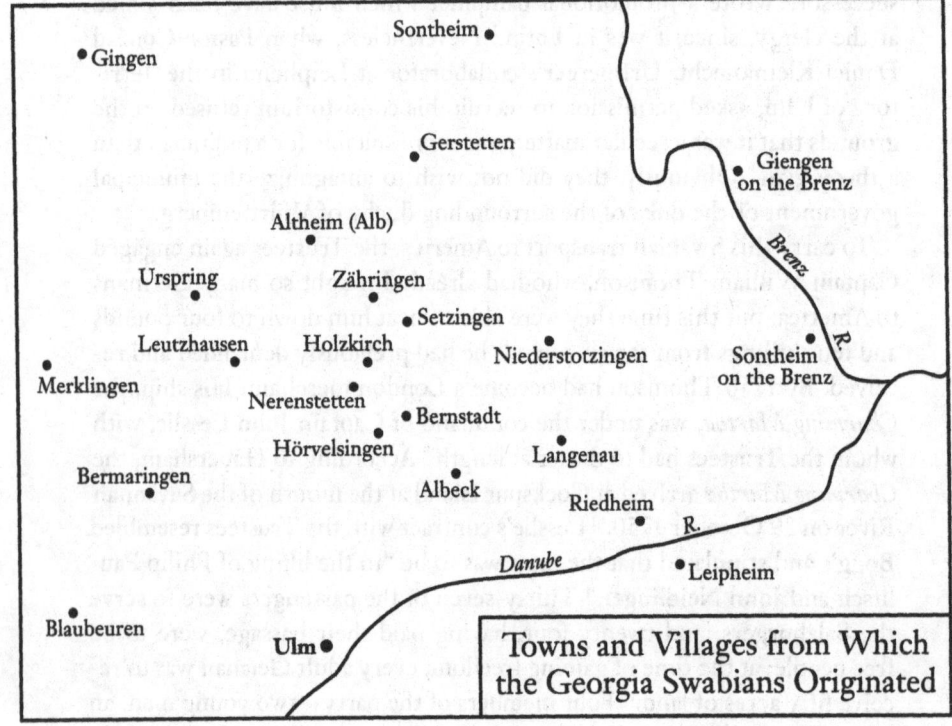

Towns and Villages from Which the Georgia Swabians Originated

arrivals.[14] On 29 November 1750 the surveyor was busy measuring out land for the Swabians as well as for some of the old inhabitants of Ebenezer who had not taken out enough. As we shall see, this measure was being urged by Habersham.[15]

Because of resulting confusion, the president's Council resolved on 18 September 1750 to find someone capable of putting things in order, and they agreed "that no Person in the Colony was better qualified to execute this weighty Trust than Mr. Noble Jones, who, notwithstanding it had not been his proper Business, had kept a private Register, and had always been ready to assist with his services therein, when desired; Therefore it was now proposed to Mr. Noble Jones to undertake it, who willingly accepted it and engaged to perform the same carefully, the Board not doubting but the Trustees will approve of, and confirm him therein."[16] We have seen Dobell's testimony that it was Jones's help that made his rosters possible.

Jones seems to have progressed considerably in the few years since he was dismissed by the Salzburgers and suffered snide remarks from Stephens and others.

At about this time the Salzburgers lost a loyal patron, but in his place they acquired an equally loyal one. Feeling the infirmities of his advanced age, Colonel Stephens stepped down. On 26 June 1750 James Habersham was appointed to the "Office of Secretary for the Affairs of the Trust in the Province of Georgia in the room of William Stephens, Esq." This was rapid social mobility for the young schoolmaster who had come to Georgia only some twelve years earlier at the Trustees' expense.[17] When Habersham and his friend Henry Parker were appointed to office, Boltzius wrote: "As they are Men of great Abilities and Probity, as also my & our People's Friends and Favourers, so I am sure, their Advancement will turn out to the Colony's and our Settlement's Happiness under the gracious Influence of the Almighty."[18] In a letter of 29 August 1747 Boltzius wrote to Martyn that as their agent in Savannah the Salzburgers had chosen "Mr. James Habersham (a true friend & promotor of our Settlement's Good, & a man of great ability & inclination to serve the Trustees & our Country)." Boltzius also assured Martyn that Habersham would do everything "for nothing, merely out of love to us & our people."[19]

Habersham's great admiration and sympathy for the Salzburgers is revealed in a long letter of 19 December 1750 to the Trustees, in which he stresses the fact that the settlers have very little good land, being crowded on a narrow strip of fertile soil surrounded by useless pine barren. Even the six-mile strip being surveyed for them on and beyond the Blue Bluff was so narrow that it would accommodate but a few families.[20] Habersham continued all his life to assist the Salzburgers both as an official and in his private capacity as merchant. In this he was aided by his business partner, Francis Harris, who could speak German. Boltzius also praised Harris, "who in company with James Habersham has begun some time ago at Savannah a Trade in several Goods, is a great friend to me & our Settlement, & is with his Partner Mr. Habersham very assistive to me in my present Difficulties."[21]

The first Swabian transport brought (Johann) Ludwig Mayer, a young man who proved to be of great use to Boltzius, serving both as surgeon and physician, although he appears to have brought no proof of previous training.[22] As we have seen, young Mayer was among those brave

James Habersham, schoolmaster, merchant, and friend of the Salzburgers (Hargrett Rare Book and Manuscript Library, University of Georgia)

souls who boarded the pestilential *Europa* to help its wretched passengers. Boltzius had hoped to turn all secular matters over to Mayer, who served as conservator of the peace despite frequent illness.[23] His younger brother, a glove-maker named (Johann) Georg Mayer, served as tailor. When Ludwig was named conservator, Thomas Bichler was again made constable.[24] The Neidlinger family, who also arrived with the first Swabian transport, developed an important tanning industry in Ebenezer.

On 5 August 1749 Boltzius and Lemke each received three hundred acres, and another three hundred was reserved for a future minister. On 21 August 1750 Boltzius received a grant for five hundred acres, which he named Good Harmony. This property was "bounded on the east by the Savannah River, on the south by James Habersham, north by lands of the German servants."[25] Unlike the Swiss pastors Chiffelle, Zubly, and Zouberbuhler, Boltzius never developed his grant for his own use but continued to live abstemiously in his crowded quarters, which served many communal needs.

Although good land was now in short supply at Ebenezer, as Habersham advised Martyn on 19 December 1750, Boltzius requested more servants in June 1751. He did not yet know that already on 24 May 1751 the Trustees had resolved to pay the passage of the impecunious members of a group of Swabians who had just reached Rotterdam.[26] These must have arrived in London soon thereafter. According to the Trustees' journal for 21 August,

> several German Protestants attended the Board, and expressed their Desire of going over to Georgia at their own Expence, in order to settle with the Saltzburghers at Ebenezer, And the following Seven Elders Viz Michael Walliser, Michael Wienkraft, Daniel Renshard, John George Gwant, John Oexlin, John Neidlinger, and John Peter Shubdrein, being Conductors of the Embarkation were called in, And They acquainted the Board that their Number would amount to One hundred and fifty Seven, Whereof fifty four Men, forty six Women, twenty Seven Boys, and thirty Girls.[27]

The Board then resolved to give each one of the applicants fifty acres of land at Ebenezer. These names were rather well rendered, except that Gwant, Renshard, and Wienkraft should be Gnann, Remshard, and Weinkauf. Peter Schubdrein had come with Captain Bogg in 1749 and had returned home to Nassau-Saarbrücken to fetch relatives.[28] Since these people traveled at their own expense, they must have been more substantial than the general run of immigrants to Georgia.

There is no list of people whom Peter Schubdrein persuaded to accompany him to Georgia, but they probably included Paul Fink, Peter Freyermuth, Johann Georg Klein, and Jacob Tussing, all of whom appeared in the Georgia records at about the same time, since people with these family names served as witnesses at Schubdrein marriages in Weiher (Weyer).[29]

On 18 November 1751 the *New York Evening Post* published a report from London, dated 2 September, announcing that "yesterday morning the *Antilope*, McClellan, sailed from Gravesend, for Georgia, with 160 German Protestants, who came from Germany on the Invitation of their countrymen, at Ebenezer, in Georgia, and go over to settle in that colony." Like the first Swabian transport, most of this group were also from villages in the Territory of Ulm. After an uneventful voyage, the second Swabian transport reached Georgia on 23 October. Boltzius assured Verelst that the passengers had been well treated by "MacClallan."[30]

This party arrived in Georgia under the conduct of Johann Wilhelm Gerhard von Brahm. Soon after his arrival, this skilled surveyor set out to explore possible places for settlement on the Ogeechee and in the neighborhood of Darien. He also inspected land around Briar Creek, far up the Savannah River. He ended up choosing a spot on the Blue Bluff, just five miles up the river from Ebenezer. He named his settlement Bethany. Habersham, who was well pleased by the healthy condition in which this second Swabian transport arrived, made this observation: "The Trustees, I believe are not mistaken in Mr. von Brahm's abilities: He has been at a great deal of Pains to view the country to fix on a Settlement and has taken Plans of all the Places he has visited, and I look upon him to be one of the most intelligent Men I ever met with, and will I doubt not make a very useful Colonist."[31]

With the second Swabian transport came a merchant named David Kraft from Ravensburg, who received five hundred acres and was expected to develop a thriving trade. He died very soon, though, leaving a widow, Anna Barbara, née Brandt. Five hundred acres apiece were also granted to Chrétien de Münch, the Augsburg banker, and to his sons Thomas, Carl, and Chrétien and his son-in-law Remigius.[32] Chrétien von Münch had long been a benefactor of the Salzburgers. Already on 26 March 1734 he had been receiving mail for Urlsperger from Newman. On 28 January 1746 Boltzius had written to Verelst that a "great Merchant at Augspurg Mr. Von Münch" had aided the Salzburgers with many gifts of goods and had even lent the pastor two hundred pounds without interest, which had been used for buying plows, horse collars, and other agricultural necessities.[33]

Because of von Münch's concern for the Salzburgers, the Trustees elected him a corresponding member of the Trust. Von Münch thanked them heartily for that honor on 12 January 1747 and again on 2 July of that year.[34] Another letter of 2 July 1747 indicates that he had sent some merchandise to Ebenezer to be sold for the benefit of the mills. On 1 August of the same year von Münch wrote that he was sending a chest containing 562 yards of white cloth for Ebenezer.[35] Five months later Boltzius requested the Trustees to repay von Münch's loan.[36] All this suggests that von Münch was trying to circumvent England's strict mercantilist restrictions.

On 12 September 1747 Boltzius wrote the following to Verelst:

> I forgot in my last letter to mention that our worthy Benefactor Mr. von Münch has wrote me and Mr. Meyer very kind Letters, in which he shews really a great inclination to do all in his power for the Prosperity of our Settlement & Colony. He approves of my imperfect Proposals to bring their Honours' laudable Scheme into execution, & writes us very wise & useful Instructions to better our Plantations, Husbandry & some Commerce upon a profitable footing which all (we believe) would be practicable, if our people had faithful Servants, and if their Honours had one or two proper, well qualify'd & disinterested Agents at Savannah & our Place, to encourage the People in a familiar and convincing manner, and to lead them in the way to attempt the making & exporting lumber.[37]

To judge from his letter of 22 July 1751 to the Trustees, von Münch had some fanciful idea about developing a hereditary estate in Georgia, which was to be directly under the English Crown and as independent of all other jurisdiction as any imperial territory in Germany. As his agent he recommended a Bavarian captain, obviously von Brahm.[38]

Boltzius sent von Münch "some seeds & curious Things" on 14 July 1746. It appears that von Brahm had expected to be the supervisor of the lands given to the von Münchs but that his plans had been "abortive."[39] Nevertheless, it does appear that some effort was made to develop von Münch's plantation, for on 25 July 1759 a slave there was struck and killed by lightning.[40]

After von Brahm settled his people on the Blue Bluff, Georgia's Red

Bluff, White Bluff, and Blue Bluff were all occupied by German-speaking settlers. The new town, named Bethany, remained ancillary to Ebenezer. The inhabitants desired a minister of their own, but, unwilling or unable to support one, they had to commute to Ebenezer for divine services. By 1759, however, the Ebenezer pastors were holding divine services in Bethany every second week.[41] Although physical conditions were now much better than when the first Salzburgers had arrived, the new settlers suffered similarly from sickness and death. By 1759 they were able to build a small church, which was served by the Ebenezer pastors. The British Museum now holds a map of Bethany in the year 1772 by von Brahm.[42]

On 13 November 1752 the *New York Gazette* reported that the "Caledonia, Capt. Alexander Harvie, of Charles Town, with German passengers, put into Savannah in Georgia on the 2nd" of October. These passengers did not stop off in Savannah but proceeded to Charleston, which had been their goal when diverted by the hurricane of 30 September 1752. They were certainly more fortunate than the Swiss on the *Oliver*, who perished in a storm off the coast of Virginia in 1738, and the Palatines who were wrecked on Block Island in the same year.

Two members of the first Swabian transport, Martin and Barthel Botzenhardt of Langenau by Ulm, must have come at their own expense, since they were free to earn money in Savannah and elsewhere. Martin visited his brother, Barthel, a hundred miles up the Savannah River, probably at Savannah Town, and found life too difficult. Discouraged and homesick, the two sent pathetic letters back home saying that their pastor had been right in trying to dissuade them from emigrating. Martin declared that there were no ministers except in Ebenezer and that one could catch no fish because there were no boats. He also announced that a Matthias Neydlinger had returned home,[43] as had Matthias Bader. Three of Martin's negative letters were published in the *Ordentlich-Wöchentliche Anzeigs-Zettel* in Ulm in 1754 to discourage potential emigrants. As in the case of Mittelberger, by these propagandistic letters the Botzenhardts ingratiated themselves with the Ulm authorities, which enabled them to return home with impunity.

Because of letters such as those from the Botzenhardts, the Highwellborn Council of Ulm issued a rescript on 29 July 1752 titled *Concerning the Emigration from Europe to Georgia, Pennsylvania, New England, Nova Scotia, and Carolina*, which listed the evils of emigration and ordered all pastors to

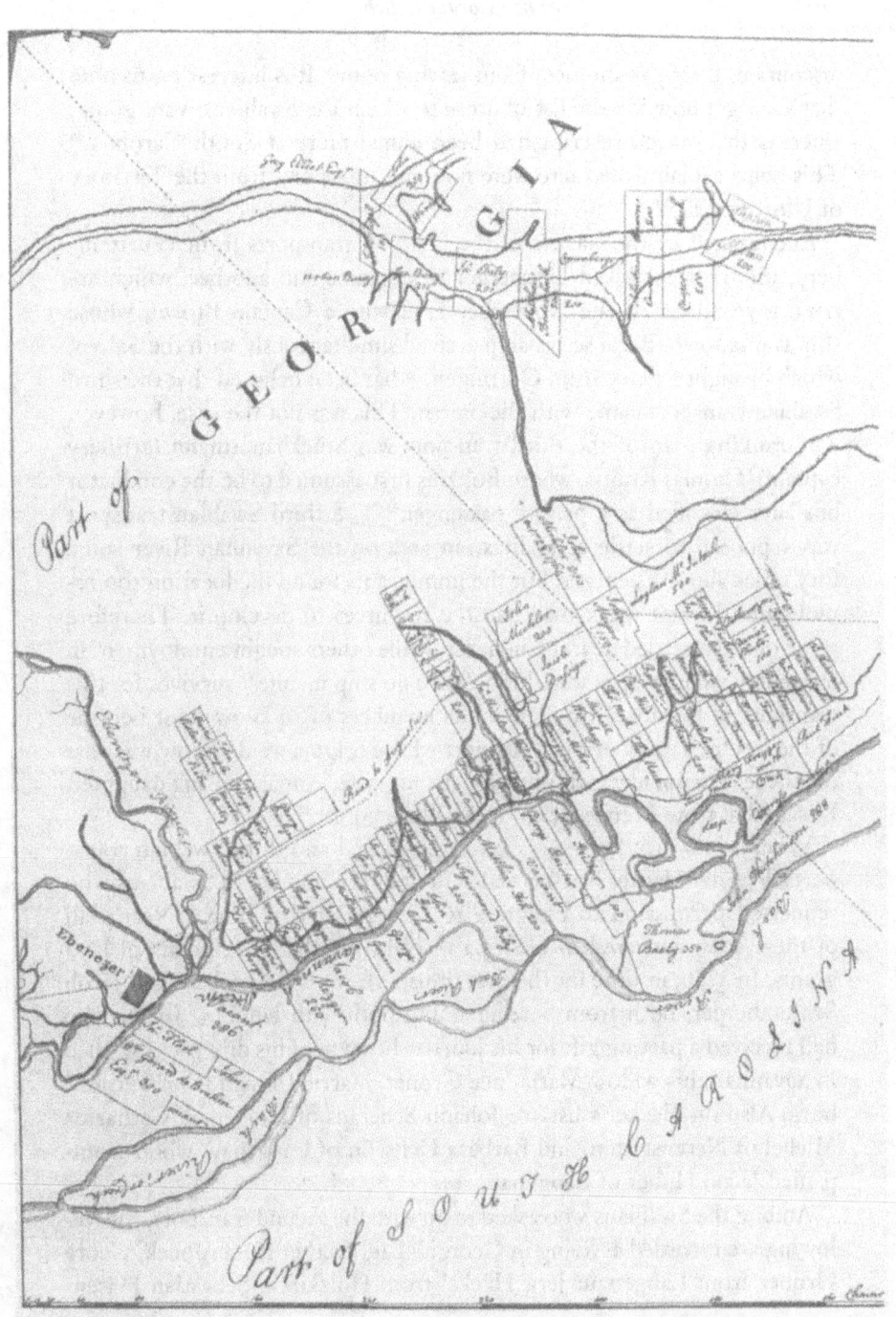

Plan of Bethany, by Wilhelm Gerhard de Brahm (by permission of the British Library)

discourage their parishioners from leaving home. It is interesting to note that Georgia now led the list of areas to which the Swabians were going, whereas the Zurich rescript had been aimed more at South Carolina.[44] This helps explain why there were no more transports from the Territory of Ulm after 1752.

Encouraged by the success of the first two transports from Württemberg, the Trustees asked Urlsperger to organize still another, which arrived a year later in late November 1752 with a Captain Brown, whose ship is unknown. Because his ship arrived simultaneously with the *Success*, which brought a party from Göttingen, it has been believed that the third Swabian transport came with the *Success*. This was not the case, however. The ranking man of the third transport was Stückhauptmann (artillery captain) Thomas Krauss, whom Boltzius first assumed to be the conductor but later classified as a private passenger.[45] The third Swabian transport was supposed to settle at Halifax, an area on the Savannah River some fifty miles above Ebenezer, but the immigrants found the location too remote and did not think they had the resources to develop it. Therefore some of them settled nearer Ebenezer, while others sought employment in Savannah, where wages were high. Since no ship manifest survives for this transport, it is difficult to identify its members or to know what became of them. One family of this transport whose origins we do know was that of Andreas Schneider, who came with his wife, Anna, and his daughter, Elisabetha, from Freudenstadt in the Black Forest.[46]

Whereas no manifests survive for the second and third Swabian transports, Werner Hacker has succeeded in finding a number of Swabians who requested permission to emigrate to Georgia at that time.[47] Nearly all of these soon appeared in Georgia records, mostly as recipients of land grants. In 1750, in time for the first transport, we find Abraham and Jacob Schlumberger, both from Setzingen and both with families. Jacob, who had received a parting gift for his journey because of his dire poverty, died in Savannah; his widow Maria, née Groner, married a man from Vernonburg. Also on Hacker's list are Johann Scheraus of Langenau, Catharina Michel of Nerenstetten, and Barbara Öchselin of Langenau, who accompanied Jacob Huber of Langenau.

Among the Swabians who asked to go with the second transport, the following are recorded as living in Georgia: Paul Gerber from Albeck; Georg Gruber from Langenau; Jerg Häckel from Holzkirch; Sebastian Hasen-

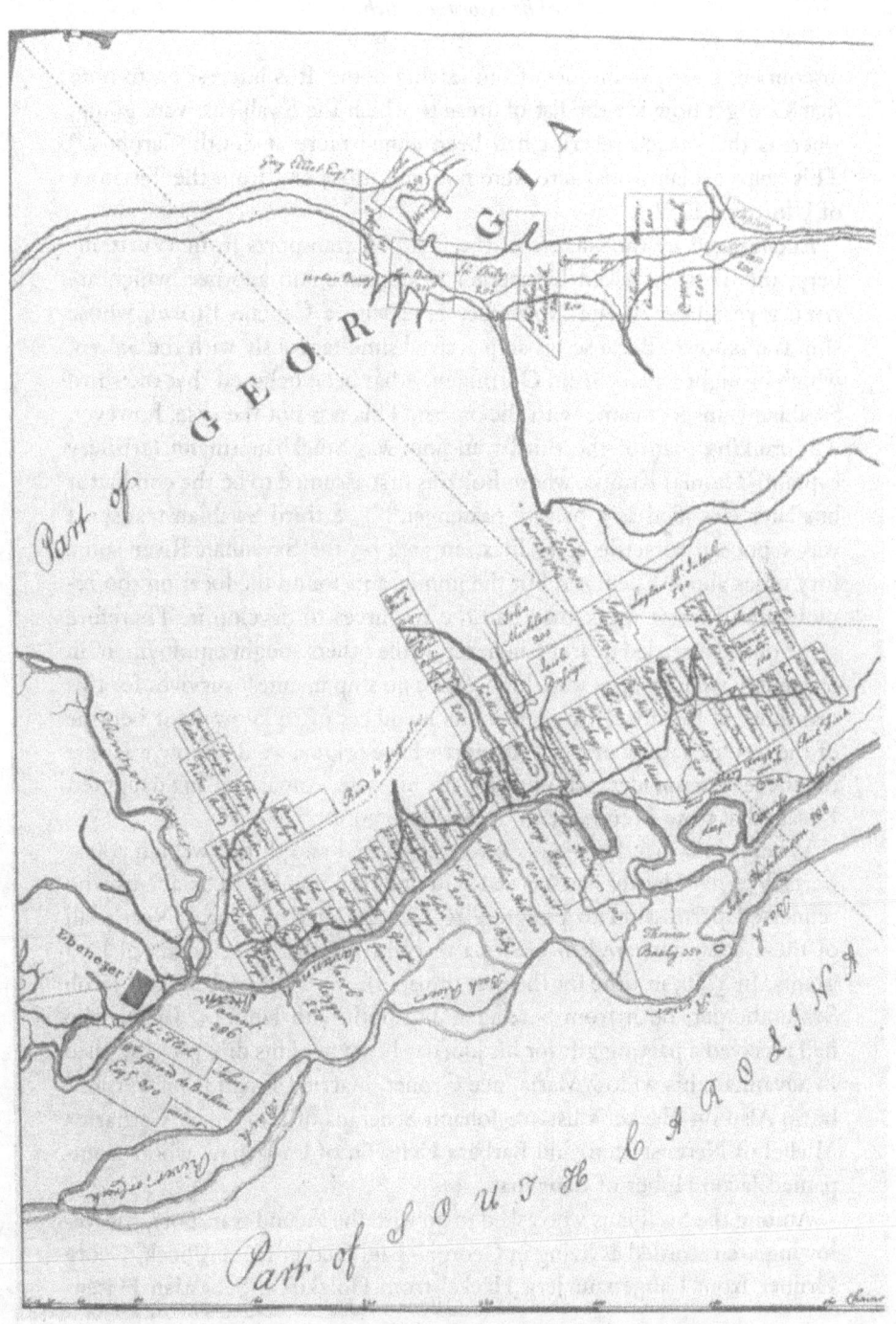

Plan of Bethany, by Wilhelm Gerhard de Brahm (by permission of the British Library)

discourage their parishioners from leaving home. It is interesting to note that Georgia now led the list of areas to which the Swabians were going, whereas the Zurich rescript had been aimed more at South Carolina.[44] This helps explain why there were no more transports from the Territory of Ulm after 1752.

Encouraged by the success of the first two transports from Württemberg, the Trustees asked Urlsperger to organize still another, which arrived a year later in late November 1752 with a Captain Brown, whose ship is unknown. Because his ship arrived simultaneously with the *Success*, which brought a party from Göttingen, it has been believed that the third Swabian transport came with the *Success*. This was not the case, however. The ranking man of the third transport was Stückhauptmann (artillery captain) Thomas Krauss, whom Boltzius first assumed to be the conductor but later classified as a private passenger.[45] The third Swabian transport was supposed to settle at Halifax, an area on the Savannah River some fifty miles above Ebenezer, but the immigrants found the location too remote and did not think they had the resources to develop it. Therefore some of them settled nearer Ebenezer, while others sought employment in Savannah, where wages were high. Since no ship manifest survives for this transport, it is difficult to identify its members or to know what became of them. One family of this transport whose origins we do know was that of Andreas Schneider, who came with his wife, Anna, and his daughter, Elisabetha, from Freudenstadt in the Black Forest.[46]

Whereas no manifests survive for the second and third Swabian transports, Werner Hacker has succeeded in finding a number of Swabians who requested permission to emigrate to Georgia at that time.[47] Nearly all of these soon appeared in Georgia records, mostly as recipients of land grants. In 1750, in time for the first transport, we find Abraham and Jacob Schlumberger, both from Setzingen and both with families. Jacob, who had received a parting gift for his journey because of his dire poverty, died in Savannah; his widow Maria, née Groner, married a man from Vernonburg. Also on Hacker's list are Johann Scheraus of Langenau, Catharina Michel of Nerenstetten, and Barbara Öchselin of Langenau, who accompanied Jacob Huber of Langenau.

Among the Swabians who asked to go with the second transport, the following are recorded as living in Georgia: Paul Gerber from Albeck; Georg Gruber from Langenau; Jerg Häckel from Holzkirch; Sebastian Hasenlauer from Langenau; Nikolaus Helme from Albeck; Wolfgang Mack from Langenau; Daniel Remshard from Langenau; Anna Schröder from Langenau, who later married Hans Georg Winkel of Niederstotzingen; David Unselt from Bernstadt, first husband of the second Mrs. Johann Adam Treutlen; and Peter Zipperer of Bernstadt.

In time for the third Swabian transport were Michael Dauner of Langensee and his servant Martin Eckhart of Nerenstetten, and Anna Eberhard of Urspring, possibly a kinswoman of Johann Eberhard, who received a grant in 1752. There were also Johann Erhard of Altheim, Georg Fischer of Zähringen, and Ambrosius and Catharina Fischer of Langenau. Also with this transport were Abraham Frey of Bermaringen, Barbara Gröner of Altheim, Michael Gross of Leutzhausen, Sebastian Haselmeyer of Langenau, Johann Häckel of Langenau, Catharina Lang of Hörvelsingen, David Lohrmann of Altheim, Johann Mayer of Riedheim, Paul Mayer of Bermaringen, and Hans Pflüger of Langenau. Bartholomäus Nübling of Langenau probably accompanied the third transport, even though his name, corrupted to Neibling, first appears in 1762 records, which identify him as a landowner. In 1766 he was a Ranger, and in 1768 he requested a legacy from Germany. Catharina Lang fared better than most. She became the mistress of the royal governor, John Reynolds, who gave her a house lot on 11 March 1756.[48] After returning to London, Reynolds sent for her and married her.[49]

In addition to those Swabians documented as reaching Georgia, there were others who declared their intention of emigrating and may have done so, even if no evidence of this has yet come to light. Among these were Johann Bauer of Altheim; Nikolaus Brezel of Albeck with his wife; Hans Geywitz of Langensee; the widow and children of Jacob Glöckler of Altheim; Hillmann of Altheim; Christoph Kreusser of Scharnhausen and his wife, Barbara Ruhland, of Leutzhausen; Regina Moser of Langenau; Angelica Schumacher of Altheim; David and Jerg Siegler of Merklingen; Johann Staudemeyer and the widow Magdalena Staudemeyer, both of Altheim; and Johann Georg Usenbenz of Altheim. It seems very probable that Schumacher and Moser did carry out their resolution to emigrate, since families with those names, surely kinsmen, arrived in Georgia during the same period.

In 1752 and 1753 grants were issued to many of these Swabians, who are designated as "late from Germany." Unfortunately, we are not told how late, so it is not always possible to ascertain with which transport the individuals came. For example, Adam Kessler and his family, who arrived at Ebenezer at about this time, must have come with the third Swabian transport. Some had to serve out their indentures before receiving a grant, as was the case with Johann Georg Niess, who received his grant on 4 April 1753.[50] Johann Caspar Greiner, who was surely the same as Jean Grenier, a substantial settler of Purysburg and originally of Fleinsheim in Württemberg, moved to Halifax.[51] There he was joined by Johann Christoph Bornemann, who established a plantation he named New Göttingen in honor of his German home. Bornemann was accompanied by his wife and her parents, Johann Heinrich and Louisa Margaretha Greve, who also settled at Halifax.

Greiner, who married Bornemann's widow, prospered. By 1762 he had three hundred acres, a wife, three children, and two slaves; he requested and received a hundred more acres on Briar Creek.[52] He would appear to have been the father of Andrew Griner, who acquired much land and was appointed justice of the peace for St. George's Parish in 1760.[53] Although the third Swabian transport did not settle at Halifax as a body, other Germans did, so that the area remained partially German-speaking. Among these German settlers was the hero William Jasper.

With the third Swabian transport came Christian Rabenhorst, an additional pastor sent by the Halle authorities, who knew that Boltzius was suffering from age, poor eyesight, and sickness and that the widespread duties of the growing settlement were too much for him and Lemke. Rabenhorst, from Pagenköpp in Hinterpommern, had been trained in Halle like the previous three pastors and therefore shared their Pietistic views.[54] Shortly after arriving, Rabenhorst married Anna Barbara Kraft, the widow of the recently deceased merchant, who proved to be a very shrewd and somewhat grasping businesswoman, even though Boltzius and Urlsperger stressed her selfless and Christian character.[55] Rabenhorst preached regularly in all Ebenezer's dependencies and also served as justice of the peace, as Boltzius did.[56]

Because the SPCK had not provided a salary for a third pastor, benefactors in Germany collected money to buy and stock a plantation for his support.[57] Francke had considered Rabenhorst too financially ambitious for the post in Ebenezer. At first this proved true, for the new pastor devoted more time to his plantation than to his pastoral duties, much to Boltzius's chagrin. He revealed his business acumen in letting Hermann Lemke,

Jerusalem Church at Ebenezer (Hargrett Rare Book and Manuscript Library, University of Georgia Library)

Gronau's successor, take over the pastor's plantation until it proved profitable.[58] Although managed by a white overseer and worked by slaves procured from Habersham, the plantation interfered with Rabenhorst's spiritual obligations.[59] His materialistic wife saw to it that he collected all fees due to him. With time Rabenhorst mellowed, became less greedy, and won Boltzius's friendship, but not before he had pushed poor self-effacing Lemke to the wall. By the time Muhlenberg returned to Ebenezer in 1774, the Rabenhorsts, who had no children, were less grasping; yet Muhlenberg was still impressed by Mrs. Rabenhorst's management of the minister's plantation.[60]

Since Jerusalem Church, which was built in 1741 with Whitefield's aid, had required constant repair because of wood rot, and since it was too small for the enlarged congregation, the Ebenezer parishioners resolved to build a more durable and more spacious building of brick, a project Boltzius had hoped for in 1764.[61] When benefactors in Germany donated eighty-five pounds for the purpose, Boltzius let Habersham ("President of the Council, Secretary of the entire province, and the Germans' right hand") invest the sum for him at 8 percent interest.[62] Lemke and Wertsch devoted much effort to the task, which was aided by the arrival of brickmakers among the Swabian transports. After much delay, caused in part by a dishonest or else incompetent contractor, the forty-by-sixty-foot building was finally consecrated on 10 March 1770 as the New Jerusalem Church.[63] Unfortunately, Boltzius, who died in 1765, did not live to see the church built. This handsome edifice, the oldest church building in Georgia, is all that remains of Ebenezer. It stands as a fitting memorial to the faith on which the settlement was based.

The Sea Islands

Several Germans and Swiss received or bought land on the sea islands east and southeast of Savannah.[64] On 1 April 1748 Johann Alther, a Swiss butcher from Purysburg,[65] and the boat builder Caspar Hoffstätter (called Gaspar Offstetter), both old inhabitants of the colony and industrious men, petitioned for a small island in Augustine Creek, a river just east of Savannah and flowing past Thunderbolt and Causton's estate, Ockstead.[66] The president and his assistants granted the request provided that Hoffstätter would surrender his lot at Hampstead, which he readily did. On 15 May 1756 Josef Alther, whose father, Johann, had died the previous year, received a grant for 117 acres on an island "in the District of the Sea Islands."[67] On 19 November of the same year he bought the remaining 117 acres from Hoffstätter and his wife.[68] On 5 June 1759 fifty acres, called Point Hope, were granted to Henry Danzler, and fifty acres called Providence were granted to Michael Radick.[69] These were "on an Island between Skidaway River and Thunderbolt Bluff." This property is now known as Dutch Island.

Georg Siegfrid lived east of Augustine Creek on Whitemarsh Island in 1760, and Salomo Schad owned property on Wilmington Island, a few miles to the east of Whitemarsh.[70] At some time Schad acquired Elba Island, a piece of marsh in the Savannah River at the head of Augustine Creek. Although too salty for planting rice, this island, as we shall see, was later worth a fortune. On Skidaway and other nearby islands grants were made out to John Gaspar Betz, John Michael Betz, Henry Danzler (Densler), Michael Illy (Ihle), Samuel Lyon, Henry Frederick Meyers, Michael Radick, Michael Reitter (Reiter), and John Michael Borman.[71] Skidaway was a large island east of Wormsloe, Noble Jones's plantation on Jones Narrows a few miles east of Vernonburg.

When the second royal governor, Henry Ellis, took office in 1757, all previous grants were reconfirmed, thus producing an accurate list of almost all "Dutch" landholders at that time.[72] Ellis soon saw the value of German settlers and wrote to the Board of Trade, which had taken over the functions of the Trustees, that "the Germans in this Province are a very Industrious People and Bolzius, who is their Minister of the Gospel, and a Man greatly esteemed among them, has informed me that his Correspondent in Wertemberg writes, that many of those People would come from thence at their own expence to Settle here, if a small support could be allowed to them, for the first year only, 'till they could raise their own Provisions."[73]

Individual Emigration from Europe

In addition to the organized and well-documented transports, individual German-speaking colonists arrived on their own all during the colonial period, sometimes recorded and sometimes not. Some of them came as the servants of individual settlers, such as Christian Dasher (Taescher), a Swiss in the employ of William Cooksey, who arrived in 1735.[74] On 5 November 1737 John Jacob Vanomaker (Wannemacher) arrived as a servant to Hans Jacob Hamm, a German who had just emigrated from the West Indies. Not wishing to leave Savannah, Wannemacher indentured himself to the Trustees, who thereupon ordered Causton to repay his freight to Hamm when the latter proceeded to South Carolina with his large family.[75] Eventually Hamm returned to Georgia. Wannemacher soon moved to Orangeburg County in South Carolina, but recently some of his descendants have returned to Savannah. One inhabitant of Ebenezer, a German boatman, paid his passage by working on the ship as a sailor, as Boltzius mentioned on 16 January 1751.

While most of the Georgia Germans and Swiss, except for their pastors, were peasants or workers, a few were of the higher orders, as we shall see in the cases of von Reck, Dietzius, von Brahm, and Bornemann. We might also include Hans Jacob Hamm of St. Christopher's, who brought the indentured servant Wannemacher and who will be mentioned later as a slave holder. The percentage of wellborn Germans was probably just as high as that among the British element, many of whose leaders had been wigmakers, carpenters, and schoolmasters in the Old World and had come to Georgia "on the charity" or as indentured servants. According to Boltzius's entry for 21 February 1751, several noble German families wished to take up land at Briar Creek, but a scouting party from Ebenezer found the area unsuitable, and nothing came of the idea.

Because of their rigorous education and sacerdotal function, eighteenth-century Anglican and Lutheran clergymen were usually socially acceptable, even if born of humble parents. It will be noted that Boltzius, although the offspring of middle-class cloth merchants, associated freely with gentlemen like Oglethorpe and enjoyed the title "Mr." or "Herr," which was denied to "mechanics" like Georg Kogler, or Noble Jones until he was promoted to captain. All the Ebenezer ministers had been poor boys supported by scholarships and teaching positions. Regardless of their social origins, they ranked far ahead of schoolmasters, who usually served under their authority. The relative standing of ministers and schoolmasters is indicated by an invoice of 29 July 1738 by Henry Newman, which gives the pastor's half-year salary at twenty-five pounds and that of the schoolmaster at five pounds.[76] We have seen that two Swiss ministers, Zubly and Zouberbuhler, consorted with the ruling class and amassed sizable fortunes. It is to be noted that the German word *Lehrer* always referred to the pastor, never to the schoolteacher, who was a *Schulmeister*. This terminology probably derived from Hebrew usage, since the word *rabbi* literally meant "teacher."

Upper-Class Arrivals

The best-born of the Germans who visited Georgia was Baron Philip Georg Friedrich von Reck, who stemmed from a patrician family of Goslar, which had been ennobled in 1627 and had produced important functionaries and diplomats, such as the baron's uncle, Johann von Reck, the representative of King George at the Diet of Regensburg both as king of

England and as duke of Hannover.[77] Although Jean Vat had been considered for the position as commissioner of the first Salzburger transport, the influential statesman's glowing recommendation of his nephew prevailed, and Vat was held back for the next transport. The uncle stressed his nephew's virtuous Christian behavior, his fine stature, his broad education, his study at the University of Helmstedt, and his knowledge of French and Italian. Von Reck had intellectual curiosity and the ability to judge what he saw, and his remarks on the Indians were sound and informative.[78] Were it not for him, we would not have the valuable illustrations of Georgia's flora, fauna, and Indians published by Kristian Hvidt.

Most who met von Reck agreed with his uncle's encomia. Captain Thomas Coram, the Trustee and former sea captain who met the first Salzburger transport at Dover, called him "a Clever Young Gentleman very much like Oglethorpe tho not altogether so thin in the face, Yet handsome to the full, he looks as much like a noble man as any I have seen, and his behavior is very engaging being of an Excellent good Humour of good understanding and Prudence."[79]

What seemed to impress the good captain most, however, was von Reck's liveried servant, Christian Schweikert. Later Coram said that von Reck was "of a healing temper" and that, the more he saw him, the more he liked him.[80] The only negative criticism of von Reck came from James Lowther, the Anglican minister at Rotterdam, who found him "a good Man," but one who had "too much Gaiety about him for the People under his Care."[81] Urlsperger described the young gentleman as "a Young active man" and also "an able, brisk, courageous, disinterested, serviceable and pious Man."[82] Henry Newman shared Urlsperger's enthusiasm and said he could not express "the Praises Mr. von Recks conduct has brought upon him for his Paternal Care of these Emigrants both in Holland and on their voyage hither"; he stressed von Reck's prudent behavior, which surpassed what one could expect from a gentleman of his years. Despite his exceptional maturity, von Reck proved unable to cope with the disappointments, friction, and backbiting at Ebenezer. Martyn wrote to Oglethorpe on 10 June 1736 that "lest the Restlessness of Mr. van Reck's temper should have any influence on the Saltzburghers, the Trustees desire that his Lott of 500 acres may be laid out at as great a distance from them as possible."[83]

Despite his good birth and charm, the young baron was quite impecunious. His uncle stated that "he has little fortune to hope for" in Germany, a situation that explains his determination to acquire a large land grant and to find servants to work it. Von Reck did eventually overcome his lack of funds, first by loyal service in a series of bureaucratic positions, and later by marrying an heiress ten years his senior. He went into Danish service at Ranzau in Holstein in 1763, a fact that explains why his valuable folio of drawings ended up in the Royal Danish Library. He worked until he was seventy-two and lived to the age of eighty-eight. Late in his life, during the American Revolution when all Europeans were curious about America, he published a short treatise gleaned from his earlier writings.[84]

Although von Reck's drawings are generally attributed to him, it is apparent that they were by hands of varying ability. The botanical sketches were obviously the work of a well-trained botanist. It may be significant that the Scottish botanist William Houston traveled in Mexico and the West Indies in quest of herbs for the Trustees and that some of his collections were sent to Charleston for the Georgia Trustees shortly after his death in Jamaica in 1733.[85] It is possible that some illustrations accompanied them. The British botanist Mark Catesby also made drawings of such quality in Georgia at about that time, and the botanist Robert Millar was supported by the Trust in 1734.[86] While Millar and Houston never set foot in Georgia, some of their illustrations of tropical flora and fauna could have come into the colony. This might explain why von Reck's folio included tropical flora and fauna such as coconut trees and crocodiles, which were not native to Georgia.[87]

Andreas Gottfried Dietzius, who had amassed money in Batavia and settled in Anhalt, received a grant in 1732 for five hundred acres and crossed over with the second Salzburger transport in 1734 with his family and ten servants.[88] Ten being a large number of servants, Dietzius must have been a man of considerable means. He later asked permission to move to "Purysbury" and surrendered his grant.[89] It will be remembered that Dietzius had complained of Vat's barbaric treatment of the Salzburgers. The Latin ending *ius* suggests that one of his ancestors may have been a cleric, like Boltzius, because German Latinists often signed Latin letters with latinized names.[90] We will see that the con artist Jacob Kurtz had affected the latinized name Curtius.

Johann Wilhelm Gerhard von Brahm, the leader of the second Swabian transport, was perhaps the most talented man ever to reach colonial Georgia. Martyn well described him as "a man of Parts, & Spirit, has been a Captain in the Bavarian Service, and is a very good Engineer." Governor

John Reynolds called him "a German Gentleman of Great Honour and Ingenuity."⁹¹ Habersham considered him one of the "most intelligent men" he had ever known. Time was to prove Martyn, Reynolds, and Habersham right. Von Brahm brought his wife, Wilhelmina, who was the daughter of Baroness von Gera and therefore of the nobility.⁹² Von Brahm's own title was merited rather than inherited, since a military commission was usually recognized as equivalent to a patent of nobility, even if not always by those born to the manor, as we shall see again in the case of Colonel von Porbeck.

Von Brahm, or de Brahm as he restyled himself soon after reaching Georgia, was born in 1717, probably in or near Koblenz on the Rhine. He served for some years as an artillery officer and engineer in the Bavarian and Imperial service and, like Oglethorpe, served under Prince Eugene against the Turks. At some point he left the Catholic Church and embraced Protestantism, and for this reason he had to leave the Bavarian service.⁹³ One might suspect that he really changed religion in order to accept English service; but his later spiritual development revealed a serious and inquiring religious mind, which led him to become a Quaker with mystical leanings.

De Brahm lost no time in proving himself: within a year of his arrival he had charted the coast of Georgia and the Savannah River from its mouth to the head of navigation and produced a map, whose baroque title is practically a table of contents: "A Map of Savannah River beginning at Stone-Bluff, or Nextobethell, which continueth to the Sea, also the Four Sounds Savannah, Hossabaw, and St Katherines with their Islands. Likewise Neuport, or Serpent River, from its Mouth to Benjehova bluff. Surveyed by William Noble of Brahm Late Captain Ingenier under his Imperial Majesty Charles the VII."⁹⁴

De Brahm's unusual skill as a surveyor was quickly recognized; within a year of his arrival in Georgia, Governor Glen of South Carolina requested his services both as surveyor and as military engineer. His labors in Georgia and South Carolina, as outlined by Louis De Vorsey, Jr., were far too vast and varied to be outlined here; but it might be mentioned that in 1751 he began to build fortifications in Ebenezer, which became a heavy burden for the inhabitants, as Boltzius complained on 27 July 1760.⁹⁵ Boltzius made little mention of de Brahm. Indeed, they seem to have feuded, and Whitefield was called upon to try to reconcile them.⁹⁶

Despite de Brahm's obstinate and sometimes overbearing disposition, which antagonized many colleagues, he performed an incredible amount of excellent work. Already by 24 March 1753 de Brahm could send a map of the province of Georgia to the Trustees, for which he hoped for some relief, since, as we have seen, his plans for his future happiness in Georgia had proved "abortive." As on his map, he signed this letter "William Noble of Brahm, Captain."[97] As suggested, the failure of his future plans may have resulted from his inability to develop the land grants made to him and the von Münch family.

De Brahm drew up grandiose plans for the fortification of Charleston, which were never approved because of the expense they would have entailed. He was also sent to build a fort to protect the Overhill Cherokees, England's Indian allies across the mountains. Here he came to blows with the military commander, Captain Raymond Demere, who was less visionary and more practical. Luckily for de Brahm, he was transferred from the fort he built shortly before the garrison surrendered to supposedly friendly Indians. Its inhabitants were massacred, and the Indians put Demere's younger brother and replacement to excruciating torture.

Despite his eccentricities, de Brahm continued to receive royal support and was engaged to survey and fortify Georgia, where he acquired land and filled public offices. He also wrote the first history of Georgia, which appears a bit biased in favor of the Germans.[98] His connection with Georgia, however, all but terminated in 1764 when he was appointed surveyor general of East Florida, which England had finally wrested from Spain. Nevertheless, even though he had feuded with Boltzius soon after his arrival, he left his only daughter with Rabenhorst to be confirmed.[99] In 1772 he completed excellent maps of Ebenezer and Bethany, giving the names of the property owners at that time.[100]

As surveyor general of East Florida and the Southern District of North America, de Brahm made unusually accurate maps of the previously unsurveyed Florida peninsula. Later, he charted the Gulf Stream more exactly than it had ever been charted before. Refusing to renounce his allegiance to the Crown, he left his possessions in America and returned to England during the Revolution. As an old man, having received a pittance in compensation, he returned to America with his third wife, the widow of Edward Fenwick of South Carolina, and settled at Bristol on the Delaware, where the couple was known as quaint old Huguenots and where de Brahm delved into mystico-mathematical theology. After his death his widow joined her children in Charleston, but she was buried next to de

Brahm in Germantown, Pennsylvania, in 1806.[101] De Brahm of Koblenz and Augustin Hermann of Prague were without doubt the two greatest cartographers of colonial America. The historian Charles L. Mowat judged well when he said: "De Brahm was a man whose versatility of genius went beyond even that of the typical eighteenth-century dilettante: a surveyor, engineer, botanist, astronomer, meteorologist, student of ocean currents, alchemist, sociologist, historian, and mystical philosopher." [102]

An interesting newcomer to Georgia in 1752 was Johann Christoph Bornemann, who has been erroneously considered a Swabian because he arrived in Georgia almost simultaneously with the third Swabian transport. Actually, he was a North German, from Göttingen in Hannover, who came to Georgia to do research for the recently founded University of Göttingen. Being a surgeon, he wished to discover new and valuable medicinal herbs in the colony. Bornemann was born in 1716 as the son of Johann Wilhelm Bornemann and his wife, née Apel. Following his confirmation in the Lutheran Church, he was apprenticed to a surgeon; later he served in that capacity in Freiberg, the Saxon mining center. After living for a while in Berlin, he served as surgeon in the Prussian army during the First Silesian War under General von Kleist. Released from military service, he returned to Göttingen for further study, some of which was under Albrecht von Haller, a famous Swiss scientist, who became his friend and supporter. He married Carolina Magdalena, the daughter of Johann Heinrich Greve and his wife, Louisa Margaretha, née Schichhoff.[103] Bornemann matriculated on 17 January 1746 at the University of Göttingen, where he was appointed surgeon to the university.[104]

Bornemann, his wife and two children, his parents-in-law, and a maid left Göttingen on 9 July 1752 and traveled, first by wagon and then by boat, via Hamlin and Minden to Bremen. Along the way, especially in Oldenburg, Bornemann made interesting observations about the agriculture he saw. Later he wrote interesting letters to von Haller about the flora and fauna of Georgia.[105]

Because of letters of introduction from von Haller, the Bornemanns were well received in London and met many interesting people, including a family named Dietze, who may have been related to Andreas Gottfried Dietzius. Bornemann gives a vivid account of the difficulties travelers had at the time with custom officials because of their baggage, especially when it was excessive like that of the Bornemanns, which filled three wagons when the family left Göttingen. Naturally, the authorities suspected that some of it was for resale. Even in London the Bornemanns bought additional things for establishing themselves in Georgia.

The Bornemann party of seven and two other people were the only passengers on Captain Isaacs's *Success*, which was destined for Port Royal in South Carolina. They left London on 18 September 1752 and were deeply impressed by the courtesy of the crew, who spent their leisure time reading books. Finding that they could not eat at the captain's table, as they had been promised, and seeing what wretched fare was given the crew, the Bornemanns put ashore at Deal to buy provisions. After a sometimes stormy and sometimes hot voyage, they finally reached Georgia on 25 November. Fortunately for the Bornemanns, the captain had miscalculated and made his landfall at the mouth of the Savannah River, where the party was courteously received and taken up to the city by James Habersham, who, along with his partner Harris, happened to own the *Success*.[106] On 27 November the Bornemanns returned to their ship to get their luggage, and they met the third Swabian transport, whose ship was commanded by a Captain Brown.[107] Boltzius met them in Savannah on 30 November 1752, but he did not give their names in his journal.[108]

After a short stay in Savannah, the Bornemanns received a grant for five hundred acres and then proceeded up the Savannah River to Halifax, where they established a plantation which they named New Göttingen in honor of their German home. Heinrich Greve, or Graeve, Bornemann's father-in-law, took out a grant at Briar Creek in 1752.[109] He lived only seven more years, however, two more than did his wife, as Boltzius reported on 1 February 1759. In the fateful year of 1756 the Bornemanns fled to Ebenezer to escape an Indian uprising, and their youngest child died on the flight. Bornemann died the next year. A year later his widow married John Caspar Greiner of Halifax.[110] Carolina Magdalena bore her first husband six children and her second seven, but only one survived from each group. She herself died on 21 July 1773. Greve, Bornemann, and Greiner all died testate. The surviving Bornemann child is not named, but it must be the same as the Benjamin Wilhelm Burnemann from Göttingen who wished to be ordained, as reported by Muhlenberg when he was in Savannah.[111]

The noblest of all the colonists, if we can take his word for it, was Carl Rudolf, a prince of Württemberg. According to his story, he had been kidnapped in London by Captain Thomson and sold into slavery at Frederica. When he wrote a complaint to London, Oglethorpe intercepted it and tore it up before Carl Rudolf's very eyes. No doubt unknown to Oglethorpe, however, he also wrote a very convincing letter verifying his identity.[112] To judge by the style of the letter, Carl Rudolf must have been very literate, or else he won the confidence of a very literate man. When the Georgia authorities ordered Boltzius to extradite him from Purysburg, Carl Rudolf's host, Theobald Kieffer, refused to allow it, as Boltzius reported on 9 December 1742. Boltzius, however, was able to persuade the imposter to surrender and remain in Ebenezer, where he was kindly treated, before going to Savannah. The next time Boltzius heard of him was on 24 August 1750, when the pastor received a letter from Vigera in Philadelphia saying that the prince had joined the soldiers in Boston but had deserted and posed as a preacher in Maryland, but only until the parishioners chased him away for seducing their daughters.[113]

Self-made Men

In addition to the colonists who were already of the upper classes when they arrived in Georgia, there were several German-speaking indentured servants who achieved status through their own efforts. If ownership of slaves was a mark of success, then we would have to include the Slytermans (Schlechtermanns), Kieffers, Burckhalters, Schads, and many others. More important for the history of the Georgia Dutch were, of course, Johann Adam Treutlen and Johann Caspar Wertsch.

We have seen that little Johann Adam, under the name Frideling, arrived in 1746 on the *Judith* and was indentured to Michael Burckhalter. Because his story has been told elsewhere, it will suffice here to review that he went to school in Ebenezer, where he won Boltzius's heart and where he later taught school while managing a little retail trade on the side.[114] Because Boltzius wrote to Muhlenberg on 16 June 1751 that Treutlen was helping Ludwig Mayer in his *Handlung*, historians have thought that he was helping him in his medical practice. Elsewhere Boltzius uses the word *Handlung* to mean merchandising, as in his bitter complaint against Treutlen on 18 May 1757.[115] Thus it is clear that Treutlen helped Mayer in his business, not his medical practice.[116] Moreover, Treutlen became a merchant, not a physician. When the Savannah merchants who advanced him his wares told him that he must either teach or keep shop, he chose the latter as being more lucrative, thus forfeiting Boltzius's favor. With his earnings from his store Treutlen bought slaves, which then enabled him to acquire grants for large landholdings. By 1760 Treutlen was able to build and consecrate a house.[117]

During his stay of more than a year in Gosport, Johann Adam must have played with the English children, for he seems to have mastered English so well that no reference was ever made to his having a foreign accent, as was the case, for example, with Zubly. Having wealth and a loyal German constituency, Treutlen entered politics and served in the Assembly, where he acquired a fine understanding of English law. Appealing to the yeoman and small planter class, he was elected to the Council of Safety in 1776 and became the first elected governor of the new state in 1777, defeating the candidate Button Gwinnett.

Johann Caspar Wirtsch, a baker's apprentice from Ansbach, arrived in 1749 on the *Charming Martha*. Like Treutlen, he first taught school on the plantations and served well and faithfully, as Boltzius reported on 17 November and 6 December 1749. On 30 July 1750 Boltzius declared him to be the most useful of the servants brought by Captain Bogg. Later Wirtsch, or Wertsch as he began to call himself, served in the community store. He served so well that he became manager and was able to buy the establishment in four years. In 1758 he married Hanna Elisabetha, a daughter of the late pastor Gronau. Wertsch was eminently successful as a merchant and amassed what passed in Georgia as a sizable fortune. Sometime before 1774 he provided an endowment of five hundred pounds to support a schoolmaster. In the same year he gave Muhlenberg a greatcoat from his store, for which he refused payment.

On 13 September 1771, in a letter to the earl of Hillsborough, Habersham declared that Wertsch was "a very worthy Man, and a useful Magistrate among these People, and is very attentive in promoting their welfare in every Respect."[118] Several days later, in reporting on the Salzburgers' silk production, he reminded Governor Wright that "you know him to be a worthy, prudent and Cautious man."[119] It was regrettable that Wertsch later crossed swords with Treutlen, as we shall see.

The German Homelands

Whereas the bulk of Georgia Germans came from former provinces of the Roman Empire, there were various individuals from elsewhere in Germany. All five of the Ebenezer pastors were North Germans: Boltzius hailed from Forst on the Elbe in Lower Lusatia, Gronau from Kroppenstedt in Sachsen-Anhalt, Lemke from Fischbeck in Schaumburg, Rabenhorst from Pagenköpp in Pomerania, and Triebner from Pössneck in Thuringia. Among the other Georgia Germans we find Franz Sigismund Hernberger from Hungary (probably from a region now in Slovakia); and from Silesia we find Georg Sanftleben and his sister, Elisabetha, and Regina Charlotta Hamilton, the schoolmaster's wife. The Bornemanns and Greves were from Göttingen, the soldier Kikar from Hamburg, Friedrich Holtzendorf from Brandenburg, Prieber and Hammer from Saxony, Hersen from Oldenburg, Samuel Schröder and Christian Fulbright (Vollbrecht) from Danzig, Anna Barbara Rabenhorst from Mecklinburg, and Johann Lichtenstein from Kronstadt in Russia. Most of the other colonial Germans in Georgia came from the headwaters of the Rhine and Danube.

German Emigration from the North

As far as we know, the first Palatine in Georgia was Friedrich Rheinländer, the carpenter-glazier from New York or Philadelphia who accompanied the first Salzburger transport from Charleston to Georgia and went up to Savannah ahead of it to fetch a pilot. Not long thereafter, he and his family joined the Salzburgers at Old Ebenezer.[120] Rheinländer soon returned to New York, where he died, leaving Boltzius with a cantankerous widow and several ill-behaved children. Two of these, Christian Colmann and John Martin, straightened out and became respectable and prominent inhabitants. Being a South German, Rheinländer pronounced, and probably wrote, his name as Rhylander, in contrast with the standard form of the name used by the pastors. Rhylander is the way that most of his many descendants in Georgia and elsewhere spell the name today.

As we have seen, there was a steady trickle of German emigrants from South Carolina, first of all from the area of Purysburg, including many Unselts, Kieffers, Strohbarts, and Metzgers. There would have been more Metzgers but for a tragic accident. The tailor Jacob Metzger, or Metscher as it is often written,[121] sent his oldest son to Charleston to bring back the two youngest children and their mother, who was begging there. On the way back their pirogue sank near Port Royal, and they all drowned, as Boltzius recorded on 14 February 1739.

Many of the Purysburgers came as brides. The first Unselt girl to marry a Salzburger was Eva Regina, who married Georg Schweiger in 1735, against Vat's objections. The next was Anna Justina, who married the tailor Franz Sigismund Hernberger and departed with him in 1740 for Pennsylvania. Their mother would have followed them to Ebenezer with her other two daughters if it had not been for the law of tail-male, which kept widows from owning land. The third daughter, Sibilla Friederica, married Boltzius's servant Henry Bishop, better known as Heinrich Bischoff, who also moved away with his bride.[122] Theobald Kieffer of Purysburg sent his four daughters to school in Ebenezer, where they lodged with Ruprecht Steiner.[123] Margaretha married Thomas Bichler, Elisabetha Catherina married Matthias Zettler, and Dorothea married Johann Flerl. The records do not show what became of Barbara. Kieffer and his son, Theobald, Jr., eventually moved to Ebenezer also.

In Captain John Bourquin's sixty-one-man Purysburg militia company of 1756 there were some thirty-three militiamen with German names, of which thirteen lived in, or moved to, Georgia or at least took up land grants there. They were Rudolf Bininger, John Lastinger, Adrian Mayer, Henry Mayerhoffer, George and John George Mingersdorf, Frederick Rester, George and Nicholas Stroubhart (Strohbart), John Walser, and Jacob, Lewis, and Nicholas Winclare (Winckler).[124] Of course, some of these may have resided in Ebenezer first and just commuted to the military musters at Purysburg, which were held at infrequent intervals. That could have been the case with Johann Michael Lastinger, the descendant of Protestant exiles from Austria who had found refuge in Langenaltheim in Württemberg, where the family's vital statistics have been well preserved.[125] Because Langenaltheim was near Ulm, it is possible that Lastinger arrived with one of the Swabian transports and was merely performing his military service across the Savannah River.

In addition to the Purysburgers, emigrants came from Pennsylvania and other northern colonies, as did Friedrich Rheinländer. In 1751 Boltzius mentioned the movement of many Europeans from Virginia, Maryland, and Pennsylvania to the area around Augusta. In this context the word *Europeans* means "whites," as opposed to Indians; yet it is safe to assume that many of them, or their parents, were Palatines who had landed at Philadelphia, since there had been a steady migration for two generations from Pennsylvania, across Maryland, down the Valley of Virginia, and along the frontier of the Carolinas.

Already in 1741 Boltzius had heard that Pennsylvania was overcrowded.

Muhlenberg sent a young man named Israel Heintzelmann, the son of a deceased preacher in Philadelphia, to Ebenezer to serve as a clerk in Treutlen's store. The young clerk proved so faithful that Treutlen decided to give him his daughter Rachel, but nothing came of this because, as Muhlenberg relates, Heintzelmann broke his neck during a horse race.[126] It was a coincidence that Treutlen had gained his second wife in the same way he lost his intended son-in-law: her husband, David Unselt, had suffered an identical accident in a "hateful race."[127]

In 1752 an Alsatian from Strassburg named Johann Georg Ebner arrived at Ebenezer looking for land, after spending six years in Philadelphia and three at the Congarees.[128] Another immigrant from Pennsylvania was Johann Wilhelm Jasper, of whom we shall hear later. Still another migrant from Pennsylvania was the previously mentioned Anabaptist. The last recorded large group of Germans from the north were on a ship full of English and German people who came to Georgia from Pennsylvania in 1760.[129]

Toward the end of the colonial era immigration from the north may have been stimulated by the Proclamation of 1763, which prohibited settlement beyond the Atlantic watershed. The British authorities feared that colonists venturing that far west would lose contact with the eastern seaboard and possibly drop their allegiance to the English Crown. While this law could not be enforced, it may well have influenced some of the backwoodsmen along the western frontier to move southward rather than westward. Also in 1763 the Georgia Indians ceded a large tract of land to the whites between the Savannah and Ogeechee rivers north from Ebenezer, thus providing free land for all newcomers from the north. A number of these "Virginians" were German-speaking. According to James Wright, the last and most popular of Georgia's colonial governors, many of the "Virginians" were a shiftless bunch of vagrants not much better than the Indians.[130] This was confirmed by a Moravian named Ettwein, who was advised to cross the Savannah River and go up on the South Carolina side en route to Augusta to avoid the trash from Virginia and North Carolina, who might well steal his horse or take it by force.[131] Boltzius gave a rather dismal description of these unruly frontiersmen, who, in his opinion, represented the convicts deported from England.[132]

Emigration from Georgia

The frequent accretions of German settlers were partially offset by emigration; for, like many other coastal regions in America, Georgia served as a bridgehead, or staging area, for immigrants. Once they had served their time, become accustomed to the climate, and learned some English, many of them preferred to move to cheaper, healthier, and more fertile lands upcountry, particularly where there was no slave competition. Whereas the confirmation of land grants in 1755 showed a large number of Dutch landholders holding modest tracts, the percentage of German names on later grant lists fell noticeably as the great slave-owners of South Carolina began crossing the Savannah River to take out large grants along the Georgia seaboard.[133]

Some redemptioners had come to Georgia reluctantly and only because they were delayed so long in Rotterdam that it was too late to find passage to Philadelphia before the Delaware froze. Despite the Trustees' attempts to hold them, many discontented servants resumed their journey as soon as they had paid their passage. A typical example was Peter Marold of Saarbrücken, who arrived at Savannah with Hewitt in 1737 and departed two years later for Orangeburg, South Carolina.[134] As we have seen, some servants, like Balthasar Zoller and the Richard boys, fled to Saxe Gotha even before completing their indenture. Boltzius noted on 28 April 1743 that many Germans who came to Georgia to be farmers soon sold their plantations, animals, and other things and moved to Pennsylvania.

Among the defectors from Ebenezer were Friedrich Rheinländer; Andreas Zwiffler; Hans Michael Muggitzer; Andreas Grimmiger; Franz Sigismund Hernberger and his wife, Anna Justina Unselt; Stephan Riedelsperger and his wife, Catherina Valentin; Henry Bishop and his wife, Sibilla Friederica Unselt; and Johann Spielbiegler and his mother, Rosina. Some, like Ruprecht Schrempf, regretted their removal and returned to Ebenezer, as Boltzius reported on 8 November 1747.

In 1775 Muhlenberg wrote that in Georgia "the children are numerous. The boys cannot remain here because there is no land left for them; consequently they must go elsewhere in America and learn to be craftsmen, merchants, clerks, or the like in order to earn an honest living and thus become not a burden but a credit to the community."[135] Muhlenberg wrote these lines in explaining why Wertsch had donated the five hundred pounds for the training of young men at Ebenezer who would inherit no land.

It sounds incongruous that Georgia, which was already larger than most German principalities, was overpopulated with scarcely more than thirty thousand souls including slaves. It is to be remembered, however, that the salt marshes along the coast, which composed much of the total area, were sterile. The pine barrens, which covered much of the remainder, were almost as sterile and served only as poor pasturage for cattle, which would degenerate into "piney wood cows" unless their natural food was supplemented. The swamps along the fresh tidal rivers would produce rice, but only with capital investment and slave labor, and the great cypress swamps were untameable. That left only relatively small areas of arable land along the Savannah River. The soil around Acton and Vernonburg produced crops for a few years but soon played out, being of a sandy nature and depending on humus from the forests, which were soon removed.

When Muhlenberg wrote that there was no more land in Georgia, he was referring to St. Matthews and Christ Church parishes, where most of the Germans had settled. Already in 1750 the freeholders of Abercorn had petitioned the Trustees to give them some swamp land because they were being boxed in on their small holdings by the large five-hundred-acre grants being given to gentlemen.[136] An informative letter of 19 December 1750 from Habersham to Martyn explained the shortage of good land at Ebenezer. Landless sons in these areas emigrated not only to other states but also up the Savannah River in the direction of Halifax and Augusta, as Boltzius mentioned in regard to the disaffected inhabitants of Acton and Vernonburg. Very few Germans moved southward.

In 1775 St. Andrews Parish, where the Scots lived, contained only three landowners with German-sounding names. These were John Lightenstone (Lichtenstein), Gaspar Starkey (Caspar Sterki?), and Michel Hamer (Hammer?).[137] In 1759 a certain John van Maajen Hoff, having a wife, two children, and seven slaves, petitioned for five hundred acres at Midway, which were granted.[138] His name could have been a corruption of either a Netherlandish or a German name. Benjamin Sheftall and his son Mordecai had grants there, too, but they did not reside there.

To make matters worse, as Boltzius had predicted, slave labor enabled the large-scale planters to displace the yeoman farmers. Whereas Germans like Georg Philip Portz and Christoph Weissenbacher were still taking out grants at Abercorn in 1759, this practice soon stopped.[139] Within fifteen years William Knox, a wealthy Englishman, bought up all the family farms at Abercorn and turned them into a single slave-operated agribusiness. By 1775 the only Germans left were two Moravian missionaries, a scholar named Ludwig Müller, and a tailor named Johann Georg Wagner, whom Knox employed to convert his slaves. James Habersham, who had meanwhile become a large planter, employed Wagner to preach to his slaves, too, even though the tailor could not yet speak English.[140]

On the other hand, in St. Pauls Parish surrounding Augusta, we find grants under the names of Charles Bentz, Leonhard Craus, Gabriel Eerhard (Ehrhard), Christian Fulbright (Vollbrecht), Michael Elly (Ihle), Michael Illy (Ihle), Christian and George Limbacher, David Millen, Jasper (Caspar) Rahn, Christopher Ring, George Roseborough (Rösberg), John Schich (Schick), and the nonresidents Mordecai and Levi Sheftall. Most of these grantees had moved up from the Savannah area.[141]

♦ *Chapter Seven* ♦

Decline of Ebenezer

In 1750 Boltzius and his wife suffered a grievous blow, the death of two of their children, Samuel Leberecht and Christina Elisabetha, who died within one week. The very precocious son was his father's pride and joy. As his father's heir, he not only attended school with the other children but also received Greek and Latin instruction from both his father and the physician Thilo. He was just preparing to go to Halle to study when he sickened and died.

Boltzius was already ailing at the time; in fact, like Gronau, he had never been free of malaria since the epidemic of 1736. By 1754 he was complaining of poor sight, and he gradually succumbed to his many years of labor and sickness.[1] In 1755 his burden was somewhat alleviated when the new royal governor, John Reynolds, appointed four justices of the peace for Ebenezer with considerable authority to maintain order. These were Christian Rabenhorst, Ludwig Mayer, Johann Flerl, and Theobald Kieffer.[2]

After the death of his firstborn, Boltzius hoped to be succeeded in office by his surviving son, Gotthilf Israel, whom he sent to Germany with Captain Krauss to study at Halle; but for a long time Francke did not consider the young man dedicated or selfless enough.[3] Meanwhile, Boltzius realized that Ebenezer would be a difficult post, for few of the original religious refugees remained alive. While the parishioners still listened to the sermons, many did not take them to heart. In one of his last letters, that of 21 June 1765 to the younger Urlsperger, Boltzius complained that the Germans of South Carolina and Georgia had become indifferent in religious matters and chose the religion and church that were most convenient and cost them nothing.[4] Moreover, Boltzius must have realized that the climate was unhealthy. He therefore decided that Philadelphia would be a better location for his son.[5] Boltzius died on 19 November 1765.[6] His son spent the remainder of his life at Halle, where he married and incurred serious debts.[7]

Ebenezer proper had not really grown much since it was first established on the Red Bluff, since most of the population had moved out to the plantations and even practiced their trades there. A few months before Boltzius's death a Moravian visitor named Johann Ettwein wrote that Ebenezer deserved no more than Purysburg to be called a city, since there were only twelve houses besides the church. During his march toward Augusta in 1778, the British commander Archibald Campbell described Ebenezer as a "small struggling town."[8] The population was widely scattered on plantations in the various dependencies, which likewise remained rural. The Salzburgers did not really need a town, since they could trade directly with Savannah.

Ebenezer's moral decline, and even its physical decay, began with the arrival of Christoph Friedrich Triebner in 1769. Boltzius's death had put the burden of office upon Rabenhorst and Lemke; but the latter was now failing fast, and the Reverend Fathers saw that Rabenhorst could not manage alone. Since Rabenhorst had never received a salary but had been supported by the "minister's plantation," Boltzius's stipend was transferred to the newcomer. Unfortunately, this led Triebner to consider himself Boltzius's successor and therefore the "first pastor" and, consequently, the superior of the "third pastor," Rabenhorst. With the chain of command unclear, Triebner refused to preach in the outlying dependencies and restricted himself to Ebenezer proper.[9]

Because of his puritanical views, Triebner won the loyalty of some of his older, more conservative parishioners, who preferred his strict ways to the laxity of the tolerant Rabenhorst. On the other hand, Triebner's high-handed manners alienated many of his parishioners. One time, for example, he demanded church penance from Mrs. Häg and fired her husband from his position as schoolmaster in Bethany because she had danced to a dulcimer while pregnant.[10] The younger Francke, who had been Triebner's professor and knew him to be brash, greedy, and emotional, did not endorse him; but other people, less well acquainted with him, had sent favorable recommendations. There had been no other candidates for the distant and unhealthy post in Ebenezer.[11]

Soon after reaching Ebenezer, Triebner strengthened his position and ingratiated himself with his parishioners by marrying Friederica Maria, the daughter of the late lamented pastor Gronau and the niece of Boltzius. This made him a brother-in-law of the influential citizen Johann Caspar Wertsch, who had married Elisabetha Gronau. Backed by a strong faction, he then accused Rabenhorst of trying to misappropriate the Ebenezer mills. Ignoring the carefully worded contracts, he trusted his own intuitions and sent denunciations to the authorities in Halle. Deceived by these accusations, the authorities put the mills under his direction.

The mill board in Ebenezer, being near at hand, were much better informed than the gentlemen in Halle and therefore ignored their commands and sent letters exonerating the popular Rabenhorst. Among Rabenhorst's chief backers was Johann Adam Treutlen, Wertsch's main competitor as merchant and community leader. Soon all Ebenezer was sharply divided into Triebner-Wertsch and Rabenhorst-Treutlen factions, or, more realistically, into Wertsch and Treutlen factions. Poor Wertsch seems to have been swept into this unhappy strife only through his marriage ties: even though he was a shrewd and determined businessman, he does not appear to have been an overly ambitious or power-mad person. When an old, sullen, and possibly demented black woman was accused of almost killing the Rabenhorsts with rat poison, Triebner called her an instrument of God; but the authorities thought otherwise and burned the old woman alive, as Muhlenberg relates.[12] Other blacks testified that she had boasted of her deed, but there is no record of what persuasion may have been used to extract their testimony.

The vestrymen at the time were Wertsch, Johann Flerl, Christoph Krämer, Matthäeus Biddenbach, Johann Paulus, and Paul Müller. These were good men; but, because they were all of the Triebner faction, the Rabenhorst party called for a new election under Treutlen's supervision and elected a new board consisting of Treutlen, Ulrich Neidlinger, Christian Steiner, Joseph Schubtrein, Samuel Kraus, and Jacob Caspar Waldhauer. Since the first group would not resign, Ebenezer now had two boards of vestrymen.[13] One Sunday, to prevent Triebner from using the pulpit to make innuendos about Rabenhorst, the Treutlen faction stood guard with drawn sabers before Jerusalem Church and kept Triebner and his followers from entering. Meanwhile, the bewildered authorities in Halle were inundated with charges and countercharges from the two feuding groups. Feeling themselves too far away from the scene to judge correctly, they requested Muhlenberg to journey from Philadelphia to

Ebenezer to assess the situation. Fortunately for historians, Muhlenberg, as a true Pietist pastor, kept a most informative journal of this unhappy journey, which supplies most of the information that follows.[14]

Already in Charleston, Muhlenberg learned from a Mr. Philips from Old Ebenezer that the friction in Ebenezer was actually a feud between two leading men, Treutlen and Wertsch, both justices of the peace and wealthy merchants, who had the common people under their sway.[15] Arriving in Georgia, the venerable minister took lodgings in Savannah and summoned the two pastors to come individually in order to state their cases and to agree to abide by his final decision.[16] Next he went to Ebenezer and convened a series of meetings, which often degenerated into shouting matches, at least on Triebner's part. At these sessions Wertsch and Rabenhorst remained more or less in the background, and the argumentation was carried on mainly by Triebner and Treutlen, emotionally by the former and calmly and collectedly by the latter.

Muhlenberg's journal shows that he was deeply impressed by Treutlen. Whenever Triebner attacked him, Treutlen

> replied coolly and laconically, for he possesses native intelligence. He has lived in this neighborhood for almost twenty-nine years; he knew the late pastor, is a confessor of our religion, has attended our religious services for many years back; has observed what was good and what was bad; for a number of years he has been a justice of the peace and member of the provincial assembly. He was deacon of the congregation during Pastor Boltzius' lifetime and still is at present, and he is accustomed to demand sufficient reasons concerning any matter. Such a man who is at home in the English ways does not easily permit himself to be shouted down with declarations, etc., still less can he be won over by untimely reprimands given in the manner in which gentlemen are accustomed occasionally to convince their bonded servants.[17]

After talking with Treutlen on 19 November, Muhlenberg wrote, "It is a peculiar pleasure for me to confer with a man who possesses an enlightened reason, Adam's natural intelligence and ability to give a name to every animal, knowledge of the laws of the land, and some discernment of practical religion."[18] Having carefully considered all evidence and arguments, Muhlenberg judged that Rabenhorst's behavior had been proper and that Triebner owed him an apology for his ungrounded accusations. The mills were then rented to a tenant.

During this second visit to Georgia, Muhlenberg performed another valuable service for his church. In composing a new charter for Jerusalem Church, Triebner and Wertsch had failed, probably unintentionally, to insert the words "Evangelical Lutheran." Had Muhlenberg and Treutlen not observed this omission, the church might well have escheated to Zouberbuhler's Anglican Church, which had become the established church after the colony reverted to the Crown. Muhlenberg's respect and affection for Treutlen lasted throughout the latter's short remaining life, as is shown by his use of the terms "his Excellency" and "my kind friend" in their later correspondence.[19]

The Revolution

While Ebenezer was embroiled in the feud between the two pastors and their backers, Savannah and the rest of Georgia were also in turmoil, for most of the younger generation were clamoring to follow the example of the northern colonies in their struggle for independence from the mother country.[20] Among their greatest grievances were the mercantilist restrictions forced on the colonies by the home government. We have seen that, when Whitefield helped the Salzburgers develop textile manufactures at Ebenezer, Boltzius suppressed this information. Boltzius also played down the fact that the British authorities discouraged the Salzburgers from manufacturing their own tools and instruments. On 10 August 1772 Habersham wrote to the earl of Hillsborough, one of His Majesty's principal secretaries, that Wertsch had advised him that the Salzburgers could manufacture silkworm reels more cheaply than they could import them from England; yet this seems to have been discouraged. We have seen that Stephens belittled the weaving done at Vernonburg in order to convince his superiors that the Vernonburgers would not compete with English weavers. Urlsperger had expressed it well: "Only such fabriques and Manufactures would be allowed to erect in Georgia, which don't hinder those in Great Britain."[21]

Although Boltzius usually refrained from finding fault with the British administration, he, too, sometimes betrayed the popular discontent with its mercantilist trade regulations. On 31 July 1748 he recorded in his journal that, despite the unlimited resources in wood for potash, sand for glass, and porcelain for pottery, the colonists were not permitted to export such processed wares for fear of hurting England's home manufactures, lest the daughter harm the mother, as Boltzius expressed the idea. He also referred to restrictive British trade regulations in discussing a possible market for sesame seed oil.[22] Nevertheless, while certain elements in Savannah were urging resistance to the Stamp Act, Boltzius urged restraint. When the older Theobald Kieffer went down to Savannah, the rabble gave him a beating, to which his death was attributed. Apparently the anger was actually directed at Boltzius. Despite the excesses of the radicals, most Georgians were still aware that they needed British protection from the Indians on their long frontier.

As has been indicated, the Georgia Germans were generally apolitical. Most of them had played no governing role in Germany, except on the village level, and then under the scrutiny of bailiffs and other officials. As long as there were only Germans around Ebenezer, the Salzburgers had to send their own people as representatives to Savannah; but, as soon as they were joined by Englishmen, they began electing men like William Ewen and Jenking Davis, who understood the English language and laws better. In 1775 none of the representatives from Acton and Vernonburg except David Zubly bore German names.[23] As a result, the German element took little initiative in the independence movement.

Moreover, the Germans tended to be conservative and to accept things as God had ordained. If God has put a tyrant over you, it is surely to punish you for your sins. St. Peter had been very explicit in this matter: "Submit yourselves to every ordinance of man for the Lord's sake: whether it be to the king, as supreme, Or unto governors, as unto them that are sent by him for the punishment of evildoers, and for the praise of them that do well" (1 Peter 2:13–14). Governor James Wright was surely included among those governors to be obeyed. In addition to obedience to divine law, the older generation felt gratitude and loyalty to the British, who had brought them to America, often at British expense, and had given them free land and more freedom than they had ever known at home. There were, however, two major exceptions to this rule of quietism: Johann Joachim Zubly and Johann Adam Treutlen.

Pastor Zubly played not only a local but also a national role in preparing the way for independence, even though he desired only the "rights of Englishmen," not separation from the Crown. Zubly felt that a monarchy was superior to a democracy. He did, however, think that the monarchy should be limited, and he did not think that was the case in the American colonies. Consequently, he composed three influential tractates, the best being perhaps *The Law of Liberty* (Philadelphia, 1775), which Habersham, as a Loyalist, declared to be "mere sophistry and jingle of words."[24]

Because of his insistence on the "rights of Englishmen," Zubly was elected to the Second Continental Congress in 1775. In Philadelphia Zubly was much admired, at least until he refused to vote for a break with the Crown and was accused of communicating clandestinely with Governor Wright. Thereupon his influence waned. He was declared a traitor, and half his property was confiscated. Upon his return to Georgia he was even taken into custody, because his going at large would, it was thought, "endanger the public safety."[25]

Many Englishmen and Germans of the older generation remained loyal to their king, whereas their American-born or American-reared sons wished independence from the Crown. The Salzburgers' friends Noble Jones and James Habersham remained loyal, but they both had the good grace to die in 1775 and thereby free their sons to join the Whig party, that is, to take part in the independence movement. Triebner, whose salary came from the British SPCK, remained loyal; it is understandable that he accused Habersham's son John of favoring independence merely to free himself from his debts to his London creditors.[26]

Most Savannah Germans, being apolitical by training, were in a quandary. For example, John Neidlinger, the sexton of Christ Church, did not know whether he should obey the committee at Tondee's Tavern, where the revolutionaries met, when he was ordered to ring the church bells.[27] The Germans in the backcountry generally stood by their rebellious English neighbors. When Martin Strohacker, a Savannah shoemaker, tried to deliver a writ against John Green for biting off the ear of John Adam Neisler, he was threatened with a flogging and tar and feathering by a gang that included John Gaspar Greiner. Thomas Lane, who reported this event, explained that "it is a Common Practice, among the People of the back parts, of the Southern Provinces when a fight or battle happens, for the Contending Parties, to bite any part of the human body, and to Gouge the eye."[28]

German Life under the Whig Government

Despite Governor Wright's orders, the Whigs of Georgia organized a Council of Safety to collaborate with the councils of the northern colonies, which were already well on the road to independence from the Crown. On 8 June 1776 the Georgia Council of Safety ordered that commissions "be issued for the following gentlemen, viz. John Flerl, as Captain; Christopher Cramer, First Lieutenant; Jacob Ihle, Sr., Second Lieutenant; Christian Steiner, Third Lieutenant, of a Company in the Lower District of the Parish of St. Matthew, Second Battalion in the First Regiment."[29]

These officers had been locally and popularly elected, probably by the recruits themselves, for the government was then in the hands of the radical Whigs, who thought that authority should derive from the people. As the Germans would say, it should come *von unten herauf* (up from below) rather than *von oben herab* (down from above). Lieutenant Colonel Archibald Campbell, a member of the gentry, was shocked to learn that rebel officers of his rank were sometimes "Cobblers and Blacksmiths."[30] On 26 June 1776 John Greiner was reappointed captain of the Volunteer Company in the Upper District of Halifax, and John Adam Niesler (Neisler) was appointed third lieutenant. On 2 July of the same year commissions in the Bethany Company were given to Jacob Tussing as captain, Matthias Rahn as first lieutenant, and Caspar Greiner as second lieutenant.[31] At the same time Frederick Restar was commissioned as a second lieutenant.[32] The First Regiment was under the command of Lieutenant Colonel John Habersham, the rebel son of the loyal James Habersham.[33]

Six months later, on 7 December 1776, the Council appointed officers for the Grenadier Company in the same Lower District: John Keebler, captain; Charles Mackey, first lieutenant; Martin Dasher, second lieutenant; Daniel Zettler, third lieutenant.[34] Previously, on 29 August 1776, the Council ordered that five pounds be paid to Peter Buckhalter (Burkhalter) for his information respecting the ships of war at Cockspur Island.[35]

The highest rank won by a Georgia German seems to have been the rank of colonel awarded to Johann Adam Treutlen. Treutlen's commission greatly pleased his admirer Muhlenberg, who often referred to "Colonel Treutlen." The good pastor was also delighted when Treutlen was chosen to be the first elected governor of the new state in 1777. Treutlen's term was not spectacular; yet he did gain funds from the Continental Congress to arm Georgia, and he prevented William Henry Drayton from campaigning to have Georgia join South Carolina by proclaiming a bounty of one hundred pounds for his capture.[36]

During the political maneuvering between Whigs and Tories in Savannah, Ebenezer remained embroiled in the feud between Rabenhorst and Triebner and their factions. Because Triebner was a Loyalist, his party was looked on as Tories, whereas the Treutlen party became Whigs, or revolutionaries. When the Whigs extended their authority to Ebenezer, the people there, as obedient Lutherans, obeyed the government it pleased the Lord to grant them and swore allegiance to it. Being dependent on his salary from the SPCK, Triebner remained loyal to the Crown as long as he could.

On 7 July 1776 Triebner and fourteen of his Loyalist followers were taken at Colonel Treutlen's orders to Goshen, where Colonel Samuel Stirk ordered them to abjure their loyalty to the Crown. Triebner refused to do so, and on 5 October 1777 he was arrested as an enemy of the state and declared a prisoner of war by John Holtzendorf, the speaker of the House. He was released, but on 2 May 1778 Christian Steiner, Ernst Zittrauer, and ten other Republicans took him to Daniel Zettler's house, where Jenking Davis, prodding him with a saber, forced him to abjure.[37]

At this time Triebner was no longer preaching in Jerusalem Church, because the vestrymen, all of them being of the Rabenhorst party, would not accept him until he faced charges of being improperly intimate with Lemke's daughter. Claiming that the charges had been trumped up just to discredit him, Triebner refused to submit, even though ordered to do so by Ziegenhagen himself. After Rabenhorst died on 30 December 1776, Jerusalem Church had no pastor at all, and Johann Ulrich Neidlinger read a sermon every Sunday. Mrs. Rabenhorst continued to manage the minister's plantation, where the slaves were orderly and diligent even without a slave driver.[38] At this time Mrs. Rabenhorst contributed thirty pounds for a nephew's schooling in Germany, but there is no evidence of whether the sum was ever remitted.

Like the Salzburgers, most of the older Germans in Savannah, Acton, and Vernonburg also went along with the majority of the population when the Whigs took over the government, for they, too, were mostly apolitical.[39] No doubt many of their young people in active military service fled with their units when the British took Savannah in 1778 and continued to fight for the cause of freedom. This was true, for example, of Treutlen, who had just finished his one-year term as governor.

British Capture of Savannah and Ebenezer

Having met little resistance in taking over the government of Georgia from Governor Wright, the Whigs called in Continental troops under

General Robert Howe to hold the city. They also gathered considerable quantities of military supplies. It was therefore a dreadful blow to the independence movement when, on 28 December 1778, Colonel Archibald Campbell landed his British and Hessian troops a few miles downstream from Savannah and captured the city, having been shown a footpath leading around and behind the American lines. The American defeat was total. The British suffered almost no losses, whereas the Americans suffered severe casualties, many men being drowned while trying to swim across a creek west of the city.

Among the prisoners taken in Savannah was Mordecai Sheftall, the "Quartermaster of the Southeastern District," who had served on the revolutionary Savannah Parochial Committee in 1775. The British were delighted to capture this "notorious rebel," because they resented the audacity of a Jew who entered politics. Although born in Georgia, Mordecai had learned German well from his parents, perhaps because of its great use in dealing with the German-speaking inhabitants; and he owned property adjacent to Boltzius's at Ebenezer. Sheftall was roughly treated by his captors until a Hessian major, whom he later remembered as Zaltmann, sympathized with him because of his German language and introduced him to a Captain Kappel, who treated him kindly.[40] The Hessian officer would appear to have been Gregorius Saltzmann of the Trümbach Regiment.[41]

As the stream of refugees from Savannah fled through Ebenezer, Pastor Triebner went out to greet the victorious British and to assure them of the Salzburgers' loyalty.[42] When the British occupied Ebenezer and made it an important outpost, most of the older Salzburgers renewed their loyalty to the Crown and swore that they had been coerced into siding with the Whigs. Triebner himself swore that he took the treasonable oath under duress. Most of the Whigs fled and found refuge, and often military service, with the patriots. Among these were Stephan Blunt, Daniel Burgsteiner, Christoph Cornberger, Christian Dasher, John Martin Dasher, Philip Greiner, William Holtzendorf, John Eigel, William Kemp, John Gottlieb Neidlinger, Adam Nessler, Rudolf Strohacker, Andrew Waldhauer, Adam Weidmann, Peter Youngblood (Jungblüt), Daniel, Matthew, and Nathaniel Zettler, and Jacob Zinn.[43]

Triebner dined daily at the English colonel's table and served as chaplain to the Hessian troops, a unit of some two hundred men of the Knoblauch Regiment under the command of Major Johann Otto Göbel. During this period the Hessian contingent in Savannah and Ebenezer steadily in-

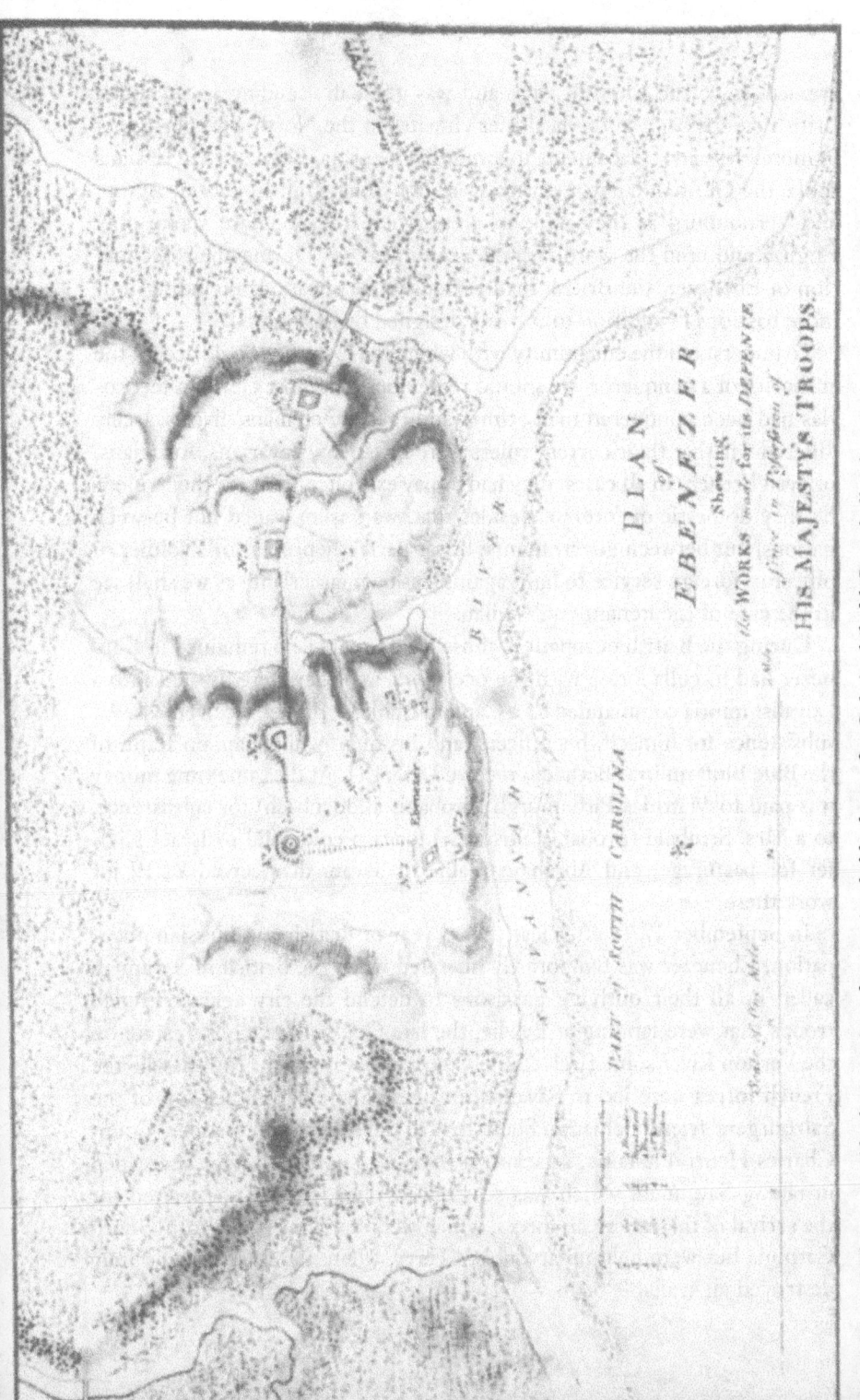

Map of Ebenezer redoubts, origin unknown (probably drawn for Col. Archibald Campbell, whose troops occupied Ebenezer in 1779)

creased, since the English command was gradually sending its invalided British troops back to the healthier climates in the North while bringing in more Hessian replacements to swelter in Georgia. Because the Hessians spoke the German language, they were not so hated in Ebenezer, Acton, and Vernonburg as they were in areas where the populace spoke only English and used the word *Hessian* as an invective. During their occupation of Ebenezer, the British made extensive fortifications including four more bastions in addition to the one designed by de Brahm.

To understand the equanimity with which the Germans could accept the authority of a conqueror, we should remember that most German territories had been conquered many times and that the civilians' lives scarcely differed whether their current rulers were Prussians, Bavarians, Austrians, or even French. In all cases, they had to pay exorbitant taxes to their rulers, be they domestic or foreign. Besides that, wars were waged not between nations, but between governments; it was perfectly proper for a soldier or officer in foreign service to fight against his own fatherland, as we shall see in the case of Lieutenant von Andlau.

During the British occupation, those Salzburgers who remained in Ebenezer had to collaborate with the occupiers, and they were drafted into a Loyalist militia commanded by a Captain Bühler.[44] Bühler received £46.9.1 subsistence for himself, his officers, and his men, while Captain Rahn of the Blue Bluff militia (Bethany) received £37.4.11. At the same time money was paid to Matthias Pittenburgh (probably Biddenbach) for subsistence, to a Mrs. Strobald (probably Strohbar) for two cows, and to Israel Kieffer for pasturage; and Abraham Gable of Savannah received £1.19 for work there.[45]

In September 1779, after less than a year of British and Hessian occupation, Ebenezer was temporarily liberated when the British in Savannah called in all their outlying garrisons to defend the city against French troops that were landing at Bewlie, the late Colonel Stephens's estate on the Vernon River some twelve miles south of Savannah.[46] From Bewlie the French forces were led to Savannah by Levi Sheftall, another son of the Salzburgers' friend Benjamin Sheftall. Had the French commander, Count Charles Henri d'Estaing, attacked at once, he might well have succeeded in taking Savannah, which was scarcely fortified. Instead, he waited for the arrival of the American forces, which were hurrying down from South Carolina but were held up at Zubly's Ferry, where the British had wisely destroyed all available boats.

By making d'Estaing believe he would surrender, the British commander, a Swiss named Augustin Prevost, was able to gain time to fortify the city and to call in the garrison at Port Royal. These troops consisted mostly of Hessians and Highlanders who had been attacked some months earlier by the Americans at Stono Ferry near Charleston but had escaped intact.[47] Through carelessness on the part of both the Americans and the French, this crucial reinforcement was able to reach Savannah by rowboat through a little-known waterway right under the eyes of the helpless and hapless French commander.

Realizing at last that Prevost was stalling for time and being advised that his supporting fleet would have to leave because of the approaching hurricane season, d'Estaing finally resolved to launch his attack. The decision was unfortunate, because both the French and the Americans suffered heavy losses and the British still held the city. Among the casualties were the two most lamented heroes of colonial Georgia, the glamorous Polish cavalryman Kazimierz Pułaski and a young sergeant named William Jasper.[48]

Jasper, who had been recruited at Halifax on 7 June 1775 for a South Carolina regiment, distinguished himself a year later at the battle of Fort Sullivan in Charleston Harbor, when a heavily armed British fleet attacked the Carolinians in their palmetto log emplacements. During the bombardment the flag on the central fort was shot down, and the garrisons of the two outlying forts, believing it a sign of surrender, held their fire. At this moment, Sergeant Jasper leaped over the embankment, recovered the flag, tied it to a spunge-staff, leaped on the parapet, and, despite shot and shell, held the colors aloft for all to see. For this heroic deed, Governor Rutledge presented Jasper with a sword and offered him a commission. Jasper accepted the sword but refused the commission on the grounds that he was unfit to be an officer, being unable to read or write.[49]

After the fall of Savannah, and of Charleston the following year, Jasper became a notorious guerrilla fighter, leading small patrols behind the enemy's lines and even capturing troops sent out to capture him. General Benjamin Lincoln, the regional commander, spoke highly of the clever noncom, who was called "a perfect Proteus."

After regaining Ebenezer in the winter of 1778, the British rounded up some patriots who had been captured fighting them after having given their parole. These prisoners, well bound and well guarded, were sent to Savannah for trial and execution. Jasper and a companion named William

Newton joined the party disguised and unarmed, purportedly for protection against the rebels. When the group was in sight of Savannah and apparently out of danger, the guards tied their prisoners to trees and placed a sentinel to guard their stacked arms while they drank from a spring. At this moment Jasper and Newton overpowered the sentinel, grabbed the muskets, shot the soldiers, and rescued the prisoners. This feat of derring-do was recorded by none other than Parson Mason L. Weems, the author who wrote about George Washington and the cherry tree, so it may not have been entirely authentic; but other more convincingly documented stories do attest to Jasper's courage and cunning.

When the French and Americans assaulted the British lines at Savannah on 9 October 1779, their main thrust was made against the Spring Hill or Ebenezer Redoubt, the point at which the Ebenezer Road entered the city. Having a skillful engineer, Captain George Moncrief, plenty of time, and four hundred black field hands, the British had prepared excellent fortifications and lines of fire and were generously supplied with ammunition. The assault was courageous but badly led, and the attackers suffered awesome casualties. Nevertheless, the South Carolina regiment broke through the abatis, crossed the ditch, and planted their colors on the Spring Hill Redoubt. When the ensign was shot down, a second officer recovered the colors, but he too was killed. Then Sergeant Jasper raised them again, at which moment he was mortally wounded in his chest. This is the scene depicted by the splendid monument erected in Savannah to honor Jasper's memory.

Because no records of Jasper or his family could be found, there was much speculation about his birth until someone, with no evidence, concluded that he was Irish. By 1888, only forty some years after the potato famine, the Irish community in Savannah was prosperous enough to erect the magnificent monument to "our great Irish hero," and thus it is inscribed. In Philadelphia at the time were records, subsequently published by Ralph Strassburger and William Hinke, revealing that John William Jasper arrived from Rotterdam on the *Minerva*, whose master was John Spurrier, and took his oath of allegiance on 29 October 1767. These facts exactly concur with all that is otherwise known of the young hero. As we have seen, when a German had two names, the first of which was Johann, he was called by the second, it being the *Rufname*, and he often ignored the first. This was the case, for example, with both (Johann) Martin Boltzius and (Johann) Adam Treutlen.

Monument in Savannah to Sergeant William Jasper, mortally wounded while retrieving his regimental colors at the Siege of Savannah in 1779 (photo by Steve Bisson)

Loyal Subjects

Having failed in the assault on the British positions, Count d'Estaing withdrew his troops quickly to avoid a counterattack by the victorious garrison while embarking, and the American troops returned to South Carolina. Those Germans remaining in and around Savannah either fled or returned to English loyalty. Among the loyal subjects requesting protection on 6 April 1780 were John Daniel Hammerer, Frederick Fahm, Herman Herson, Nicholas Hanner, John Heisler, Jacob Theiss, Philip Snider, J.J. Zubly, and Christopher Frederic Triebner.[50] Another list names these and also John Retter (Ritter).[51] A testimony of loyalty to the king was also signed by John Lightenstone of Christ Church Parish.[52] Of these German Loyalists, two had been frank about their views beforehand, for Lightenstone and Zubly had both been accused as traitors by the revolutionary government on 1 March 1778.

Among the "Distressed Subjects" recompensed by the British government were George Limebecker (Leimbacher) and Samuel Lyons.[53] Those inhabitants who would not swear allegiance to the Crown were blacklisted on 1 July 1780. Among these were John Treutlen, William Holzendorf, Rodolph Strohager, Philip Densler, John Snider, Philip Minis, and Mordecai, Levi, and Sheftall Sheftall.[54] Among the Germans who profited from confiscations, we find the surgeon Friedrich Rehm, who bought land taken from Joseph Johnston, and Friedrich Schick, who bought land taken from John Graham.[55]

On 4 May 1782 the revolutionaries, on top once again, banished or confiscated property from all those who had sided with the British, among whom were John Lightenstone, the heirs of John Joachim Zubly, David Zubly, Levi Sheftall, Christopher Triebner, and Wilderick (Friedrich?) Gruber.[56] Triebner's name might be expected on this list, but not that of Levi Sheftall, who had previously been blacklisted by the British and had led d'Estaing's troops from Bewlie to Savannah. He was pardoned in 1785.[57] Indeed, old animosities seem to have been forgotten quickly after the Revolution. In the case of multiple families, like the Sheftalls, it is possible that the brothers agreed to be on different sides to be sure that one would be with the winners.

The only German not forgiven was Triebner, who wished to return to Ebenezer but was not allowed to. Legend says that, when he asked whether he might return, the Whigs assured him that he was perfectly free to do so, but that he would hang on the nearest tree if he did. Although earlier historians assumed that he ended his days in shame and want, this was not the case. In English eyes he was loyal; for that reason he was granted a pension of forty pounds, plus twenty pounds per annum, beginning when his SPCK salary terminated. He was also granted £700 as compensation for the £2,260 worth of property he claimed to have lost in Ebenezer.[58] That would certainly have been excessive wealth for a man of God to amass in one decade in a poor parish.

Triebner served as chaplain in Florida and in the West Indies and then sailed with his family, taking the heiress Hannah Wertsch along on the *Commerce* to New Providence in the Bahamas, whence he wrote lengthy justifications for his actions.[59] Later he served as a minister in England and spent much time defending his character. His son returned to Georgia, where his grandson married one of Treutlen's granddaughters. His niece Hannah Wertsch returned to Ebenezer and married Hergen Herson, who quickly ran through her fortune.[60]

The Ebenezer Loyalists could vindicate themselves by serving in the Continental forces. Many offered to do so, but they were never called up, because by then the Continental Congress no longer needed them and had no funds to support them.

The Hessians

Many Germans had served in the assault on Savannah. Some of Pułaski's men were Germans or German Americans; in fact, at the battle of Brandywine the Polish count had rallied some scattered troops by shouting, "Vorwärts, Brüder, vorwärts!" ("Forward, brothers, forward!").[61] There were many Germans in the Continental line. There were also many individual Germans in the British units. After the British troops evacuated Savannah in 1782 and were stationed at St. Augustine, they included the Sixtieth Regiment, which had been quartered in Ebenezer three years previously. Triebner, who had fled with them, stated that "a large part" of the regiment was German, enough in any case to justify employing him as their chaplain.[62] Because eighteenth-century armies tended to be international, there were many Germans and German Swiss troops in the various French units at Savannah, and there were six hundred men in an Anhalt regiment.[63]

Of course, the largest German element in the British army was the so-called Hessians, the auxiliary troops rented to the British government by the rulers of Hessia, Waldeck, and other German principalities. When Colonel Campbell captured Savannah, he was supported by two highly trained Hessian units, the Wöllworth and the Wissenbach regiments. The latter of these became the Knoblauch Regiment upon a change of command.[64] Troops from the Wöllworth or Trümbach Regiment supported the unsuccessful attack launched in 1779 against Charleston by General Augustin Prevost, the Swiss commander of occupied Savannah. These Hessian troops distinguished themselves by fending off an American attack by General Benjamin Lincoln. Later, the troops were joined by units from the Wissenbach, or Knoblauch Regiment, in the successful siege of Charleston in 1780. Other Hessians from Savannah (actually Waldeckers), were captured with Prevost at Pensacola by the Spaniards, who paroled them under the promise that they would not fight again against the king of Spain or his allies. That left them free to fight again against the Americans, who were not so allied.

The senior officer of the auxiliary troops in Savannah, and for a time the military commander of royal Georgia, was Colonel Friedrich von Porbeck, an officer who had risen from the ranks. He suggested a very advantageous sortie before d'Estaing's assault and was in command of the British flank containing the Spring Hill Redoubt during the French and Americans' futile attack. For his excellent service he was commended by Prevost.[65] This professional soldier was a totally dedicated and militarily ambitious man, so it is not surprising that he came to blows with the reinstated civil governor, James Wright, during the period that Prevost was in Florida and von Porbeck was in military command at Savannah.

Although von Porbeck's reports to his superiors in Germany were always respectful, in fact servile, they were nevertheless a continuous complaint against conditions in Georgia, particularly against the unhealthy climate and the poor treatment accorded the German troops by the British. He complained bitterly against the high prices demanded for food, wine, and lodgings, the best of which were reserved for the wealthy English merchants. He also complained that the British had held back the booty in the form of "Moors," indigo, silver plates, cows, and merchant wares that the combined British and German troops had garnered in South Carolina in their abortive attack on Charleston.[66]

Most interesting are von Porbeck's reports of the desperate attempts of the Hessian troops to desert to the enemy, an undertaking made difficult by mounted patrols of blacks and Indians, who carefully guarded all the routes out of the city and received two guineas for every deserter they brought in dead or alive. It is hard not to sympathize with the poor involuntary conscripts in their attempt to flee the unhealthy and dangerous British service. In one of his letters von Porbeck well describes such an attempt in his vivid, if not always syntactical, style. When it is reported to Lieutenant Colonel Alured Clarke, the British commander, that five men have deserted, he sends out a patrol that sees from the footprints in the dew seven miles from town

> that the deserters have gone to a plantation belonging to a Jew named Sheftall whose father fled here from Berlin and whose son still speaks good German. The Creeks pursue in the swamp and find the deserters together in a thicket. A Creek by the name of Werner, who can speak good German, too, calls to them in the British language, also in German, that they should surrender. "We will not surrender," and immediately raise their muskets. Hereupon the Creeks open fire and kill some, and they still defend themselves with their sabers in their hands, as the enclosed report to His Serene Highness shows.[67]

These unfortunates, who deserted on 9 March 1782, were all killed and scalped. They appear to have been the privates Christoph Bracke of Valbrück in Hannover, Georg Friesland of Verden in Hannover, Johannes Schelhaas of Messel by Darmstadt, and Wilhelm Eckstein of Lorch in the Territory of Mainz. Bracke was twenty-three years old, the others all twenty-five. On 26 March four more deserted, of whom one was shot by the Royal Militia.[68] Despite such harsh measures, James Wright had to report that the men "still continue to desert."[69]

Von Porbeck's regimental reports give the names of the troopers who deserted. The rate of desertion accelerated even more after the American commander General Anthony Wayne, encamped at Ebenezer, smuggled many copies of a gubernatorial proclamation into Savannah offering good terms to deserters. The proclamation, signed on 20 February 1782, was distributed by slatternly women (*liederliche Frauen*) from Ebenezer. It reminded the Hessians that they were being mistreated, against all contracts and agreements, and being forced to fight against an innocent and upright populace that wished to welcome them into their own homes. It promised that every deserter would receive two hundred acres of land, a good cow, and two brood swine.

The British were naturally furious at this proclamation and offered five guineas to anyone who would report a person who helped distribute it.⁷⁰ The invitation to desert was most effective, however. Apparently word of it had come in advance, for on the very morning after it arrived a party of Hessian and Loyalist deserters arrived at Ebenezer under the command of Sir Patrick Houston.⁷¹ Lieutenant Colonel Clarke was seriously concerned with the Hessian desertions and notified his immediate superior, General Alexander Leslie in Charleston. Leslie in turn wrote to his superior in New York, General Sir Henry Clinton:

> I find that the Hessian Regiment has been there too long, they desert fast, and I am afraid little dependence is to be put in them, I shall for this reason be under the necessity of withdrawing them, I am very much at a Loss whom to send to replace that Corps. I am sorry to observe that when the Hessian troops are sent out to Posts Desertion takes place, they being so long here has been the means of their forming too many connexions, and the Enemy have taken every care to encourage desertion as much as in their power, this together with the assistance of their friends within our walls enables them to seduce the foreigners from the encouragement they give them.⁷²

The "Hessians" who deserted were mostly not real Hessians, for these usually felt some loyalty to their colors and also feared that their families might suffer reprisals if they defected. Most of the deserters were the non-Hessians with whom the Hessian recruiters filled their quotas after the Landgrave, as a good mercantilist, stopped exporting more of his "children" for fear that their absence would harm his agricultural and industrial output. The high percentage of foreigners among the "Hessian" deserters is indicated in the desertion rosters published in the *Journal of the Johannes Schwalm Historical Association*.⁷³ It will be noted that none of the five unfortunate deserters of 9 March was actually from Hessia.

With only one exception, all the deserters were enlisted men, mostly privates, since officers were volunteers and career men whose professional reputations demanded loyalty. The exception was Freikorporal Franz von Andlau, a young officer from Alsace, then under French sovereignty although still German in culture. As von Porbeck wrote, the senior French officer at Yorktown, Count Rochambeau, had announced that, if any French subject persisted in fighting against the king of France, he would forfeit his right ever to return to France. Von Andlau took the hint and deserted from the British service.⁷⁴ Eventually, all the surviving Hessians left Georgia, the last detachment arriving in New York on 13 August 1782.⁷⁵

There are no records relating where the successful deserters went. Some merely transferred to the American forces, who now seemed to constitute the winning side. Some may have taken up the promised two hundred acres right away and become farmers, but we may be sure that few lingered on the sweltering and malarial coast.[76] Only one Hessian deserter is recorded as dwelling in Ebenezer, namely a Pastor Bernhardt.[77]

The Wöllworth Regiment had been formed from the redeemed prisoners taken by Washington on Christmas Eve, 1777, when he captured the entire Rall Regiment. These prisoners had been stationed in the Lebanon area and given much freedom to work for the local German farmers. It is not surprising, therefore, that some deserted from Ebenezer to return to Pennsylvania, that El Dorado of all German immigrants. One of these, Nikolaus Bahner, made the dangerous seven-hundred-mile journey to Lebanon, often through Loyalist territory, and married the girl he had left there.[78]

Aftermath of War

The British had hardly evacuated Ebenezer the second time before a raiding party under Charles McKay invaded Ebenezer, plundered the property of some forty families, and killed Georg Schiele, while the terrified populace fled to the swamps. To be sure, General Wayne arrived in time to send McKay to South Carolina for punishment; but by then the damage was done. Despite this destruction, many refugees returned to Ebenezer after the Revolution and tried manfully to rebuild the town, but the task was immense. Jenking Davis wrote to Muhlenberg on 18 March 1783 to describe the sorry situation in Ebenezer when peace finally came.[79]

The town had been almost totally destroyed, and most of the inhabitants had died or had been scattered by the war. Davis also claimed that Triebner had absconded with all the money and bonds of the church. Time was to tell, however, that, despite his many personality faults, Triebner was correct in taking everything along with him to St. Augustine for safekeeping until he could be sure that it would be properly received.[80] In this he probably did well, because the British left Ebenezer to the mercy of partisans from both sides, who felt justified in liberating property from the members of the other party. According to Jacob Caspar Waldhauer, the chief spokesman of the community, among these plunderers and murderers was

Martin Dasher.[81] The property of Stephan Millen, who lived three miles from Ebenezer, was plundered by a troop of seventy men under Colonel Jackson.[82] This may have been the raid mentioned by Governor Wright on 3 February 1780 as having occurred three weeks earlier, in which a Captain Müller was killed.[83]

In a letter of 5 May 1783 to Muhlenberg from the newly appointed elders of Jerusalem Church, Josef Hangleiter told how he had been robbed and stabbed. After Mrs. Rabenhorst's death, the "Third Minister's Plantation" had been looted and everything taken, including the younger blacks who had served her so loyally. The church, which had served the British first as a hospital and later as a stable, had been stripped of all woodwork, including shutters, pews, and altar. Worst of all, the British had broken through the mill dam to make Abercorn Creek more navigable.[84]

Most of the prerevolutionary leaders having died, the current elders were Johannes Hangleiter, Nikolaus Schubdrein, Johannes Muchler, Caspar Heck, Jacob Gnann, Christoph Krämer, Samuel Kraus, and Johann Gottlieb Neidlinger. Despite the wretched conditions then prevailing, these men hoped to attract Muhlenberg's son Friedrich August Conrad to come and live on the third minister's plantation, which was managed by Waldhauer until he delegated the burden to a poor German, but the young divine did not accept the unattractive offer.[85]

The successful revolution brought an end to Georgia's colonial status, and it therefore ends this account of the Dutch of colonial Georgia. The colonial period in Georgia all but ended with the evacuation of the British and Hessians in the summer of 1782, even though independence was not official until the Treaty of Paris in 1783.

✦ *Chapter Eight* ✦

Diaspora

Although a majority of the German residents of the Georgia coast left because of the climate or because of slave labor competition, many remained in Effingham County, as the larger part of St. Matthews Parish was renamed in honor of a British friend of the colonies. Salzburger and other German names are found throughout Georgia; even deep in the Okefenokee Swamp one finds Snyders (from Schneider) and Roddenberrys (most probably from Rottenberger). An idea of the number of descendants of the Ebenezer Germans is given by Pearl Rahn Gnann's excellent book, *Georgia Salzburger and Allied Families*, which is now being greatly expanded.

It would be impossible now to ascertain where all the many Germans and Swiss went who left Georgia and how many of their descendants have survived elsewhere. An interesting case is that of Salomo Schad, whose "infentoray" omitted a small island he owned in the Savannah River. Because the water around Elba Island is too brackish for raising rice, it was all but forgotten until about 1975, when a power company paid three million dollars for it. It was then discovered that Schad had left hundreds of descendants, most of them living in New England and other northern states, where the climate was more salubrious. The largest share, $365,000, however, went to a Savannah man, whose name was of more recent German extraction.

While, as Muhlenberg observed, few Georgia Germans could fetch up many children, this difficulty diminished as they trekked inland away from the coast. We may be sure that, once away from the subtropical and malarial coast, many of the Georgia Germans obeyed the Lord's commandment to be fruitful and multiply.[1] Even those who removed to the extreme south of Georgia multiplied, as one may see in the Dasher Cemetery south of Valdosta, where one finds the names Wisenbaker, Dasher, Hineley, Flerl, and others of Salzburger derivation.

When, as Boltzius had predicted, slavery drove the yeoman farmers away from coastal Georgia, most inhabitants of Acton and Vernonburg moved inland to the Piedmont or else northward. Some, however, joined the German community in Savannah, which included many descendants of the Salzburgers. Among them we still find families by the names of Arnsdorf, Blackwelder, Burckhalter, Burgstiner, Dasher, Densler, Exley, Geiger, Gnann, Griner, Groover, Grovenstine, Grover, Gruber, Gugel, Heidt, Helmly, Hinely, Kessler, Kieffer, Meyer, Mingeldorf, Nease, Neidlinger, Nongasser, Rahn, Reiter, Rentz, Rieser, Schubdrine, Seckinger, Shearouse, Snyder, Stine, Swiger, Walthour, Wannamaker, Wideman, Winkler, Wisenbaker, Youngblood, Zeagler, Zettler, Ziegler, Zipperer, and Zittrauer. Being a minority in the city, the Germans quickly lost their language and, with it, their sense of being German. Within a century after the first Germans reached Georgia, all the early immigrants except those in Effingham County had been completely assimilated and were now Americans rather than Germans. Even in Effingham County only the older generation still preferred the German language. A Mr. Niess of Effingham County could still speak German in 1880.

The linguistic assimilation proceeded most rapidly in Savannah, where the German children grew up bilingually and gradually dropped their parents' language as foreign and useless. We may safely assume that the Savannah Germans passed through the stage experienced by all immigrant groups during which they spoke in their own native tongue to their children and were answered in English in a bilingual conversation. This tendency was noticed in Pennsylvania already in 1784 by Johann Schoepf, a physician who had served the Hessians.[2] Because English and German are both Germanic languages and employ the same dynamic accent, Germans learn English much more readily than the French, Italians, or Spanish. What Newman said of Matthäus Friedrich Degmair, the chaplain who accompanied the second Salzburger transport from Augsburg to Rotterdam, held for many Germans: "He daily improves in acquiring the English Tongue, as indeed I find all Germans do with a facility beyond any other nation that comes among us."[3]

While the Germans of Savannah, Acton, and Vernonburg soon lost their native tongue, those of Effingham County clung to theirs much longer. Since the SPCK would no longer provide a pastor for Ebenezer after the colonies had won their independence, the elders of the church there turned again to the benefactors in Halle. The third minister's plantation had been partially salvaged and provided sufficient income for a modest stipend. Therefore the Reverend Fathers selected Johann Ernst Bergmann, who arrived in Ebenezer on 20 December 1786.

This young divine was a pious and diligent pastor, yet he contributed to the decline of Jerusalem Church in two ways. The first was his refusal to preach in English, and the second was his ecumenical tolerance. Unwilling to insult the Lord with his broken English, he insisted upon preaching in German, to the delight of the older generation but to the despair of the younger people, who generally preferred English. As a result, many of the younger people followed the English-speaking Methodist and Baptist ministers whom the tolerant Bergmann permitted to preach in Jerusalem Church. Bergmann's ecumenical views even allowed his son to study at a Presbyterian seminary, and a Catholic monk was allowed to take up a collection for his cloister in Switzerland.[4]

Upon Bergmann's death his son, Christopher F. Bergman, was persuaded to return to his family's faith and take his father's position at Ebenezer, where he served faithfully until his death in 1832.[5] Since he had grown up bilingually and preached in English, the exodus from Jerusalem Church stopped; but grievous damage had already been done. The church did, however, survive. It has recently regained many descendants of the old congregation, who can now come from greater distances by motorcar. The handsome church, the oldest in Georgia, has been joined by a Sunday school and a Lutheran retreat. Pride in the Salzburger heritage is shown by an active and growing Salzburger Society.[6]

Oral tradition says that Bergmann gave the church at Goshen to the Methodists, and this appears to have been true. On 1 February 1793 Bishop Francis Asbury, who was touring Georgia, wrote in his diary: "I came to Ebenezer, and had a pleasing interview with Mr. Bergman: he cannot speak much English. The Lord has certainly something in design for this man, more than to be buried in this place." On the next day he added: "I suppose there are five hundred houses of all sorts; and if I guess well, about two thousand inhabitants. There is one Lutheran Church with, perhaps, fifty or sixty members. Goshen Church is about forty by twenty-five, well finished. Mr. Bergman and the congregation have given it to us, on condition that we supply them with preaching on Sabbath days—once in two or even three weeks."[7]

The descendants of the early German-speaking colonists in Georgia are often not recognized as such, chiefly because so many names have been anglicized. Few people recognize Staley as an anglicization of Staeheli, or Ash as a corruption of Eischberger. The Schlechtermanns could hardly have expected the English scribes to write their names correctly, and they probably found it practical to accept forms like Sliterman, Slyterman, and Slighterman. A good method of detecting whether an English-appearing name is really English is to ascertain whether it is actually found in England. Names like Fulbright, Hight, and Lightner appear to be English; yet they rarely if ever appear in England and have no meaning in the English language. The reason is that they are derivatives of Vollbrecht, Heidt, and Leitner, which mean respectively "very splendid," "heathen" or "heath-dweller," and "resident of a *Leite*, or slope."

In many cases the Germans just resigned themselves to the anglicization of their names, seeing that it was as advantageous as it was inevitable. For example, one branch of the Burckhalter clan accepted the spelling Buckhalter, which is the way both forms of the name are pronounced in the local dialect. Some names, like Kessler, Kieffer, and Rieser, needed no orthographic change to preserve their correct pronunciations. Heinle, Helmle, Oechsele, and Weidmann suffered little phonetic change in becoming Hinely, Helmly, Exley, and Whiteman. The name Treutlen, now pronounced "Trootlen," was still pronounced correctly when Colonel Archibald Campbell, who captured Savannah in 1778, destroyed "Troitland's" plantation.[8] An Andrew Lambert of Briar Creek, who pursued and shot some Indian horse thieves in 1756, was clearly Andreas, the son of Georg Lamprecht, a Palatine who had arrived on 2 October 1749 on the *Charles Town Galley* and served the Salzburgers as a herdsman.[9] Therefore the James Lambert who accompanied him was probably a brother or other kinsman. Three of his companions, Andrew Clements, Joseph Clements, and Solomon Kempt, have suspiciously German-sounding names. Solomon was possibly the son of Johann Kemp, who had come over with Captain Hewitt; Andrew and Joseph were possibly sons of the widow Clements, who came over with Captain Thomson. The English form of this name is Clement, and the French form is Clemence, while the German form is Clementz or Clemens. Incidentally, even if never noticed, the name Samuel Clemens was possibly of German origin, too, just as William Faulkner might well be related to the Falcker of Vernonburg, even if latter-day genealogists may have found them more suitable English ancestors.

The Germans left relatively few place names in Georgia, mostly in or near Ebenezer or Vernonburg. Among these are Burckhalter Road, the Dutchtown Road, and the following places and terrain features: Dasha Landing, Dasher Creek, Dutch Island, Gnan Hammock, Haner's Creek, Hangleiter's Creek, Heck's Branch, Herb River, Keiffer Branch, Keiffer Pond, Kogler's Creek, Lockner's Creek, Michael's Creek, Neidlinger Lake, Sweigoffer Creek, and Walthour Swamp. Among the towns and villages named for colonial Germans we find Dresler, Exley, Gruber, Hinesville, Huber, Hubert, Jasper, Keller, Millen, Neese, Quitman, Rahn, Rentz, Walthourville, Weber, and Zeigler. There are also many places and towns named for colonial Germans who migrated from the North to Georgia after the colonial period.[10] Other place names honor later German arrivals.[11]

Even after the Ebenezer Germans had lost their ancestral language, they retained many of their inherited characteristics. In 1848 George White wrote of Effingham County, the home of the Salzburgers:

> The majority of the people are the descendants of Germans, and they still retain many of the customs of their forebears. Honesty and industry are their leading traits. Very few of the citizens are rich, but generally speaking, in comfortable circumstances. Although the soil is barren, they manage to get the necessaries of life by industry and frugality. . . . The prevailing religious denominations are Lutherans, Baptists, and Methodists. Provision is made for the instruction of the children of the poor. The county academy is richly endowed.[12]

The number of Ebenezer names still present in Effingham County in the early nineteenth century is indicated by *Effingham County Records*, volume 2 of the *Annals of Georgia*.[13]

The contribution of colonial Georgia's German-speaking element was truly great. First, Germans were far more numerous than most histories indicate. Boltzius wrote to Francke on 4 May 1743 that there were more Germans than English in and around Savannah and that they prospered more because they were used to work.[14] De Brahm may have been prejudiced when he claimed that, upon his arrival in 1751, there was little else in Georgia but the Germans and the British officials; yet, as we have seen, this same view was shared by both William Seward and Joseph Avery. Most of the free British immigrants quickly migrated northward, and even the indentured ones found it easy to do so, whereas German renegades were more easily recognized by their speech. Despite their constant complaints, the British officials repeatedly said that the indentured Dutch servants were the only reliable labor and that they were even better when redeemed. Oglethorpe, Stephens, and Avery all stated that the Dutch were the only people seriously engaged in agriculture, and de Brahm agreed with them. It was largely the Dutch who fed the infant colony. The Salzburgers were the only important producers of silk, and their mills were the first successful industrial enterprises in Georgia.

While only a moderate number of Germans actually fought against the Spaniards, the large number of Dutch militiamen served as a "fleet in being" to discourage Spanish aggression. The governor of Florida kept amazingly well informed on conditions in Georgia, and he must have known that the colony was inhabited by yeoman farmers ready and able to defend their homes.

The Georgia Dutch contributed much to the spiritual life of the colony. Religion was a serious matter not only for the Salzburgers and the Moravians but also for the German and Swiss Reformed. The Anglican pastors looked enviously at the large and enthusiastic congregations enjoyed by Boltzius, Driessler, and Zubly. Perhaps the most lasting, even if indirect, influence of the Germans on Georgia's religious life was the Moravians' influence on Wesley, whose brand of personal religion won so many followers in Georgia in later years.

Whereas the Presbyterian Church in America is normally attributed to Scottish immigrants, in Georgia the German and Swiss Reformed played an important role in the beginning. The First Presbyterian Church of Savannah was initially administered by Zubly and was attended by many Reformed members, even though it was organized by Lowland Scots. After Georgia escheated to the Crown, the Anglicans tried to realize their prerogatives as the established church but were resisted by the Dissidents. Ironically, both parties in this religious struggle were led by men from St. Gall and its enclave Appenzell. While the Lutherans lost members by adhering to their German language, these members took their faith and piety with them into the churches they joined. As one Lutheran minister said sadly but proudly, the Lutherans of Ebenezer produced some of Georgia's most outstanding Baptist and Methodist ministers. The German-speaking element of Georgia also furnished far more than its share of the intelligentsia, which included Boltzius, Prieber, de Brahm, Zubly, and Bornemann.

Summaries

Because, so far, the events in this study have largely followed in chronological order, many items that belong together thematically have been sadly dispersed. This section will attempt to reassemble some of them and summarize the various subjects to which they belong and thus give a more comprehensive and composite picture of German life in Georgia. This will unavoidably occasion a bit of repetition. Therefore, whenever a fact has been documented previously, the documentation will not be repeated, since the reader can easily find it by recourse to the index.

When civilized people are thrust into a wilderness, they somewhat recapitulate the experiences of their primitive ancestors. Although at first supported with provisions from Europe and the northern colonies, the Salzburgers and other Germans on the frontier went briefly through the stage of gathering natural products and hunting, as their ancestors had done many millennia earlier, before developing a "field grass economy," or cattle grazing. Agriculture would not follow until later, and manufactures still later. Before treating these "external matters," as Boltzius called them, however, we will discuss religion, the factor that brought the Salzburgers and Moravians to Georgia and caused many Palatines to leave their homes.

The settlers' progress had been retarded primarily by sickness and death, so the second section of the summaries will deal with the nature of their ailments, the cures used, and the practitioners who applied them. Next it will show what efforts were made to educate the children for the next world and for this, and then it will review the settlers' daily lives, their art, music, and creature comforts.

The third section of the summaries will treat the settlers' relations with their native American neighbors, their initial opposition to and final acceptance of slavery, and their participation in the colonial wars and the Revolution.

◆ *Summary One* ◆

Manna from Heaven and Earth

To understand the Salzburgers, or the other German-speaking people of Georgia, we must remember that religion played a far larger part in their lives than it does in ours. We have seen the eagerness expressed by the Dutch in Savannah, Vernonburg, and Frederica to have a pastor, and we have witnessed the excellent attendance enjoyed by those who preached to them. While many eighteenth-century European burghers had become skeptical of the church and sometimes even downright anticlerical, this was not the case among the farm folk, who needed an intermediary between themselves and God. Like their medieval forebears, the Georgia Germans were constantly aware of Death, a grim reaper ever lurking behind them. This awareness must have intensified during their voyage to and sojourn in Georgia, where the mortality rate was so frightfully high. Their longing to see their lost loved ones can only have strengthened their faith in an afterlife. To die unprepared was a dreadful thing: we need only think of the horror the Salzburgers felt at the death of Bartholomäus Roth, who died unrepentant at Fort Argyle, while almost all of the other Salzburgers died happily in the Lord.

As Colonel Stephens observed, there was a certain lack of charity between the Lutherans and the Reformed, which is explainable historically. While the closest human tie among the ancient Germans was that of kinship, the next was that of cult; those clans that worshiped at the same grove or at the same spring were normally politically and militarily united against devotees of all other cults. Political loyalty presupposed religious loyalty to the tribal gods, an attitude that lingered and was expressed by the law of *cuius regio eius religio* (He who has the rule determines the religion).

Although Christianity was supposed to be a universal religion that transcended all barriers, the pagan Germans adopted it as an exclusive cult belonging to their in-group. This explains the innocence with which medieval Christian knights could slaughter Muslim or pagan women and children in the name of Christ, and how the Holy Office could burn fellow Christians for interpreting their common religion differently.

When the Reformation divided Western Christendom, the old exclusiveness reappeared, each emerging denomination possessing the true faith and fearing all others. This helps explain why the Vernonburgers were kind to one another but not to outsiders, as Avery observed, and why they refused to attend Zouberbuhler's services even though he was their compatriot and preached in their language. They even preferred the grasping Reformed minister Chiffelle, despite his poor command of German. The enlightened Johann Tobler was exceptional in questioning his Calvinist principles, at least with respect to predestination.

As mentioned, the British ban on Roman Catholic immigration betrayed less religious bigotry than political prudence, it being feared that Catholics might aid and abet their Spanish and French coreligionists. Tolerance was shown by the admission of dissenters and Jews. Despite the ban on Catholics, there were some German Catholics in Georgia, such as the surgeon Georg Ludwig Roth and a family of refugees from the Cherokee war who passed through Ebenezer in 1760 on their way to lands south of the Altamaha.[1] On 27 January 1751 Boltzius opposed the admission to Ebenezer of a Catholic German stocking-weaver from Savannah and his wife, who claimed to be a Salzburger. On 16 March 1760 he visited a sick Catholic man in Savannah, who, even though he betrayed no popish dogma, still refused to become a Lutheran. Some of Boltzius's flock had been reared as Catholics and joined the Lutheran exodus, possibly for family or economic reasons. As he reported on 7 July 1742, one of them, apparently Mrs. Hans Flerl, was first converted in Ebenezer.

Throughout the colonial period Ebenezer remained a tight little theocracy. By good fortune, all the pastors came from Halle and therefore preached the same creed; thus, there were no schisms as in so many American congregations. Rabenhorst, the fourth pastor, was more enlightened and liberal than the first three; yet Triebner, who arrived later, was as conservative and puritanical as the first three. Although Boltzius complained on Whitsuntide Sunday, 7 June 1747, that the land was full of all sorts of sects and hawkers of strange beliefs, he never really suffered any competition, as the Reformed minister Christian Theus in Orangeburg suffered from the Weberites.² Boltzius appeared more amused than annoyed on 2 January 1752 when he learned that there was a German Sabbatarian at Mount Pleasant, who celebrated Saturday instead of Sunday and whose almost grown children were not yet baptized. Even the wolf in sheep's clothing, the prince of Württemberg, claimed to be an orthodox Lutheran. When discord finally arrived in Ebenezer, it was due more to personalities than to dogma.

The pietism brought to Georgia from Halle had its roots in the Middle Ages. Jacob Spener, who introduced the movement to Prussia, was from Alsace in southwestern Germany, the home of many medieval mystics, men who tried to approach the Godhead through contemplation and prayer, with a minimum of formality and outside intercession. Luther himself was strongly influenced by mysticism, as evidenced by his editing and publishing the anonymous *German Theology*, a mystical fifteenth-century treatise attributed by some to a Philip Frankfurter.³

Boltzius's most insistent message to his flock, repeated frequently in sermons and conversations, was that they must turn from the Old to the New Testament, from the law to grace. Those who feared punishment from a just God were legalistic (*gesetzlich*). These were the people plagued by "temptations" (*Anfechtungen*), the temptation to fear that even Christ, the Redeemer who died for our sins, cannot save sinners as wicked as we are. Boltzius assured such legalistic people that all they had to do to be saved was to acknowledge their utter depravity, confess and repent their sins, and be reborn in their Savior. The greatest danger to a Christian was self-made security (*selbstgemachte Sicherheit*), an assuredness based upon civil respectability (*bürgerliche Ehrbarkeit*) and civil righteousness (*bürgerliche Gerechtigkeit*), which are but snares of the devil. Boltzius well expressed this view on 9 September 1739 when he lent a copy of Arndt's *True Christianity* to an indentured couple in Old Ebenezer: "They depend upon external honesty and consider themselves better than other people. I recently tried to demonstrate to them their perdition and the inadequacy of civil righteousness and of a virtuous and quiet life and consequently of the necessity of a true conversion, all of which they will find even more clearly and thoroughly in the book I have given them, provided they read it without prejudice, as they have promised."

It should be remembered that eighteenth-century Lutheran divines received a rigorous training, based on a thorough grounding in Greek and Latin and a mastery of Luther's Bible. Theology (*Gotteswissenschaft*) was a science (*Wissenschaft*), just as precise and demanding as any natural science. Many of Luther's religious writings were painstakingly documented, each argument being justified by a *Grund*, or reference to a scriptural passage. This approach would appear to be the origin of modern scholarly research, which first reached its present state in the nineteenth century at the very same German universities in which theological studies had flourished and were still flourishing. It should be noted that all the Ebenezer pastors had composed learned Latin dissertations on complicated subjects. Christoph Friedrich Triebner, the fifth Ebenezer pastor, wrote *The Nature of Man before, in, and after Conversion*.[4]

Being professors in a rationalistic age, the Halle Pietists made theology into a science. The Bible, as the unquestioned word of God, furnished all the material they needed: the Christian merely had to understand it correctly and build a rational structure around it. Theologians make a sharp distinction between the true rationalists like Christian Wolff and Sigmund Jacob Baumgarten and the first generation of academic Pietists such as August Hermann Francke, Paul Anton, and Joachim Justus Breithaupt. It should be noted that Boltzius studied at Halle while Francke, Anton, and Breithaupt were teaching there.

Both the rationalists and the academic Pietists drew logical conclusions. For example, the Bible tells us that God is almighty, omniscient, and all loving. Consequently, anything He does can only be for our benefit. If your sick child recovers, you thank God for sparing him; but, if he dies, you thank the Lord for having saved him from this sinful world and having taken him directly to heaven. If we can trust Boltzius, almost every sick Salzburger realized that his illness was a gift of God; for a loving father chastiseth his son, and sickness was most salutary for one's soul. This Christian optimism, best expressed in the *Theodicy* of Boltzius's countryman Gottfried Wilhelm Leibniz, lasted unchallenged in Europe until the Lisbon Quake of 1755, and probably even longer in Georgia.

Although the Pietists' God was a jealous God who punished conformity to the world, He was also a loving God. The Salzburgers never heard the sadistic fire-and-brimstone sermons heard in New England churches. The most a sinner had to fear was exclusion from heaven and the chance to see loved ones again, and even that could be avoided by heartfelt repentance. Boltzius constantly declared, as he did on 26 November 1749, that he followed the symbolic books of the Lutheran faith, so it is not surprising that he was appalled when he learned that the physician Seelmann had been contaminated by Johann Conrad Dippel's heretical views.

Once the mills were operating, the Salzburgers returned to the task of building the church urged by Whitefield, who had collected money expressly for that purpose. Work was begun on 29 December 1740. Kogler, the master builder, was helped by other carpenters, who received "Christian" wages, while the other parishioners worked gratis.[5] This church, which was consecrated on 20 November 1741, is well described in a letter of 10 March 1743 from Boltzius to Councilor Wallbaum, a benefactor in Germany.[6] This was the second church building in the English colony of Georgia. The oldest had been built one year earlier at Frederica.[7] In Savannah both the English and the Germans had to hold divine services in the courthouse building.[8] Years later, in a letter of 19 August 1747, Boltzius thanked the Trustees for the gift of "brushes and tools for painting our churches."[9]

Shortly before the church was completed, Boltzius received a parsonage, having lived miserably for three years after renouncing his comfortable quarters in Old Ebenezer for the sake of his congregation. On 12 December 1738 Boltzius wrote to Henry Newman that his hut was "almost rotten, & very inconvenient for preserving my health."[10] Boltzius had requested a parsonage three years earlier; now at last Oglethorpe, thoroughly reconciled, lent him twenty pounds for the purpose, and Thomas Jones advanced him £28.5.10 from the public store.[11] The parsonage was begun on the second day of 1739. All these expenses seem to have been reimbursed on 6 January 1742 by the Trustees, who allowed forty pounds for Boltzius's house. Eight years later, on 24 May 1750, they allowed twenty pounds more for its repair.[12] Gronau had already received a dwelling, his priority being due to his earlier marriage and children.[13]

As soon as land was granted along Abercorn Creek, many inhabitants of Ebenezer established plantations there, where they were joined by newcomers. Being too far away to commute by foot to Ebenezer, these people desired a church and school of their own. They began building the church on 6 December 1742 and completed it on 7 March 1743 without any outside aid, an amazing accomplishment for such a small number of people who had not yet established their own households. The building was named Zion Church. On 9 March 1743 Boltzius wrote the SPCK that Zion Church was larger than Jerusalem Church.[14] By this time Boltzius and

Gronau could write the SPCK a long letter about the flourishing state of the Salzburgers, which appeared on 6 May 1743 in the *London Daily Post*.[15]

Charities

Ebenezer's poor were supported by the Salzburgers' own poor box, to which individual Salzburgers left small legacies. The larger part of the funds, however, came from collections made in Germany. To assure the donors that their contributions had actually reached the proper recipients, the gifts were listed fully, albeit anonymously, in Urlsperger's *Ausführliche Nachrichten*, often in great detail, at the beginning of each volume. Those that came via the SPCK are also very well recorded.[16] Some charities came from as far away as Venice, where the donors were German Lutheran merchants such as Schalkhauser, Flügel, and Jastrum.[17] One legacy continued to send interest to the Salzburgers for nearly a century and a half.[18]

The Salzburgers of Ebenezer even received thirty-three guilders from East Prussia, as Boltzius reported on 15 June 1743. This had been collected by Archpriest Schumann, the chaplain to the Salzburger exiles there, who could have well used this money for his own congregation. Salzburgers also received gifts from the older American colonies, including some of the largesse brought by George Whitefield. On 27 February 1753 a German from Savannah Town, the trading station up the Savannah River, offered a hundred local pounds, or fourteen pounds sterling, for the church in Ebenezer.[19] He may have been the elusive German trader often mentioned but never identified.

In addition to monetary aid, the Salzburgers received large chests of linen, household utensils, and other useful supplies. The amazing thing is that not one of these chests went astray despite the war with Spain. In fact, the Salzburgers even received one well-filled chest that had been destined for the Lutheran missions in East India but was misdirected at London. An idea of the magnitude of these gifts is given by Boltzius's letter of 12 September 1747 thanking the Trustees for the chests they had forwarded and itemizing the contents.[20]

The Malcontents and other envious people in Savannah claimed that the Salzburgers succeeded only because they were "yearly supported from England and Germany."[21] It is true that help was generous. When divided by the number of inhabitants, however, it was far less than the Salzburgers were contributing by their own labor. Still, the pastors' salaries and the sums donated for schools, churches, and other institutions served as a catalyst, being passed around many times in the town before being drained off for purchases in Savannah.[22] Besides, there were many monetary gifts to the orphanage and to various sick or indigent Salzburgers.

On 8 March 1749 Boltzius mentioned the support given Maria Lemmenhofer and other widows "from the benefactions which God lets come from Europe." Even greater than these gifts from outside was the benevolence shown by the Salzburgers to one another and to newcomers. For example, on 26 November 1738 they completed and consecrated a house for the Palatine widow Catharina Dorothea Arnsdorff, even though she was not one of them. They also cultivated the fields of Bartholomäus Zant, a Swiss, when he was incapacitated by an eye ailment, and they contributed thirteen bushels of corn to the Silesian carpenter Sanftleben when he was sick, as Boltzius revealed on 26 January 1743. In addition, they contributed more than nine pounds for Muhlenberg's church in Philadelphia, as Boltzius reported on 21 July 1743, as well as to the Lutheran missions in India.

While the Salzburgers looked after their own poor, the indigent Germans of Savannah and Vernonburg were the responsibility of the Trustees. As Colonel Stephens mentioned in his letter of 2 October 1747, some of the Vernonburgers applied to the Council for relief. On 1 February 1746 the widow Nungazer received twelve shillings; on 16 December 1749 Margaret Gamphert, a widow who had been in the colony for fourteen years, received two shillings per week from the president and his assistants.[23] We have seen that Whitefield took three miserable German orphans into Bethesda. The Savannah Germans were not only recipients of charities but also donors, for Boltzius reported on 21 July and 9 August 1743 that, like the Salzburgers, the Germans in Savannah had collected four pounds for the construction of Muhlenberg's church in Philadelphia.

Now that we have considered the religious situation, we can examine the problem of survival in this world.

Forest Products, Hunting, and Fishing

Although seldom mentioned, honey and wax were important products in colonial Georgia. Already in their first year the Salzburgers had learned from their African sawyers how to find wild honey in the forests, and honey was also brought them by the Indians.²⁴ As we have seen, von Reck lost his temper when a Salzburger woman wished to buy honey from an Indian with whom he was already negotiating a sale.²⁵ It did not take long for the Georgia Germans to domesticate the bees, as Boltzius recorded on 12 August 1738. Bornemann commented that the honey and wax were softer in America than in Germany, but perhaps he failed to take the warmer temperature into account.²⁶ We have seen that the Salzburgers were gathering acorns for their swine when they discovered the Red Bluff, and Boltzius mentions numerous occasions when his parishioners brought in grapes, nuts, and other gifts of nature.

While rice and indigo culture required large capital investments, production of naval stores did not. Nor did it require outside help or organization. All the entrepreneur needed was an ax and some vessels to contain the rosin, as a Hessian officer, Captain Johann Hinrichs, observed.²⁷ That may be the reason that Boltzius scarcely mentioned the production of tar, pitch, and turpentine, whereas he did mention their use in Ebenezer. The Kieffers in Purysburg understood tar making, as indicated when Boltzius would not let them use their slaves for that purpose in Georgia. Indeed, the Germans were important in the naval stores industry in America, as Hinrichs mentioned. The "damned Dutch" at Jamestown and the Palatines in New York had been sent expressly to produce them.

Having lived under the archbishop's strict game laws, the Salzburgers were slow to take advantage of their new freedom to hunt; yet by 26 April 1735 Boltzius could report that many Salzburgers had shot deer. It was a long time, however, before they had enough hounds to protect their crops from the destructive rabbits, opossums, and raccoons. On 20 December 1738 Boltzius was offered an indentured hunter. He refused the offer, no doubt through clerical prejudice against hunters.²⁸ The pious Moravians in Savannah, however, had a professional hunter, a man named Peter Rose.²⁹ Hunting on the Sabbath was particularly sinful, as Boltzius tried to persuade his parishioners, as he did on 30 July 1753. Perhaps Boltzius minimized the quantity of game taken by the Salzburgers lest the benefactors think that they no longer needed provisions. Also, some of his more pious patrons may have resented their protégés' indulgence in the hunt, a sport fit only for gentle folk.

The Palatines in Savannah started hunting promptly and even shot cattle, if we can believe the allegations made against Hewitt's passengers.³⁰

The Palatine killed by John Fallowfield had gone hunting instead of working for Thomas Causton. Stephens tells a charming tale of a Palatine who shot a "ravenous wild Beast" of a kind that was doing great damage to livestock. When the widow Harris's Dutch servant fired at one, his first shot only wounded the animal, which then turned on him. Luckily, the hunter's little dog held the creature at bay until his master could reload and fire another shot. Stephens, who doubted that the beast was a tiger as people called it, gave a detailed and accurate description of a cougar, or mountain lion (*Felis concolor*).[31] Even though the Salzburgers never killed a cougar, they did have to join forces to chase one from their area.[32] Stephens also tells how two Dutch friends went hunting together, and how the musket of one went off accidentally and killed the other. Fortunately, the death was judged accidental.[33] As usual, Stephens did not bother to name the subjects.

Whereas the Salzburgers never saw the nocturnal cougars, they saw many bears. On 26 June 1736 a bear killed and mauled a hog, but a Salzburger chanced to come by and was able to chase the bear away and recover the pork. During the following year bears were more destructive, killing calves, hogs, and chickens. In return, the bears furnished good oil for lubrication and salad dressing.[34] Only one large beast ever harmed a Salzburger. When Peter Reiter fired at a bear in a tree, it fell on him "like an ox" and dislocated his hip. The injury required protracted and excruciating setting by the Purysburg surgeon Bourquin. This salutary injury did, of course, bring Reiter much nearer to God, as Boltzius assured his readers on 12 January and again on 19 February 1742. The Salzburgers never reported seeing any of the wolves of which they complained, as they did on 11 March 1742, which suggests that the major culprits were the mountain lions.

It is not surprising that the Germans at first made so little use of their right to fish, for in their homeland piscatorial privileges were restricted mostly to the gentry and the clergy. As an old Swiss saying stated, "Fish, know ye, is a food for lords" (*Fisch, wiss, das ist ein herren speis*). Although the Savannah River teemed with bass, bream, sturgeon, catfish, and eels, all luxuries in Central Europe, the Salzburgers scarcely profited from the fact. Indeed, Boltzius was amazed on 10 April 1738 when the English miller at the cowpen emptied the millrace and gave him a fine string of "trout," as the English colonists had already misnamed the largemouth black bass. Even after that, fishing seems to have been practiced only by youngsters like the naughty young Rheinländer and Helfenstein boys, whereas, as we have seen, the Savannah Dutch kept their boys out of school to hunt and fish. The Purysburgers did so, too, as Boltzius reported on 12 September 1742. When, on 9 August 1749, Boltzius mentioned the great quantity of eels in the Mill River, he did not praise their deliciousness but complained of their digging holes in the dam. Bornemann seems to have been the first person to describe the unusual art of "skittering," a method of fishing no doubt learned from the Indians.[35]

Cattle Raising and Cultivation

Like Moore and Martyn, other visitors to Ebenezer were impressed by the Salzburgers' success with cattle, which was stressed in nearly all reports. For example, the "State of the Province of Georgia," which was sworn to on 10 November 1740 by the leading citizens of Georgia, especially mentions that the Salzburgers had "a great deal of Cattle."[36] They had received their first cattle at Abercorn while on their way from Savannah to Old Ebenezer: on 24 April 1734 Boltzius learned that God had awakened some wealthy South Carolinians to donate twelve cows and twelve calves, which were soon followed by others. On 18 May a Carolina planter named Bryan brought a large herd. Boltzius does not tell which of the two brothers, Hugh or Jonathan, made the gift, but it was most likely Hugh, who is recorded as bringing cattle across the Savannah at that very time.[37] On 5 June 1735 one of the Bryans brought thirty-five cows and thirty-five calves as a gift from the SPCK; he returned six days later with some more, which the Salzburgers bought readily. These cows were thin, either because they had been raised on salt marsh or because they had lost weight on the long trek up the Savannah River to the crossing place. Fortunately, no matter how poor most of the soil was at Old Ebenezer, the canebrakes there quickly fattened the cows.

To appreciate the importance of cattle at Ebenezer, as well as at Acton and Vernonburg, one should keep in mind that all the Indo-Europeans had been closely attached to their cattle. The various Germanic tribes, who had lingered longest in the old homeland, continued this intimacy with their bovine livestock. In his *Germania*, Tacitus states that cattle were the Germans' dearest form of wealth. It should also be noted that the German word *Vieh* (cattle) is cognate with the English word "fee," just as

Latin *pecus* is related to "pecuniary," while "chattel" is related to "cattle." In parts of Germany, as in Pennsylvania, the farmers lived under one roof with their cattle, thus being on hand to care for them and also profiting from the warmth created by the animals and their manure. Cattle were treated with a certain affection. In a short thirteenth-century tale written in Austria not far from the Salzburgers' homeland, a peasant boy named Helmbrecht, who has returned home in the guise of a knight, proves his identity by naming all his father's cattle.

Whereas most Georgians allowed their cattle to roam wild, at the mercy of bears and wolves, the Salzburgers employed herdsmen to guard the community's cattle jointly, a fact noted favorably by all commentators.[38] Jacob Schartner of the second Salzburger transport, who could not manage the herd alone, was later helped by Andreas Grimmiger, whose service was a penance for a theft, and still later by Palatine redemptioners. Despite this precaution, many cows were killed by nocturnal predators, probably less by the wolves, which the Central Europeans blamed, than by mountain lions. Bears, too, were destructive to livestock, as we have seen. Also, some cows became homesick and attempted the long journey back home to South Carolina. To prevent the cows from straying unnoticed, the Salzburgers attached bells to them; but these sometimes tempted passing Indians to shoot the cows just for the bells. More effective was the practice of cropping the cows' ears in various ways and branding the animals. The names of many Salzburgers and other German ranchers, along with their brands and method of cropping ears, are listed in the colonial Marks and Brands Book, now at the Georgia Department of Archives and History.

Even though the "poor Salzburgers" had little money for anything else, they did seem to have cash on hand whenever Bryan or other South Carolina planters brought cattle for sale. Soon the Salzburger herds were the largest in the colony. Some calves were sold in Savannah, a few were slaughtered for local consumption, and others were altered to furnish work oxen for plowing and hauling logs. On the other hand, all heifers were kept for breeding, for in Salzburg not only a peasant's diet but also his status depended on the number of cows he owned. As Mark Twain observed, in the Black Forest a man's social standing could be measured by the size of the manure pile in front of his house. Unfortunately, the cows, which were acquired from South Carolina and were probably of English provenience, are never described; but they seem to have pleased the Germans well and to have flourished under their care. The greatest benefit from the cattle was, of course, the dairy products they produced for domestic consumption. By 24 May 1735 the Salzburgers were already making butter.

Despite the losses caused by predators, rustlers, and bovine homesickness, the Salzburgers' herds continued to increase. In November 1738 Ruprecht Steiner wrote to his brother in Lindau that he now had five cows, Georg Kogler six, Matthäus Brandner four, Simon Steiner four, Christian Riedelsperger five, and Stephan Rottenberger three.[39] By 1739 the Salzburgers had 250 cows, as Boltzius reported on 27 July of that year. Kogler alone had fourteen, whereas he had not owned a single one back in Salzburg.[40] On 22 April 1741 Boltzius could state that cattle breeding was half the Salzburgers' livelihood.[41] Although the Salzburgers impressed all early observers with the way they herded their cattle, by 1742 they, too, had found it more practical to let the cattle roam free and to guard only the milk cows, which were brought home every evening.[42] Thus, after following Central European practices for several years, the Salzburgers now adopted the open range method of the South Carolinians, a method ultimately derived chiefly from western Britain and Senegambian Africa.[43] It is to be remembered that the Salzburgers' cattle suffered far less from the distemper than the cattle at Vernonburg, even though the disease did reach Ebenezer in 1743.[44]

It has been mentioned that, in the great destruction of wild cattle in 1748, the Salzburgers renounced their claim to their large share of the cattle in favor of the Vernonburgers. Boltzius had been, in fact, a prime mover in this operation, having asked the Council in Savannah for such a destruction a year earlier.[45] On 5 March 1750 Boltzius sent the Council in Savannah a most informative letter concerning the Salzburgers' planned purchase of the Trustees' cowpen, in which he enumerated the advantages to the colony and the difficulties it would cause the purchasers.[46] The Salzburgers' cattle business continued to prosper throughout the colonial period, while public interest and propaganda gradually shifted to the silk and lumber businesses. In addition to cattle, the Salzburgers also acquired some sheep by 1748, but these never became economically important.[47] On 7 August 1747 Boltzius reported that Johann Georg Köcher was weaving some wool, some from Bethesda and some from the "modest supply" at Ebenezer.

Whereas almost no crops had been harvested in Old Ebenezer because of the sterile soil, the prevailing sickness, and the need to make roads and build shelters, agriculture improved rapidly as soon as fertile land was allotted on the Red Bluff. This was especially true of the bottom land along Abercorn Creek, which was covered with rich silt in winter when the river flooded. For lack of horses, all cultivation had to be by hoe, which made it laborious work. Such primitive means of cultivation sufficed for Indian corn, field peas, and sweet potatoes, which remained the major crops as long as there were no plows. On 14 March 1739 Boltzius reported good crops of corn, peas, (sweet) potatoes, and rice despite the failure of the "Pennsylvania" corn, which had been so highly recommended.[48]

From 1739 on these crops were encouraged by a "corn-shilling," a subsidy of one shilling per bushel.[49] It was not, however, until 1743, after many petitions, that Boltzius could finally distribute the "bownty" of 1739, as he recorded on 17 March 1743. The first impressive harvest was that of 1741, as shown by the itemized report Boltzius submitted on 18 November of that year for each Salzburger's crop of corn, beans, rice, and sweet potatoes. The following year brought a good crop of wheat, rye, barley, and oats, which Boltzius recorded on 21 May and itemized in the crop report of 6 November. Boltzius's figures were the basis of Colonel Stephens's official report of 22 January 1743, which showed that Ebenezer had produced two thirds of all the crops raised in the Northern District.[50]

Without horses and plows, "European" grains like wheat, rye, oats, and barley could not be profitably raised. Even if horses had been available, they could not have drawn plows while heavy roots still lay under the newly cleared land. As long as the Salzburgers had to depend upon hoes, they produced only enough food for their own consumption, and what little money they earned came mostly from the calves they sold in Savannah. Commercial production of grains would have to wait until the roots rotted and horses and plows were obtained. Another reason that plows were necessary was to combat the crab grass that grew between the furrows and became so tough that it could not be chopped with a hoe. Misled by the Salzburgers' Upper German dialect, Boltzius first called it "Crop Grass." Later he called it "Grab Grass," apparently thinking that it had to be grubbed up by hand. Eventually he learned the meaning and called it *Krebs Grass*.

On 30 October 1741 the Salzburgers' first plow was manufactured at the orphanage; but it was of little use as long as Ruprecht Kalcher, the manager of the orphanage, had only one horse partially trained to plow, as Boltzius mentioned on 30 October 1741. The few horses at Ebenezer were trained only for riding, not for plowing. On 17 February 1742 Oglethorpe donated forty pounds for seven horses, and by 1743 Boltzius could write that, having horses, the Salzburgers were now expecting a good crop of "Europian grains."[51] In view of Oglethorpe's military interests, it is easy to assume that the chief purpose of these horses was reconnaissance. By 15 May 1751 Boltzius reported that there were so many horses that everyone rode—men, women, and even children. European farmers seldom rode; they usually led their horses. On 18 October 1746 Boltzius reported to Urlsperger that the Trustees had donated twenty plowshares along with many other useful gifts.[52]

On 28 May 1735, while still at Old Ebenezer, the Salzburgers received several bushels of seed rice, which they obediently planted, but apparently without success. Whereas the Salzburgers later planted rice for their own consumption, they could not hope to compete in the market against the Carolina planters with their slave labor and capital investments in ditches, dikes, and floodgates. Besides that, the heavy labor in the muck ruined their clothes, shoes, and health. Later on, when the Salzburgers added a rice-stamping mill to their gristmill, they could grind rice to perfection.[53] It is probable, though, that most of the clients were from across the river in South Carolina.

The Spanish War of 1740 caused a practical embargo against the export of rice from South Carolina; the price fell so low that the Salzburgers hardly bothered to plant any rice. As Boltzius reported in his entry for 10 November 1749, when normal commerce was restored and the price rose again, the Salzburgers began to produce more rice, which they could now stamp at their own mill. In his entry for 13 August 1750 Boltzius mentioned a new and very much improved stamping machine for rice.

On 13 December 1754 the Salzburgers sold some indigo of excellent quality in Savannah, and in 1759 indigo was growing well, especially on the alluvial soil along Abercorn Creek.[54] The Salzburgers did not follow this up, however, perhaps because indigo culture required a great capital outlay. The fourth minister to arrive, Christian Rabenhorst, had the capital and slaves needed to build a suitable trough for processing the dye, which he fully described along with the art of preparing it.[55]

The Salzburgers planted many other crops, mostly for their own consumption. Sweet potatoes, prominent in their annual crop reports, were a staple food, as were squash, peanuts, and watermelons. In 1751 Boltzius listed two score of vegetables and herbs being planted by the Salzburgers, as well as many kinds of flowers.[56] The peach trees that thrived so well at

Ebenezer provided not only fresh fruit but also dried fruit, cured in the sun or in ovens.[57] Ruprecht Steiner and Matthias Brandner made peach brandy with a still donated by the SPCK and sold it as far away as Frederica. Others also made brandy from plums and cornstalks.[58] Having little cash to buy clothes, the Salzburgers planted and processed both flax and cotton. On 15 February 1740 Boltzius mentioned that many people had begun to plant cotton and to spin it on spinning wheels made by Friedrich Wilhelm Müller, the clock maker who joined the third Salzburger transport in Frankfurt. Boltzius reported that cotton flourished even on only moderately good land, but he stressed the great effort involved in removing the seeds, whose value had not yet been discovered. Boltzius also hoped to develop a foreign market for the oil of sesame seed, or benne seed, as the English called it.[59]

The cultivation of "European grains" could assume no importance until the establishment of gristmills.

The Mills

When the Salzburgers arrived at Old Ebenezer, they brought small iron handmills for grinding their grain; but these proved entirely unsatisfactory, consuming much time and energy, producing very poor meal, and constantly breaking down, as Boltzius reported in many entries.[60] Already by 10 May 1736 Boltzius began requesting millstones from the Trustees. At last, on 4 October 1737, the millstones arrived and a mill was built; a year and a half later two more stones arrived and were mounted and operating successfully by 20 November 1739.[61] While better than the iron handmills, these new mills were also hand-driven. Therefore the work was slow and laborious; two men required a whole day to grind only one bushel of grain.

As one might expect, the Salzburgers soon began agitating for a power-driven mill. For this they had the wholehearted support of Oglethorpe, who was most anxious to have the people of Georgia plant "European" grains such as wheat and oats, perhaps wishing the wheat for his English soldiers and the oats for his horses and Highlanders. Boltzius could easily show him that Ebenezer was the ideal place for a mill, having waterpower, skilled carpenters, industrious laborers, and a location on navigable water. Oglethorpe made the first contribution toward the mill, one of twelve pounds, as mentioned by Boltzius on 24 June 1740. A site was chosen on Abercorn Creek because it provided sufficient waterpower as well as navigation on a rather sluggish waterway, and also because it was close to the plantations on which most of the grain was produced.

Even though ten able-bodied men had served at the siege of St. Augustine, where one died and several were enfeebled, and even though some token work had to be done on the church to pacify Whitefield, work on the gristmill and rice-stamping mill was begun on 20 August 1740 with humble prayers, catalyzed by Oglethorpe's advance of twelve pounds. The head of Abercorn Creek was blocked off where it flowed out of the main channel of the Savannah River, and work progressed steadily until impeded by high water, which eroded the soft soil from the mill dam. Nevertheless, the dam withstood the exceptionally high water of 9 September. By 16 December Georg Kogler, the master builder, could grind six bushels of flour in one night even at the lowest water. These results so pleased the Trustees that they contributed seventy-seven pounds, which, when added to Oglethorpe's contribution, covered the modest costs of eighty-nine pounds.[62]

Because the water above the dam was not much higher than the water below it, the water of the millrace had to pass under the wheels, rather than over them.[63] In February 1741 milling had to be suspended for a while because the water behind the mill was as high as that in the millrace, but this fault was remedied by raising the wooden walls of the millrace one foot. For the next few years repairs, improvements, and additions were constantly made to the mills. For example, in September 1744 Boltzius had to ask Avery to help prevent the mill from being undersapped by water.[64] Despite such expenses, the mills became a source of income for the Salzburgers and a great satisfaction for the Trustees. A stamping mill for rice and barley was added, which was operating by April 1745. In that year Boltzius described it in a detailed letter to Verelst. In 1747 the Trustees again sent millstones to Ebenezer.[65] Avery, who designed the additions and improvements to the mills, did not live to see them completed. Feeling sick, he returned to Savannah to recuperate, but he died there. Fortunately for the Salzburgers, he had drawn his plans so well that Kogler could carry them out unaided.[66]

The Salzburger mills brought clients from far away. On 20 December 1749 six men brought a large cargo of grain to Ebenezer by water all the way from Vernonburg. Their load was so large that they had to wait several days for it to be ground. Boltzius noted that this gave them a chance to attend church, a privilege they enjoyed at Vernonburg only every other month when a pastor from Ebenezer visited them. On 4 September 1750 Boltzius requested millstones once again, his justification being that the Salzburgers' success in milling had encouraged the Purysburgers to grow more grain. These heavy millstones reached Ebenezer on 18 August 1751.[67]

There were a series of millers. On 26 May 1742 David Eischberger of the fourth Salzburger transport took over the task from Thomas Bichler when the latter became captain of the Rangers, and it was agreed on 1 June that the corn earned by the miller would be ground and sold in Savannah. Ruprecht Zimmerebner was serving as miller in both 1749 and 1760, and probably the whole period in between. In addition to the miller there were two indentured servants, Johann Heinle and his wife, who had come with Captain Lesslie and served faithfully, as Boltzius recorded on 9 May 1751. The administration of the mill is well described in a letter from Boltzius delegating the management to Lemke, which is cited by Muhlenberg.[68]

With the dams and millraces completed for the gristmills, the grounds were laid for ending the laborious task of sawing boards by hand. Sawing boards had been one of the most arduous tasks for the Salzburgers at Old Ebenezer, even though they had been aided by Negro and English sawyers and by gifts of lumber. When they abandoned that location against Oglethorpe's wishes, they had to leave all their hard-earned boards behind them and start all over again. In 1743 the Trustees at last allowed the Salzburgers to pick out some lumber from Old Ebenezer for their own use, much of which must have been damaged in the interim by weather and termites.[69] Needless to say, the Salzburgers saw the necessity of a power-driven saw.[70] In his letter of 2 August 1745 concerning the gristmills, Boltzius had indicated that there was also enough waterpower for a sawmill; he soon requested and obtained the timber, chains, and other ironwork from the Trustees' sawmill at Old Ebenezer, which had recently been destroyed by a flood.[71]

Since the dam and millrace were already functioning, the sawmill was erected quickly. By 20 January 1746 it could cut a thousand board feet in twenty-four hours.[72] In a letter of 18 July 1746 to Stephens, Martyn expressed the Trustees' pleasure "that the Saltzburghers have brought their Saw Mill to Perfection" and that they hoped that "such an Example of Industry will have its proper Influence on the other Inhabitants of the Province, especially when they see the Saltzburghers reaping the Fruits of their Industry."[73] Because the water was sometimes too low to turn the wheel, Boltzius decided to dig a ditch some 1,500 feet long to bring additional water from the main channel of the river to the sawmill so that it could run uninterruptedly.

Boltzius was equally aggressive in marketing the lumber, which found ready purchasers because the Salzburgers sold only the heart wood and used the slabs for domestic purposes.[74] Since ships sometimes arrived in need of a cargo of lumber while Abercorn Creek was too low for rafting, Boltzius acquired a wharf under the bluff at Savannah next to that of Habersham, where there would always be some lumber on hand for immediate sale.[75] In addition to the wharf, Boltzius also requested a crane for lifting the lumber up to the high bluff such as had existed in Causton's time. The wharf and crane enabled him to make the lowest bid on the lumber for the Anglican church that was then to be built in Savannah.[76] By 17 August 1748 Verelst had received a certificate from the Council that the Salzburgers had supplied 11,500 feet of boards and planks.[77]

In order to help create a West Indian market for the Salzburgers' lumber, the Trustees permitted the sale of rum in Georgia after 13 April 1747, possibly at Boltzius's suggestion, after fourteen years of prohibition.[78] That Boltzius requested the import of rum is indicated in his letter of 16 June 1746 to Ziegenhagen.[79] Boltzius seems to have hoped for a market on the European mainland, too; on 13 December 1751 he sent to Europe a cypress chest filled with samples of all sorts of rare woods sawed at the mill. Boltzius also appears to have suggested the manufacture of prefabricated houses (*zusammengelegte Häuser*).[80]

The success of the first sawmill called for the construction of a second, since tall trees seemed unlimited in the lands drained by the Savannah River. Boltzius's long journal entry for 26 March 1750 gives very convincing reasons why a second mill would be profitable. According to his letter of 4 September 1750, the Salzburgers' carpenters and laborers were then busy building a strong dam for another sawmill. A letter of 29 November of that year gives interesting details of the sawing and marketing of timber,[81] and Boltzius's journal entry of 16 January 1751 explains the details of the sawmill operation. On 27 April 1751 the second sawmill was consecrated. Habersham was now urging the Salzburgers to produce for export, rather than remain subsistence farmers as the Trustees had originally intended them to do.

The best market for lumber was in the sugar islands of the West Indies, where the forests had given way to cane fields. The success of the second sawmill may have been owed in no little measure to Habersham's letters of 19 December 1750 and 5 March 1751 to Martyn, in which he praised Boltzius and stressed the value of the sawmill. Construction of the mill was completed by 26 April 1751 at a cost of more than a hundred pounds. This included the making of a two-hundred-foot dam, which furnished a good road on the way from Ebenezer to Goshen.[82] When the Trustees surrendered their charter for Georgia to the Board of Trade in 1752, they mentioned that "a considerable Trade for Lumber is now carried on with the West Indies to the great Benefit of the Province in general, and in particular of the Saltzburghers who have two very good Saw Mills at Ebenezer."[83]

Doubtless taking a cue from Habersham, Boltzius complained to the Salzburgers that, by persisting in farming, they were going against the providence of God, who had set them into a different climate, where they could earn twenty-four pence in the timber business but only four pence by farming.[84] On 26 March 1750 Boltzius had quoted the high wages that timbermen, sawyers, and rafters could earn, and on 23 July of the same year he wrote that it had been suggested that the servants brought by Captain Bogg should redeem themselves by cutting six thousand barrel staves each. On 31 July, however, he wrote that the plan was unfeasible because all the nearby white oaks had been destroyed. Despite many difficulties, the timber business continued to prosper, and in 1759 Boltzius obtained nine hundred acres of woodland for the sawmill, as he reported on 6 January of that year.

During this lumber boom, a German named Jacob Friedrich Kurtz, or Curtius as he liked to call himself, arrived from the North, served for a while as schoolmaster, and won everyone's confidence.[85] Claiming to be the son of an old Württemberg preacher, Kurtz also claimed to have learned all about barrel staves, shingles, paneling, and other wood products from a wealthy cousin, a dealer in New York. He then organized an extensive timber operation, which was to have the financial backing of his wealthy connections in Philadelphia. It soon turned out, however, that he was a swindler, for he departed with the cash and left the Salzburgers, especially Bichler, with large debts in Charleston and elsewhere.[86]

Boltzius mentioned this theft often in his letters and reports. On 24 August 1750 he reported a letter from Pastor Brunnholtz of Philadelphia stating that Curtius was there, clad in silk and satin, having just sold a load of redemptioners and Rhine wine. A Lutheran there had extracted a promise from him to repay Boltzius, yet Curtius seemed to have intercepted a letter from Brunnholtz to Boltzius requesting a power of attorney, which Boltzius could not send until 4 September. On 26 February 1751 Boltzius was still struggling with this problem. When Kurtz reappeared some years later in Philadelphia as a wine merchant, Boltzius swore out an affidavit against him, but without success.[87]

Wine and Silk Culture

Dear to the hearts of the Trustees was the cultivation of wine, for they hoped a bountiful export of wine to the mother country would reduce the amount of good English money spent on imports. In the first years of the colony a little progress in viticulture had been made by the Spanish Jews in Savannah, but they found it unprofitable even before their flight from the Spaniards in 1742. A major purpose of Riemensperger's transport on the ill-fated *Europa* was to bring Swiss and German vine dressers, but most of these died en route. Hans Schutz, one of the few surviving vintners, was assured of "Encouragement as a Vine Dresser" after devoting himself to the more immediate task of planting for food, but there is no evidence that he ever tried cultivating grapes.[88]

Although the Salzburgers expended much effort, they were just as unsuccessful as vintners as the inhabitants of Savannah were. This was surprising, in view of the luxuriant native vines around Ebenezer and the rapid growth of the imported vines when planted. On 4 June 1741 Boltzius reported that Stephens had recently given the Salzburgers twelve vines from Madeira. These had sprouted en route and then dried out and appeared to be dead upon arrival, yet they sprouted again as soon as they were planted. Attempts at vine growing were made in 1742, when on 2 February Boltzius planted some vines next to his house. There were few vines available, however, until Oglethorpe supplied some.[89]

The Salzburgers' failure to produce wine profitably may have resulted from the excessive rain during the ripening season or from harmful bacteria in the often wet soil. Boltzius summed up the whole situation in a remarkable entry of 2 August 1751, in which he explained that the colonists should not try to grow European grapes in Georgia, where they did not prosper. Instead, they should cultivate the native vines, which had borne well ever since the Salzburgers arrived. These should not be domesticated as in Europe but planted in their natural habitat in the humus-filled swamps, where they would climb up the shady trees.

Another of the Trustees' major purposes in establishing the colony of Georgia was to produce silk and thus spare England from sending good money to Piedmont, Italy, and other silk-producing regions. As a labor-intensive industry, silk culture hardly suited an underpopulated province; yet the prevailing mercantilist views made the Trustees overlook the fact. Even the Prussian "Soldier King" Frederick William, who had invited so many Salzburgers to East Prussia, was then subsidizing a silk industry in Brandenburg in order to prevent importation. As early as 17 March 1736 Oglethorpe had given the Salzburgers some mulberry trees. In 1739 these trees were damaged by cold weather and did not bloom, as Boltzius mentioned on 30 April of that year.

In 1741 Boltzius explained to the Trustees that conditions in Ebenezer had been too severe during the first years for anyone to think of raising silk and that few people had planted mulberry trees. In that year two girls, instructed by a resident of Purysburg, had made a small beginning. In the same year Oglethorpe gave the Salzburgers five pounds for buying white mulberry trees.[90] On 21 May Boltzius could report that the Ebenezer orphanage had earned £2.19.6 for fourteen pounds, fourteen ounces of silk.

On 1 May 1743 the orphanage and several individual Salzburgers sent a good quantity of silk to Savannah, which was only a small part of what was still to be spun by the worms. For fourteen pounds, fourteen ounces they received £2.19.6, as Boltzius recorded on 21 May. Nine days later Martyn wrote Stephens that Boltzius should attest that all silk balls delivered from Ebenezer were actually raised in Georgia so that none could be smuggled in from Purysburg to qualify for the Georgia subsidy.[91] After another ten days the Trustees remitted the Salzburgers' debt of thirty-seven pounds, apparently to encourage them in silk production. On 15 September 1743 Boltzius requested a house for raising worms and reeling silk.[92]

On 29 August 1744 Stephens reported that the Salzburgers had distinguished themselves both by their production of silk balls and by their willingness to learn. Boltzius sent two girls to Mrs. Camuse in Savannah to learn the art of winding silk, but she used them for other purposes and would not let them learn anything. Because of this, Boltzius employed a Piedmontese or Swiss widow named Barriky to instruct the girls in Ebenezer.⁹³ On 21 November 1744, however, he wrote that she, like Mrs. Camuse, wished much money for no work and that, while she would let the Salzburger women watch her work, she would not instruct them. Like Mrs. Camuse, she wished to keep the art a secret. To thwart her, Boltzius determined to buy the necessary implements and let his women try the art without any more instruction. As a result, in July 1745 the Trustees sent silk-making implements to Ebenezer. Boltzius had already brought some silk balls to Savannah on 24 April 1745.⁹⁴

On 22 February 1746 Boltzius expressed his thanks to the Trustees for "the Machine for winding Silk & and for the Books, by which our people can be instructed in the art of Manufacturing Silk." On 3 June 1746 he sent a report to Urlsperger on the progress made since the receipt of the machines.⁹⁵ Averse to bringing the cocoons down to Savannah, where the major profits went to other people, Boltzius requested a filature for Ebenezer. On 18 July 1746 Martyn wrote that the Trustees approved of a filature in Ebenezer and were thinking of giving some assistance; yet they delayed five years before doing so.⁹⁶ On 12 May 1747 Boltzius reported to Verelst that, instead of the 200 pounds of silk he had predicted, the Salzburgers had delivered 366 pounds, 7 ounces to the store.⁹⁷ On 19 March 1748 the Trustees resolved to give five pounds sterling to each of the Salzburger women who "learnt the Art of winding Silk from the Coquons."⁹⁸ In a letter of 29 August 1747 to Verelst, Boltzius thanked him for the instructions for using the winding machine the Trustees had donated, and he stated that Harris was bringing to London a sample of silk made by two women at Ebenezer.⁹⁹

In 1748 the Salzburgers were waiting "most eagerly for that Instruction to draw off the Silk from the Cocoons" which Verelst had promised but apparently failed to send. Although the cold had killed many mulberry leaves, a satisfactory quantity of silk was made that year. By the very next year the silk business was prospering, and the Trustees made good the bill of exchange that Boltzius had borrowed to remunerate the workers.¹⁰⁰ On 16 May 1749 Boltzius reported to Martyn that the inhabitants of Ebenezer had produced seven hundred pounds of silk.¹⁰¹

On 30 May 1750 Boltzius reported that the Salzburgers had received some silkworm seed from Italy but that it had hatched en route and that the worms had died. Yet the Salzburgers seemed to have had enough seed to surpass all other producers in Georgia, of which Boltzius claimed there was only one.¹⁰² In September of the same year Boltzius sent a box of silk to the Trustees with the humble wish that they would continue their encouragement. On the fourth of that month he wrote that he had requested Mr. Beaufain of Charleston to help him get some Portuguese silkworm seed, but Beaufain could not fulfill the request.[103]

On 5 January 1751 Boltzius wrote very highly of Mr. Pickering Robinson, a well-qualified gentleman sent over from London to supervise the silk industry in Georgia. He assured the Trustees that, with Robinson's help, the Salzburgers would correct all their blunders and mistakes. He was very pleased that the Salzburgers' enemies had not been able to win Mr. Robinson over to their side, and he promised to encourage his congregation to sow their ground with mulberry seeds and to have inexpensive seed available for others.[104]

On 17 April 1751 Robinson visited Ebenezer and promised to take the Ebenezer produce to Savannah to be spun by the Ebenezer girls there on six large machines. On 17 May Boltzius reported that the inhabitants of Ebenezer had sent 1,500 pounds of silk down to Savannah, for which they were paid at once. The largest producer of silk was Mrs. Boltzius, and there are indications that she was operating a *Verlag*, a commercial enterprise that furnished supplies for cottage industries and served as distributor for their products.[105]

On 24 May 1751 the Trustees resolved that the "Allowance of forty shillings to Each White Woman in Georgia, Who shall acquire the Art of reeling Silk, be continued for One Year from Midsummer 1750."[106] As we have seen, some Salzburger women had already been receiving a subsidy for more than two years. On 18 June 1751 Boltzius wrote to Verelst to thank the Trustees for their support of the silk industry and to report that the Salzburgers' cocoons were being sent down to the filature in Savannah to be spun off under the direction of Mr. Robinson, who would teach the Salzburgers this noble art. Harris and Habersham, now business partners, had already paid them the sum offered by the Trustees.[107] On 19 December 1751 the Trustees finally resolved to subsidize a filature in Ebenezer at a cost of one hundred pounds. Boltzius described this filature in great detail on 12 July 1752, even stating that the well had been dug deep enough to supply the entire community with water when the other wells went dry.[108]

In January 1754 Joseph Ottolenghe prevailed upon the Salzburgers not to use their filature because their work was so poor and because they refused to accept instruction. He claimed that he would rather teach ten of the dullest Englishwomen than one of the Salzburgers, who can be neither "led nor driven."[109] He really gave himself away a few lines later, however, when he said that there were not enough cocoons in the colony to supply two filatures. Obviously, he was protecting his own livelihood. Toward the end of 1754 the newly appointed governor, John Reynolds, visited Boltzius on his way to Augusta and was pleased by the arrangements at Ebenezer. It did not take him long to realize that Ottolenghe was "very Jealous of a Rival, and extreamly desirous of making himself Solely necessary," so he sent a sample of the Salzburgers' wound silk directly to the Board of Trade.[110] Reynolds listened to the Salzburgers' petition to wind their own silk, but Boltzius doubted that the authorities in Savannah would change their minds.

According to William Little, the governor's private secretary, "In the year 1756 there was raised at Savannah 1024 lb. 14 oz. of Cocoons, at Ebenezer 1232 lb. 11 oz."[111] Although the Ebenezer silk business flourished for some time, it eventually declined: in 1770 it had fallen to 291 pounds.[112] The next year, however, it rose to 438 pounds.[113] In 1772 Johann Caspar Wertsch, the leading entrepreneur in Ebenezer, reported to Habersham that he had shipped only 485 pounds of raw silk, a decline he blamed on the sudden changes in weather.[114]

In order to produce and process the gifts that God had bestowed, the Georgia Germans had to practice certain skills and crafts.

Skills and Trades

Benjamin Rush commented on the valuable skills the Germans brought to Pennsylvania, and it appears that this held equally of the Germans who came to Georgia.[115] Most of the farms in southern Germany, as well as those in Switzerland, had become so small that they could just barely feed their owners, forcing farmers to gain their cash by maintaining trades on the side. As a result, rural homes often maintained cottage industries, as we have seen in the case of Michael Burckhalter's diligent household in Vernonburg. Because of strong competition, European artisans had to excel merely to survive. The few townspeople who had served out their apprenticeships successfully were, of course, highly skilled. On 2 July 1736 Boltzius mentioned that Ebenezer had many tradesmen, such as carpenters, tailors, shoemakers, glaziers, and coopers, who could not ply their trades because of their obligation to perform communal work. Some of the skilled Salzburgers may have learned or improved their trades while sojourning in the South German cities after the expulsion, as was the case of Martin Lackner, who, as Boltzius reported on 14 September 1743, had learned blacksmithing from a skillful master in Augsburg. Seeing the economic and social need of more urban inhabitants, Boltzius frequently encouraged the settling of tradesmen in Ebenezer. He discussed this policy very ably in his long and well-composed entry for 7 December 1751.

On 5 October 1743 Boltzius wrote:

> If Kogler moved to the orphanage, we would assign some boys, especially from the orphanage, who would learn from him carpentry and mill construction and also cabinet making, in which he is the most skillful man among us. It is too bad that we have no pious and skilled handworkers in this country or at our place. To be sure, we have shoemakers and tailors, but still too few carpenters. We could also use a good cooper or barrelmaker. We have no tanner for red or white leather here, who would have enough work to do all year. We also lack a wheelwright. We have smiths and locksmiths, who also have enough work even though the community is small.

Although Boltzius contended that the Salzburgers lacked sufficient carpenters, they do seem to have had a number. Among these were the Palatine carpenter-glazier Friedrich Rheinländer, who did not remain long in Georgia before he went north to seek his fortune but found his death. The most productive worker seems to have been the highly appreciated master-carpenter Georg Kogler, who built the mills and the church and was aided later by Paul Zittrauer and the Swabian carpenter Christian Fetzer. Boltzius also referred to "Carpenter Balthasar Bacher" on 8 September 1749, and he mentioned on 5 November that Andreas Piltz of the fourth Salzburger transport had been a carpenter. Smaller work was performed by the Swiss cartwright Hans Krüsy and by Stephan Rottenberger. More delicate and inventive work was performed by the clockmaker Friedrich Wilhelm Müller, whose wooden clocks were very much in demand.[116] Müller also worked in other media, and Georgia's earliest silver artifact, a cloak or coat stud, is attributed to him.[117] All three of the Schubdrein boys were good carpenters, as was their father. There were several German carpenters in Savannah, including Abraham Gabel, Caspar Garbut, and Caspar Whitehard (Weisshard).[118] We have seen that Wesley declared the Moravians to be the best carpenters in Georgia.

As long as there were few horses and no real roads, carpenters like

Krüsy and Rottenberger sufficed to make the few wheels needed; as late as 5 October 1743 Ebenezer had no wheelwright. As Boltzius reported on 28 April 1744, Kogler and Rottenberger built a heavy wagon for hauling wood from Old Ebenezer. Nevertheless, on 17 April 1747 the captain of the fort at Mount Pleasant sent his Indian serf to request that some wheels be made in Ebenezer. By 1752 the community could support a true wheelwright, Georg Mayer, who died on 26 December of that year. John Schick, who refused to serve as a juror on 17 October 1775, was a wheelwright in Savannah.[119] Like other colonial Germans, those of Georgia excelled as wainwrights and performed much of the drayage. De Brahm extolled a wagon devised by a German for transporting cocoons to Savannah without damaging them; it was provided with drawers to prevent the cocoons from resting too heavily on each other.[120] The German cabinetmaker recorded in Savannah, Caspar Gerber, must have been the same person as the carpenter Caspar Garbut.[121]

While well supplied with carpenters, the Salzburgers at first lacked good shoemakers and shoe repairers, as Boltzius noted on 22 May 1735. The Purysburg cobbler Jacob Reck was capable when sober; but that was not often enough, and Boltzius ejected him from Ebenezer. Salomo Ade, the cobbler from Tübingen, also had to be removed on 15 May 1739, even though his work was good. Since, as Boltzius mentioned on 27 October 1738, Ade was a compatriot of Reck, the latter must have been a Swabian, too. Johann Caspar Ulich, who came with Sanftleben on his second voyage in that same year, was both competent and pious; but he practiced only a few weeks before his untimely death. Peter Kohleisen of the fourth Salzburger transport was a cobbler and received cobbler's tools among the gifts distributed in 1742.[122]

As we have seen, two Ebenezer boys were sent out as apprentices, both to questionable masters. Young Martin Rheinländer worked in Savannah under Tannenberger, who was unblemished except for being a Moravian.[123] Matthias Zettler, who had come over as a youngster with the second Salzburger transport, apprenticed himself in Purysburg to the drunkard Reck, who made him fight in the St. Augustine campaign and held back half his military pay. By 1752 Ebenezer was so well supplied with shoemakers that the newcomer Johannes Groll could not support himself and his family, so he moved to Savannah, where the only cobbler was a young German man.[124] The old Jacob Metzger of Purysburg, who had lost several children in the boat wreck, was practicing the cobbler's trade in Ebenezer in

1760, as were Ludwig Weidmann and Johann Hangleiter.[125] Savannah had its quota of shoemakers, including Martin Strohacker.

Leather was used not only for shoes but also for harnesses and saddles. Bichler served as a saddler and also made horse collars, as Boltzius mentioned on 28 January 1748. In 1759 an itinerant saddler resided for several months in Ebenezer, served the people well and reasonably, lived soberly, and won the people's confidence. Taking advantage of the credit extended him, he absconded without paying his debts.[126] There were many references to the saddler Friedrich Holtzendorf. This may have been the same as Saddler H., who, in Boltzius's estimation, was far beyond any hope of being converted or saved.[127]

Nikolaus Riedelsperger of the second Salzburger transport could tan leather, as Boltzius noted on 21 May 1735; but he had no equipment and he died the following year. Among the people von Reck picked up along the way, apparently in Savannah, was the large family of Johann Jacob Helfenstein, a Swiss tanner who died before reaching Ebenezer. Eventually his widow, with the aid of her sons, began a tannery business. Surely she is the N. of whom Boltzius said on 30 May 1740 that she "has been tanning for some time and seems to understand that craft right well." Nevertheless, her work was insufficient for the needs of the community, and on 23 July 1750 Boltzius was still on the lookout for a tanner.

When a tanner offered on 13 September 1750 to train two Salzburger boys for forty pounds, Boltzius found the tuition too high. By 16 January 1751, soon after the arrival of the first Swabians, the tanner Neidlinger and his sons established a true tanning mill, which was possible because Abercorn Creek had been harnessed. Boltzius's entry of that date describes the undertaking in detail, particularly the stamping mill that pulverized the oak bark.[128]

Tailors were also indispensable before the age of ready-made clothing, as is suggested by the frequency of the name Taylor and of its German equivalents, Schneider and Schröder. The third Salzburger transport had brought two tailors, Gottfried Christ, the convert from Reicheltsheim by Frankfurt, and Franz Sigismund Hernberger from Hungary. According to Boltzius, Christ had learned his trade badly and could survive only through lack of competition. Hernberger, being better trained, prospered despite constant illness. On 5 January 1737 he took Mrs. Helfenstein's fifteen-year-old son, Friedrich, as an apprentice, but the boy tired of the trade and apprenticed himself to the Moravian cobbler in Savannah but soon quit.[129]

A soldier named Kikar, who had been a tailor apprentice in Hamburg, was too sick with dysentery to practice in Ebenezer when he first arrived there. His long sickness had exhausted his money and had cost him his horse; yet a Salzburger couple took him in.[130] On 27 December 1742 Boltzius reported that "the German tailor from Savannah has fully resolved to move to us." He mentions that the man had previously served with the French as a soldier, but he does not say whether he was the same man as Kikar, nor does he tell us whether the tailor carried out his resolution to move to Ebenezer. With the first Swabian transport came Ludwig Mayer's younger brother, (Johann) Georg, who was a purse maker by profession but easily adapted to tailoring when he found little market for purses in Ebenezer. With the second Swabian transport came another tailor, Michael Weinkauf. Somewhat later, there were several German tailors in Savannah, such as Sigismund Biltz, Heinrich Steermann, and Georg Uhland.[131]

On 21 May 1735 Boltzius mentioned that the Salzburgers had a smith, but that he had no tools. In order to have their horses shod and their tools repaired, they depended on the services of a poorly trained and unreliable smith in Abercorn or else did the repairs themselves. On 18 April 1738 Boltzius advanced a Salzburger three pounds to buy a smithy in Purysburg, but it is not clear whether or not he did so. The locksmith Veit Lechner established a smithy on 2 April 1742; it must have been insufficient, however, for his stepson, the locksmith Ruprecht Schrempff, also opened up a smithy. On 14 September 1743 Boltzius reported that, now that Leitner had set up shop, the Salzburgers had a good smithy.[132] He does not say what became of Lechner's smithy. Schrempff moved to South Carolina but later returned and died in Ebenezer.[133]

On 10 September 1749 "the locksmith," who had moved unnecessarily to South Carolina and suffered losses and declining health, wrote to Boltzius asking permission to return to Ebenezer. This was Schrempff, whose departure Boltzius had overlooked or Urlsperger had suppressed. It should be noted that, in the reports, few people left Ebenezer, yet a large number returned. Georg Streigel was a blacksmith at Halifax, and Georg Faul died as a blacksmith in Ebenezer in 1768, after training Lucas Ziegler as an apprentice.[134] The Loyalist Frederick Fahm of Savannah was a blacksmith.[135] After Schrempff changed from locksmith to blacksmith, Christoph Krämer assumed the task of locksmith. Late in 1759 Boltzius mentioned a "locksmith Krämer, who had previously managed the minister's plantation."[136]

There being no stones on the Georgia coastland, bricks were essential for fireplaces, chimneys, wells, and other purposes. Since good clay and firewood were abundant in the vicinity of Ebenezer, Boltzius made great efforts to introduce brickmaking, as he reported on 7 February 1739. His attempts in 1742 were unsuccessful, as he recorded on 6 March of that year. In 1750, however, two of the Schubdrein boys, whom Boltzius had redeemed, made good progress in the trade despite their lack of previous training.[137] Visitors to Ebenezer are still impressed by the large handmade bricks of which the beautiful Jerusalem Church is made. Apparently British mercantilism discouraged the making of bricks.

The Germans in Georgia not only made bricks but also laid them. Already on 13 April 1736 William Bradley hoped to have a "Dutch Bricklayer & his Wife" as indentured servants.[138] Johann Eppinger of Savannah was a bricklayer, as was Johann Spielbiegler after he absconded to Charleston.[139] Boltzius was less successful in encouraging pottery manufacture, even though Andrew Duchee, a gifted potter from Pennsylvania, had found excellent clay near Ebenezer.[140] In 1760 Boltzius referred to the "Potter Gnan" and also to *die Häfnerin Gnannin* (Mrs. Gnan, the potter's wife).[141]

As the population increased at Ebenezer, labor became more diversified; even everyday chores became specialized trades, as in the case of baking, a profession practiced by Johann Rentz.[142] On 14 April 1743 Boltzius reported that "our butcher" accompanied him to Savannah, and on 26 November 1750 he referred to Riedelsperger as "our butcher." This shows that butchering had become a profession by that time. As late as 3 August 1747, however, Boltzius could remark that the Salzburgers followed the custom of their homeland and ate butter and lard rather than meat. Savannah received most of its meat from the "German butcher," who appears to have been the Swiss Johann Altherr, who married Boltzius's servant Amalia Schiermeister.[143]

Whereas Ebenezer had a series of storekeepers, including Ortmann, Riedelsperger, Ludwig Mayer, Wertsch, and Treutlen, the Germans in Savannah seem to have relied on English and Jewish merchants. They did, however, have their own taverns, such as that of Solomon Schad and also "the King of Prussia." By 3 May 1759 Boltzius maintained that all artisans in Savannah, of which he gave a list of individuals mostly concerned with woodworking, were prosperous if they did not drink and that they had more work than they could do.

Boltzius did not stress manufactures at Ebenezer, perhaps because he realized that the Trustees obtained their funds from a Parliament interested in raw materials, not in industrial competition. America was to be a market for, not a supplier of, manufactured goods. As we have seen, Stephens felt compelled to assure Martyn that the weaving at Acton would not compete with the manufactures of the home country. We have also seen that, despite the aims of the Trustees, Whitefield supplied some Salzburger women with flax, cotton, looms, and spinning wheels to help them set up a manufactory, a fact that Boltzius failed to mention in his journal. Governor Wright also belittled the manufactures in Georgia. In 1766 he reported that Georgia had no manufactures and were supplied "from and through Great Britain. Some few of the poorer and more industrious people make a trifling quantity of coarse homespun cloth for their own families, and knit a few cotton and yarn stockings for their own use."[144]

Perhaps Governor Wright was not apprised of all the activity going on among the Georgia Germans. In 1741 Mrs. Pletter spun fourteen pounds of flax for Mr. Whitefield; in 1749 Boltzius reported that the people of Acton and Vernonburg were showing good skill in weaving both flax and cotton.[145] At Ebenezer Georg Köcher, the schoolmaster, had assembled the necessary utensils and tools for weaving flax and wool by 7 August 1747, whereas Georg Held had recently moved to South Carolina in order to teach slaves to weave.[146] The widow Graniwetter, who had been a knitter and weaver in Germany, continued these occupations in Ebenezer, and the widow Anna Rau was spinning both flax and cotton in 1759.[147]

♦ *Summary Two* ♦

Health, Medicine, and Daily Life

It has been obvious that the greatest impediment to progress for the Germans, as well as for the other colonists in Georgia, was the high incidence of sickness. Many immigrants had been in poor health by the time they reached Amsterdam, nearly all were weakened still more by the poor diet and crowded conditions on shipboard, and many arrived afflicted with scurvy or other diseases. It is not surprising, therefore, that their mortality rate was especially high soon after landing but gradually decreased with time. Although many of Boltzius's reports concern sickness, often mortal, he occasionally reports that everyone is well, as on 11 May 1735, by which he means well enough to drag themselves to church. A year earlier, on 13 April 1734, when all was going so badly, he had written that the Salzburgers "live in a very good Health."[1] On 5 October 1739 he wrote that they were "in a very good Condition of Health."[2] Like Oglethorpe and most others in Georgia, Boltzius argued that the climate there was salubrious and that the fevers were due to indulgence or to the people's failure to protect themselves from changes in weather. Jean-Pierre Pury had already expressed this view very convincingly, and Gottlieb Spangenberg repeated it somewhat later.[3]

The apparently acquired resistance to the new diseases is generally attributed to "seasoning." That means that the colonists gradually built up immunity to the prevalent illnesses. Although immunity can be developed against many diseases, even malaria,[4] I think that the so-called seasoning was often a case of the survival of the fittest. Those individuals who had strong constitutions could resist the diseases, while the others could not. In time, only those with strong constitutions were still alive. This does not mean they developed resistance, but merely that they already had it.

Some families, like the Hubers of the first Salzburger transport and the Ferrier family of Vernonburg, died out completely, while in other families, like the Kieffers and Helfensteins, nearly all survived. Boltzius reported on 27 May 1754 that Michael Schneider was healthy at seventy and had seen little sickness during his sixteen years in the country.

On 28 July 1737 Boltzius wrote to Captain Coram that half the Salzburgers who had stopped off at Dover had died.[5] On 30 July he reported that thirty-one adults and twenty-five children had died so far and that eighty-nine adults and forty-three children were still alive. In less than two and one-half years, then, more than a fourth of the adults and a third of the children had perished. Of all the many children born in Old Ebenezer, only three were still alive in 1750, as Boltzius reported on 12 October of that year.[6] On 29 April 1747 Boltzius noted that the children who should then have been twelve or thirteen years of age and therefore useful to their parents had died. By 1747 Georg Schweiger had lost six of his seven children, and the surviving three and a half year old was sickly, as Boltzius reported on 7 January 1748.

Whereas twenty-seven of the first thirty-nine children born in Old and New Ebenezer died by 13 December 1738, Boltzius could report "a very good state of Health" by 1743.[7] Most of the new arrivals who were prone to die of Georgia's diseases had done so by 1741; but in that year the fourth Salzburger transport arrived "unseasoned," with the result, as we have seen, that many of them died during the following summer. Consequently, the mortality record for 1742 was nearly as bad as in earlier years. On the other hand, in the year 1747, after the community had grown much larger, only four adults and seven children died, and seventeen were born.[8] In other words, at this time the population was more than renewing itself without immigration. Nevertheless, in 1750 Boltzius reported burying nine adults and ten children, while baptizing only thirteen.[9] It has been noted that each new contingent suffered the so-called seasoning, or really "culling out," even though living conditions had greatly improved.

Despite the gradual improvement in health, some people simply could not fetch up any children. After losing many children and their mothers, Georg Schweiger finally married the widow Margaretha Zittrauer and took on her sons, whom he adopted and remembered in his will. There were, fortunately, a few exceptions to the rule of infant mortality. Upon reaching Savannah in 1774, Muhlenberg mentioned a Mr. Schick, who "had nine living children, which is a rare thing here, for parents are not able to keep many children alive because of the climate."[10] Oglethorpe had mentioned a German at Frederica who had nine children, whose wife may have been the woman who sought refuge in South Carolina during the threatened Spanish invasion and gnawed her arm in her grief at losing all her children during their flight, as Boltzius reported on 22 August 1750.

One of the most prevalent shipboard diseases was scurvy, a consequence of vitamin C deficiency. Scurvy struck some of the members of the first and second Salzburger transports and also afflicted most of the third transport.[11] Boltzius described the symptoms of this loathsome illness in lurid detail on 6 April 1736. The fourth transport, however, was spared and arrived relatively healthy; it may be pertinent that the commissioner, von Müllern, had bought lemons in Rotterdam and that a Dutch sea captain had donated some more to the transport on the high seas. The Bornemann party were also spared, in part because their captain took on a large load of oranges.[12]

Scurvy disappeared as soon as the settlers planted their kitchen gardens and were no longer dependent on imported salted beef. Like the Germans of Pennsylvania observed by Benjamin Rush, those in Georgia were also prompt in planting vegetable gardens. According to Boltzius's journal entry for 2 September 1734, the Salzburgers followed this custom. On 22 April 1735 Boltzius noted that Zwiffler had found a kind of wild celery, which he hoped could be grown, because "some people report that it has done them much good to eat even one turnip, or the tops of turnips, or anything else that is green."[13] We have seen Francis Moore's favorable comment on the Salzburgers' "Pompkins, Cabbages, and other Garden Stuff."

The first fatal disease to scourge the Salzburgers, like the other settlers, was the *rote Ruhr*, or "bloody flux," which they contracted already on their way from Savannah to Old Ebenezer and which caused the death of Tobias Lackner on 10 May 1734 in Abercorn. This ailment was chiefly dysentery; but, since illnesses were diagnosed only by their symptoms, the term may have included typhus and typhoid when they manifested themselves through bloody bowels.

One disease suffered by all the Salzburgers, and apparently by all the other Europeans in Georgia, was malaria.[14] Malaria was not uncommon at the time even in Northern and Central Europe, being known in England as the "Kentish disease." It would appear to have attacked the Dürrenberger exiles in Cadzand, too. The varieties in Georgia, however, were far more virulent, having been brought to Carolina with the slaves from Africa. Long exposure to these virulent strains had somewhat inured the blacks to them, perhaps less through "seasoning" than by culling out the most susceptible victims and preserving the more immune, including those with sickle cells.

The newness of the African strains of malaria may explain why even the aboriginal Indians seem to have caught it, as Boltzius reported on 9 September 1736. Malaria did not afflict the Salzburgers at Old Ebenezer, probably because the area was uninhabited and the anopheles mosquitoes there were not yet infected. As soon as the Salzburgers moved to the Red Bluff, they all succumbed, because the mosquitoes there were infected by both European- and African-born carriers across the river.

Although most of the Salzburgers were debilitated by their high fevers, Boltzius noted on 24 July 1736 that no one had yet died of them. Malaria was not a killer; it merely weakened its victims and made them susceptible to fatal diseases. In 1736 the prevailing type was tertian, as Boltzius noted on 7 August and 22 October of that year. In other years quartan fever predominated. Because the ague struck only every third or fourth day, Boltzius praised the Lord that either he or Gronau was nearly always functioning. On the other hand, in the summer of 1753, although there were three pastors, some days all three were down with malaria. A strange side effect of malarial fever was the "fever clot" (*Fieber-Kuche*), a lump in the left side, which appears to have been an enlarged spleen.[15]

Boltzius often reported death from "epilepsy."[16] Once again, he was diagnosing the symptom, for the word *epilepsy* denoted any violent paroxysm, no matter what the cause. Anyone who died in convulsions died of "epilepsy."

The "disease" that baffled the Salzburgers and their physicians most was "clay-eating," a symptom of Ancylostomiasis, a disease associated with an iron deficiency in the system caused by hookworms. Bare feet, warm moist soil, and ignorance of field sanitation exposed people, especially children, to this tragic disease. On 21 April 1748 Boltzius wrote to Urlsperger that the children were eating raw Indian corn and rice, dirt, clay, and charcoal and that some more of them had died.[17] The carpenter Rottenberger lost all three of his children to this disease, as Boltzius reported on 13 September 1748. The symptoms of hookworm disease are pallor, greatly bloated bellies, and an uncontrollable craving (called pica) to eat dirt, unmilled grain, and other inedible substances. Boltzius preached against the sinful practice of eating dirt, which he considered a form of suicide, and he warned of damnation. Nevertheless, many naughty children did not heed his loving advice, including children of Matthias Burgsteiner, Thomas Bichler, Hanns Maurer, and Georg Schweiger.[18] On 13 May 1759 Boltzius was still reporting the presence of such craving among the children. This disease caused death indirectly through malnutrition, which made the sufferers more susceptible to other diseases.

A very typical case of hookworm disease was that of Georg Adam Leinbacher, an orphan who arrived in Georgia on the *Judith* along with Johann Adam Treutlen. Both children reached Ebenezer, but, whereas Treutlen prospered, Leinbacher contracted hookworm disease and persisted in eating inedible substances against Boltzius's admonitions, thus sinning grievously. Fortunately, as Boltzius reported, before his painful death he freely acknowledged his sin of suicide, was truly penitent, and was surely saved through the merit of our reconciling Savior.[19]

The Salzburgers were frequently afflicted by *Seitenstechen* (side stitches), which Boltzius often mentioned but never described. On 13 August 1753 he reported that in a calendar Benjamin Franklin had described an infallible cure for this affliction by way of a recently discovered Seneca snakeroot, with which Dr. John Tennent had achieved many successful cures in Virginia. Whether or not Boltzius was able to obtain this medicine, his flock continued to suffer from side stitches, as Peter Arnsdorf did on 11 February 1759. Boltzius read everything he could lay his hands on to find cures for his ailing parishioners.

Fortunately, Ebenezer was not visited by the yellow fever epidemics that were so rampant in Charleston, probably brought with the slaves from Africa. Yellow fever was feared in 1752 when Elisabeth Prickel, who had recently married Martin Lackner, died suddenly of *Gelbsucht*. The symptom of dark blood in the vomit suggested yellow fever, but Thilo convinced Boltzius that it was merely yellow jaundice.[20]

The Salzburgers were also spared smallpox for a long time. Stephens was very indignant at a servant at the Trustees' cowpen named Sommers, who went about "with the Small-Pox out full upon him" and thus endangered everyone. He had contracted it in South Carolina, but luckily he did not spread it in Georgia.[21] Ebenezer did not suffer seriously from smallpox until the British occupation during the Revolution, at which time some fifty people died within two months.[22] On the other hand, in 1750 Ebenezer did suffer from *rote Friesel*, or "the purples," as Boltzius mentioned on 11 December of that year. It was still present on 27 January and 28 February 1751 and carried off many children. It also claimed two adults: Maria Niess, née Öchsele; and Martin Rheinländer's young wife, Maria, née Kalcher, who caught it while working in the filature in Savannah.[23] "The purples" may sometimes have been diphtheria.

In January 1760 Boltzius reported that there was still no whooping cough in Ebenezer, but in May of the same year he had to report that God had visited it on the children there. In 1760 Lemke reported both whooping cough and measles in Ebenezer.[24]

In all his reports Boltzius appears to have made only one veiled reference to venereal disease. When, on 13 July 1741, Margaretha Stout confessed her sins against the seventh commandment at Fort Argyle, she was frightened because the men she had sinned with had suffered in their bodies. We never learn whether her saintly second husband, Christian Leimberger, also suffered in his body, but we know they had no children.

In view of the high incidence of illness, it is surprising not only that Pury and Oglethorpe praised Georgia's salubrious climate but also that Boltzius could contend on 24 August 1752, "Our climate is one of the healthiest in the world according to my and many people's experience and according to the testimony of Mr. Thilo."[25] On 7 May 1759 Boltzius stated that most of the inhabitants of Savannah were English and Germans, who were reproducing greatly and living healthily and well.

Medical Personnel

When the first Salzburger transport left Augsburg it brought with it an apothecary named Andreas Zwiffler, who hailed from Hungary. For some time Zwiffler was held in high regard and was even appointed as Ebenezer's first constable. He also received various gifts such as twenty pounds from the SPCK on 17 February 1736. Nevertheless, because he was only an apothecary and not a learned physician, Boltzius ridiculed his attempts to use fancy medical terminology. Finding himself totally unable to cope with malaria and other ills, unable to preserve the bride who followed him from Europe, and no longer appreciated by his patients, Zwiffler left for Europe but stopped off in Philadelphia, where he remained and was accused of having become a Moravian.[26] After his departure, the Salzburgers received some medical treatment from the Moravian physician Jean François Regnier in Savannah and from Friedrich Holtzendorf, a surgeon from Brandenburg then residing in Purysburg, who not only gave medical advice to the Salzburgers and bled them but also taught Gronau to do the same.[27]

Francke's fulsome recommendation for the physician Christian Ernst Thilo, written in Latin, stressed not only his excellent training but also his piety and dedication to serving the poor.[28] It overlooked certain personality traits, though, that were to plague Boltzius. Concerning the new doctor, Newman wrote that Francke and Ziegenhagen had "prevailed on Dr. Thilo a Learned Gentleman of great acquirements in the Knowledge and Practice of Physick to relinquish all advantages he could propose to himself by staying in Germany, to embark on a voyage to Ebenezer to assist You and your Congregation in the Quality of Physician Surgeon and Apothecary." Thilo had studied at the Martin Luther University in Halle-Wittenberg while lodging and presiding at the sick bay of the Francke Foundation and teaching anatomy to the students there.[29]

Thilo left Halle on 8 September 1737, stopped off in London to receive the Trustees' promise of provisions, and arrived unexpectedly at Ebenezer on 13 January 1738, having traveled on the *Georgia Pink* with a load of provisions from Ireland. In Ebenezer he was welcomed enthusiastically by all the inhabitants, who had prepared a dwelling for him. Although Boltzius concealed the fact in his regular reports, his letters reveal that he was appalled by Thilo's erratic behavior, which indicated that he was mentally unbalanced and prone to prophetic visions and conversations with God. He wished to cure not only his patients' bodies but also their souls, and he often changed his treatment in midstream, even withdrawing a spoonful of medicine from the patient's mouth when divine voices told him to do so.[30]

To make matters worse, Thilo refused to attend church services, complaining that the congregation had made idols of the two pastors. He was also too free in calling on the young ladies of the congregation, at least until he was severely admonished by Francke. After that he married Friederica Helfenstein, a daughter of the Reformed widow of a Swiss tanner. Boltzius finally accepted Thilo as he was and even went to great effort to obtain his promised rations. On 27 January 1744 he wrote, in Thilo's name but in his own hand, a request to the Trustees for him and his wife.[31] There were such constant complaints about Thilo's indolence and hypochondria that Francke thought it advisable to hold back an anonymous gift until the physician improved.[32]

The Thilos had two daughters: Anna Maria Friederica, who died on

24 December 1757, and Hanna Elisabetha, who married Johann Jacob Heinle on 5 January 1773. Thilo had studied at the famed University of Halle; yet, despite his good training, he was hardly more effective than poor Zwiffler had been. Thilo practiced medicine lackadaisically for the rest of his life in Ebenezer, going as far as Purysburg to treat the sick. When the surgeon (Johann) Ludwig Mayer arrived with the fourth Salzburger transport, he too practiced medicine and acquired the larger practice, even though Thilo remained nominally the chief doctor.

The Trustees paid for Thilo's passage and a year's support, but they expected him to support himself after that from his practice. This, however, was not possible. As the Philadelphia physician Benjamin Rush explained in a letter dissuading an English doctor from settling in a prosperous Pennsylvania Dutch community, the Dutch would not spend their good money on medical treatment, preferring to rely on herbs and charms. Even the relatively well educated Moravians hesitated to buy expensive medication for one of their grievously sick colleagues; instead they boiled oak leaves. This concoction caused a sweat, which immediately cured the man so that he went right back to work.[33] Despite Thilo's odd behavior, Boltzius requested support for him on 2 August 1742; the Trustees granted five pounds. Later on, the Trustees engaged Thilo to attend the sick in the northern part of the colony gratis, but his allowance was not to exceed fifty pounds per year.[34]

Being a physician, Thilo lacked the training and the instruments necessary for setting or amputating limbs, so the Salzburgers had to go to Purysburg to be treated by Jean Baptiste Bourquin, a Swiss who had served for nine years as a surgeon in the duke of Marlborough's army. As we have seen, Bourquin treated Peter Reiter's grievous dislocation, and he also amputated Josef Ernst's hand (just below the armpit) and treated a growth in Maria Maurer's throat, apparently to everyone's satisfaction, despite his questionable methods.[35] Bourquin died in 1784 at the age of ninety-three, as reported by the *South Carolina Gazette* for 30 January 1784.

Although Ludwig Mayer practiced medicine in Ebenezer, it would appear that he had never received any formal training. This was probably a good thing, since formal medical training then went back to Hippocrates and Galen, whose works were often wrong even before being mangled in translation from Greek into Arabic and from Arabic into Latin. The barber-surgeons, who were shunned by the learned physicians as empiricists, seem to have had a far better grasp of the ailments they treated. If a leg set by a barber-surgeon failed to mend, he could not blame an unhappy constellation of the stars or an improper balance of the patient's four humors, or vital body fluids. As we shall see, the folk at large still preferred charms and incantations. We have seen that Mayer dared to go aboard the *Europa* to help the sick passengers. In addition to his medical practice, Mayer kept the store in which little Johann Adam Treutlen worked.

After Mayer left Ebenezer and Thilo died, they were succeeded by Gronau's son Timothy, who had been trained by Thilo and was much beloved during his short life. Later on, the people of Ebenezer had the services of the English doctor Jenking Davis, who became a close friend of the community and represented them in the provincial assembly.

Since many German doctors were in the British colonies, it is not surprising that one practiced in Savannah and Purysburg. On 25 July 1759 Boltzius reported that a doctor named [Georg Friedrich] Meissner, who was then practicing in Savannah, conducted himself well for a while but then resorted to drink and bad behavior. He had been everywhere in America and had served on a British privateer, and he was then on his way to St. Augustine and Havana.[36] While in Purysburg Meissner ordered some medicines from Halle.

Women in childbirth were helped by midwives, not by physicians, since men were not permitted to witness births. At about the time the Salzburgers were flourishing at Ebenezer, a doctor was burned at the stake in Hamburg for dressing like a woman to attend a childbirth. Among the midwives in Ebenezer were Maria Anna Rheinländer, Anna Maria Bischoff, and Maria Bacher. Mrs. Hernberger nearly died in childbirth on 15 February 1739, but she was saved by a French Swiss midwife brought over from Purysburg, as Boltzius wrote on 15 February 1739. When Boltzius recorded on 25 September 1739 that Colonel Stephens was donating his Palatine maid, Anna Maria Bischoff, to Ebenezer as a midwife, he failed to mention that Mrs. Boltzius happened to be pregnant at the time. The Trustees and benefactors in Germany were mindful of the importance of midwives and donated many personal gifts for them as well as utensils for their profession. When Muhlenberg visited Ebenezer in 1742, he brought gifts for them from a Christian midwife in N., as Boltzius reported on 4 October of that year. In 1759 the two midwives at Ebenezer were Mrs. Lackner and Mrs. Rieser, as Boltzius recorded on 12 April of that year.

Medications and Treatment

Of all the medications used at Ebenezer, the most popular by far was Schauer's Balm, a panacea for all ills and ailments. It was a distillation, probably high in alcoholic content, which was manufactured in Augsburg by Johann Caspar Schauer. Schauer himself donated fifty bottles, which Boltzius acknowledged on 28 June 1739. Boltzius praised it highly and often as a cure-all, perhaps aware that his praise would be good advertisement for the donor. It appears that Ebenezer was actually in business supplying the remedy to outsiders, as was indicated on 4 June 1740 when Captain Holtzendorf requested six bottles of it for the preacher in Purysburg and on 14 October 1760 when Dr. Meissner ordered medicines from the Ebenezer storekeeper.[37]

Because malaria was the chief ailment, the Salzburgers experimented with chinchona, which went under the names Peruvian bark and *china de china*.[38] The prescriptions obtained from Savannah were exceedingly complicated and far from convincing. Typical of the prescriptions relied upon was one from a benefactor, Counselor Wallbaum, which Boltzius recorded on 15 September 1742. Certain that it not only suppressed the fever but actually cured it, Thilo prescribed it for Mrs. Boltzius. It required the following: "A few quarts of good wine, *china de china*, juniper berries, and Virginia or local snake-weed. For the vomiting, however, which must come before one drinks the fever potion, it required ipecacuanha and cardiobenedicti boiled in water, which is drunk at the same time." Since this was costly, the poor were aided from the poor box. A more convincing treatment for quartan fever was prescribed by Privy Counselor Carl Wegen and forwarded to Thilo, as recorded by Boltzius on 15 September 1743.[39] Boltzius also learned the prescriptions for many remedies from the Charleston papers, for example, the tar water recommended by Mr. Prior, which Boltzius reported in 24 August 1743.

Among other medicines frequently mentioned in the *Ausführliche Nachrichten* were *essentia dulcis*, *essentia amara*, *pulvis vitalis*, *pulvis antispasmodicus*, and polychrest pills.[40] Spangenberg also recommended polychrest pills and *essentia amara* as well as red powder (*rothes Pulver*) and bezoardic powder (*pulvis bezoardicum*).[41] Being made of gold dust, the *essentia dulcis* was especially esteemed, for most doctors still agreed with Chaucer's doctour that "gold in phisick is a cordial." A good insight into the medicines used at Ebenezer is offered by the list of the drugs sent gratis from Halle on

16 July 1758.[42] One medication, which Boltzius seemed to question on 19 September 1739 despite its apparent efficacy, was a strap of human skin, which cured a withered arm. Somehow, he did not ask who donated the skin. As we have seen, the Moravians cured fever with an oakleaf brew, and they also found some very effective herbs in Savannah.[43]

When the Salzburgers reached Georgia, they knew little more about snakes than that serpents were more subtile than any beast in the field that the Lord had made and that a serpent had beguiled Eve and thus caused man's fall, for which deed God cursed it above all cattle and made it go on its belly and eat dust all the days of its life. Despite its lack of grace, it was so wise that St. Matthew (10:16) advised men to be "as wise as serpents." The Salzburgers also knew that God had chastised the Children of Israel by sending fiery serpents to bite the people, until Moses raised a brazen serpent on a pole. From their pre-Christian past they also knew it was lucky to have a house adder (*Hausnatter*) dwelling under their house, for this was the embodiment of some ancestor.[44] Some adders in Northern Europe were poisonous, but not nearly so poisonous as the rattlesnakes and cottonmouth moccasins found in Georgia. (There is no evidence that the Salzburgers ever saw any coral snakes or copperheads.)

Unfamiliar with Georgia's snakes, the Salzburgers acquired as much information as possible from the South Carolinians, most of it entirely wrong. Even Boltzius accepted the belief that a certain root was a cure for snake bite, as he mentioned on 27 April 1734. When a small child was bitten on 27 June 1740, a tourniquet was applied below her knee and the poison sucked out. Unfortunately, someone in Purysburg knew a better way; so, when Ruprecht Steiner was bitten by a rattlesnake on 27 April 1742, he was buried naked in the ground to draw out the poison. Luckily, Dr. Mayer arrived in time to dig him up and scarify the bite. On 11 September 1742 Mrs. Kieffer was bitten on the finger by a small unidentified snake. The wound was scarified, covered with salt, and bound with a tourniquet so tightly that the finger became numb and the tourniquet had to be loosened. She was then given theriac.

When Paul Müller's wife was bitten on 15 August 1749, she killed the snake. Her husband put its lung and liver and also the posteriors of living chickens on the bite and gave the patient theriac and brandy, "which means, it appears, God blessed," as Boltzius piously added. After reporting this event, Boltzius recommended some rather dubious cures, such as holding the bitten limb up in the air, since poison rises rather than descends. It is probable that the limb was held up only until proper medication could be given. A Salzburger serving as a herdsman at the cowpen cured himself of a snakebite on 1 June 1751 by killing the snake and putting it twice on the bite. On 1 July 1751 a young Salzburger, who had been bitten by a rattlesnake, saved his life by tying the snake over the wound and thus keeping the blood from his heart.

The North European immigrants to South Carolina and Georgia had not lived for centuries in mortal dread of vipers; indeed the Irish there were not even acquainted with snakes, if we can believe the legend about St. Patrick. Consequently, the Salzburgers must have learned much of their unscientific herpetology from the Indians, especially with regard to antidotes such as snakeroot.[45] They may have learned even more from the African slaves, who had perhaps been even more threatened by poisonous vipers. Boltzius reported that people in Georgia feared to eat the meat of a rattlesnake that was angered before being killed. This superstition still lingers on the sea islands along the South Carolina coast, where "not everyone will eat [rattlesnakes] because the flesh is believed to be poisonous if the snake was angered before being killed."[46] Since blacks constituted the vast majority of the population on these islands, it is generally assumed that their superstitions were part of their African heritage.

On 1 June 1751 Boltzius entered into his journal some information about rattlesnakes, which "are from 21 to 22 feet long"; and he recommended some rather questionable remedies. He soon discovered that his informant had said "seven feet," not "seven yards." By 1754 the Salzburgers agreed that the best antidote was Venetian theriac, a disgusting brew that often contained sixty-four antidotal ingredients worthy of Shakespeare's Weird Sisters.[47]

The only fatality from a snakebite was that of Valentin Depp in 1758, but we do not know what cure hastened his death. In return for the harm they did, rattlesnakes furnished snake oil, popularly used to treat various eye ailments.[48] Because of either biblical or African prejudice, the Salzburgers did not avail themselves of rattlesnake meat, now an expensive delicacy, or of the even more delicious meat of the water moccasin.

With modern medical hindsight, we can see that the cures for snakebite were not much worse than those for other ills, most of which were as useless as the frequently recorded bloodletting. Knowing nothing of germs or viruses, the doctors could treat only the symptoms, not the cause; and they knew little of prevention. In most cases, as on 19 October 1754, fevers were attributed to sudden changes in the weather. It pains a modern to see the trust the Salzburgers put in their cures, for example the praise that Gronau gave to his cure by bleeding on 7 December 1742.[49] Boltzius does not indicate whether or not his parishioners read any of the irrational folk medicine texts so popular among the Pennsylvania Dutch.[50]

Education

Education in Ebenezer was, of course, subordinate to religion.[51] In Protestant areas of Germany even the peasantry had been helped to literacy so that they could read the gospel and articles of faith, whereas in Catholic areas reading was discouraged lest the common people be contaminated by subversive books. As a result, most of the Germans who came to Georgia, being Protestant, could at least read the Bible and their articles of faith in Luther's *Small Catechism* and Freylinghausen's *Order of Salvation*. Many could also read other edifying authors like Arndt and Schaitberger.

The old former marine schoolmaster Ortmann began his classes on the way from Rotterdam and tried to continue them during the lean years in Old Ebenezer, with the assistance of the pastors for the older children.[52] After his dismissal, Ortmann was replaced as teacher by Ludwig Mayer. When Ludwig took sick, he was succeeded by his brother Georg and later by Philip Paulitsch and his brother Johann Martin, while the pastors Boltzius, Gronau, and Lemke continued to bear the major load. Boltzius's own sons attended the town school with the other children, but they also received more advanced education in Latin and music from Thilo.[53]

When the Salzburgers began moving out to their plantations on Abercorn Creek, which were too far away from town for the children to walk to the school, a school was begun there. Among its teachers were Ludwig Mayer, Georg Mayer, Georg Köcher, Johann Flerl, Ruprecht Steiner, Lucas Geiger, Christian Ernst Thilo, Martin Lackner, Johann Adam Treutlen, and Johann Caspar Wertsch. By 1755 the inhabitants of Abercorn, Goshen, and Joseph's Town were able to build their own school, which also served as a church. In 1760 Lemke reported that a school was operating in Bethany, but the teacher, Häg, was fired by Triebner because his pregnant wife danced. In 1774 Muhlenberg stated that the schoolmaster there was a certain "Bühler of Philadelphia," who also oversaw Rabenhorst's plantation.[54] Some of the adult Salzburgers were illiterate, having lived in a Catholic country; for them several attempts were made to maintain adult education classes, as on 22 January 1736 and 5 May and 23 November 1742.

We have seen that Driessler gave good instruction to the German children at Frederica and that Ortmann taught those at Acton and Vernonburg. We have also seen reference to a German teacher at Savannah who officiated as a layman at divine services, but we are not told his name or who supported him. Whoever he was, he must have had few children over twelve years of age in his classes, because the indentured children were, to use Whitefield's apt words, "used to exceedingly hard labor." Boltzius commented on 13 September 1742 that the German children in Savannah had to work instead of going to school. Even the free children had to help their parents in the field or to fish or hunt for them. This helps explain why John Dobell was unable to get even one Dutch child into his school in Savannah, even though the parents blamed it on their silly notion that they were waiting to receive a German schoolmaster.[55] The SPCK continued to support a schoolmaster in Ebenezer; the incumbent in 1759 was Johann Martin Paulitsch, the husband of Ursula Schweighoffer, as Boltzius recorded on 20 April of that year.

Boltzius realized the economic and political necessity of English in a predominantly English-speaking environment, and he worked diligently to improve his own and his parishioners' use of that tongue, even though it meant exposing them to English customs and values. In this regard he agreed with Muhlenberg, who said, "In school German for our religion, English for temporal and civic welfare."[56] Ortmann was supposed to teach English, but Boltzius soon realized that his command of the language was inadequate, the language spoken by British seamen not being suitable for small children. The English lad Bishop was of some help, but he could not maintain order in his classes. Hamilton, the wigmaker from Breslau, spoke German well enough, but he was a discontented person. Nevertheless, he seems to have taught later in Savannah, as we saw in the records regarding his testimony for Ortmann. On 14 May 1747 Boltzius expressed a wish for an English schoolmaster, one of his reasons being that he was kept too busy reading, writing, and interpreting English for his parishioners.

To encourage reading, Boltzius instituted a church library, which was functioning by 26 May 1738, most of its volumes being gifts from Halle. This library naturally contained mostly theological, devotional, and inspirational books, but there were also some medical texts. While a majority of these books were in German, some were in Latin and English. These books were lent freely to readers in Purysburg, Savannah, Orangeburg, and other outlying areas. Johann Tobler of New Windsor mentioned with gratitude Boltzius's generosity in lending good books.[57] On 29 June 1749 Boltzius reported sending books to the people of Saxe Gotha for use at their meetings and in their homes. Recently, a number of these volumes, some signed by Boltzius, Gronau, and later ministers, have been found in the archives of the Lutheran Theological Southern Seminary in Columbia, South Carolina. In his *History of Georgia* de Brahm highly praised the "free library" at Ebenezer, and apparently also that of Johann Tobler, who was perhaps best known locally for *The South-Carolina and Georgia Almanack for 1764*, which was printed in Savannah.[58] The finest library in Georgia was that of Zubly, which de Brahm must have had chiefly in mind when he wrote that in Georgia there were libraries containing volumes in "Caldaic, Hebrew, Arabic, Siriac, Coptic, Malabar, Greek, Latin, French, German, Dutch, Spanish, besides the English, vide, in thirteen Languages."[59]

Domestic Life, Customs, and Superstitions

Perhaps the best picture we get of "Dutch" domestic life, in this case German Swiss, is Joseph Avery's depiction of the activities of the large and industrious family of Michael Burckhalter at Vernonburg in his letter of 31 January 1743 to the Trustees. As a minister of the gospel, Boltzius gives us glimpses into the spiritual life and righteous behavior of his parishioners, but he does not tell us as much as we might wish about their secular lives. Written mainly for inspirational and promotional purposes, his letters and reports ignored many everyday secular conditions and occurrences, which he always denigrated as "external" matters. Sometimes, however, even spiritual affairs have secular interest. For example, Boltzius often tells of house consecrations, which, of course, consist mainly of hymns and benedictions. It is probable, however, that, upon the pastor's departure, the consecrations degenerated into housewarmings, with fun, food, and frolic.

Boltzius had to warn Gottfried Christ on 22 January 1741 and Sigmund Ott on 11 February 1742 against consorting with frivolous young men, and this fact seems to imply that frivolous young men actually lived in Ebenezer, even if we do not learn the nature of their frivolity. We have seen that some of the Salzburger wives had begun to rebel from their divinely ordained subservience to their husbands, perhaps emboldened by the greater freedom enjoyed by Englishwomen. After Boltzius's death the inhabitants seem to have indulged in horse racing, which caused the deaths of both David Unselt and Israel Heintzelmann.

Boltzius took disappointingly little note of the Salzburgers' native customs, which differed so much from those in his own native Lower Lusatia. Yet he did mention on 13 April 1734 that the Salzburgers used coffins only for women who died in childbirth, all other corpses being wrapped in a shroud, carried to the cemetery on a board, and buried without a coffin. On 10 August 1736 Boltzius complained that the Salzburgers tended to choose a single godparent for all their children. The Catholic Church had forbidden marriages between cosponsors, and therefore people tried not to disqualify too many neighbors as potential mates.

In 1760 Boltzius thought it noteworthy that at Ebenezer the godparents brought food to the child's mother, instead of being entertained by her.[60] Since the Salzburgers had been in Georgia for twenty-six years, it is possible that they had acquired this reasonable custom from their English neighbors. Boltzius also mentioned that the Salzburgers preferred to attach their plow to the ox's horns, as in Salzburg, rather than to a yoke or collar. We have seen that the long lot, which still exists at Vernonburg and Ebenezer, was an importation from Central Europe, and we shall see that Ebenezer's first barn was built in the Salzburg manner.

Unfortunately, the Effingham County Germans never found their anthropologist or folklorist, as did the Pennsylvania Dutch and the Dutch Fork Germans in South Carolina. Dr. Benjamin Rush, the "Tacitus of the Pennsylvania Germans," gave excellent insights into the life of his German neighbors, and Orlando B. Mayer preserved some lore from his Dutch Fork homeland, but no one recorded the beliefs and superstitions of the Georgia Germans.[61] Since the German settlers in Pennsylvania, South Carolina, and Georgia came from the same parts of Germany at the same time, we can assume that they shared the same beliefs, some of which had not changed in centuries. For example, Mayer records a magic charm written down sometime between 1847 and 1861 at Dutch Fork in South Carolina, which differs little from its forebear recorded in a tenth-century German manuscript. It commands an ailment to go out of the marrow into the bone, out of the bone into the flesh, out of the flesh into the blood, and out of the blood into the skin: "O swiney go out of the marrow in the bone. O swiney go out of the bone in the flesh. O swiney go out of the flesh in the blood. O swiney go out of the blood in the skin. For this is good for the swiney."[62] It stops there, whereas the earlier German version has the ailment go out of the skin into an arrow, which the medicine man then shoots away.[63] The same charm also survives in Low German. The word *swiney* is a corruption, surely not understood, of the German word *Schwinde*, meaning consumption or, by extension, any other ailment.

Boltzius suppressed mention of such superstitions, yet on 1 and 21 March 1750 he did report that he had to admonish a widow not to allow her servant to exorcise her cattle. Unfortunately, he did not relate the nature of the "heathen" charm used, but it was surely some pre-Christian magic incantation similar to the one used at Dutch Fork and was apparently followed by a petition to God. Despite the tendency of most colonial Germans to put their faith in witchcraft, the first case of black magic Boltzius records was that of a Frenchman, by which he may have meant Swiss, in Savannah. This magician ascertained a man's guilt through divination and thus involved Georg Dresler with the law.[64] It is probable that black magic flourished in Ebenezer; but either it was concealed from Boltzius or he suppressed it, or else Urlsperger deleted it from the reports.

When Boltzius used two kettles in making a decision on 17 July 1742, the practice was preceded by a prayer; therefore the decision was made by God, not by Dame Fortuna or the personal power of a magician. This was also the case on the many occasions that lots were drawn in the distribution of land. The Moravians also left most decisions to the judgment of God. Predicting the future by drawing lots was an ancient custom among the Germanic peoples and was well described by Tacitus in chapter 10 of the *Germania*. Because of Boltzius's and Urlsperger's censorship, we know nothing about the Salzburgers' superstitions, but we might surmise that they had the same beliefs in haunts and hexes as their compatriots in Pennsylvania. The only surviving ghost story is of late vintage: reportedly, the white ghost of the greedy Mrs. Rabenhorst vainly seeks the treasure she buried during the Revolution.

A vestige of an ancient German custom still lingers, or at least lasted until recently, in the Okefenokee Swamp in south Georgia. The custom of putting out a saucer of milk for a snake, which is unknown in Great Britain, must have come from Germany, where it is widespread.[65] Cecile Hulse Matschat tells of an old "Snake Woman" who put out a saucer of warm milk for her king snake, which came at her call and drank the milk.[66]

When German peasants set out a saucer of milk for their house adder (*Hausnatter*) in return for the good luck it brings them, they are probably unaware that the custom dates from pagan days and originally served to propitiate the human spirit residing in the serpent. One might ask how a German custom found its way into the heart of the Okefenokee, but one might just as well ask how the Snyders (Schneiders) and Rodenberrys (Rottenbergers) found their way to the area of the Snake Woman.

When the Salzburg emigrants left their mountain homes, they were wearing quaint Alpine costumes as seen in the pictures reproduced by Angelika Marsch. The men wore broad floppy felt or leather hats, tight jackets, and voluminous knickerbockers, a style popular at court a half-century earlier and associated in America with Peter Stuyvesant and his cohorts. The women wore high bodices and full skirts down almost to their ankles. All these jackets, trousers, bodices, and skirts were in lively colors, not somber ones such as those worn by so many Protestant refugees. No doubt such costumes disappeared soon after the Salzburgers reached Georgia. The first tailors, Hernberger and Christ, were from Hungary and Reicheltsheim by Frankfurt, respectively; and all clothes bought in Savannah would have been of English manufacture, as were the gowns worn by Boltzius and Gronau. The generous donations of linen shirts from Halle would probably have represented North German rather than Alpine styles. A reversion to older styles occurred on 17 December 1747 when Whitefield donated nine shillings for bonnets for nine widows, because these happened to be similar to some received previously from Salzburg.

When the first Germans reached Georgia, they had to make do with British provisions brought from Great Britain or the northern colonies. They soon became dependent on local, and often unfamiliar, food, such as Indian corn, sweet potatoes, squash, and rice; and it is likely that they prepared them as the other colonists did. The later German settlers introduced "European grains" and had more leeway in preparing them to their own taste. Since they slaughtered their own beasts, they probably butchered them as they had done in the old country, and they surely cured their hams and made their sausages as they had done at home. As we have seen, the people of Savannah bought meat from the "German butcher," Johann Altherr of Purysburg. Later on, Levi Sheftall served as butcher, too. In order to be assured of kosher meats, someone in each Jewish community had to know how to slaughter. It might be of interest for some culinary expert to ascertain whether Central European cuisine is reflected in smoked hams, blood sausage, souse, chitterlings, cracklings, and other current Georgia dishes.

Like Luther, and unlike the Quakers and Presbyterians, Boltzius approved of music for the church, but only as an offering to God. When little boys volunteered for the choir, they had to promise that they would sing with their hearts as well as with their mouths, by which Boltzius meant that they should not sing just for aesthetic or worldly enjoyment. To improve the singing in church, Boltzius gave singing lessons, which he described in his journal entries for 18 June and 6 August 1738. The women with good voices sang along with Boltzius, then the men and the children repeated the words softly. The quality of the singing probably improved after 14 February 1740, when Thilo began teaching part singing. On Christmas Eve, 1747, Boltzius recorded that he was employing Mr. Thilo to teach his two sons to sing and that he and his wife, along with Thilo, who had a bass voice, were singing with the two little sopranos for the enjoyment and encouragement of the congregation. When Muhlenberg admired the Salzburgers' singing on his visit in 1774, he attributed it to Boltzius's expertise.[67]

Being an accomplished musician and the founder of a Collegium Musicum, or music club, in Halle, Boltzius always desired a clavichord or an organ for the Ebenezer church. He never succeeded in getting one, even though, as he stated on 16 November 1750, he had an organist named Neidlinger in the congregation. The nearest organ to Ebenezer seems to have been one belonging to Johann Tobler in New Windsor, which Boltzius mentioned on 15 February 1740. On 8 July 1753 Boltzius reported that some of the earlier inhabitants of Ebenezer collected money so that Captain Krauss might buy an organ in Germany, yet nothing came of this.

In his reports, Boltzius identifies most of the hymns he taught his flock, and he often jotted down the notes they sang.[68] Nearly all these songs were Pietistic, yet they avoided exaggerated emotionalism; one would look in vain among the songs for any "vermiform" hymns, in which the singer confesses to being a "miserable worm" or a "dead dog." A majority of the Salzburgers' songs are found in the Halle songbook of Johann Anastasius Freylinghausen, who had been one of Boltzius's mentors in Halle.

Boltzius never referred to any secular songs sung by his parishioners, possibly for fear that such mention might lead their benefactors to think them worldly and less deserving of benefactions. His disapproval of secular songs explains why one of his parishioners confessed to having misused her voice to sing "secular and shameful songs." Obviously the Salzburgers found occasion to sing their native songs, probably including yodels, a form of falsetto singing still reflected in Georgia's hog-calling, which the swamp dwellers call "hollerin'."[69]

Even Boltzius found a use for secular music: he mentioned on 30 December 1748 that Habersham had given him twenty-four arias by Handel.[70] These must have been secular songs, since Boltzius planned to make contrafacts (*Parodien*) of them. Dancing was, of course, taboo, as we saw in the case of the schoolmaster's wife who had to do penance for dancing to a dulcimer. It is probable that other musical instruments were used in Ebenezer, even if they were not mentioned in the published reports. Boltzius himself called dancing a "godless activity" on 28 December 1747, and on 6 April 1752 he expressed the view that dancing was "senseless and common" and was "accompanied by coarse and subtile impurity."

While Boltzius loved music, he revealed little enthusiasm for the visual arts, perhaps associating them with graven images. Of course he tolerated religious pictures, for on 14 February 1740 he distributed some little engravings depicting the life of Christ, which Mr. Martin Engelbrecht of Augsburg had engraved and sent as gifts for the children at Ebenezer. The same was true of an engraving of Field Marshal von Seckingdorf, which Boltzius received on 3 August 1748 and showed to his parishioners, not for aesthetic enjoyment, but so they could see the likeness of their great benefactor, a true "German Gideon."

The Salzburgers also received a large allegorical painting representing the voyage of the fourth transport, which Boltzius described fully on 17 August and 7 September 1743. This gift, which had been given to Vigera by people in Strassburg, portrayed a ship under full sail on a rough sea, watched by the eye of God and pulled by a rope from God's hand.[71] The two shores are marked as "Europa" and "America," people are praying on bended knee, and over the picture are Bible verses. It is significant that Boltzius hung this picture in his study, perhaps thinking people might find it objectionable in church.[72]

On 7 September 1743 a German Swiss painter in Charleston, surely Jeremias Theus, produced some Bible verses for Vigera but refused payment. Theus was the artist who, in 1753, painted the portrait of Boltzius that is now lost and known to us only through an engraving made by Johann Jacob Haid of Augsburg in 1754. On 21 November 1750 the Salzburgers received a five-by-seven-foot painting of the Last Supper from

Mezzotint of Johann Martin Boltzius, first minister at Ebenezer, after a painting by Jeremias Theus (Hargrett Rare Book and Manuscript Library, University of Georgia)

Salzburger cottage. Note mortise construction. (Hargrett Rare Book and Manuscript Library, University of Georgia)

Ziegenhagen, which they mounted on the wall behind the Communion table. Boltzius was far more concerned with its edifying effect than with its aesthetic value.

Boltzius mentioned that von Reck's servant, Christian Müller, painted a likeness of Oglethorpe, which pleased the general so much that he gave the artist free passage back to Europe.[73] Boltzius made no mention of the beautiful drawings collected by von Reck and recently published by Kristian Hvidt.

Like most other Germans in America, those in Georgia did not burden themselves with traditional practices unsuited to their new homeland. This was clearly the case with architecture; there were no stones in coastal Georgia, and Alpine cottages and chalets would hardly have fitted the Georgia climate. Only once does Boltzius mention that a house, that of the widow Lemmenhofer, was "built in the style of the Salzburger houses," as he wrote on 5 August 1750. In both Old and New Ebenezer the Salzburgers built huts of planks like those in Savannah. Gradually, toward the end of the eighteenth and the beginning of the nineteenth centuries, the Georgia Salzburgers developed a typical dwelling that is known as the Salzburger cottage. This style of cottage, with its wide veranda and overhanging roof, was probably based on houses in the West Indies, which in turn had been influenced by the bungalows of the East Indies. It is possible, of course, that the mortised joints are of Salzburger origin. Likewise, the squared timbers of these houses may have reflected German practice, since English barns of the period were usually half-timbered, the interstices being filled in with clay-covered wattles or masonry.[74] It is to be remembered that Oglethorpe praised the squared-timber houses built at Frederica by Heinrich Michel and Heinrich Meyer. To be sure, the Salzburgers built a barn in the Salzburg fashion, but Boltzius did not tell how it differed from other German or English barns.[75] Nor is there any evidence whether or not it influenced other barns as the Dutch barns did in Pennsylvania.

Descriptions and Anecdotes

Our colonial records and journals offer us practically no descriptions of people's physical appearance: they almost never tell us whether a person was blond, brunette, or redheaded, or whether he had blue or black eyes. Seldom do we learn whether a man was fat or thin or tall or short, or whether his nose was straight or crooked. Of all our informants on the Georgia Germans, only Captain Coram deigned to describe physical characteristics, and he did so sparingly. He said of Boltzius and Gronau, for example, "The minister is a thin little man about 31 Years of Age, and resembles Mr. Vat at a Distance. The Catechist is about 25 Years a Tallish ruddy looking young man, they seem both to be very sober persons." About von Reck he wrote, "De Reck is a Clever Young Gentleman very much like Oglethorpe tho not altogether so thin in his face, Yet handsome to the full, he looks as much like a nobleman as any I have seen." The remainder of the description concerns von Reck's behavior, humor, prudence, and his liveried servant.[76] From all this we learn that Boltzius was small and thin and that Gronau was tall and ruddy, hardly enough for a police report. Yet this is more than anyone else has told us.

Whereas Boltzius was a profounder student of the human condition, Colonel Stephens was a wittier and more entertaining reporter on mundane affairs. He was also a bit of a gossip who enjoyed reporting scandals. He tells, for example, of a Dutch serving girl living with the widow Vanderplank who was made pregnant by Lieutenant William Francis.[77] Francis married the girl and took her to his fort at Mount Venture, where she and her child were later murdered by Spanish Indians.

Stephens also devotes many words to William Norris's affair with the

Dutch serving girl Elisabetha Penner. As a good Anglican parishioner, Stephens stood by his minister until the evidence became overwhelming.[78] He was also very disturbed when Whitefield began to preach the insidious dogma of predestination, which Stephens well summarized: "The main Drift of his Sermons, Morning and Afternoon, was to maintain the Doctrine of a peculiar Election, of such as were predestined to be saved, condemning utterly an universal Redemption by Christ's Blood, which terrible Doctrine was shocking to all such as by a sincere Repentance, and true Faith in Christ, hoped for Salvation thro' his Mediation."[79] In this matter Stephens fully shared Boltzius's conviction that all sinners could achieve salvation through repentance and faith.

Although Stephens never bothered to learn the Palatines' names, he does seem to have cared about their welfare. In his journal entry for 2 February 1741 he wrote: "An unhappy Accident happened this morning, by a little Child belonging to a Dutch Woman's Servant; who playing near its Mother, fell (unseen by her) into a Tub of Water, and was drowned; whereupon a jury was summoned to make Inquisition after its Death."[80] Elsewhere Stephens tells how a German servant was gravely injured by a falling tree on 12 August 1738, but again he failed to give a name.[81] Stephens also tells of a Dutch woman who lost a sum of paper money she had hidden in her corset. The blame was first put on a poor little indentured English boy, whose excuse was that he had slipped out into the woods, not to hide the money, but to relieve himself because he had diarrhea. Eventually, it was proved that the woman's own son-in-law had purloined the money.

On one occasion Stephens tells how some of the Vernonburgers took joy rides back home from Savannah on horses they had stolen for the occasion. The riders then released the animals, causing their owners much loss in recovering them. When a warrant was sworn out against two Vernonburgers on 9 November 1743, they confessed and gave drunkenness as their excuse. They were put in stocks for two hours but spared a whipping in order to encourage them in the improvements they were making.[82] While less witty than Stephens, Boltzius did tell some amusing stories about ordinary, everyday life in Ebenezer. These sometimes reveal a bit of malicious joy, especially where poetic justice is concerned. For example, on 7 February 1741 he reported the divine justice done to Josef Ernst, who, like Michael Rieser, had refused to work on the gristmill because he was secretly planning to leave Ebenezer. When the mill was completed, he was denied its use and therefore had to use the old handmill. While he and his wife were doing so, she let the shaft of the mill strike him in his face and knock out one of his teeth. Thereupon he cursed and beat her, thus adding sin to sin.

Boltzius was particularly annoyed by the widow Rheinländer, who demanded much help, constantly complained and accused, and never showed gratitude. When her house burned on 5 April 1741, the Salzburgers rushed from church and salvaged many of her possessions. Instead of thanking them, however, she accused them of stealing a large amount of paper money she had concealed. This amazed Boltzius, because for years the widow had been begging and borrowing without repaying.

Some of Boltzius's reports are exciting, as when a small child fell in the millrace on 12 March 1748 and was carried rapidly almost to the mill wheel before being rescued. Only a short time earlier a huge alligator had been crushed by the powerful wheel, and the Salzburgers had great difficulty in extracting it. On 16 January 1750 Boltzius seemed to get satisfaction in telling of the narrow escape of a shoemaker, who, like the unfortunate Arnsdorf, was given to drink. Once, while a bit intoxicated, he missed his step in crossing a footbridge over the millrace and fell in it only nine feet ahead of the wheel. Fortunately, a repair had just been made on the wheel that saved his life, but Boltzius does not explain how.

Wills and Inventories

A family's domestic life is partially revealed by its material possessions, which are best recorded in wills and inventories. Although most of the German-speaking settlers in Georgia had arrived with few possessions, many of them prospered and died possessed of enough wealth to justify a will.[83] In the early days at Old and New Ebenezer, last testaments were usually made orally in the presence of witnesses, and Boltzius saw to it that the stipulations were carried out. The procedure is given, for example, in Boltzius's journal entry for 1 September 1742. The legacies were usually modest and consisted mainly of clothes and utensils, and later also cattle, which were bequeathed to relatives, friends, helpers, and the poor box. Even for these Boltzius had to send inventories to Savannah, which, unfortunately, have been lost.[84] Fortunately, a few wills were recorded in the daily reports, such as those of Christian Riedelsperger in Boltzius's entry of 23 April 1742 and of Maria Maurer in Boltzius's entry for 3 and 4 August of the same year.

Whereas many wills list only land, cattle, and slaves, inventories give more detailed lists. Inventories of widely ranging values survive for the following German-speaking people: John Alther, Sigismond Beltz, John Boltzius, C. John Borneman, Christian Burck, Michael Burghalter, Andrew Clemmands (Clemenz), Peter Dowle (Diehle), Christoph Fulbright (Vollbrecht), John Gable, Balthasar Gimmell, George Heid, Frederick Holtzendorff, Theobald Kieffer, Matthias Kugel, Martin Lyons, John Meyer, John Lewis Meyer, Philip Portz, George Rentz, Adam Riedelsperger, George Lewis Roth, Solomon Schad, Ruprecht Schrempf, Michael Schweiger, William Slighterman (Schlechtermann), John Smith, Henrick Steerman, Gottlieb Steheli, George Sybold, George Uhland, Christoph Wiesenbacher, Thomas Whitehard, Gaspar Whitehart (Caspar Schargold Weisshart), Matthias Zettler, Peter Zipperer, and Bartholomew Zouberbuhler.[85]

Very informative, as well as amusing, is the "Infentoray of Solomon Shad Deceased taking [taken] this 4 march 1768." This "infentoray," recorded by John Eppinger, John Schick, and John Neidlinger, is easy to read, provided one knows Swiss German:

4 Cowse at 25/ [shillings] in the woods	£ 5. 0.0
3 Cows and Calfs at 32/6	4.17.0
6 heavers [heifers] at 15/ five in the woods	4.10.0
12 Sheep one Ram at 5/	3. 5.0
2 Sows with beeks [pigs] at 12/6	1. 5.0
2 Barrows at 7/6	0.15.0
1 horse in the woods	3.10.0
1 Negerow thom	15. 5.0
1 Negerow wench Selvey with a boy 3 years old	35. 0.0
2 tables 5 Cheeres	0. 5.0
1 bowter [pewter] Dish 2 passen [basins?] 10 bleats [plates]	0. 6.3
4 Iron poat [pots]	0. 4.6
1 pair of Iron Donggs [tongs]	0. 5.0
1 great Iron & 1 tea Cadle [kettle] 1 fire Dongs	0. 4.5
1 powter tea poot Cobbe & Sassors [cup & saucers] & Sundery	0. 2.3
1 Cune [gun?] Shorte back & Catlach pouter [powder] horne	0. 4.6
1 feather beth 1 beth Sheats 2 Pillows & Bolsters 2 blankets 4 Sheets	1.15.0
1 Caffy mell	0. 2.6
2 old Chests one trung [trunk]	0. 2.3
waring apearel	2.10.0

1 Carth	0.18.6
one pair mell Stones	0.15.0
one Boat in Savannah	10. 0.0
Books accompts good and pat [bad] Debts	72.10.1

This inventory shows that Schad did a good deal of farming, certainly enough to support his family and slaves. The relatively large number of cooking and eating utensils was needed for the tavern he ran, whereas the small supply of bedding suggests that the tavern was not an inn. It will be noted that everything was functional; there is no mention of musical instruments, pictures, or anything of an aesthetic or recreational nature. The inventory represents a sizable fortune for a man who had begun his American career as an indentured rower, had served as a Ranger, and had been captured by Indians and displayed as a trophy in St. Augustine.

♦ *Summary Three* ♦

Indians, Slaves, and Soldiers

This study is about the Germans in Georgia, not about the Indians; so the native Americans are seen only as they affected the Germans, that is, through German eyes. It is now popular among cultural historians to hold that all cultures are intrinsically equal and, therefore, that the Indian cultures were just as good as the European ones.[1] I disagree. If all cultures are equal, then Western civilization is no better than the barbarian culture of the Indo-Europeans, and in that case we owe no thanks to Aristotle, Jesus Christ, Dante, Gutenberg, Luther, Voltaire, Beethoven, Pasteur, or anyone else. In the Indians' favor, it can be said that they lived symbiotically with nature and did less damage to Georgia's ecology in twenty thousand years than the white men did in two hundred, even if they did set fire to the woods when hunting.

The Georgia Germans' poor opinion of the Indians was due to observation, not to preconceived ideas, for most of them had heard little in Europe about the North American aborigines. On the other hand, when they first arrived in Georgia, they heard only complimentary things about the noble savage from Oglethorpe, who had both idyllized and idealized the redskins. On the first Salzburgers' third day in Georgia, someone took several of them to see the local Indians on Yamacraw Bluff, and they felt "compassion and sorrow" because of the Indians' heathen condition.[2] Boltzius thereupon resolved to learn the Indians' language.

On 5 December 1734 Oglethorpe wrote to Samuel Wesley, the father of the great religious leader, to persuade him to become a missionary to the Indians in Georgia, who "are mighty desirous to hear Instruction, and have high Notions of a Deity."[3] A similarly favorable account of the Indians was given by the Moravian David Nitschmann.[4] In his account of his

1 Carth	0.18.6
one pair mell Stones	0.15.0
one Boat in Savannah	10. 0.0
Books accompts good and pat [bad] Debts	72.10.1

This inventory shows that Schad did a good deal of farming, certainly enough to support his family and slaves. The relatively large number of cooking and eating utensils was needed for the tavern he ran, whereas the small supply of bedding suggests that the tavern was not an inn. It will be noted that everything was functional; there is no mention of musical instruments, pictures, or anything of an aesthetic or recreational nature. The inventory represents a sizable fortune for a man who had begun his American career as an indentured rower, had served as a Ranger, and had been captured by Indians and displayed as a trophy in St. Augustine.

◆ *Summary Three* ◆

Indians, Slaves, and Soldiers

This study is about the Germans in Georgia, not about the Indians; so the native Americans are seen only as they affected the Germans, that is, through German eyes. It is now popular among cultural historians to hold that all cultures are intrinsically equal and, therefore, that the Indian cultures were just as good as the European ones.[1] I disagree. If all cultures are equal, then Western civilization is no better than the barbarian culture of the Indo-Europeans, and in that case we owe no thanks to Aristotle, Jesus Christ, Dante, Gutenberg, Luther, Voltaire, Beethoven, Pasteur, or anyone else. In the Indians' favor, it can be said that they lived symbiotically with nature and did less damage to Georgia's ecology in twenty thousand years than the white men did in two hundred, even if they did set fire to the woods when hunting.

The Georgia Germans' poor opinion of the Indians was due to observation, not to preconceived ideas, for most of them had heard little in Europe about the North American aborigines. On the other hand, when they first arrived in Georgia, they heard only complimentary things about the noble savage from Oglethorpe, who had both idyllized and idealized the redskins. On the first Salzburgers' third day in Georgia, someone took several of them to see the local Indians on Yamacraw Bluff, and they felt "compassion and sorrow" because of the Indians' heathen condition.[2] Boltzius thereupon resolved to learn the Indians' language.

On 5 December 1734 Oglethorpe wrote to Samuel Wesley, the father of the great religious leader, to persuade him to become a missionary to the Indians in Georgia, who "are mighty desirous to hear Instruction, and have high Notions of a Deity."[3] A similarly favorable account of the Indians was given by the Moravian David Nitschmann.[4] In his account of his first journey to Georgia, von Reck gave a very interesting and generally objective report on the Georgia Indians; fifty-three years later he published a speech by Tomochichi in which the chief declared a keen wish to hear the word of God.[5] Von Reck did, however, seem to echo Oglethorpe in telling about the Indians' generosity and magnanimity. One Indian, who had donated venison to a group of Englishmen, returned and discovered that it had not been distributed fairly. Returning again with more venison, he supervised a more equitable distribution.[6]

Boltzius tells how, when an English malefactor was to be flogged, a compassionate Indian thrust his body against the culprit to guard him from the lash, while shouting, "No Christian, no Christian." This favorable report was immediately followed by one of a different nature: an Indian cut off the hair and ears of an Indian widow who had been too familiar with an Englishman.[7] Von Reck was informed that the Creeks, unlike the other Indians, were quite civilized.[8] The first gift the Salzburgers received from an Indian was a deer, brought to them on 2 May 1734.[9]

Although Oglethorpe tried to sell Boltzius his high regard for the noble savage, Boltzius more often observed poor behavior, especially when the Indians were drunk, as they usually were when he saw them. On 20 February 1735 Boltzius confided in his journal that "so far we have failed to find in any of them the good traits they were said to have when we first arrived in America." It was not long before Boltzius wrote to a friend in Berlin that "you find in them not the least trace of any knowledge or fear of God, but rather they live just like cattle." Appalled by the Indians' laziness, he added that "not even hunger and want can force them to work"; what little work was done was done by the women.[10] Even the tolerant Moravians gained a bad impression of the Indians. Töltschig wrote back to Herrnhut, "The Indians live worse than cattle, drunk every day so that they roll around on the ground."[11]

Unable to win the Indians to Christianity, Boltzius wrote on 4 February 1742 that "we hold it as an example of God's love that so few Indians come to us." On 14 December of the same year he wrote, "We may thank God that we have so little traffic with them." Boltzius did, however, occasionally see virtue in an individual Indian, such as an elderly man who visited him on 9 November 1737. On 11 July 1739, when Boltzius gave something to one of two Indians, the recipient immediately shared it with his companion, for, Boltzius wrote, the Indians "have no greed, selfishness, or jealousy." Boltzius's journal for 7 March 1739 gives an amusing, albeit not entirely favorable, picture of some "foreign Indians," perhaps Creeks or Cherokees, who visited Savannah to collect gifts. Boltzius gave a very informative, even if secondhand, description of the Creeks and their life-style in his entry for 9 July 1751.

Before being disillusioned by the Indians, Boltzius honestly tried to carry out the urgent injunctions of his superiors to learn the Indian language, and he even made a list of Indian words, some of which he wrote in his journal entry for 30 December 1734.[12] His efforts at learning the language failed because the Indians he met were passersby who seldom stayed long. Also, they represented different tribes and therefore spoke widely varying languages. As late as July 1747, however, Boltzius was still hoping to learn the Indian languages.

During his second sojourn in America, von Reck mentioned seeing a German Indian-trader whom he had previously known. This may have been some German trader whose name is not recorded, or possibly recorded only in some completely anglicized form. On 3 August 1738 Boltzius mentioned the visit of a former friend of Baron von Reck, a German trader who had lived among the Creeks, Chickasaws, and Cherokees and must have been the person who advised the baron so well about Indian lore. In any case, von Reck's rendition of Indian words and his understanding of Indian customs indicate that he had been tutored by someone very familiar with the Indians.

The only trader definitely connected with Ebenezer was Johann Paul Francke of Purysburg, whose widowed mother had sent him to school in Ebenezer at great sacrifice. Although he had done well in school, Francke ran away to the Indians, where he served a trader, probably as teamster. When he finally returned after twelve years among the Indians, he had completely forgotten his German and had to relearn it as well as his catechism, as Boltzius remarked on 8 July 1750. Despite his long sojourn in the wilderness, Francke became a respectable member of society once he had outgrown his wanderlust.

The Indians' behavior put Boltzius on the horns of a dilemma. Oglethorpe was a stalwart champion not only of the Salzburgers but also of the Indians, whose rights he always respected and protected. As late as 1741 he wrote to Boltzius to remind him that the Indians had been the rightful owners of America.[13] On 31 July 1748 Boltzius repeated Oglethorpe's views in his journal and stated that, since the Indians were the first and legitimate inhabitants, it was a sin for the common people to wish to destroy

Indian busk, from von Reck's folio. Original in color. (Det Kongelige Bibliotek, København)

them; yet on the sixth of the next month he requested military protection against the Indians. Three days earlier he had revealed his prejudice by saying that the crops in the field were endangered by "Indians and other bad people." It was largely because of their loyalty to Oglethorpe that the Georgia Indians refrained so long from committing massacres like those perpetrated against many early German colonists from New Bern to New Ulm. It was not until 1759 that the Cherokees went on the warpath against the whites, and that occurred mostly in the Carolinas.

Boltzius frequently complained against the rowdiness of the Uchees, his nearest native neighbors, who had little respect for private property. Oglethorpe argued that the Indians always shared whatever they had and that the whites should do so, too. To this Boltzius parried that the Indians raised nothing and therefore could not pay back the favors they took for granted. The Salzburgers could not understand the practice of "Indian giving." For them, a bargain was a bargain which could not be undone at the whim of one of the parties. Boltzius was never sure whether a piece of venison was a gift or whether the donor would return demanding a reward. As a result, he tried manfully to enforce the Trustees' injunctions against trading with the Indians.

The Salzburgers and other Georgians never suffered attacks from the Indians under British protection such as the Uchees, Creeks, and Cherokees. Except for a few murders committed by Spanish Indians, the Georgians suffered little violence, and then only far upcountry. It was fortunate for the whites that the Indians still had no national feeling. As late as Bloody Knee each Indian tribe hated their Indian neighbors even more than they did the palefaces, with whom they were always glad to cooperate in annihilating their fellow Indians. Luckily for the whites, the Indians depended on them for both firearms and firewater. Most of the Indians' violence around Ebenezer was committed against fellow Indians, as we have seen in several examples. Another incident occurred in 1782 when a drunk Indian shot another. He then reloaded his musket and gave it to his chief to execute him, which the chief promptly did.[14]

Boltzius's disgust at the Indians increased when he heard on 16 July 1750 of the brutal tortures, such as the "petit feu," that they inflicted on their helpless prisoners.[15] He also complained of their ingratitude when, after receiving gifts in Savannah, they stole some horses at Ebenezer on their way home, including a fine one belonging to Hanns Schmidt. Boltzius mentioned this event on 16 and 25 July 1750. On 1 July 1751 Boltzius again described the Indians' cruelty, and he also explained the difficulty of fighting against them. It is therefore surprising when, in 1760, he justified the actions of some Cherokees who shot cows, stole horses, and killed some white people because they had been mistreated by the whites.[16] On the other hand, he was still indignant at their cruelty.[17] For many years Boltzius seemed to think that a scalper cut off the top of the cranium, but by 1760 he realized that only the skin was taken.[18]

We have seen that the Indians who scalped Gabriel Bach, the Ranger, were Florida Indians and not allies of Oglethorpe. The same was true of the Indians who murdered the German wife and child of Lieutenant Francis at Mount Venture on the Altamaha River. Besieged by Yemassee Indians, the four-man garrison surrendered with a promise of safe conduct. The Indians at first spared the mother and her infant and started off with their four prisoners; but on the way they had a change of mind, killed two of their prisoners, and returned to the fort to tomahawk the mother and child before resuming their trip to St. Augustine with their surviving captives. John Dobell gave an account of this incident, which survives in fragmentary form.[19] The two men, Salomo Schad and Josef Ubjer, were both German-speaking.[20] They reached St. Augustine alive, where they were displayed as trophies.[21] As we have seen, Schad later prospered. Boltzius, who recorded this event on 27 November 1742, attributed the woman's fate to her sinful life, but that did not explain why God punished the child also.

Georgia Indians did come close to killing some Salzburgers in 1741, when a party of Creeks captured the German settlers on their way from Ebenezer to Savannah, thinking them to be Spaniards.[22] It was fortunate for the Salzburgers that they did not resist but allowed themselves to be bound, for otherwise the Indians would surely have killed them. That might well have pleased Boltzius, because Veit Landfelder, Michael Rieser, and John Spielbiegler, his most difficult parishioners, were on their way to complain about him in Savannah. On 30 November 1754 some Indians bound the English overseer of the Trustees' cowpen and molested him until they were driven off.

The first German death caused, even indirectly, by the Georgia Indians occurred much later, after Oglethorpe was no longer present to restrain them. Because of the Cherokee War, an Indian uprising in the hinterland, the Bornemanns of New Göttingen fled precipitously to Ebenezer, and their youngest child died on the way.[23] The Bornemanns were not the only Germans who fled unnecessarily from the rumors of war; much of the backcountry as far from the front as Halifax was abandoned when the settlers fled to the coast for safety.[24] Boltzius suspected that the Creeks, allies of the English, spread stories of massacres by the Cherokees so that the settlers would leave their farms as easy pickings for the Creeks.[25] Perhaps the greatest loss caused to Ebenezer by the Indians was the military service, decided by lot, which took the men away from their cultivation. This duty, both by day and night, fell most heavily on the people of Bethany, Ebenezer, and Goshen, who were commanded by Captain Theobald Kieffer, Jr.[26] About this time Andrew Lambert (Andreas Lamprecht) pursued some Indian horse thieves and killed one of them in self-defense.[27]

When von Reck first requested land across Ebenezer Creek, Oglethorpe ordered Causton to prevent people from settling beyond the creek and to dislodge any who had done so, "for we will never break Faith with the Indians and not at this time disoblige them." He ended this letter of 16 March 1736 to Boltzius by writing, "Neither the Saltzburghers the English or any other persons are to take up and cultivate Lands beyond the River Ebenezer."[28]

In his account of his voyage to Georgia in 1735, Francis Moore reported that the Uchee king and his people "had taken some Disgust at this Colony, by reason of an indiscreet Action of one of the Saltzburghers, who had cleared and planted four Acres of Land beyond the Ebenezer River, contrary to Mr. Oglethorpe's Order, and without his knowledge; they had also turn'd their Cattle over the River, some of which had stray'd away and eat the Uchee's Corn twenty Miles above Ebenezer."[29]

In Oglethorpe's account of the same incident, he says that a certain Captain Green had "advised the Uchi Indians to fall upon the Salzburgers for setting upon their Land."[30] When Boltzius desired some land downstream from the Red Bluff on a high bank called Indian Hut, he saw fit to explain in his report on 4 November 1735 that the name did not imply that Indians lived there: it was called Indian Hut only because the first Salzburgers had built a hut there in the Indian style. James Vernon was very displeased at the Salzburgers' request for land across Ebenezer Creek, as Boltzius recorded on 30 November 1737.

Boltzius's complaints against the Indian ravages began at once.[31] They were most frequent in 1741.[32] This, however, may have served to reinforce his request for the Uchee lands across Ebenezer Creek, which he mentions on 25 September 1741. On 12 December 1741 Oglethorpe sent Boltzius some gifts for "the bad Uchi Indians," as the pastor called them. Despite these gifts, Boltzius was still complaining against the Uchees in 1743 and 1745.[33] On 24 February 1746 he wrote to Verelst asking him to urge the Trustees to acquire the land across Ebenezer Creek for some expected settlers. Only five months later, on 18 July 1746, the Trustees ordered Stephens and his assistants to ascertain whether the Uchees were disposed to relinquish their land across Ebenezer Creek for gifts not to exceed fifty pounds. The land should then be surveyed for the Salzburgers.[34]

Two and a half years later, on 2 January 1749, the Trustees directed the president and his assistants to "use their Utmost Endeavours to engage the Uchee Indians to give up to the Trust the Lands lying a little above Ebenezer in Order for it to be added to that Township."[35] This time it was not only for the Salzburgers but also for many distressed Protestants from "Swisserland" who were petitioning to be settled in Georgia.[36] On 2 January 1751 Habersham, now the vice president of the Council, wrote to the Trustees that the Council had advised Boltzius to settle a number of people on twenty-four fifty-acre lots across Ebenezer Creek. These lots were for the second Swabian transport.[37] Meanwhile, Boltzius should settle some Salzburgers there; but he hesitated to do so lest the settlers be unable to defend themselves. Whereas the Uchees were amenable, he feared trouble from the Creeks, who claimed to be the Uchees' overlords.[38] By now, Oglethorpe, the champion of the Indians, was no longer in Georgia. It should be noted that in 1760, at the height of the Indian disturbances, Lemke, like Boltzius, justified their behavior on the grounds that white men were settling on their land and shooting their game.[39] Perhaps he felt differently a week later when describing their practice of tormenting their captives with the "petit feu."[40]

Boltzius never really blamed the Indians for their barbarism, for, as he wrote on 6 January 1754, they were blind heathens, whose condition was such that "it might well move a Christian heart to prayer and pity. For they show us as in a picture how we would look without the means of grace. And we must note that these are not given to us because we are by birthright or nature better than the Indians; we must thank Jesus Christ and the Lord God and His mercy for them."

The Slavery Question

While the Trustees wished to keep Georgia free of slavery, their stand owed less to a moral repugnance against slavery than to a desire to further their goals for Georgia, which was to be a land of yeoman farmers able to defend their homes.[41] Besides, the Trustees saw the danger of having discontented slaves, whom the Spaniards might tempt to run away to Florida or even to rebel. Besides that, slave labor would degrade honest work and corrupt the master class.[42] Even those Trustees who personally abhorred slavery probably did not wish to offend their many friends who profited from slavery in the West Indies and South Carolina, including those Trustees who had invested in the African Company. George Whitefield saw no incongruity in maintaining a slave-operated plantation in South Carolina to support his orphanage in Georgia. As previously shown, the Trustees and Oglethorpe permitted Paul Jenys to lend the Salzburgers some slaves to help them with their sawing at Old Ebenezer.

It did not take the Georgians long to discover the difficulty of competing against slave labor. Already on 14 December 1734 Thomas Christie, the recorder in Savannah, wrote that the Carolinians with their slaves could undersell the Georgians' rice and corn.[43] We have seen that Robert Parker could not make his sawmill profitable without slave labor as long as his South Carolina competitors used it. Von Reck's first report from Georgia explained how, in the slave colonies, the slave-owners let their clever slaves learn a profession, while the remainder cultivated the fields. Von Reck continued, "Then, because everything is occupied by Negroes who have to work hard and with miserable sustenance day and night and even on Sunday, which is a terrible thing, a white man in these lands, if he cannot buy a slave, must work himself like a slave."[44]

While slavery was still illegal in Georgia, the Salzburgers had observed the fourteen slaves lent them by Jenys. These had been people apparently newly arrived from Africa. One of them stabbed another, one ran away, and a third committed suicide in order to return to Africa.[45] After that, the Salzburgers often saw black rowers on the river, including the Kieffers' slaves, who sometimes brought their masters to church. Being resident in South Carolina, the Kieffers were permitted to have slaves, but Boltzius would not allow them to use their slaves in Georgia. He did allow a Kieffer slave to attend church on 11 April 1742 and was impressed by his good behavior.

The Georgia Germans made keen observations about slavery. Von Reck, who witnessed it in South Carolina, described it well, especially the fact that the slaves had to work on the Sabbath to feed themselves, since the masters provided little or no food, and that some had to hire themselves out and to give the money to their masters. Gronau was somewhat inconsistent in his remarks about the black slaves. He often referred to their treachery and thieving, yet he attributed such behavior to the bad treatment they received. He was also lenient when obliged to have an unruly slave punished.[46]

Boltzius considered slavery not only unproductive but also dangerous, having been alarmed by the bloody uprising at Stono Ferry in South Carolina, which he mentioned on 13 March 1739, and by an attempted rebellion at Santee, which he mentioned on 14 July 1740. He also considered slavery immoral, since the slaves were snatched away from their own country, as he explained on 19 July 1740. Boltzius consistently upheld the Trustees' stand against slavery. For example, in 1741 he would not allow the Kieffers to employ their three slaves in making tar on the Georgia side of the river, as he reported on 27 August of that year; on 28 December of the following year he remarked that white people could not find employment in South Carolina where there were enough slaves. He also thought there could be no blessing in the un-Christian life of slave holders, as he wrote on 8 February 1743. On 24 December 1745 he wrote Whitefield a long letter refuting, one by one, the latter's arguments in favor of slavery.[47] This letter brought him favorable comments from the Trustees.

On 2 January 1746 Boltzius sent Urlsperger a similar letter of seventeen pages in German, brilliantly summarizing all the economic, social, moral, and military arguments against slavery.[48] This letter may well have been the stimulus for Urlsperger's spirited letter of 1 August of that year to the Trustees urging them not to introduce slavery into Georgia.[49] According to Ziegenhagen, it was the reason that several wavering Trustees were won back to their stand against slavery.[50] When the land around Parker's Mill was given to the Salzburgers on 18 July 1746, this appeared to be a reward for their opposition to slavery, for Parker had tried to operate the mill with slave labor despite the Trustees' prohibition.

As late as 6 May 1747 Boltzius was still writing persuasively against slavery, which would drive out free labor and present a danger to life and property.[51] On 29 August 1747 he wrote to Martyn that he was hated for upholding the Trustees' stand on slavery.[52] In this very long letter, in which he well summarized the Salzburgers' previous hardships, Boltzius assured Martyn that, lest people believe he forced his own will on his parishioners, he let Ludwig Mayer question them privately. Mayer found the Salzburgers unanimously opposed to slavery.[53]

On 20 May 1748 Boltzius wrote an eloquent letter against slavery to his friend and admirer John Dobell, who had fled to Charleston to escape the wrath of the proslavery faction in Savannah. The Malcontents had branded both Boltzius and Dobell "mercenary slaves" of the Trustees.[54] Without Boltzius's permission, Dobell sent a copy of this letter to the Trustees, and thus it has survived. In it Boltzius renews his arguments against slavery and informs Dobell that he is resolved to suffer "heinous reflectings, revilings, and reproaches" rather than "lend the least finger to promote the Introduction of Black Slaves to the apparent destruction of our Well situated and fertile Province as an intended Asylum for many poor laboring Protestants." He assures Dobell that he will not waver in his views although in mortal danger from those who look upon him as a stone in their way. He gives no credence at all to the restrictions promised on slavery, since such restrictions are ignored in South Carolina.[55] Despite this, in a letter of 7 September 1748 to Francke, Boltzius said he would no longer oppose slavery since the Trustees could not populate the province with white labor.[56]

By 1749 the Malcontents had so greatly intimidated Boltzius that he thought his life in danger and ceased opposing them; yet he continued to disapprove of slavery, as he did on 23 April 1749 when Whitefield notified him that it was to be introduced. His views, however, were still maintained by many of the Salzburgers. On 28 April 1749 Christian Leimberger, Ruprecht Steiner, Matthias Brandner, Simon Reiter, and Thomas Gschwandl petitioned against slavery and declared they would not have come to Georgia had they known that it would be permitted. They would have preferred to go to Prussia to be among whites and safe from thieving people who would take away their livelihood, and now they were ready to go to any of the king's territories where no slaves were allowed.[57] Agreeing with the petitioners and seeing no other remedy, Boltzius saw their complaint as grounds to petition in the Salzburgers' name all the land from Abercorn to Mount Pleasant and from Ebenezer to the Ogeechee so that they would have no slave holders as neighbors. On 24 August 1749 he prayed that God would not let him be tempted to desire blacks or to do anything to have them introduced.

Nevertheless, during the same year the people of Savannah heaped "so much heinous reflection" on Boltzius for his fight against slavery that he began to question his stance and actually besought the Trustees to disregard his previous petitions against slavery and to allow the introduction of black slaves, but only "under such wise restrictions that it be not a discouragement but rather an encouragement to poor white Industrious people to settle and live in this happy Climate."[58] On 10 October 1749 Boltzius reported that the new stipulations concerning slavery were not only just but also pleasing, and on 30 October of that year he wrote that they were such that slavery would not hurt in view of the shortage of white labor. When Habersham offered to supply the Salzburgers with slaves on credit, Boltzius decided on 1 February and 23 July 1750 not to stand in the way. He was, however, always sympathetic toward the slaves, and he preached against cruel treatment. On 17 May 1752 he was shocked that a slave was tortured with a thumbscrew, but we can hope that the cruelty occurred across the river.

Boltzius's change of heart was facilitated by a letter from Urlsperger, who had written on 11 July 1750: "If need is such that one can do nothing else, then one may take slaves in faith and for the purpose of leading them to Christ. Then such a deed will not be a sin, but rather it may lead to a blessing."[59] Until the letter arrived, Boltzius still questioned whether a Christian could buy slaves with a clear conscience and keep them in perpetual slavery, as he wrote on 3 August 1750. When on 19 April 1751 at the Council in Savannah, Boltzius revealed his scruples about buying and selling slaves, he was assured that the slaves had already been slaves in Africa under tyrannical conditions and had been sold and bought legally. Therefore Christians should feel no more scruples than the patriarchs, or even Philemon, to whom St. Paul returned the slave Onesimus. Besides, the slaves would have a chance to become Christians. Despite these assurances, Boltzius expressed his scruples on 23 August of that year and again on 18 September.

Once slavery was legalized, however, Boltzius resigned himself to it. Backed up by Urlsperger's letter, he told his flock that it was permissible to keep slaves if one looks out for both their bodies and their souls, as he wrote in his journal on 3 April 1751. By October 1751 Boltzius admitted that one could accomplish more with black slaves than with white indentured servants. Only a short time later, on 3 January 1753, he justified slavery again when he needed labor for his uncultivated lands. Boltzius always insisted on good treatment, which would not spoil the slaves but would make them loyal, since they would not run away from kind masters. Whatever maliciousness they had was due to brutal treatment. No sooner had Boltzius withdrawn his objections to slavery than the Salzburgers began to buy slaves, some of them being financed by Habersham at 8 percent interest.[60]

Muhlenberg observed that many Germans considered it unprofitable to keep slaves. As seen in the comparison of free and bonded white servants, those work best who work for themselves. We may assume that many small German farmers in Georgia would have agreed with Philip Eisenmann of Old Indian Swamp, fifty miles from Charleston. According to Muhlenberg, Eisenmann and his wife worked their plantation by the sweat of their brows; this proved that one could live and find food without slaves, provided, as Muhlenberg added, "one is godly and contented and does not desire to take out of this world more than one brought into it."[61]

For years Theobald Kieffer of Purysburg insisted that he was just about to move to Ebenezer to be nearer Jerusalem Church, yet something held him back. It is easy to suspect that he remained in South Carolina in order to profit from the use of slaves, even though he was constantly complaining of their uselessness. On 30 March 1747 Boltzius recorded that one of Kieffer's slaves committed suicide, one of them died, and one tried to run away but was caught. His feet must have been bound too tightly, for both of them had to be amputated, thus greatly lessening his value. He was sold for a cow, which died.

By 27 January 1750 Habersham was arguing convincingly that the Salzburgers should buy some slaves and that Boltzius should use some at the mill, for the poor Salzburgers would not be able to live long without them. Except for the slaves of the Carolina-based Kieffers, the first two slaves in New Ebenezer were two rented by a Salzburger on 8 May 1750, probably from a Carolinian. The Salzburger wished to work them on Sunday, the only day he could rent them, but Boltzius insisted on upholding the law of the Sabbath.

By 17 July 1750 Christian Leimberger and other Salzburgers had earned enough money through lumbering to buy black labor to help them in their work. Some time before 14 January 1751 the shoemaker Matthias Zettler bought a black woman to help his wife in her silk business. The Zettlers christened the slave's child Sulamith and reared the child in a Christian way along with their own. When they wished to get rid of the surly mother yet keep the child, however, Boltzius read them the law on 15 March 1751 that parents and children were not to be separated. On 12 May of that year Zettler was still complaining of his uncontrollable slave woman. Boltzius said that slaves on the block in Charleston often warned would-be purchasers that they would run away.

On 27 September 1750 Jacob Caspar Walthour requested a grant for four hundred acres "setting forth that his Father had enabled Him to cultivate and improve the same" by giving him thirty pounds for a slave.[62] The grant system greatly stimulated the purchase of slaves. First, the grantee had land but no slaves. Then he bought a slave on credit, giving his improved land as collateral. Having a slave, he could request more land; then, having more land, he could get credit for another slave. It was probably by this method that the poor orphan Peter Sliterman (Schlechtermann) of Fort Argyle acquired six hundred acres and ten slaves by August 1771.[63]

Habersham remained the chief source of slaves for the Salzburgers, in part because he let them buy on credit, a failing they had learned from the other colonists. In April 1753 he brought a shipload of twenty-six blacks from St. Kitts and St. Christopher and fattened them for sale; Boltzius attended the auction and bought five slaves for £145. One of these bondsmen, a Catholic man named Thomas, could speak excellent English; but Boltzius saw little hope of converting the others. He was especially pleased with their performance when they rowed him back to Ebenezer. Six years later he and Rabenhorst bought a youth for thirty-five pounds, who would have brought forty pounds if he had not been so emaciated.[64] The following year a group of Salzburgers went down to Savannah and bought nine or ten more slaves.[65]

One of the first Germans in Georgia who owned a large number of slaves was Johann Hamm, who brought slaves from St. Christopher in the West Indies and proceeded to the slave colony of South Carolina. His German servant Wannemacher did not follow him there but remained behind in Georgia. Hamm bought five more slaves in Savannah on 18 October 1755 and sold fourteen slaves four days later. Subsequently, having become a "Gentleman," Hamm requested five hundred acres of land with the Germans at Black Creek near Pastor Lemke. He also requested a lot in Savannah, which was granted on 6 August 1755; yet two years later his five hundred acres had not yet been run out. He served as collector and assessor for Abercorn and Goshen in 1755 and also as surveyor of the highways.[66] Some of the indentured Palatines in Savannah also rose to the rank of "planter"; the term was gradually restricted to those farmers whose work was done by slaves. For example, Jacob Ihle had twelve slaves by 1771.[67]

Among the slave holders one might be surprised to find the Moravians' Swiss physician, Jean François Regnier, who returned to Georgia on 6 June 1769 with a wife and three slaves and received two hundred acres. After returning to Europe in 1738, when most of the Moravians left Georgia, he had gone to Surinam in South America and then to Pennsylvania, where he feuded with the Moravians.[68] Because his paper money had been burned in Savannah on 1 February 1773, the Council made it good on 29 September of that year.[69] By then Regnier seemed to have recovered from his religious zeal and insanity, for which his host, Conrad Beissel of Ephrata, had to confine him soon after his first arrival in America.[70]

During the Revolution slaves were a major form of booty, as mentioned by Colonel Friedrich von Porbeck, the Hessian commander at Savannah.[71] The Hessians, who felt less prejudice against blacks than many other whites did, recruited many of them into their service, mostly as drummers but also as packmen and grenadiers.[72] The labor of four hundred slaves was crucial in the successful defense of Savannah by the British in 1779. Like other slave-owners, the Salzburgers had to furnish slave labor for whichever government was in power during the Revolution. Because Zubly was a clergyman, his slaves were exempted from work on the roads, but Matthias Ash (Aschbacher) had to give over his slaves for public works in 1782.[73]

It has been mentioned that the Kieffers, as residents of South Carolina, owned slaves before slavery was permitted in Georgia. They truly tried to convert their slaves; one of the sons borrowed a primer from Boltzius on 14 May 1739 to try to teach his slave enough German to understand the catechism. On 11 April 1742 the young Kieffer came to church with his slave, who paid close attention even though he did not understand the language well.

In his journal entry for 17 October 1742 Boltzius repeated a discussion he had had with a blasphemous slave-owner in which he gave reasons why it was the man's Christian duty to convert his slaves. The slave-owner could merely repeat the standard arguments: the slaves could not comprehend Christianity, it would corrupt them, and so on. Boltzius never doubted the native intelligence of blacks. In his often-quoted *Questionnaire* of 1751 he wrote:

> To be sure, people have often told me that you cannot teach the Negroes anything, that they are stupid and disinclined to learn and that they take advantage of Christian and gentle treatment. But I consider all this a fiction of those people who take no trouble with the souls of these black people and do not wish to keep them in a Christian way with regard to food, clothing, and work. They are intelligent enough and can learn arts and crafts and even writing and mathematics, as is known of some in Carolina. It is also known that many Negro men and women of Christian and righteous masters have achieved the Christian religion and a righteous behavior in Christ.[74]

As late as 21 August 1750 Boltzius delayed accepting a plantation because he could not bring himself to buy slaves, not because he questioned their usefulness but because he questioned the morality of keeping them in bondage.

In his journal entry for 3 December 1752 Boltzius still contended that blacks were just as intelligent as whites; on 3 November of that year he advocated teaching the slaves German for their proper religious instruction.[75] Seven years later he repeated his conviction that blacks are just as intelligent as whites, and he regretted that they could speak neither English nor German. The English they acquired, now called Gullah, made it hard for Boltzius to convert them.[76]

The Salzburgers fulfilled their duty to convert their slaves and provide them with Christian nurture, for baptisms of blacks are recorded along with those of white children, as Lothar Tresp has shown and as is evident in the *Ebenezer Church Records*. It would appear that the first black child baptized in Georgia was baptized by Boltzius, not by Zouberbuhler as is usually believed. It was a child belonging to Theobald Kieffer, Jr., which was baptized on 30 March 1747. This was probably the same child who later took catechism instruction from Boltzius along with his master's children. When Muhlenberg visited Rabenhorst in 1774, he noted that the old minister's slave children came to his house every evening to pray with him.[77] According to Boltzius, the Rabenhorsts, who were childless, loved their slave twins as if they were their own children.[78] In 1760 Boltzius baptized two black girls and three black boys; by 1764 the number had risen to four girls and four boys.[79] When Boltzius baptized the child of a slave woman at the mill on 21 August 1760, he reminded the congregation that by nature black children were just as good as white children.[80] It was his policy that slave holders had to stand as godparents to their slave children and give them a Christian education. As a result, the black child owned by the Kieffers attended Sunday school along with their own white children.[81] Just as the blacks received the same baptism as the whites, they also merited identical funeral rites, as we see when Lemke held the funeral ceremony for Captain Kieffer's slave child on 10 June 1760.

Some of the Germans who could not afford slaves profited from slavery by serving as overseers or slave drivers. On 18 September 1737 Boltzius mentioned a German overseer from South Carolina who came to Ebenezer to attend Holy Communion; on 10 February 1738 he reported that Hans Michael Muggitzer had engaged himself as a slave driver and that Stephan Riedelsperger had probably done so, too. The renegade Ruprecht Zittrauer also became a slave driver, as Boltzius wrote on 24 May 1748. On 15 December 1751 Boltzius reported that Ebenezer had just received a soap boiler from Stuttgart who had served as a slave driver in South Carolina. On 15 August 1759 the widow of carpenter Hirsch married a slave driver from South Carolina named Johann Christoph Heintz. Conrad Fabre (no doubt Faber) and Matthias Zophi, who served Henry Laurens as overseers in 1769, were clearly German or Swiss. The slave driver Joseph Weatherly, mentioned by Betty Wood, may well have been a member of the Vetterli family that came over on the *Europa*.[82] On 10 February 1739, while still supporting the Trustees in their stand against slavery, Boltzius expressed his view that overseeing slaves was a very evil profession. Ordinarily, "only such people are used for this task as can be quite merciless with these poor slaves."

Even though German slave drivers were available, the widow Rabenhorst preferred to do without one. This seems amazing, in view of the allegation that a slave woman had tried to poison her and her husband. Perhaps the threat of employing a slave driver was sufficient to persuade her slaves to serve faithfully. On 26 September 1777 she wrote to Muhlenberg, saying that "My Negroes have behaved very well, and have been orderly and diligent. I have a good harvest of all crops, also a great deal of cotton for Negro clothing. That also was done by the Lord. I was a little afraid on account of them, but He has guided their hearts. I often wondered about it quietly; I will not be forced to hire a white man if they continue this way." She ended her letter saying that she had told her slaves that she had written Muhlenberg that they loved her and that they promised to behave well and be diligent in the future and that they sent him their love.[83] After her death two years later the slaves were sold, we hope as a group and to a good master. As we have seen, however, even if they remained on the plantation for a while, they were scattered during the Revolution.

The Military

Although German-speaking people played a significant role in the military life of colonial Georgia, they have been largely ignored by most historians. For example, in his otherwise excellent book *British Drums on the Southern Frontier*, Larry E. Ivers makes no mention whatever of the Swiss and Palatines, who constituted a large part of the local militia. For him, the fighting was done almost entirely by Englishmen and Scottish Highlanders, though he does make fleeting reference to the Salzburgers. Among the latter he wrongfully includes Captain Hermsdorf and the Dutch of Frederica; when he relates the death of Gabriel Bach, he uses the anglicized form of the name, Baugh. While he mentions that Lieutenant Francis's wife, who was murdered by the Spanish Indians at Mount Venture, was German,[84] he fails to recognize that the two soldiers who survived the massacre and captivity, Solomon Shad and Joseph Ubjer (Salomo Schad and Josef Upshaw), were also Germans. As we have seen, Upshaw arrived in 1738 with Captain Thomson, and Schad arrived in 1741 on the *Europa*. In 1747 Schad served as a rower for one month and twenty-six days for £1.10. He died possessed of a comfortable estate. Dr. Hirsh, the surgeon with Captain Mackay's troop of foot mentioned by Ivers, would appear to have been a German.[85] *Hirsch*, the German word for "stag," was a popular name, which was present in Ebenezer in the persons of the Swabian Johann Michael Hirsch and his widow, Barbara, who married the slave driver Heintz.

While no German units served under Oglethorpe in Georgia, many of his soldiers were German. This is understandable in view of the compulsory military service in nearly all German states, in which a surplus of trained officers and men were unemployed during the brief intervals between wars. Marlborough's spectacular victories in Central Europe had been fought to a large extent by German auxiliaries rented from their greedy rulers and by German career officers attracted by the high British pay. One such officer was Adolf von Hermsdorf, who came over with the Moravians and volunteered for service with Oglethorpe. We have seen that the Swiss laborer Abraham Grüning served at Frederica and rose to the rank of captain at Cartagena. Although de Brahm had been a captain in the Imperial army, he preferred to serve in Georgia as a surveyor and engineer rather than as a line officer. The soldier Kikar, who took ill near Ebenezer, was from Hamburg.

When Charles Dempsey, the Trustees' emissary to the governor of Florida, went to St. Augustine in 1736, he was accompanied by von Hermsdorf and Major Richard as far as the boat landing in Florida, where von Hermsdorf remained behind. Later, when Major Richard sent a communiqué to von Hermsdorf at the landing, it was in the German language.[86] The two men may have used German because they thought the Spaniards could not read it, but even this would indicate that Major Richard could write German. Subsequently, Oglethorpe put von Hermsdorf in charge of Fort St. George. Unable to trust his mutinous men, von Hermsdorf abandoned the fort, much to Oglethorpe's annoyance, and fled back, very sick, to the Moravians to escape his commander's wrath.[87]

Oglethorpe had fought under Eugene of Savoy against the Turks in Eastern Europe, where there were many Swiss and German troops and where German was perhaps the language best understood by the enlisted men and the horses. Before Boltzius or von Reck found time to learn English, they appear to have conversed rather freely with Oglethorpe; this suggests that Oglethorpe had acquired a functional command of German while serving on the Continent. According to Jean-Pierre Pury, Oglethorpe loved the Germans.[88] This may help explain why, after returning from Georgia and being accused of treason for his leniency toward the Scottish rebels, Oglethorpe served for some years under Frederick the Great.[89]

It would seem that, except for Oglethorpe, the only prominent Englishmen in Georgia who could speak German were the storekeeper William Russell and James Habersham's business partner, Francis Harris. Although Stephens depended on German labor at Bewlie and was heartily concerned with the welfare of the Trustees' Palatine servants, he was too much of an Englishman to learn their language or even to give their names in his journal.

As Boltzius reported on 14 April 1740, the shoemaker Jacob Reck of Purysburg recruited ten inhabitants of Ebenezer for Jacques Richard's polyglot battalion that served at the siege of St. Augustine. He almost engaged the Rauner woman; but Boltzius refused to accept her children into the orphanage during her absence, as he reported on 6 May 1740. While army women usually served as housekeepers, cooks, nurses, and canteen women, a German woman named Maria Ludwig, but affectionately called Molly Pitcher, actually operated a cannon at the battle of Monmouth in the Revolution. Boltzius put great pressure on his parishioners not to join the St. Augustine expedition. On 12 April 1740 he expressed the view that "righteous people do not let themselves be used for this purpose, but rather those who like to roam around and find pleasure in such a life." As a result, none of the true Salzburgers enlisted except for Zettler, who was forced to do so by his master, Jacob Reck. The only parishioners who volunteered were the Swabian Bach and those Palatine servants who hoped to redeem themselves in the short period of four months.

On the Florida campaign there was a large contingent of Swiss and Germans from Savannah and Hampstead, as one might expect in view of the enthusiasm Stephens observed there at military musters. When Major Richard tried to take one of Gronau's rowers, his plan was thwarted by a rugged tithingman who seized one of Richard's men and held him as hostage until Gronau's rower was released.[90] After the unsuccessful siege, the Dutch volunteers had to go to Charleston to collect their pay in person. Fearing that this was a ploy of the Carolina authorities to induce the veterans to remain in South Carolina, the Trustees sent Noble Jones to chaperon them and bring them back to Georgia, as Stephens relates.[91] Since the authorities in Charleston were responsible for compensating the veterans, they must have made and kept a careful list of their names, yet no such list is known. There are various references to the service performed by the Dutch in Florida, but usually these do not include names. For example, on 14 April 1741 a young German in Savannah asked Boltzius for Holy Communion, having been sick ever since the campaign.[92]

When the threat of Spanish invasion ended in 1742, the Salzburgers' good friend and neighbor William Ewen wrote: "Mr. Boltzius offer'd his People to come down with what arms they had there, and join the English and Dutch that were in Savannah, they would then have made about two hundred men, who, under the conduct of a good Commander might have repulsed six or seven hundred of the enemy, if any had come."[93]

Although Boltzius had tried to dissuade his parishioners from serving in the siege of St. Augustine, he surely approved of defending Georgia. Had the Spaniards succeeded in their purpose, the Salzburgers would have once again been exiles, for the Spaniards' purpose was to devastate Georgia by "sacking and burning all the towns, posts, and plantations and settlements."[94] Having played the role of Moses for so long, perhaps Boltzius would have enjoyed playing Joshua and leading the armies of the Lord in person.

Soon after reaching Georgia, Oglethorpe organized a troop of Rangers, or mounted scouts, to keep an eye on the Indians allied with the Spaniards.[95] Some of these were Germans, as we have seen in the case of the sick tailor-apprentice Kikar of Hamburg. We have also seen that Gabriel Bach was serving as a Ranger when killed by the Florida Indians. Gradually other German colonists joined the Rangers, such as two unnamed Germans who visited Ebenezer on 25 December 1742. Eventually the Germans supplied a high percentage of the unit. Seven of the Salzburgers' first horses were supplied to help them in the task of patrolling their area. On 13 May 1742 they received the trappings for their horses, and Thomas Bichler was made captain of the troop.

One of the Trustees' main purposes in limiting the size of most grants and restricting inheritance to tail-male was to provide the largest possible number of yeoman farmers to protect their homesteads, and no time was lost in organizing a militia. Influenced by the theories of the popular social theorist James Hamilton, the Trustees thought that land could be best defended by those who owned and occupied it. We have seen that one of Boltzius's main grievances against Vat was the large number of men he (at Oglethorpe's command) demanded for standing watch. When the militia was mustered in Savannah on 29 June 1742, Stephens noted that the men of Highgate, Hampstead, Acton, and Vernonburg consisted of twenty-seven "hearty and resolute" men and that the Trustees' German servants made up another body of twenty-two.[96] As we have seen, to command the foreign militia Stephens chose Pierre Morel of Highgate, who could speak the "Dutch and French" languages. After attending another muster nearly a year later with Morel, Stephens wrote: "Having a while since committed the Charge of our German and Swiss Settlers, at Vernonburgh and Acton, to Mr. Peter Morelle who talked those Languages well, being Born a Swiss, and Bred a Soldier, and looked on by us as a Man of Resolution withall Interested in the Colony by Tenure of Land at High Gate in his own Right, as well as a Freehold Lot in Town in Right of his Son, I thought none so well qualified for that Service."[97]

On 4 May 1743 Stephens thought that "Vernonburgh and Acton can Muster near as many effective Men as Savannah, for the Defence of this Country." While reviewing a muster on 18 June of the same year, he found that the "Out Settlers at Vernonburgh, Acton, Hampstead and Highgate, outnumbered the Freeholders and Spare men in Savannah." He also observed that the foreigners distinguished themselves in firing "their Pieces singly, and afterwards in Volleys."[98] Whereas, according to Stephens, the Germans and Swiss of Acton and Vernonburg could "find the alternate use of the Sword & plough share," those at Savannah would not work as long as there were so many opportunities to enter some form of military service.[99] It seems that, at the time, military service was the chief business in Georgia.

Like the other inhabitants of Georgia, those of Ebenezer had to perform military service, which was required of all males between sixteen and sixty years of age. In a letter of 16 February 1755 to Urlsperger, Boltzius wrote that, as of that date, his parishioners were permitted to elect their own officers and to drill at Ebenezer every two or three months.[100] Military service became especially burdensome during the Cherokee disturbances of 1760, when the men of Bethany, Ebenezer, and Goshen had to draw lots to patrol for two weeks at a time.[101] We have seen that compulsory military service was the cause, or at least the excuse, for the Moravians' abandoning Georgia.

While most of the German servicemen during the colonial period were enlisted men, perhaps for linguistic reasons, there were some exceptions. On 30 September 1746 Habersham wrote to Verelst concerning an "Alexander Linder, Son of Linder of Pourisbourgh" who "is a Cadet in G. Oglethorpes Regiment at Frederica." Stephens referred to the cadet's father as "Mr. Lyndar, A Gentleman of Purysburgh well known."[102] We have seen that Abraham Grüning rose to the rank of captain. As soon as Georgia declared independence, the German element filled its due quota of the commissioned ranks.

In addition to combat service, the Georgia Germans did their share of work on fortifications. Already on 17 June 1736 Oglethorpe reported that he had sent "a Detachment of Germans, English & Americans to build another Fort upon Saint George's Point."[103] We have seen that many Vernonburgers neglected their farms in order to work on fortifications. One of these, a Catholic turned Reformed, turned Moravian, turned Lutheran, who had been working around Savannah, had been saved by God from drowning, as he related to Boltzius on 12 May 1747. The Salzburger Ruprecht Zittrauer also worked at a fort south of Savannah, as Boltzius reported on 24 May 1748.

Notes

Abbreviations

AG	Samuel Urlsperger, *Americanisches Ackerwerck Gottes*
AN	Samuel Urlsperger, *Ausführliche Nachrichten*
CGHS	*Collections of the Georgia Historical Society*
CO	Colonial Office Papers, British Public Record Office
CR	Candler, *Colonial Records*
DGB	Coleman and Gurr, *Dictionary of Georgia Biography*
DR	Jones, *Detailed Reports*
GHQ	*Georgia Historical Quarterly*
MA	Missionsarchiv, Franckesche Stiftungen, Halle, Germany
RR	Candler, *Revolutionary Records*
SCHM	*South Carolina Historical Magazine*
SPCK	Society for Promoting Christian Knowledge, London
UA	Unitätsarchiv, Archiv der Brüder-Unität, Herrnhut, Germany

Preface

1. Adalbert Stifter, *Gesammelte Werke* (Bielefeld, 1956), 3:18.

Chapter 1: The European Background

1. The chieftain was not named Hermann, as German poets would have us believe, but probably Siegward or Siegfried. He appears to have been the historical personality behind the Siegfried legends.

2. *Cellarius* (cellar master), *cuparius* (barrel maker), *cupellus* (bucket), *faber*

(smith), *murus* (wall), *matiarius* (sausage maker), *tegulum* (tile), *torcularius* (wine-presser), *winum* + *caupo* (wine + merchant). The English and German agent suffix *er* is derived from Latin *arius*.

3. Perhaps the most scathing of these denunciations were by the thirteenth-century poet Walther von der Vogelweide.

4. The history and geography of the Palatinate is well covered by the contributions to *Pfälzische Landeskunde*.

5. Trautz 8. Some of the French names, if borne by Württembergers, may have been inherited from Waldensian ancestors.

6. A Widow Owens of Ebenezer was the granddaughter of Huguenots who had been expelled from France and had become German Reformed (Universität Tübingen, Tübinger Kapsel 714).

7. Hacker, *Kurpfälzische Auswanderer* 48. For careful documentation of many incidents of religious persecution, see Hacker, *Auswanderungen aus Rheinpfalz* 78–80.

8. CO, class 5, vol. 609, pt. 2, pp. 238–39, 361–363v; *CR* 21:389–92, 406.

9. *CR* 21:407–13. See their supplication, in French, of 24 May 1736 to Walpole (*CR* 21:99). For the religious situation in the Palatinate, see Trautz 19–20.

10. In 1733 the Trustees published a promotional pamphlet entitled *Reasons for Establishing the Colony of Georgia*, edited by Benjamin Martyn. The title page stated that Georgia would afford employment and support "to great Numbers of our own Poor, as well as foreign persecuted Protestants." Rodney M. Baine and Phinizy Spalding have proved that this pamphlet was based on Oglethorpe's unpublished manuscript "Some Account of the Design of the Trustees for establishing Colonys in America" of 1731.

11. CO 5.639.2.252; *CR* 1:287; *CR* 21:397.

12. The Palatine emigration is well told by Knittel, as well as by Yoder, *Pennsylvania*.

13. Most history books state that the Palatines had met the Schohari Indians at London, but chronology disproves this.

14. An excellent summary of this Palatine emigration, with bibliography, is found in Trautz. Interesting documents concerning the Rhinelanders who immigrated to Pennsylvania are found in Yoder, *Rheinland Emigrants*.

15. See Wust, "Palatines," "Wm. Bird II," and "Emigration."

16. This name was given by John Greenleaf Whittier in his poem about the ship. Its true name was the *Princess Augusta*. See Wust, "Emigration" 40–42. Johann Heinrich Keppele sailed in 1738 on the *Charming Nancy*, which lost three fourths of its passengers to typhus (Trautz 25).

17. See Rupp 138; Howard M. Chapin, "The Discovery of the Real Palatine Ship," *Rhode Island Historical Society Collections* 16, no. 2 (1923): 33–38.

18. *AN* 3:590.

19. *AN* 3:635. This may have been the *Friend's Goodwill*, a Palatine ship that, as Klaus Wust has written me, left Rotterdam in 1749.

20. Mittelberger.

21. A good account of the expulsion is given in Florey.

22. *CR* 22, pt. 1, pp. 144–45.

23. *Verzeichnis der zu freien Kauf feilstehenden Güter der Emigranten* (Salzburg, 1733).

24. See excellent reproductions in Marsch.

25. See Oglethorpe's plans for Georgia in Baine and Spalding.

26. *CR* 32:291. See note 10 above.

27. *CR* 1:77–78.

28. *CR* 1:78–79. See also pp. 137–41. The instructions sent to Urlsperger on 12 Sept. 1733 differed slightly in wording toward the end (*CR* 32:222–23).

29. CO 5.666, p. 4.

30. Typical of their publications was *An Account of the Sufferings of the Persecuted Protestants in the Archbishopric of Saltzburg* (London, 1732). This and other accounts are found in the DeRenne Collection of the University of Georgia's Hargrett Collection. See *Catalogue of the Wymberley Jones DeRenne Georgia Library* (Wormsloe, Ga, 1931) 1:11–49.

31. Newman 42–45. A list of the transport, written in French, is given in *CR* 20:505–6, English translation 507–8.

32. Egmont 20.

33. *Georgia, Oder: Kurtze Nachricht Von dem Christlichen Vorhaben Der Königlich-Englischen Herren Commissarien.*

34. Newman 336. The passenger list is reproduced in *DR* 10:130–33.

35. The journey from Augsburg to Rotterdam is well summarized by Urlsperger in his introduction to the *Ausführliche Nachrichten* (*DR* 1:7–10).

36. Boltzius also wrote his name as Bolzius, but in both cases it was pronounced Boltsius. He relates his and Gronau's journey from Halle to Rotterdam in *DR* 1:25–30. His commission from the Trustees is preserved in *CR* 32:200–201.

37. For vital statistics on Boltzius and Gronau, see Winde 157–74, and Jones, "In Memoriam."

38. *CR* 1:137. The journey from Rotterdam to Savannah is described in *DR* 1:30–59.

39. Salley 97, 101, 104. Cf. "Et de mensibus quidem . . . julium heuuimanoth, augustum aranmanoth, septembrem uuitumanoth, octobrem uuindumanoth, novembrem herbistmanoth." Einhard, *Vita Karoli Magni*, cap. 29. It will be seen that there had been some changes in terms and sequence.

40. For a good history of Switzerland, see Dürrenmatt.

41. This did not betray religious bigotry on the part of the British, who accepted Jews and Baptists. They were afraid that the Papists would aid and abet their French or Spanish coreligionists.

42. Dürrenmatt 301–2.

43. One of the most successful of these pamphlets was Josua Kocherthal's. Despite his praise of South Carolina, Kocherthal soon led a party to New York.

44. For a good account of these rascals, see Voigt, "German" 14–20. For the punishments they received, see Faust, "Swiss" 35.

45. A good example is in Faust, "Unpublished" 22–28.

46. "Hoffe auf den Herrn und thue Gutes; bleibe im Lande und nähre dich redlich." The King James version states a fact, not an injunction: "Trust in the Lord, and do good; so shalt thou dwell in the land and verily shalt thou be fed."

47. Staatsarchiv Zurich, Mandatensammlung, Signatur III, AAb1. For one of the earlier mandates, see Schelbert 245–47. A similar mandate was issued by Basel (Faust, "Documents . . ." 128–30). Many such rescripts against emigration issued by the various petty rulers in the Palatinate are reproduced in Hacker, *Auswanderungen aus Rheinpfalz*, see Faust, "Swiss Emigration" 40–41.

48. A complete list of (legal) emigrants from Canton Zurich from 1734 to 1744 is found in the Zurich Staatsarchiv A.174. They amounted to 2,310 persons.

49. CO 5.636.1.10; *CR* 20:115. These emigrants belonged to a party recruited by the questionable pastor Moritz Götschi of Zurich, see Pfister.

50. Saunders 4:18.

51. *CR* 20:328–29 (new). Original French in *CR* 20:196–200 (unpub.).

52. Pury and three other Swiss composed a little propagandistic pamphlet about South Carolina, titled *Description Abrogée de l'Etat présent de la Caroline Meridionale, nouvelle Edition avec des Eclaircissemens*. This was also published in German by Samuel Benjamin Walther in Leipzig in 1734.

53. Noted by Boltzius (*AN* 3:937).

54. Purry.

55. Meriwether cites Henry Smith 201, but Smith mentions no Salzburgers and merely repeats a report of November 1734 that some Piedmontese were expected later. Meriwether renders Chiffelle as Chisselle.

56. For the efforts to prevent, alter, or contradict all favorable magazine articles, see Faust, "Swiss" 41–42.

57. *CR* 20:607–8 (unpub.). The new edition of this volume of the *Colonial Records of Georgia* gives only the contemporary English translation, which contains some inaccuracies.

58. *CR* 20:333–34.

59. Robbins, "Swiss and German" 46–47.

60. Wesley 89.

61. Faust, "Unpublished" 15–21.

62. CO 5.636.3.331v–332v.
63. CO 5.636.3.329–329v; *CR* 20:332–34 (new); *CR* 20:330 (new).
64. For biography of Tobler, see Türler 8:4.
65. Newman 556–57; *DR* 4:60.
66. Egmont 265. The name also appears as Zauberbuhler and Zouberbuhler.
67. *DR* 4:69. Steiner wrote to his brother-in-law on 6 Nov. 1738 that the Salzburgers had had a good harvest and were happy and that he had forty-eight acres and several cows (*AN* 1:2045). Another of his letters was excerpted in Urlsperger's *Zuverlässiges Sendschreiben* 10–13.
68. Hans Trachsler, *Kurtz-Verfasste Reiss-Beschreibung* (Zurich, 1738); Voigt, "Swiss"; Schelbert 116–17, 145; Faust "Documents." For the Council of Bern's attempt to discourage emigration, see Faust, "Swiss" 29.
69. For his account of his possessions, see Schelbert 332–35.
70. Robbins, "John Tobler"; Schelbert 332–35.
71. *AN* 3:916–21.
72. Five years after its founding, a certain Dr. Hilti wrote a negative and sarcastic description of the "world-famous and beautiful" city (Schelbert 328–32).
73. Saunders 4:159–62.
74. For a brief history of Württemberg, see Weller and Weller.
75. A medieval song claimed that "Quando Suevus nascitur / Tunc in cribro ponitur / Dicit ei pater / Simul atque mater / Foramina quot cribro / Hoc ordine sunt miro / Tot terras circumire / Debes, sic vitam finire."
76. Edict of 7 July 1768, by Joseph II, State Archives, Bremen, section A2, no. 351. See van Ham. For the efforts of the Ulm magistrates to discourage emigration to South Carolina and Georgia, see Wiegandt 99–102.
77. Prinzinger 32–33.
78. The Swabian dialect is also reflected in present-day Milwaukee: the name of the Goethe Hotel is pronounced Gaytee, and Professor Schroeder of that city pronounces his name Shrader.
79. *AG* 242, 244.

Chapter 2: Arrival in Georgia

1. *CR* 1:73; 3:15.
2. *CR* 3:15.
3. *CR* 2:393. It is possible, however, that in this case a comma was intended after *Swiss*.
4. British Public Record Office, State Papers, George III, vol. 27, no. 4.
5. Dürrenmatt 265–75.
6. Faust and Brumbaugh 1:37.

7. Küffer, from Latin *cuparius*, was pronounced and written in most South German dialects as Kieffer, just as Kübler was written Kiebler.

8. *DR* 1:60, 65. See also p. 70.

9. UA R.14 A 6, 1, pp. 100, 103.

10. *DR* 1:141–42; *CR* 2:130.

11. UA R.14 A 2, 16, p. 55. The Bohemians refused to go because von Reck could not provide them with a Czech-speaking minister (CO 5.637.2.215–16).

12. UA R.14 A 2, 18, p. 21.

13. Reck and Boltzius 19–20; CO 5.637.1.76v.

14. Reese, *Our First Visit* 50; *CR* 20:170.

15. Reck and Boltzius 21.

16. *CR* 20:52 (new); Reese, *Our First Visit* 52.

17. *CR* 20:52 (new).

18. "Then Samuel took a stone, and set it between Mizpah and Shen, and called the name of it Ebenezer, saying, Hitherto hath Jehovah helped us."

19. *CR* 20:191 (new).

20. *CR* 20:493.

21. Newman 46, 56, 486, 489–92, 497–502, 538–42, 578–83; *CR* 20:223–27, 359–67 (new).

22. CO 5.636.1.18.

23. *CR* 2:111. For efforts to recruit Carinthians, see *CR* 20:469–77.

24. See diagram of their quarters superimposed on picture of vessel in Hvidt 57, and Jones, *Salzburger Saga*, pl. 8.

25. Stephens 1:16. In his entry for 27 April 1741 Egmont wrote that "One Theary alias Terry a Frenchman by extraction but who has been sixteen years in England" wished to go to Georgia (*CR* 5:505). On 10 Sept. 1741 the Trustees appointed Mr. John Theary alias Terry recorder at Frederica (*CR* 5:545).

26. See Jones, "Secret Diary."

27. CO 5.638.2.186.

28. See Boltzius's letter of 28 Feb. 1736 (CO 5.638.1 and 2.196–197v). Oglethorpe dignified this letter with a detailed reply on 16 March 1736 (*CR* 21:132–33). See also his letter to Causton of 17 March 1736 (CO 5.638.2.230).

29. CO 5.638.2.149, 232–42. See Oglethorpe's letter of 16 March 1736 to Vat (CGHS 3:22).

30. See Oglethorpe's letter of 16 March 1736 to Wesley (CO 5.638.2.235; CGHS 3:22–23).

31. CO 5.638.2.149–149v. For Oglethorpe's reaction, see p. 186. See also pp. 232–33.

32. CO 5.638.3.302–3; *CR* 21:169–72 (French), 172–75 (English). See also his letter of 7 March to Oglethorpe (*CR* 21:127–28 [French], 129–30 [English]).

33. CO 5.638.3.304.

34. CO 5.638.2.237. See also p. 239; *CR* 21:131–32.

35. *CR* 21:134. See also Oglethorpe's letter of 16 March 1736 to Vat (*CR* 21:131) and Verelst's letter of 17 March 1736 (MA 5.A.3.54).

36. CO 5.638.2.241–42; *CR* 21:136–37. See CGHS 3:25–26.

37. CO 5.638.3.302v; *CR* 21:174. See his promise of 7 March 1736 (CO 5.638.2.233).

38. See Hvidt; Jones, "Commissary von Reck's Report."

39. *DR* 3:185.

40. CO 5.666, p. 114.

41. Jones, "Von Reck's Second Report," 332. David Nitschmann claimed on 17 Sept. 1736 that von Reck had come to the Moravians "sick and miserable" and that he departed on 10 October (UA R.14 A 6d, 7, pp. 443, 445).

42. *CR* 21:88, 90, 640.

43. *CR* 21:227, 489, 493; CO 5.640.2.30.

44. Pastor Quincy also complained that Jones had laid out the glebe lands in Savannah in sterile pine barrens (CO 5.637.1.117). It was Jones who made the map of Ebenezer, which von Reck referred to as "le plan de Mr. Jones" (CO 5.638.2.232).

45. CO 5.639.3.376. Ross was sometimes called Rose (*CR* 2:444; 6:4). On 24 June 1740 Boltzius rightly blamed the lack of success in farming on the granting of land without regard to its quality.

46. Jones, "Pastor Boltzius."

47. CO 5.639.1.34–35; *CR* 21:245–47; *CR* 21:488–89.

48. CO 5.637.1.40–40v; *CR* 20:338–39 (unpub.). As the previously cited letter to Lord Harrington suggests, Thomson maintained a good image among the Swiss (see Chapter 1).

49. This fascinating story is told in documents in J. Franklin Jameson, *Privateering and Piracy in the Colonial Period* (New York, 1970), 337–566. After years of effort, the Spanish captain finally won his case in the New York courts, but the opposition appealed. Myerhoffer had been wrecked on the coast of Yucatan with Caleb Davis, a rather questionable merchant and privateer resident in Savannah. He may have been the "German" smuggler mentioned by Boltzius on 16 Oct. 1750, who had his own ship.

50. *CR* 2:86, 88. Bishop Spangenberg, one of the Moravians on the ship, referred to all the other passengers as "Swiss" (UA R.14 A 6a, 5–7, p. 117).

51. *CR* 29:122.

52. *CR* 2:101–2.

53. *CR* 32:473; Coulter and Saye 40; *CR* 2:103; Coulter and Saye 24. To judge from a letter of 30 April 1735, the *James* would appear to have belonged to Simon & Co. (CO 5.636.2.185). Although Adelhait (in English, Adelaide) is usually feminine, Adelhait Hoffmann appears to have been a man.

54. *DR* 2:113; *CR* 2:119. The passenger list is reproduced in *DR* 10:137–38.
55. *CR* 29:143. Daubuz also appears in the records as Daubas.
56. *CR* 32:473.
57. For the history of Romansh, see Robert Henry Billigmeier, *A Crisis in Swiss Pluralism* (The Hague, 1979). Dialect map on p. 7.
58. *CR* 29:148; Coulter and Saye 45. In German the inhabitants of Grisons are Graubündtner, or just Bündtner.
59. *CR* 29:148. Captain Horner, the master of the ship, certified that the Grisons were Protestant (*CR* 2:86).
60. Egmont attests to this (Coulter and Saye 52). The name is erroneously written Fayssoux (*CR* 29:148).
61. *CR* 29:151. See also pp. 147–48.
62. *CR* 21:63.
63. Coulter and Saye 45.
64. *CR* 5:554.
65. *CR* 5:319, 354–555.
66. Coulter and Saye 45.
67. *CR* 29:151; 23:275.
68. For good accounts of the Moravian Church, see J. Taylor, *History of the Moravian Church* (Bethlehem, 1967), and Helmut Beck, *Brüder in vielen Völkern* (Erlangen, 1981).
69. August the Strong converted to Catholicism in order to become king of Poland.
70. A copy of the exceedingly long and wordy grant is found in the Moravian Archives in Herrnhut (UA R.14 A 1, 16; 2, 41). This entire venture is copiously covered in UA R.14 A 1–10, in German, Latin, and French, often in duplicate and sometimes in triplicate.
71. *CR* 2:81, 92; Egmont 73.
72. For the conditions of the contract, see UA R.14 A 1, 21–35.
73. UA R.14 A 2, 44b. He also brought a very warm letter of introduction from Oglethorpe (UA R.14 A 2, 45).
74. CO 5.636.3.225–26. A copy of the daily allowance of provisions survives in the Moravian Archives in Herrnhut (UA R.14 A 2, 44b). Captain Thomson was now a merchant and let others, such as Captain Horner, command his ship.
75. UA R.14 A 3, 47. Spangenberg was named bishop in 1744.
76. *CR* 20:440 (new).
77. UA R.14 A 1, 17.
78. *CR* 29:91–92.
79. A list of these Moravians is found in *DR* 10:135–37.
80. This was noted by A. G. Voigt in *The Lutheran Quarterly* (Gettysburg) 27 (1897):370–76.
81. UA R.14 A, no. 5.

82. UA R.14 A 281.
83. UA R.14 A 6a, 6, pp. 446–47.
84. CO 5.666, p. 43; *CR* 2:82; *CR* 29:79–80. Spangenberg understood the surveyor's name to be Johnsen (UA R.14 A 6a, 57, p. 148), which Fries (72–78) rendered as Johnson.
85. The Moravians' Georgia sojourn is well told in Fries.
86. Egmont 215.
87. *CR* 4:394–95; *DR* 5:225; *DR* 8:163.
88. Egmont 236.
89. UA R.14 A 1, 30.
90. UA R.14 A 9a, 4. For other letters and reports about this endeavor, see 9 a–d.
91. *CR* 29:478.
92. Fries 188–89; *CR* 29:478.
93. UA R.14 A 1, 28. Nearly a century later, however, the Moravians were successful among the Cherokees in the mountains of Georgia.
94. *CR* 29:407, 449; Egmont 303.
95. See Benjamin Martyn's letter to the Moravians dated 23 Sept. 1737 (UA R.14 A 1, 29).
96. CO 5.639.2.195–96; *CR* 21:364–65. A copy is in the Moravian Archives in Herrnhut (UA R.14 A 2, 69).
97. UA R.14 A 2, 70b. Many years later Oglethorpe sent a letter on their behalf (UA R.14 A 1, 38; A 2, 72).
98. *CR* 21:364. This error seems to have occurred on the original petition, a copy of which is preserved in Herrnhut (UA R.14 A 1, 38).
99. CO 5.639.2.266–67.
100. *CR* 21:404–5; 29:452; 30:4; 2:252.
101. Fries 221–24, 239; *DR* 8:4; *CR* 2:252.
102. *CR* 5:374.
103. UA R.14 A 1, 3, pp. 308–9.
104. UA R.14 A 2, p. 62.
105. UA R.14 A 8, pp. 384–88.
106. Stephens 1:116, 186; 2:120.
107. See Gerhard Reichel, "Die Entstehung einer Zinzendorffeindlichen Partei in Halle und Wernigerode," *Zeitschrift für Kirchengeschichte* 23 (1902):549–92, esp. 560–64.
108. Holtstaller and Dester are probably corruptions of Hoffstätter and Textor (Latin for Weber). Elsewhere Holtstaller is called Holsteter (*CR* 6:213), and Dester is called Peter Tester (*CR* 25:53) and Peter Deshter (*CR* 3:426). Oglethorpe ordered "Deshter the Palatine" to instruct Spangenberg how to "cultivate his Land" and also to serve as an interpreter (UA R.14 A 2, p. 45).
109. *CR* 2:258, 261; Egmont 308.

110. CO 5.640.2.240.
111. Faust and Brumbaugh 2:38.
112. Bryan 111.
113. Ibid.; *CR* 1:404, 405; *CR* 2:406.
114. *CR* 1:138. Morel wrote his name with one *l* (CO 5.639.2.145).
115. Stephens 1:101; 2:119.
116. *CR* 6:80; *DR* 6:106.
117. Reese, *Clamorous* 153.
118. CO 5.641.2.439–439v. Meyer fled to South Carolina but later surrendered in Savannah (Stephens 2:265).
119. CO 5.641.2.442v–445; *CR* 30:628–29.
120. CO 5.641.2.444; Stephens 2:265; *CR* 24:323–324; Stephens 2:147, 157; *CR* 24:313, 323–28; *CR* 30:629.
121. CO 5.636.2.197v; 666, p. 38. See index to *DR*, vols. 2–3, also *CR* 20:222–23; *CR* 29:71.
122. *CR* 29:71; *CR* 20:62; Jones and Exley 99.
123. *DR* 6:81, 106–9. The real name was Staud or Staude.
124. This church penance is carefully recorded in *DR* 7:31–32.
125. *CR* 35:491; *CR* 28, pt. 1, p. 9.
126. *DR* 6:332, 259.
127. Reese, *Clamorous* 115.
128. The soldier was named Shannon. The doctor (Mazzique) claimed to be named Masig and to hail from Cologne (*DR* 6:171).
129. *CR* 35:52; 2:188.
130. *DR* 4:129; 5:239–40. Faust and Brumbaugh 2:47.
131. CO 5.640.3.430.
132. CO 5.640.3.433–35.
133. *DR* 6:331–32. The spelling Shanbacker for Schönbacher suggests Swabian influence.
134. Coulter and Saye 53.
135. The Gaelic name Donald must have been a corruption of a German name, unless the Meyers' son was renamed in honor of a Scot.
136. *CR* 30:620.
137. *CR* 5:591; 22, pt. 1, p. 16.
138. CO 5.640.3.434v; *CR* 22, pt. 2, p. 292.
139. CO 5.640.3.435; *CR* 2:328; *DR* 6:331; *CR* 30:247; *CR* 22, pt. 2, p. 293.
140. Margaret Davis Cate, *Frederica-Georgia: Town Lot Ownership* (Frederica, Ga., n.d.).
141. CO 5.641.1.4v; CGHS 3:113. On 29 June 1741 Oglethorpe again wrote that the machinations of the Spaniards could be thwarted by "the importation of Germans and married recruits" (CGHS 3:117).

142. *CR* 5:171.

143. *CR* 5:283; 22, pt. 2, p. 353. Shats is listed elsewhere in the records as John Peter Shantze (*DR* 6:333).

144. CGHS 3:90; *CR* 22, pt. 2, p. 251. On the *Loyal Judith* on 21 Sept. 1741 were "43 Highlanders, two of whom speak some English" (*CR* 5:549).

145. *CR* 1:446. Heron mentions a William Ruf, not otherwise recorded, who raised a quantity of tobacco.

146. *DR* 8:318–19. The striking thing revealed in this letter was Oglethorpe's ability to occupy himself completely with other people's welfare. Here we see his concern not only for the Salzburgers but also for the lad Bishop and for the spiritual needs of the Germans at Frederica. A reader would hardly guess that he had taken out time from the pressing business mentioned in other letters of the period (CGHS 3:112–18).

147. *DR* 2:194. On 26 Aug. 1735 Bishop wrote a very affectionate and florid letter to his parents praising Boltzius's kindness (CO 5.638.1.122).

148. CO 5.640.2.468; CGHS 3:92.

149. Information about Driessler comes chiefly from Winde 174–77.

150. *CR* 24:203; 30:573; 24:221. See Boltzius's letter of 24 Feb. 1744 (CO 5.641.2.289v–290).

151. *AN* 3:6; Stephens 2:75–76. Driessler often complained to Boltzius, as on 3 March 1745 (MA IV Fach J 10).

152. MA 4.C.1.

153. *CR* 2:460; 30:631; 5:706, 716.

154. *CR* 24:266.

155. *CR* 25:121.

156. *CR* 24:406–7; *CR* 24:254–55.

157. *CR* 25:20, 22, 110. The name Sutor is Latin for Schumacher.

158. Stephens 2:265–66; *CR* 25:20–23.

159. *CR* 25:34; 24:266.

160. *CR* 24:255; *CR* 4Sup:95, 97, 107, 176–77.

161. This was Jacob Ruf, Jr. His father, Jacob Ruf, Sr., testified on Colonel Heron's behalf when the latter was accused of buying up supplies and selling them at an unjust mark-up. He signed as Jacob Rouff (*CR* 36:429).

162. *CR* 24:313; 30:629.

163. *CR* 24:402; 5:634. Stephens 1:19, 21, 23, 25. Stephens consistently called him Holzendroff, which may have been correct.

164. Henry Smith 216.

165. *CR* 2:254; Egmont 339.

166. *CR* 5:250–54; 2:306; 5:50,287; 29:433; 2:306.

167. *CR* 5:254, 289–90; 2:314.

168. CO 5.641.1.12–13; *CR* 2:313; *CR* 5:466–67.

169. Charleston Courthouse, Mesne Conveyance Records. It is of interest that the attorney involved was the Reverend Bartholomew Henri Himeli of Charleston, surely a Swiss. See also *CR* 8:451.

170. See Crane; Knox; Newton Mereness, *Travels in the American Colonies* (New York, 1966), 239–40; Samuel Williams, *Early Travels in Tennessee* (Johnson City, Tenn., 1928). According to the Indian trader Joseph Watson of Savannah, who had lived among the Cherokees, Prieber was a doctor of law from Upper Saxony (*AG* 147). He states that Prieber's dissertation bore the title "Usu Doctrinae Juris Romani de Ignorantia Juris in Foro Germaniae" (Knox 329). For further bibliographical information, see *DGB* 2:814.

171. *CR* 1:218.

172. Watson (see note 170) told Boltzius on 20 June 1747 that the Cherokees despised Prieber because of his conduct and attire. As a trader, Watson was naturally prejudiced. The trader Ludowick Grant knew that Prieber was a Saxon, yet twenty years later he still attested that he was a French agent. See "Historical Relations of Facts Delivered by Ludowicus Grant, Indian Trader," *SCHM* 10 (1909):54–68, esp. 58–61. This cannot be the Ludovik Grant discussed in the *Dictionary of National Biography* 8:399–400, who lived from 1650 to 1716, but the trader may have been a grandson.

173. CO 5.655.2.171–271v. This was published by Katherine de Baillou in *GHQ* 44 (1960):100–101. It is also found in *CR* 36:129–31.

174. As proved by Clement de Baillou, *GHQ* 42 (1958):112. See also Mellon Knox, Jr., "Christian Prieber and the Jesuit Myth," *SCHM* 61 (1960):75–81.

175. Crane.

176. *CR* 6:165.

177. *CR* 25:248.

Chapter 3: The Georgia Palatines

1. *CR* 2:101. See also *CR* 2:111; *CR* 32:291–93; Egmont 83, 99. On 2 March 1735 the Trustees' accountant, Harman Verelst, reported that £102.10.0 was spent "For Agency for engaging men from Germany" (*CR* 32:463).

2. *CR* 2:98. See letter in *CR* 29:144. The contract of 7 May 1735 was very carefully worded.

3. Egmont 183.

4. Edited by Benjamin Martyn, the secretary to the Trustees. Reprinted in Reese, *Most* 159–98. A somewhat later German version was Johann Matthias Krämer, *Neueste und richtigste Nachricht von der Landschaft Georgia* (Göttingen, 1746). See *CR* 21:437–38; Egmont 264.

5. See Krämer.

6. *CR* 2:193, 199. The Trustees' instructions of 11 May 1737 to Krämer are found in *CR* 32:608–11.
7. Original French petition, CO 5.632.2.176–176v; French original and English translation, *CR* 21:98–101.
8. CO 5.638.2.179–179v; *CR* 21:98–99.
9. CO 5.640.2.290–92.
10. Jones, "Fourth Transport" 15.
11. CO 5.643.2.316–317v; *CR* 26:310.
12. *CR* 26:31.
13. CO 5.639 pp.274–75; *CR* 21:420–23.
14. *CR* 21:437. See also *CR* 29:396, 397, 402.
15. *CR* 22, pt. 2, p. 21. For ship list, see *DR* 10:140–46.
16. British Public Record Office, State Papers, vol. 42, p. 138.
17. CO 5.654.1.129. See also pp. 127–30.
18. CO 5.654.1.116; *CR* 34:118.
19. British Public Record Office, State Papers, vol. 42, p. 287.
20. *CR* 32:283 (new). See *CR* 19:446–49.
21. *CR* 22, pt. 1, p. 50; 4:54–55; 22, pt. 2, p. 21.
22. *CR* 4:54–55, 57; Egmont 326; *CR* 2:119; *CR* 2:232; *CR* 30:4; *CR* 5:232, 251.
23. *CR* 22, pt. 1, p. 261; Egmont 313.
24. *CR* 4:512; Temple and Coleman 249.
25. CO 5.640.3.471–72, 504.
26. Clark 1012.
27. *CR* 22, pt. 1, p. 262.
28. *DR* 4:228; 6:35. Both Egmont and Stephens agreed with Boltzius concerning the relative merits of Hewitt's bad passengers and Thomson's good passengers (*CR* 5:107; 22, pt. 1, p. 322).
29. *CR* 4:117.
30. *CR* 4:256, 301–2.
31. *CR* 4:268.
32. *CR* 4Sup:256; Stephens 1:90.
33. *CR* 4:292–93; *DR* 6:34–35.
34. *DR* 6:170, 192.
35. *AN* 1:2540.
36. *CR* 29:579; 22, pt. 2, p. 21. Ship list reproduced in *DR* 10:146–50.
37. Gemeentelyke Archif Rotterdam, Notorial Acts, Jacob Bremer, no. 2332/159, 18 July 1738.
38. University of Georgia, Phillips Collection, Egmont Papers, vol. 14,269, p. 126. This would appear to have been the group who petitioned Lord Harrington and who wished to sail with Thomson.
39. *CR* 30:247. For complete disposition of passengers, see *CR* 2:326–28; *DR*

6:329–34; and Oglethorpe's letter of 29 Dec. 1739 (CO 5.640.3.433–35; *CR* 22, pt. 2, p. 290).

40. Abbot E. Smith 21–22.

41. *CR* 30:282.

42. Verelst's list, written on 11 June 1740, was inaccurate. It omitted Schneider and gave the name Kunigunda Knowart instead of Catherina Custobader (*CR* 30:283). See *DR* 5:249, 263. The names Gephart and Heinrich also appear as Gebhart and Henrich. Oglethorpe mentioned the need for unmarried women (*CR* 22, pt. 2, p. 291).

43. *DR* 5:286; *CR* 22, pt. 1, p. 297, *CR* 22, pt. 2, p. 464; *DR* 5:280.

44. CO 5.640.3.430. See also Oglethorpe's letter of 29 Dec. 1739 (CO 5.640.3.433–435v).

45. *DR* 5:287; 6:329–34. *CR* 5:195; 2:286.

46. *DR* 5:248.

47. *CR* 4Sup:271. Although Stephens calls them "children," they were actually grown, as Boltzius recorded on 30 Aug. 1739. The girl, Anna Magdalena, moved to Ebenezer and married Carl Sigismund Ott on 16 Feb. 1743.

48. *DR* 8:380, 412, 418.

49. CO 5.641.1.29v.

50. *AN* 1:2290.

51. *CR* 5:107. Boltzius also saw that servants were unproductive, as he argued eloquently on 24 June 1740. Oglethorpe and the Trustees had wished the Salzburgers to work communally (*CR* 29:110).

52. *CR* 22, pt. 2, p. 494. Two years later Stephens was even more convinced that, after being redeemed, the servants would do four times as much work (Stephens 2:4).

53. CO 5.641.1.48v.

54. CO 5.654.2.328v; *CR* 35:318–19.

55. *AN*, vol. 1, foreword to 2nd Continuation.

56. *CR* 33:123–25, 131–33; 2:357–59.

57. The "soul catchers" (Seelenfänger) may have derived their name from the devils in medieval morality plays who snatched the souls of impenitent sinners. For the tactics of, and measures against, the newlanders, see Hittel 67–79.

58. *CR* 30:357. Verelst requested a pass for Riemensperger and Galliser on 28 Feb. 1741 (*CR* 33:123–24).

59. *CR* 2:385; 30:393–99. Reproduced in *DR* 10:153–58.

60. *CR* 30:400.

61. *CR* 23:363. See *CR* 5:611, 551; 23:217; 30:400. CO 5.641.1.119v.

62. *AN* 2:1217; Stephens 1:18, 25.

63. Stephens 1:25; *DR* 8:540. See Boltzius's letter of 4 Feb. 1742 (CO 5.641.1.90).

64. CO 5.641.1.95v; *CR* 23:222.
65. *CR* 33:219.
66. Stephens 1:36, 196.
67. Stephens 1:65, 70, 19.
68. *CR* 2:410; 30:427. See also *CR* 5:595. Gambert is called "joubert."
69. As mentioned, a naturalized Georgian named Henry Myerhoffer was captured by a Spanish privateer in 1756.
70. *CR* 24:178.
71. *AN* 1:2276.
72. Stephens 2:16.
73. *AN* 1:2276; *DR* 8:147. This was common among German communities in America. For example, the Reformed congregation at Frederick, Maryland, depended on Johann Thomas Schley except on the rare occasions that an itinerant minister visited them.
74. *AN* 1:2276; Jones, "John Martin Boltzius Reports" 217.
75. *DR* 2:141.
76. *CR* 5:557; *DR* 6:65.
77. William Davis 392.
78. *DR* 8:212–13.
79. *DR* 8:188, 215.
80. *CR* 4Sup:267.
81. Stephens 2:146, 184.
82. CO 5.641.1.266–266v; *CR* 24:32 (French), 33 (English), see also pp. 35–36. Several errors appear in the English translation. Oglethorpe thought twenty-one pounds a reasonable allowance for the minister (CO 5.641.2.265).
83. *DR* 1:47; CO 5.637.1.194. The correct spelling seems to have been Becu, as indicated by a letter in the man's support (CO 5.637.1.194).
84. Beckemeyer 30, 238.
85. MA IV Fach J 10.
86. Newman 118.
87. Newman 588.
88. UA R.14 A 6a, 5–7.
89. *CR* 21:306.
90. *CR* 4:525, 621; 4Sup:78, 92–94.
91. *CR* 24:41.
92. *AN* 1:2274–78.
93. For his trial, see R. D. Barnett, "Dr. Samuel Nunes Ribero and the settlement of Georgia," in *Migration and Settlement*, ed. Aubrey Newman (London, 1971), 63–100.
94. *AN* 1:2277; *AG* 260.

Chapter 4: Acton and Vernonburg

1. CR 5:574. See CR 2:406. The last six of these were aboard the *Europa*.
2. CR 6:20; Stephens 1:xxv.
3. CR 30:619.
4. CR 6:4, 21.
5. CR 5:663; 2:406.
6. CO 5.641 p. 29; CR 23:56–57.
7. Stephens 1:36.
8. CR 6:45–46.
9. CO 5.641.1.180.
10. CR 5:668, 680–81; Stephens 1:153.
11. Stephens 1:139. See also pp. 142, 150, 175.
12. CR 6:56; 5:663; 30:393.
13. CR 2:406. See also CR 1:405.
14. CR 2:406.
15. CR 6:63. See CR 5:691.
16. CR 5:691; Stephens 1:197–98.
17. CR 30:448.
18. Stephens 2:4.
19. CR 2:406; 5:663; 1:405; 30:503.
20. CR 5:663; 6:30.
21. DR 10:12; Weller and Weller 63.
22. See Avery's letter of 10 Aug. 1743 (CO 5.641.2.299).
23. CR 24:80–81, 172.
24. AN 2:2151; Stephens 2:249.
25. Rush 6; CR 26:101.
26. DR 10:17–18, 26.
27. UA R.14, 6a, 7, p. 104.
28. CR 5:656, 669.
29. CO 5.640.1.212; CR 23:476.
30. Stephens 1:175; CR 24:226.
31. CR 5:660; Stephens 1:197; CR 6:70.
32. Joseph Falcker and Joseph Folcker were probably the same person.
33. CR 6:74, 78.
34. CR 6:83.
35. CR 2:406; 5:653; 30:504.
36. CR 1:402; Stephens 2:115.
37. Stephens 2:51, 245.
38. CR 23:477.

39. *CR* 24:64–65.
40. *CR* 24:142–45. See *CR* 1:472.
41. *CR* 1:440. See *CR* 2:467.
42. Egmont's data go through 1741. See Coulter and Saye.
43. Stephens 2:38.
44. *CR* 2:487. See *CR* 2:406.
45. CO 5.641.1.194, 196v. *CR* 23:439; 1:404.
46. Stephens 2:60; 1:163.
47. *AN* 2:2097.
48. *AN* 2:2217.
49. *AN* 2:2234.
50. Stephens 2:59. See also p. 104.
51. Stephens 2:67.
52. *CR* 24:81; Stephens 2:51.
53. Georgia Dept. of Archives and History, Marks and Brands Book K.
54. *CR* 6:61, 65, 134, 136. Stephens 2:205; 1:222; 2:13.
55. James C. Bonner, "The Open Range Livestock Industry in Colonial Georgia," *The Georgia Review* 17 (1963):89.
56. *CR* 30:583; Stephens 2:14.
57. *CR* 31:212. See also *CR* 25:332.
58. *CR* 30:619.
59. Stephens 2:139.
60. *CR* 30:428.
61. *CR* 31:213; 26:145.
62. *CR* 2:480–83. This volume, published at London in 1733, was inscribed to the Trustees.
63. Johannes Urlsperger 252.
64. *CR* 24:144; *AN* 3:674.
65. *CR* 26:21; 31:304.
66. CO 5.641.1.214. See Stephens 2:200; *CR* 23:484. See also *CR* 23:534.
67. *CR* 23:534. See Stephens 2:200. For Zubly's origins, see Türler 8:688.
68. CO 5.641.1.214.
69. *CR* 23:484.
70. Bryan 118.
71. The child had to assume the names of all his godparents.
72. *CR* 11:316; *CR* 12:121; CGHS 3:302.
73. This explains why the earl of Shaftsbury appears as Carl of Shaftsburg in Krämer 15.
74. *CR* 5:603; 2:393.
75. Stephens 2:200.

76. Even Boltzius, a neighbor of the Zublys, did not know the correct form of the name, for he used both Züblin and Zübli on two successive pages (Johannes Urlsperger 238–39).

77. *SCHM* 58 (1957):43. Perhaps the best account of Zubly's origins is Martin; see also Miller. Recent bibliography in *DGB* 2:1108.

78. See indexes to *DR*, vols. 5–9.

79. *CR* 1:442; 31:8. *SCHM* 58 (1957):43.

80. Stephens 2:199–200.

81. Martin 131.

82. Stephens 2:216. See also pp. 200, 204, 222, 224, 227, 237.

83. *CR* 6:138; 31:107. Hemperley, *English Crown Grants* 25, 65.

84. Johannes Urlsperger 156.

85. Johannes Urlsperger 154.

86. Newman 60. In England Gerdes wrote his name as Guerdes to retain the proper pronunciation.

87. SPCK MS/A/2.

88. Boltzius complained of Ortmann's English on at least two occasions (CO 5.640.2.330–31, 351).

89. It is first mentioned in vol. 8. It helps explain several trips by Ortmann or his wife to Charleston.

90. Newman 585. See also *DR* 2:55.

91. CO 5.640.3.351.

92. CO 5.641.2.280–281v; *CR* 24:43, 53–54, 109, 117, 180, 200. See *CR* 24:319; *DR*, 28 June 1743.

93. *CR* 2:479. See Stephens 2:183–84.

94. CO 5.641.2.373v.

95. CO 5.642, p. 114v.

96. CO 5.642, pp. 123–123v.

97. *CR* 25:227; 31:213.

98. This undertaking is copiously recorded in *CR* 1:467–71, 474; 31:9, 25–27, 41–48, 294. Manifest in *CR* 31:45–48.

99. *CR* 33:294–310; 31:25–30.

100. *CR* 31:45, 30–31. Lemke, who was aboard, said the illness was spotted fever (Fleckfieber; *AN* 3:48).

101. CO 5.642, pp. 34–35; *CR* 25:8; 2:467.

102. *CR* 25:94; 2:469; 33:294–309. CO 5.642, p. 34.

103. *AN* 3:70. For ship list, see *DR* 10:158–60.

104. CO 5.641.2.373; *CR* 25:23.

105. *CR* 31:9, 27; 1:471; 31:47. The widow's name also appeared as Treutlin, which suggests that it was the feminine form of Treutel ("Sweetheart," from MHG *triutl*).

106. CO 5.642, p. 5.
107. For Zouberbuhler's biography, see Türler 7:687. The name also appears as Zuberbiller and Zoberbiller.
108. DR 5:155. Bibliography in DGB 2:1107. On 3 Nov. 1739 Boltzius reported that, after the old Zouberbuhler had died, Oglethrope engaged his son to preach to the Swiss who would move from New Windsor to his barony near Palachocolas.
109. CR 33:312–16; Martin 132.
110. CR 31:54–55.
111. CR 2:469; 31:52; 33:312, 315, 318–19, 412.
112. CR 25:222; 31:106. See also Stephens 2:200.
113. CO 5.640, pp. 35, 54; CR 25:95, 125.
114. CR 31:104, 107; 2:478; 25:123.
115. CO 5.642, pp. 185–185v.
116. CR 25:225. See also CR 31:184–86; CO 5.642, pp. 119, 123. Because the wedding was performed at Ebenezer, Martin (133) erroneously assumed that the Toblers resided there.
117. Miller 21.
118. SCHM 58 (1957): 43; George Howe, *The Presbyterian Church in South Carolina* (Columbia, S.C., 1870), 266; Muhlenberg 2:601.
119. CR 31:249.
120. CR 2:493–94.
121. CR 31:300; 2:493–94; 18:261. In 1749 the Trustees resolved to continue Zouberbuhler's salary of fifty pounds (CR 1:523, 532).
122. *Letters to the Reverend Samuel Frink*, in Miller 83–94.
123. CGHS 6:95, 99; Muhlenberg 2:601.
124. CR 31:116–17.
125. CR 1:492; AN 2:2245. By chance Saxe Gotha in South Carolina had 280 souls in 1750 (AN 3:672).
126. CR 25:232–34.
127. CO 5.642, pp. 125v–126; CO 5.656, pp. 72, 75, 76. See also Stephens 2:154.
128. CR 31:198.
129. CR 2:482.
130. See AN 2:2124, 2151.
131. CR 25:280–81.
132. CR 18:244, 274.
133. CR 25:280.
134. Georgia Dept. of Archives and History, Conveyance Book C–1, p. 152. The name Blasse, which also appears as Plessi, was derived from Blasius.
135. CO 5.697, pp. 10v–11r.
136. There is no definite proof of Denny's nationality. Because he was a cashiered soldier from Frederica, he may have been British. His name is usually found

along with German names, and it is to be noted that he chose to settle among German people. It may be significant that the widespread Denny family in Virginia had previously been named Thöney (German for Anthony).

137. *CR* 8:209–13, 245–47.
138. *CR* 8:379.
139. CGHS 5, pt. 1, p. 1. This was the same representation as in 1761 (*CR* 34:431).
140. *CR* 20:234 (new); Newman 566; *CR* 29:124.
141. *CR* 26:21.

Chapter 5: Success at Ebenezer

1. William Davis 436.
2. Whitefield 2:6. Boltzius noted on 13 Oct. 1737 that Whitefield had visited Ebenezer during his absence in Savannah.
3. Moore 159–60.
4. Reese, *Clamorous* 132.
5. Reese, *Clamorous* 5. Oglethorpe joined the chorus of praise on 28 May 1742, noting that "the Darien Settlement flourishes exceedingly so does the Town of Ebenezer" (CGHS 3:122).
6. For detailed accounts of the orphanage, see Tresp, "Salzburger Orphanage"; Winde 146–48.
7. Whitefield 2:6. See *AN* 2:348–49.
8. CO 5.641.2.388–89; *CR* 24:219. Later we will see that the Salzburger farmers had now become unwilling to let child labor be wasted.
9. CO 5.640.2.213–214v, 301–2.
10. MA 5.A.11, fol. 43–46, no. 13.
11. MA D.24a, fol. 131. Further information on Thilo comes from Winde.
12. *DR* 5:285; 6:53.
13. *DR* 4:213; 5:29; 4:218; 6:46, 117, 119, 120, 173, 174.
14. *DR* 8:358, 359; *CR* 4Sup:263.
15. Schelbert 334; *DR* 12:33. Schelbert gives the name as Krüse.
16. CO 5.640.2.330. The story of Sanftleben's expedition is well told in *DR*, vol. 6.
17. CO 5.640.3.383.
18. Newman 219, 483; *CR* 30:40.
19. *CR* 22, pt. 2, p. 297; 5:374.
20. William Davis 436. On 1 July 1740 Whitefield sent Newman a translation of this letter, which appears in *AN* 2:348–49.
21. *CR* 22, pt. 2, pp. 298, 420.

22. Ver Steeg, 97–98.
23. A copy of their letter of 25 Nov. 1738, with the names of the Salzburgers and their domiciles in Germany, is found in the British Public Record Office (CO 5.640.2.237–238v; see also p. 241). A list of the emigrants, with the names of their Salzburg homes, appears near the middle of Urlsperger's unpaginated introduction to the 7th Contribution of the *Ausführliche Nachrichten*.
24. Letter reproduced in *DR* 6:43–45, and *CR* 3:428–31. See also *CR* 39:474–75, and Boltzius's letter of 14 March 1739 (CO 5.640.2.301–2).
25. Urlsperger, *Zwei Sendschreiben*.
26. CO 5.640.3.413–14.
27. SPCK MS/A/3 under 25 April 1746.
28. *DR* 8:175; *AN* 2:984–91. Published in *Der Salzburger* (quarterly of the Salzburger Verein in Bielefeld, Germany) 3, no. 51 (1976):10.
29. *CR* 30:351; 2:403. Le Comte Jacques d'Orléans, archivist in Strassburg, has kindly informed me that Vigera was without a doubt the son of Johann Heinrich Vigera, born at Rettert in Nassau. The family records are preserved at the municipal archives in Rettert.
30. *CR* 30:351. See Jones, "Fourth Transport."
31. One of these unnamed victims seems to have been the husband of Maria Mayer, the daughter of Matthias Bacher, and therefore named Mayer. There is, of course, the possibility that the three men abandoned the party, preferring a journey to Pennsylvania, and only feigned drowning.
32. *CR* 5:549; 30:374–77. Reproduced in *DR* 10:150–53.
33. *CR* 2:383–84. The fourth transport received £282.2.6 support during its first six months in Georgia (*CR* 33:219).
34. *CR* 2:365; 5:483. See also *CR* 30:311; 24:301.
35. CO 5.141.2.431.
36. *CR* 23:222.
37. See Boltzius's journal entry for 8 June 1742.
38. *CR* 24:110, 202–3.
39. MA 5.A.10, fol. 165–78, no. 45, item 11.
40. Muhlenberg 1:62–63; Jones, "Journal." For the hardship of Muhlenberg's voyage to Philadelphia, see his letter of 3 Dec. 1742 (Aland 38–39).
41. See indexes to Muhlenberg, and Aland.
42. CO 5.641.2.468; *CR* 24:352; *AN* 3:24.
43. Winde 178–81.
44. Lemke's journey from Halle to London is recounted in MA 5.A.11, p. 32.
45. MA Abt H IV, Fach b, Nr. 2, p. 295.
46. *AN* 3:59.
47. Universität Tübingen, Tübinger Kapsel 675.
48. *DR* 5:171.
49. See *DR* 8:427.

50. *DR* 8:424. Wesley and Spangenberg visited Ebenezer together (MA 5.A.13, p. 14; Schmidt 160).
51. *DR* 8:12, 82, 423.
52. Boltzius had discredited "Calvin's dangerous error" in a dispute with Herzog on 20 Sept. 1738 (*DR* 5:213).
53. *AN* 2:1237.
54. Stephens 1:36, 44; *AN* 2:1259.
55. Jones, "Fourth Transport" 53.
56. UA R.14 A 10, 15, p. 81.
57. *DR* 5:304–5. It is very probable that this was the Gabriel Falk who was active in Pennsylvania at about this time.
58. *DR* 4:98, 112, 175.
59. *DR* 4:78, 146, 175.
60. *DR* 8:33, 59, 98.
61. *CR* 6:316–17.
62. The Richards were probably named Ritschard, a relatively frequent name in Switzerland. A Jacob Ritschard was named in the trial of a newlander in Bern (Faust, "Swiss" 39).
63. CO 5.641.1.110; *CR* 26:48–51.
64. *DR* 8:47.
65. CO 5.642, pp. 117v–118.
66. According to Spangenberg, already in 1735 Boltzius was hurt when he saw a published translation of his reports which revealed personal references that he had meant to keep private (UA R.14 A 6a, 1, p. 161).
67. Newman 420.
68. *CR* 2:354; 30:337; 24:105. Typical of his many reminders are his letters of 5 Oct. 1739 and 6 Aug. 1740 (CO 5.640.3.383v, 548. See also p. 503).
69. *CR* 30:461, 502.
70. *CR* 24:202, 222. Boltzius had noted on 22 Feb. 1743 that no mail had yet been lost, and on 18 Feb. 1746 he wrote that no mail from Europe had been lost (*AN* 3:56).
71. CO 5.642, p. 169v; *CR* 25:288; *DR* for 30 March 1748.
72. *CR* 24:359; 25:10; 31:9.
73. *DR* 16:120. See Stearns 289.
74. CO 5.642, p. 108.
75. *CR* 25:325, 332.
76. *AN* 2:2120.
77. Robbins, "John Tobler" 148.
78. Ibid. 149.
79. *Alter und verbesserter Schreibkalender auf das G. Gnadenrieche Christjahr 1755 ... Neben anderen nuz-ergözlichen Erforderlichkeiten, mit einer merkwürdigen Beschrei-*

bung von Süd-Carolina versehen, St. Gall, published by Hans Jacob Hochreutiner. Part of this was censured as encouraging emigration. Tobler's *South Carolina and Georgia Almanack* was published by James Johnston in Savannah but printed in Charleston. His *The Pennsylvania Town and Country-Man's Almanack* was printed by Sauer (Sower) in Philadelphia.

80. For an excellent example of church penance, see the one demanded of Margaretha Stout (*DR* 7:31–32).

81. *CR* 23:503. See also *CR* 24:327. This Jacob Züblin, who disappeared from Georgia records at this time, must be the Jacob Zübli who died in Philadelphia (*DR* 12:45).

82. CO 5.641.2.271.

83. *CR* 24:38–43. See also *CR* 24:318; CGHS 2:121–23.

84. Ver Steeg 97.

85. CO 5.641.1.202–202v; 2.271–272v.

86. *CR* 24:330.

87. *CR* 1:456.

88. *CR* 24:304. On 9 Aug. 1744 Boltzius wrote to Francke confirming that he had no authority to punish (MA 5.A.11, fol. 46–49).

89. *The Saltzburger Settlement in Georgia* (1772), by de Brahm. British Museum, King's MS 210, p. 45 (811732). Reproduced in De Vorsey 142.

90. *CR* 1:496; 6:347–50.

91. *AG* 206; Winde 82.

92. CO 5.697, pp. 146–146v; Muhlenberg 2:625.

93. *CR* 25:10; 31:8. See *CR* 24:315; 31:5, 15, 40 (new).

94. *CR* 2:507; 26:70; 31:415. See Boltzius's letter of 5 March 1750 (CO 5.642, p. 294v).

95. *CR* 31:431.

96. CO 5.643.2.261.

97. CO 5.642, p. 114; *CR* 26:117; *CR* 25:255.

98. CO 5.641.2.388v–390; *CR* 24:192, 358.

99. *CR* 31:77–79.

100. *CR* 20:248.

101. See his letter of 12 March 1735 (*CR* 20:262–63 [new]). His other letters must have been dictated to, or copied by, English scribes.

102. *CR* 25:254, 290; 31:220–21.

103. *CR* 31:308; 2:495.

104. *CR* 25:495. See also *CR* 6:350; 31:301. An adult was one "freight." A child under twelve was half a freight, while an infant at the breast did not count. The passenger list is reproduced in *DR* 10:160–62.

105. CO 5.643.1.20; *CR* 26:21; *CR* 6:294. Kübler was probably the farmer Jacob Kübler of Magstadt, who disappeared from Swabia in 1747. His wife was Anna

Catharina and his children were Johann Jacob (b. 1740), Rosina (b. 1744), and Gottlieb (b. 1748). Yoder, *Pennsylvania* 79.

106. *CR* 6:304, 336, 338.

107. *CR* 26:98.

108. *CR* 33:389–93. A similar menu is given for 1741 in Hacker, *Kurpfälzische Auswanderer* 65. For an excellent study of ship's fare, see Wust, "Palatines."

109. *CR* 26:48.

110. A follower of Johann Conrad Dippel, a radical Pietist and Spiritualist.

111. *CR* 26:48.

112. He could do so because Bogg's passengers were redemptioners, able to redeem themselves for six pounds. Boltzius merely had to advance the Schubdreins the money.

113. The birth records of the Schubdrein family are still preserved at the parish church in Weiher in Saar-Brücken (now Weyer in Alsace Lorraine), a copy being in the possession of Mrs. Hilde Schuptrein Farley of Overland Park, Kans.

114. *CR* 26:20, 47–51; 26:69; 31:416. CO 5.642, p. 263v.

115. *CR* 31:433; *DR* 15:18. For letters on the subject in mutilated French and Latin, see *CR* 20:481–87. The new edition of the *Colonial Records of Georgia* deletes this correspondence (*CR* 20:328–29).

Chapter 6: Swabian and Later Immigrants

1. *CR* 26:20, 47, 48, 80–82, 131.
2. CO 5.642, p. 274.
3. *CR* 31:430.
4. *CR* 31:430; *CR* 26:49–51; *DR* 10:162–64.
5. See Urlsperger's letter of 7 April 1741 (CO 5.641.1.4–5).
6. J. A. Urlsperger was made deacon in 1763 (Johannes Urlsperger 4). After his father's retirement, he was elected corresponding member of the SPCK and edited the last volume of the *Americanisches Ackerwerck Gottes*. For his biography and extensive theological writings, see Horst Weigelt, "Johann August Urlsperger, ein Theologe zwischen Pietismus und Aufklärung," *Zeitschrift für bayerische Kirchengeschichte* 33 (1964):67–105.
7. Johannes Augustus Urlspergerus, *De praestantia coloniae Georgico-Anglicanae prae coloniis aliis* (Augusta Vindel [Augsburg], 1747). This was a shortened version of J. A. Urlsperger's dissertation of that year and included a map of Georgia and a plan of Ebenezer.
8. Wiegandt 100. Nevertheless, Kleinknecht published his extensive *Zuverlässige Nachricht*, a copy of which is in the DeRenne Collection of the University of Georgia Libraries (DER 1740/K4). He had already helped Urlsperger with the fourth Salzburger transport (Urlsperger, *Die Sammlung* 36).

9. *CR* 1:547; 33:461.
10. CO 5.643.1.63. There were sixty-one Germans on board (*CR* 31:412, 430; 1:546–47).
11. *CR* 33:462–66; 31:25, 412, 430–31; 2:518; 26:47.
12. CO 5.643.2.206.
13. CO 5.643.2.205–206v.
14. *CR* 31:412; 26:248.
15. CO 5.643.2.20.
16. *CR* 6:341.
17. *CR* 2:508, 498, 365.
18. *CR* 26:70.
19. CO 5.642, p. 108.
20. CO 5.643.1.93–96v; *CR* 26:91–103.
21. *CR* 25:119.
22. At first the name was consistently written as Mayer, later also as Meyer.
23. *CR* 25:218–19. See his entry for 30 Sept. 1743 and his letter of thanks dated 24 Oct. 1748 (CO 5.642, p. 198).
24. *CR* 25:325, 330, 332. See also *CR* 6:313.
25. *CR* 26:164; *AN* 3:730; Bryant, St. Matthews 11.
26. *CR* 2:508.
27. *CR* 1:565. Passenger list in *DR* 10:164–66.
28. *CR* 26:150. At Boltzius's request, Habersham wrote Martyn a most favorable recommendation on Schubdrein's behalf when the latter returned to Germany (CO 5.643.1.145).
29. Mrs. Hilde Schuptrein Farley of Overland Park, Kans., has kindly sent me a list of witnesses and Schubdrein marriages from 21 Dec. 1714 to 25 July 1747.
30. *CR* 26:314. See *AG* 70–71.
31. *CR* 26:319–20. See also *CR* 31:240 (new).
32. *CR* 1:567; 2:518; 31:240 (new).
33. Newman 100–101; CO 5.641.2.529–30; *CR* 25:14.
34. *CR* 25:187, 261–64; 31:42, 46 (new); 39:433. See also *CR* 31:60 (new); CO 5.642, p. 93. Urlsperger seems to have been elected to the Trust at the same time. See his letter of 13 Aug. 1747 (CO 5.642, p. 99).
35. *CR* 25:14, 224. See also CO 5.642, p. 121.
36. *CR* 25:273. See also von Münch's letter of 2 July 1747 (*CR* 25:187). My student, Mrs. Renate Wilson, has treated von Münch's enterprise in her University of Maryland dissertation.
37. CO 5.642, p. 116. See von Münch's letter of 12 June 1747 to Benjamin Martyn (*CR* 25:261–64).
38. CO 5.643.2.250–253v.
39. *CR* 25:80; 26:348.
40. Johannes Urlsperger 58.

41. Ibid. 48.
42. British Museum, King's MS 210, p. 47 (811732).
43. Wiegandt 100–101. Like the propagandistic Gottlieb Mittelberger, this Matthias Neidlinger wished to be an organist or schoolteacher, as Boltzius reported on 17 Nov. 1750.
44. This rescript is in *Der Hoch-Obrigkeitlichen Rescripten, Circular-Schreiben, und Special-Befehlchen, an die Land-Geistliche löbl: Stadt-Ulmischer Herrschaft, Anno 1665 bis 1788 incl.* Stadtsarchiv Ulm. Erich Broy of Leipheim kindly found and transcribed this for me.
45. *AG* 262–63. Nevertheless, Krauss did accompany Boltzius to the meeting of the Council.
46. Yoder, *Rhineland Emigrants*, 44.
47. Hacker, "Auswanderer aus dem Territorium" 197–247. Because there is no manifest for this party, it has been compiled from other sources in *DR* 10:166–68.
48. Walker 47.
49. I am indebted to the Reverend John Reynolds of Oxford, England, a descendant of the governor, for this information.
50. *CR* 6:379–81, 435–38, 391.
51. Henry Smith 13, 14.
52. *CR* 8:769. When Archibald Campbell fought his way from Ebenezer to Augusta, he passed through "Grenier's Plantation." Campbell 49.
53. CO 5.697, p. 143.
54. For documentation on Rabenhorst, see Winde 181–86.
55. Their marriage is described, and justified, in the unpaginated introduction to *AG*.
56. Universität Tübingen, Tübinger Kapsel 210–13.
57. For details of the collection, see Urlsperger's introduction to *AG*.
58. *AG* 516.
59. Christoph Krämer managed the minister's plantation until he quit in 1759 to farm for himself, at which time the position was taken by Jacob Ihle, a former servant of Colonel Stephens's (Johannes Urlsperger 74, 107, 161, 206).
60. Rabenhorst's behavior is well summarized and documented in Winde 48–50. Muhlenberg 2:616.
61. Johannes Urlsperger 9. Boltzius had already discussed the possibility on 30 Nov. 1751.
62. Ibid. 31.
63. Winde 8.
64. See Bryant, *Islands in Georgia*.
65. Stephens regularly referred to him as "the German butcher."
66. *CR* 3:713. This creek is not to be confused with the Augustine Creek flowing into the Savannah River near Abercorn. It is now called Wilmington River, the

name Augustine Creek being restricted to a short stretch south of Elba Island.
67. CGHS 3:50, 51.
68. *CR* 7:346; Georgia Dept. of Archives and History, Conveyance Book C–1, p. 208.
69. Bryant, *Islands in Georgia* 19.
70. Clark; Bryan 136.
71. Bryant, *Islands in Georgia* 19, 37, 38, 40, 47, 48, 50, 52; *CR* 6:227.
72. CO 5.645, pp. 12–35.
73. CO 5.645, pp. 86–87.
74. *CR* 29:115–16. Michael Schweitzer, who was indentured to James Haselfoot for five pounds, had come as a Trust servant.
75. *CR* 29:475; University of Georgia, Phillips Collection, Egmont Papers, vol. 14, 204, p. 63.
76. Newman 217. When Boltzius's half-year salary appears as fifty pounds, it may include the assistant pastor at twenty pounds and the schoolmaster at five pounds (SPCK MS/A/3).
77. Vital statistics with copious documentation by Herbert Franke in *Schleswig-Holsteinisches Biographisches Lexikon* (Neumünster, 1976), 4:192–93.
78. Newman 329; *GHQ* 47 (1963):95–110.
79. Newman 396.
80. Ibid. 407. Newman also discovered von Reck to be a "Person of Prudence as well as Zeal for Serving the Protestant Interest."
81. Newman 387.
82. Ibid. 567.
83. *CR* 29:263. See pp. 292–95.
84. Reck.
85. Stearns 329.
86. *CR* 32:311–12.
87. Stearns 315–16, 329–33.
88. *CR* 2:70; 32:236. See *CR* 1:189.
89. Egmont 66.
90. Examples are Faber for Schmidt, Agricola for Bauer, Mercator for Crämer, Prätorius for Schultz.
91. *CR* 31:242 (new); *CR* 27:103 (new); Egmont 103. See *CR* 31:508.
92. Facts about de Brahm's life are taken mainly from De Vorsey.
93. *CR* 31:240 (new).
94. MS in Library of Congress (G 3922 S3 1752 D4 Faden 45).
95. Winde 281, n. 311. In 1757 people complained that building the fort had devalued some lots (*CR* 7:631).
96. Gallay 40.
97. CO 5.643.2.345; *CR* 26:348.

98. Reprinted in De Vorsey 72–166. Published in 1849 by George Wymberley Jones (later DeRenne) in forty-eight copies.
99. Johannes Urlsperger 35.
100. British Museum, King's MS 210, pp. 45, 47 (811732). Reproduced in De Vorsey 142–43.
101. *Savannah Republican* for 28 March 1806. See *SCHM* 14 (1903): 7–9.
102. *The Florida Historical Quarterly* 20 (1940):323.
103. The family history and the description of their voyage are based on Bornemann's journal, which is in the possession of Mr. A. G. Burney of Brooklet, Ga. A copy of the manuscript and a translation by Ms. Bertha Reinert are in the archives of the Georgia Historical Society in Savannah.
104. Information kindly provided by Professor Hermann Wellenreuther of the University of Göttingen.
105. Four of these letters are preserved in the Burgerbibliothek in Bern; copies at the Georgia Historical Society, Savannah.
106. *AG* 265. Boltzius's statement seems confirmed by Habersham's letters of 21 April 1750 and 31 Jan. 1753 (*CR* 25:487; 26:331), but it is possible that Habersham merely leased the vessel. It is not known whether it is the same *Success* that was mastered by John Ewell and William Thomson in 1743 (see under *Success* in index to *CR*, vol. 24).
107. *AG* 262.
108. *AG* 265; *DR* 15:263–64.
109. *CR* 6:379. He is also called John Henry Groeve. See *AG* 4a:14.
110. Jones and Exley.
111. Muhlenberg 2:664.
112. *CR* 36:167–71 (English), 172–74 (German).
113. "In 1745 came an adventurer to Monocacy calling himself Carl Rudolf, Prince of Wurttemberg. He pretended to be an ordained minister of the German Lutheran Church and supported his claim with forged documents." T. J. C. Williams, *History of Frederick County* (Baltimore, 1979), 4.
114. See Jones, "John Adam Treutlen."
115. *AG* 34; Winde 306, n. 919. Boltzius later used the word *Handlungsdiener* of Wertsch when the latter was working in the store (Johannes Urlsperger 191). There is a reference to Treutlen, but unidentified, as a future helper in Mayer's store in the entry of 16 June 1753.
116. On 29 Nov. 1750 Boltzius stated that Mr. Mayer "keeps a public Shop in our town."
117. Johannes Urlsperger 129.
118. CO 5.651, pp. 148–148v.
119. CGHS 6:146. See also p. 188.

120. *DR* 1:59,99; *CR* 20:169 (new).

121. Metzger must have been Swiss, for he pronounced his name in such a way that it was sometimes written Macher.

122. CO 5.642, p. 118.

123. *DR* 4:40.

124. Weir 231.

125. Now in the possession of a descendant, Mr. Mario Casteleiro of Middleton, N.Y.

126. MA 5.B.3, p. 149; Muhlenberg 2:599.

127. Jones and Exley 133.

128. *DR* 15:162.

129. Johannes Urlsperger 151.

130. *CR* 28, pt. 1, p. 334. On 5 June 1759 Boltzius reported that the Virginians south of the Altamaha were causing so much trouble that the governor of Georgia had to send troops to control them (Johannes Urlsperger 78).

131. UA R.14 A 10, p. 82.

132. Johannes Urlsperger 215.

133. See CO 5.645, pp. 115–122v; and 647, pp. 15–20v.

134. Coulter and Saye 34; Robbins, "John Tobler" 151.

135. Muhlenberg 2:669.

136. *CR* 26:4–6, 100–102.

137. Bryant, *St. Andrews Parish*.

138. CO 5.697, p. 10.

139. CO 5.697, p. 35v.

140. Muhlenberg 2:666, 683.

141. Bryant, *St. Pauls Parish*.

Chapter 7: Decline of Ebenezer

1. *AG* 522. On 8 April 1765, shortly before Boltzius's death, a Moravian named Johann Ettwein visited Ebenezer and commented that Boltzius was old and weak (UA R.14 A 10, 15, p. 81). See Jones, "Report of Mr. Ettwein's Journey."

2. *AG* 512.

3. *AG* 387; Winde 161–63, 319–21.

4. Johannes Urlsperger 33.

5. Universität Tübingen, Tübinger Kapsel 250–51.

6. Rabenhorst related Boltzius's final illness and death in Johannes Urlsperger 42–43.

7. Tübinger Kapsel 268–73.

8. UA R.14 A 10, 15, p. 81; Campbell 34.

9. Rabenhorst defended himself convincingly, even if one-sidedly, in a letter of 2 June 1773 (Tübinger Kapsel 228–35).

10. Muhlenberg 2:636.

11. This unhappy friction between Triebner and Rabenhorst is well summarized and documented in Winde 53–66; Muhlenberg 2:584–86.

12. Muhlenberg 2:650, 585.

13. Winde 60.

14. Muhlenberg 2:584–658.

15. Muhlenberg 2:585. It may be relevant that both Treutlen and Wertsch had taken out liquor licenses in 1764 (*Georgia Gazette*, 19 Jan. 1764, p. 1; 7 Feb. 1765, p. 3).

16. In Georgia Muhlenberg played the role of an ancient man and called himself a "dead old tree" even though he was actually only sixty-three (Muhlenberg 2:650).

17. Muhlenberg 2:611.

18. Ibid. 624.

19. Muhlenberg 2:624; 3:42, 44, 85–86.

20. The best account of the Revolution in Georgia is Coleman, *American Revolution*.

21. CGHS 6:201, 206; CO 5.636.3.329v; CR 20:234.

22. *AN* 3:964; *AG* 494.

23. CGHS 5, pt. 1, p. 1.

24. CGHS 6:185.

25. *RR* 1:148. Biography in *DGB* 2:1108.

26. Tübinger Kapsel 737–58.

27. *CR* 38, pt. 1, p. 532.

28. *CR* 38, pt. 1, pp. 617–23.

29. CGHS 5, pt. 1, p. 60; *RR* 1:137.

30. Campbell 37.

31. RR 1:199, 149. Tussing was surely the son of Johann Jacob Tussing of Weiher, who was a baptismal sponsor for the Schubdrein family on 29 April 1729. The name seems to have been derived from Dusseign or Toussaints.

32. *RR* 1:137. See also pp. 199, 220.

33. *RR* 1:213.

34. *RR* 1:220. CGHS 5, pt. 1, p. 121. Zettler was erroneously recorded as Tretler.

35. *RR* 1:194.

36. Treutlen's various proclamations are reproduced in *RR*, vol. 1.

37. Tübinger Kapsel 705; Winde 66–68.

38. Lewis 428–29, 431.

39. It should be noted that the people of Acton and Vernonburg, like those of Ebenezer, elected mostly Englishmen to represent them in the Georgia Provincial Congress in 1775 (list in *RR* 1:229).

40. From Sheftall's original letter, now in the possession of his descendant, Mrs. Marion Levy of Savannah.

41. *Hetrina*, vol. 3. The Hessian archives at Marburg do not mention a Captain Kappel. For bibliography on Mordecai Sheftall and his brother Levi, see *DGB* 2:882–85.

42. Tübinger Kapsel 702.

43. Hemperley, *Military Certificates* 9, 10, 11, 18, 30, 34, 35, 38, 54, 71, 78, 81, 84.

44. This was surely Jacob Bühler, who appeared often in entries of that time in the *Ebenezer Record Book* (see Jones and Exley).

45. *CR* 38, pt. 2, pp. 610, 620, 625. Nikolaus Schubdrein was compensated for "Forage and Labor as a Carpenter at Sundry times for the Continental troops" in Georgia under the command of generals Lincoln and Wayne in 1779 and 1782 (Georgia Dept. of Archives and History, Auditor Ledger, 1782–1792, p. 3).

46. The area is still pronounced Bewlie but written Beaulieu.

47. See Jones and Lipscomb.

48. For d'Estaing's assault, see Alexander Lawrence, *Storm over Savannah* (Savannah, Ga., 1951).

49. All statements made here about Jasper are documented in Jones, "Sergeant Johann."

50. *CR* 38, pt. 2, pp. 313–14.

51. Robert Davis 3:303.

52. *CR* 38, pt. 2, p. 20. John Lightenstone (Johann Lichtenstein), a Russian subject from Kronstadt, had served under Oglethorpe. Elisabeth Lichtenstein Johnston, *Recollections of a Georgia Loyalist* (New York, 1901), 24, 37.

53. *CR* 38, pt. 2, p. 612.

54. *RR* 1:348–56.

55. *RR* 1:508, 472. Frederick Rolf, who acquired the land of James Herert, may have been a German (*RR* 1:528).

56. *RR* 1:376, 378, 381, 382, 613. In 1760 a grant was made to William Grover in St. Matthews Parish (Bryant, *St. Matthews Parish* 60).

57. *RR* 1:613.

58. British Public Record Office AO 12, vol. 102, p. 10; vol. 109, p. 290, item 738.

59. Tübinger Kapsel 679, 692. He also refuted Muhlenberg's accusations concerning the destruction of the mills (Tübinger Kapsel 688–90). Even Triebner's banishment was repealed in 1800 (*RR* 1:630).

60. Anne Mary Triebner married Christian E. Treutlen on 8 Jan. 1819 (Caroline Wilson 103). After Herson died, Hanna married a worthier man, Christopher Hudson (Winde 312).
61. Rupert Hughes, *George Washington* (New York, 1930), 3:172.
62. Winde 89.
63. Franklin B. Hough, *The Siege of Savannah* (Albany, N.Y., 1866), 95. For the role played by the Wöllworth and Wissenbach regiments in Georgia, see "Welworth" and "Wissenbach" in index to Campbell.
64. See Jones and Lipscomb, 371–81.
65. Jones, "Note" 378.
66. Jones, "Georgia's German" 24.
67. Ibid. 26.
68. *Journal des Regiment Knoblauch*. Murhardsche Bibliothek, Kassel, 4 Ms. Hass. 205, pp. 287–88; Hessisches Staatsarchiv, Marburg, 12 Kriegsministerium 8869/61, 63, 64.
69. *CR* 38, pt. 2, p. 592.
70. Jones, "Georgia's German" 287–88.
71. Coleman, *American Revolution* 143.
72. CO 5.536, p. 90.
73. See Jones, "Hessian Deserters."
74. Jones, "Georgia's German" 25.
75. *Journal des Hochfürstlichen Grenadier Battalion Platte von 16 Feb. 1776 bis 24 Mai 1784 von Carl Bauer*, p. 376 (Hessisches Staatsarchiv, Marburg, Signatur 1.B.a.16).
76. M. A. Schwalm has kindly written me that the gun-maker Jacob Rüssel received a grant in Franklin County, Ga.
77. Tübinger Kapsel 754.
78. Three other former prisoners of war escaped from Ebenezer, two of them successfully. Jacob Strube, Georg Giesler, and Conrad Kramm deserted on 11 April 1782, but Kramm was captured. I am indebted to M. A. Schwalm, a Hessian descendant, for this information.
79. Winde 70; Lewis 434–35.
80. Tübinger Kapsel 752.
81. Lewis 451.
82. Tübinger Kapsel 715.
83. *CR* 38, pt. 2, p. 270. This could have been an error for Captain Jacob Bühler.
84. Lewis 441.
85. Lewis 443, 450.

Chapter 8: Diaspora

1. Mrs. Roberta Rhylander of Katy, Tex., wrote me on 18 Dec. 1984 that her husband's ancestor, William Israel Rhylander, a descendant of Friedrich Rheinländer of Ebenezer, arrived in Texas with eleven sons. The youngest of these, Few Anthony Rhylander, had fourteen children in Buda, Tex.
2. *Journal of German-American Studies* 13 (1978):4.
3. Newman 145. See also p. 159.
4. Winde 192–95.
5. Christopher Bergman's very flowery funeral oration, by the Reverend Stephen Albion Mealy (from Mühle) of Charleston, was published in Savannah by Purse and Styles in 1832.
6. All readers who recognize an ancestor in this volume are invited to join this group by writing to the Georgia Salzburger Society, P.O. Box 916, Rincon, Ga. 31326.
7. *The Journal and Letters of Francis Asbury*, ed. Elmer T. Clark (rpt., Abingdon, Va., 1958), 745–46.
8. Campbell 21, 22, 27. Nevertheless it is written as Tritland's on a contemporary map (*Roads and Country that Col. Campbell marched through*, Library of Congress G 3921 S3 1779 R6 Vault). This suggests that the informant must have spoken a dialect that confused *eu* and *ei*.
9. CR 26:50; AG 486.
10. Samples appear to be Funkhouser, Offerman, Ruckersville, Shelman, Shelman Bluff, Snellville, Thalman, and Troutman, and possibly Butts, Coleman, and Hagan.
11. Examples include Meinhard, Saffold, and Ludowici.
12. George White, *Statistics of the State of Georgia* (Savannah, Ga., 1848), 224.
13. See Caroline Wilson.
14. MA 5.A.10, fol. 117; MA D.24a, fol. 117.

Summary 1: Manna from Heaven and Earth

1. Johannes Urlsperger 210.
2. Jacob Weber, a Swiss, proclaimed himself Christ and immolated the Holy Ghost, in the person of one of his colleagues. He was hanged for the crime, but his accomplices were freed. See Muhlenberg's vivid account (2:577–80).
3. On 25 Jan. 1751 Boltzius defended Luther and the *German Theology* from criticism by John Wesley.
4. *Die Beschaffenheit eines Menschen vor, in, und nach seiner Bekehrung* (Greiz, 1767).

5. According to medieval theory, "Christian" wages were modest, reflecting neither greed nor the sinful desire to better one's position in the world.

6. *AN* 2:1914–15.

7. *CR* 5:348; 3:213. There had, of course, been missions along the coast during the Spanish occupation.

8. CO 5.642, pp. 109, 110v.

9. Johannes Urlsperger 157.

10. CO 5.640.2.241v, 350.

11. CO 5.640.3.548v.

12. *CR* 22, pt. 2, pp. 421, 298. See also *CR* 1:543; 26:69; 2:507; 31:416, 431. *DR* 13:131.

13. See Boltzius's letters of 6 Nov. 1736 and 11 July 1739 to Verelst (CO 5.640.2.215, 344).

14. SPCK CR 1/22, no. 17,025.

15. Copy in SPCK CR 1/22, no. 17,025.

16. SPCK MS/A/1.

17. Newman 219. The Venice merchants donated fifteen pounds per annum for many years (SPCK MS/A/2–3). For example, on 23 Sept. 1747 they transmitted £16.1.0 to Harris and Habersham for the Salzburgers (SPCK CR 23, no. 18732. See also no. 18889).

18. A fund of 1,572 marks left by a General von Dagenfelt provided interest up to the 1880s (letter of Pastor W. S. Bowman dated 15 March 1887 in the archives of the Evangelical Lutheran Church of the Ascension in Savannah).

19. *AG* 333.

20. CO 5.642, p. 115.

21. Ver Steeg 136.

22. Besides the SPCK's salaries of fifty pounds, thirty pounds, and ten pounds for the pastor, catechist, and schoolmaster, respectively, other charities were used to support the remaining schoolmasters, such as Wertsch (*AG* 202, 6 June 1752). Schoolmaster Köcher received a gift from Ziegenhagen on 13 March 1745 (MA IV Fach J 10).

23. *CR* 5:687; 6:301. Ten years later, in 1759, a Christian Gampert, apparently Margaret Gamphert's son, took out fifty acres, so we can hope the widow was then provided for (*CR* 8:210). See also *CR* 8:272, 342, 480; 1:496. In 1774 Christian Campher left modest landholdings to his wife and son Jeremias (Georgia Dept. of Archives and History, Colonial Wills, Book AA, pp. 95–96).

24. *DR* 3:133, 185, 250.

25. *DR* 3:185.

26. Georgia Historical Society, Bornemann's four letters.

27. Uhlendorf 345. Hinrichs gives a good description of tar making.

28. This prejudice may have been influenced by the double meaning of the word *venery* and by the use of the hunt in love allegories.
29. "Peter Rose, a gamekeeper," Fries 48.
30. *CR* 4:256. See also p. 283.
31. *CR* 4Sup:41. Later Georgians called the cougar "painter," from *panther*.
32. *AG* 505.
33. *CR* 4:177.
34. *DR* 4:14, 80, 148, 186, 203.
35. The bait, a mass of hooks and feathers, is tied directly to a long pole and thrust under logs and cypress knees where a line cannot be cast. When the bait is jostled violently on the surface, the bass strike it, apparently to protect their eggs. See Georgia Historical Society, Bornemann's four letters.
36. *CR* 35:307.
37. See letter of Thomas Gapen, dated 13 June 1735 (CO 5.637.1.102). For more on the Bryans, see Harvey H. Jackson, "The Carolina Connection: Jonathan Bryan, His Brothers, and the Founding of Georgia," *GHQ* 68 (1984):147–72; and Gallay, *The Formation of a Planter Elite: Jonathan Bryan and the Southern Colonial Frontier* (Athens, Ga., 1989).
38. William Stephens commented on the use of herdsmen much as Moore had done (*CR* 5:59, 60).
39. *AN* 1:2055–56.
40. *AN* 2:357.
41. *DR* 8:166.
42. *DR* 9:151, 201, 228–30.
43. John S. Otto, "The Origins of Cattle Ranching in Colonial South Carolina, 1670–1715," *SCHM* 87 (1986):117–24; James C. Bonner, "The Open Range Livestock Industry in Colonial Georgia," *The Georgia Review* 17 (1963):85–92.
44. SPCK CR 21/22, no. 16,967; *CR* 24:222. See *DR* 9:100, 225, 201.
45. CO 5.642, p. 95v; *CR* 25:190; *CR* 31:28, 211–12; *DR* 13:17, 28.
46. CO 5.642, pp. 294–295v.
47. CO 5.640.2, p. 141; *CR* 25:255; MA 5.A. 11, fol. 245–48.
48. CO 5.640.2.301.
49. *CR* 24:105; *DR* 3:260. See Boltzius's letter of 18 Dec. 1742 (CO 5.641.1.202).
50. CO 5.641.1.209.
51. *AN* 2:1865; *CR* 24:105. On 17 July 1745 Martyn wrote to Stephens that the Trustees had sent over some "Plough Shares" for the Salzburgers (*CR* 31:10 [new]). Nevertheless, on 16 March 1745 Boltzius wrote that many farmers in Ebenezer still had to cultivate their corn with a hoe, since the plowshares promised by Ziegenhagen had not yet arrived (MA IV Fach J 10).
52. *AN* 3:58.

53. *CR* 24:372.
54. Johannes Urlsperger 47.
55. Ibid. 54–56. For a brief and excellent account of indigo cultivation, see "The Rise and Fall of South Carolina Indigo," in *Carologue* (news bulletin of the South Carolina Historical Society) (Winter 1990): 4–5, 14–17.
56. *AN* 3:974 (page misnumbered as 674).
57. See Renate Wilson, "Halle," chap. 4, p. 50.
58. *DR* 11:130–31; 8:62, 93.
59. *AG* 493–94.
60. *DR* 3:129, 132, 137, 141, 160. For further details, see Jones, "Salzburger Mills."
61. *DR* 4:173; 5:276.
62. *DR* 7:231, 263; *CR* 23:222; *CR* 30:337.
63. See fig. B in *AN* 3:74. Reproduced in Jones, *Salzburger Saga*, pl. 16; also, larger with correspondingly more legible commentary, in Mills Lane, *The People of Georgia* (Savannah, Ga., 1975), 37. This picture was engraved by Tobias Conrad Lotter of Augsburg, possibly from a draft made by Joseph Avery. My student, Renate Wilson, has recently found a clearer sketch, probably that used by Lotter for his engraving, with a most informative commentary, in the Halle Archives, Missions-bibliothek AFS VD 12.
64. *DR* 8:55; Stephens 2:142. See *AN* 3:18–21.
65. *CR* 24:373; 2:481; 25:276.
66. *AN* 3:18.
67. CO 5.643.1.52–53v; *CR* 26:53–54; *AG* 65.
68. *DR*, vol. 13, for 13 Dec. 1749; Johannes Urlsperger 123; Muhlenberg 2:620–21.
69. *CR* 24:220.
70. The sawmills are discussed in detail in Jones, "Salzburger Mills."
71. *CR* 2:469; 24:220; 26:71. See also *CR* 2:211; *CR* 31:194 (new); *AN* 3:856.
72. CO 5.641.1.529. *CR* 25:13; 31:7, 74.
73. *CR* 31:39, 42, 74 (new).
74. *CR* 26:74; *DR* 12:18.
75. CO 5.642, pp. 192–195v; *CR* 25:259, 322, 334, 385; *AN* 3:898.
76. *CR* 25:157–59, 259, 275, 286; 2:478.
77. *CR* 31:110 (new). See Boltzius's letter of 12 June 1748 (CO 5.642, p. 175).
78. *CR* 31:157, 159; *AN* 3:72.
79. MA 5.A.11, fol. 245–48.
80. Ibid.
81. CO 5.643.1.72–73v; *CR* 26:53–54, 73–77.
82. CO 5.643.2.205–206v; *CR* 26:100–102, 114, 197.
83. *CR* 33:566.

84. *AG* 22. See also *AN* 3:682.

85. Either Lemke or Boltzius wrote to Francke on 25 Feb 1746 in praise of the helpful preacher's son (MA D.24a, fol. 155–58). The swindler is not to be confused with the honest Jacob Kurtz of Vernonburg.

86. *CR* 25:118–19, 167; 31:123. Boltzius discussed Kurtz in a letter of 31 Aug. 1746 to Francke (MA 5.A.11, fol. 155–58, 280–83) and also in a letter of 16 Sept. 1746 to Verelst (CO 5.642, pp. 50–51).

87. Aland 462.

88. CO 5.641.1.115v.

89. *AN* 2:1856.

90. *DR* 8:173, 509.

91. CO 5.642, p. 125; *CR* 30:512.

92. *CR* 24:104–5.

93. *CR* 24:297–98, 302, 343. Mrs. Barriky must have been the widow of Joseph Baraquier, who is falsely listed as Banaquier in Henry Smith 213.

94. Stephens 2:218, 226.

95. *CR* 25:5; *AN* 3:61–63.

96. *CR* 31:83.

97. CO 5.642, p. 89v.

98. *CR* 2:487.

99. CO 5.642, p. 111. See also pp. 113, 125.

100. *CR* 25:287, 372.

101. CO 5.642, p. 226. This letter contains a most informative description of the silk business. See also Boltzius's letters of 29 May 1749 and 14 June 1750 (CO 5.642, pp. 230–31, 237–40v, 302–3, 304–5v, 314–15v).

102. He stated on 14 June 1750 that Ginther (Günther) of Highgate was the only other person producing silk (CO 5.640, p. 304).

103. CO 5.643.1.53; *CR* 26:46, 54–55.

104. CO 5.643.1.123–24; *CR* 26:130. See also *CR* 26:47, 163, 247; *AG* 9–11.

105. This may explain the people "who work for wages," whom Boltzius visited in their homes to keep them from losing work time (*DR* 16:173–74).

106. *CR* 2:507.

107. *CR* 26:246. See also 26:46, 151.

108. *CR* 2:519; *AG* 216–19.

109. *CR* 26:426.

110. CO 5.465, p. 95v; *CR* 27:115 (new). See Boltzius's comment of 13 June.

111. CO 5.642, p. 21. See Johannes Urlsperger 101.

112. *AG* 520; *CR* 28 1:125.

113. CO 5.651, p. 148.

114. CGHS 6:206.

115. Rush 30.

116. In 1741 Müller made six striking clocks for Gen. Oglethorpe (*DR* 8:41).

117. *Hidden Heritage, Recent Discoveries in Georgia Decorative Art, 1733–1915*, High Museum of Art, Atlanta, 1990, p. 17.

118. AWC 57, 124, 144. In Savannah, Weisshart was known as Whitehard. On 18 Oct. 1749 Boltzius called the Salzburger Leonhard Krause a carpenter but did not mention the nature of his work.

119. *CR* 38:2.7.

120. *CR* 38:464; see De Vorsey, pp. 161–62.

121. *DR* 15:259.

122. *DR* 9:14.

123. *DR* 3:243. That this previously unidentified Rheinlander boy was Martin is suggested when he was called a shoemaker in 1760 (Johannes Urlsperger 119).

124. *DR* 15:259.

125. Johannes Urlsperger 242, 176; ACW 141. Weidmann is referred to several times as *Schumacher W.*

126. Johannes Urlsperger 49–50.

127. Johannes Urlsperger 60, 64.

128. See Boltzius's letter of 1 May to Martyn (CO 5.643.2.206v. See also *CR* 26:200). Boltzius also refers to shoemaker Metzger.

129. *DR* 4:2, 8, 14–15.

130. *DR* 5:88, 108, 162, 239, 307.

131. *AG* 237; ACW 13, 132.

132. In a letter of 9 March 43 to Francke, Boltzius requested some smithing tools and horseshoes for Leitner (MA 5.A.10, fol. 165–68, no. 45, item 12) and on 29 March 1745 he referred to "Schmidt Leitner" (MA IV Fach J 10).

133. *DR* 16:28.

134. ACW 134, 48; *AG* 4.b, 68, 113.

135. *CR* 38.2.623.

136. Johannes Urlsperger 107, 161.

137. *DR* 14:98–99.

138. CO 5.638.2.254.

139. ACW 45; *CR* 24:40.

140. ACW 45; *CR* 24:40.

141. Johannes Urlsperger 173, 279.

142. Johannes Urlsperger 138, 253.

143. Stephens 2:167.

144. Reese, *Colonial Georgia* 121.

145. *DR* 8:209; *CR* 25:363.

146. *DR* 11:90.

147. *DR* 13:26.

Summary 2: Health, Medicine, and Daily Life

1. CO 5.640.1.80.
2. CO 5.640.3.384.
3. Purry 136; UA R.14 A 7d, 1, p. 138.
4. Darret B. Rutman and Anita H. Rutman contend that, depending upon the type and strain of the malaria, the human body can acquire some immunity, making later attacks somewhat less severe (34). The fact that immunity had to be developed against each type and strain of the disease explains why Boltzius and others who had been exposed to malaria for twenty years still suffered from it so severely in 1754.
5. Egmont 285.
6. They were Johann Martin Rheinländer, Ursula Kalcher, and Maria Brandner (*AG* 243).
7. *CR* 24:106.
8. *CR* 25:254.
9. In 1751 and 1752 Boltzius reported twenty-five deaths and fourteen baptisms (*DR* 15:317, 315).
10. Bryan 124; Muhlenberg 2:604.
11. *DR* 2:3, 31, 34, 37, 75; *DR* 3:48, 92, 98; *CR* 21:110.
12. Jones, "Fourth Transport" 17, 55; Georgia Historical Society, Bornemann's travelogue.
13. Rush 8; *DR* 2:78. See also *DR* 2:107, 143; *AN* 2:2146.
14. For a clear explanation of the nature and transmission of malaria, see Rutman and Rutman.
15. *DR* 7:84, 127.
16. Schweiger's child died of it on 2 July 1740 (*DR* 7:181). See also *DR* 8:516.
17. MA 5.A.11, fol. 382. See *DR*, entries for 7, 11 Jan., 16, 22 March, 10, 11, 16 April, and 16 July 1748.
18. *DR* 7:84; *AN* 3:269, 703. See also *AG* 65.
19. *DR* 12:30.
20. *DR* 15:249.
21. *CR* 4:161.
22. Winde 69.
23. Johannes Urlsperger 204, 218. According to Fielding H. Garrison, "measles, rubella, and 'the purples' (military fever) were usually grouped together and not sharply defined." Garrison, *History of Medicine* (Philadelphia, 1914), 237.
24. Tübinger Kapsel 259.
25. *AG* 233. On 17 Oct. 1749 he called Georgia a "healthy and well-situated Colony" (CO 5.642, p. 262).
26. Aland 39, 42.

27. *DR* 4:68, 115.
28. CO 5.639.3.407–8.
29. Newman 209. *Matrikel der Martin Luther Universität Halle-Wittenberg, I, 1690–1730* (Halle, 1960). MA 5.A.11, fols. 48–49, 54–57, 61–64, 71, 114. I am indebted to Renate Wilson for these references.
30. Winde 151–54.
31. *AN* 3:75; CO 5.141.2.282.
32. MA 5.A.10, fols. 117–22, 127, 144–47, and 181–82, item 2.
33. UA R.14 A 6a, 1, 5–7.
34. *CR* 6:87; 2:393.

35. God punished the wicked Josef Ernst by letting a dislocated thumb develop gangrene. The entire arm was amputated successfully, but the patient died. Maria Maurer had some cancerous growth, which was also treated most painfully. See index of *DR*, vol. 8.

36. Johannes Urlsperger 102.

37. Ibid. 260. A large shipment to the orphanage could not be sold because too much in each bottle had evaporated (*DR* 8:165).

38. *DR* 4:137; see index to *DR*, vol. 7, under "medicines."
39. MA 5.A.10, fols. 218–19.
40. *DR* 3:85, 197; 2:151; 3:70; 4:116, 137; Muhlenberg 2:666.
41. UA R.14 A 6a, 5–7. Another remedy used was Württemberg fever powder (*DR* 9:184).
42. MA A E 7, fol. 204.
43. UA R.14 A 6a, 5–7.

44. For German snake lore, see *Handbuch des Deutschen Aberglaubens*, ed. Hanns Baechtold-Stäubli (Berlin 1935–36), 6:1114–99.

45. See under "snakeroot" in index to Stearns.
46. Patricia Jones Jackson, *When Roots Die* (Athens, Ga., 1987), 16.

47. *AG* 491. According to Samuel Evans Massengill, Venetian theriac contained sixty-one ingredients, one of which was from vipers. Massengill, *A Sketch of Medicine and Pharmacy* (Bristol, Tenn., 1941), 63, 65.

48. *AG* 491.

49. In the eyes of modern medical historians, I am a "presentist" because I deplore the sad state of medical science in earlier centuries. I deny, however, that this is a sign of arrogance; rather I think it a sign of humble thanks and admiration for the dedicated Listers, Pasteurs, and Kochs who discovered the germs that cause disease so that physicians can treat the disease rather than its symptoms. Harold E. Davis, writing in 1976, could still risk the accusation of presentism when he wrote, "That some of the medicines hurried patients to their graves can scarcely be doubted. This was especially true when they were combined with bleedings, purgings, blisterings, and sweatings, all then regarded as excellent remedies" (93).

50. These books, some of them first published in Germany in the seventeenth century, were still being reprinted in Pennsylvania in the nineteenth century. Among the worst of these were those like Christian Paillini's *Dreckapotheke* of 1696, which recommended the use not only of various animal parts but also of excrement, including human. For prescriptions, which this author does not endorse, see Cowen.

51. For a good summary of education at Ebenezer, see Winde 135–41.

52. *DR* 2:3, 45, 47, 54, 69.

53. *AN* 3:152.

54. *AG* 516; Universität Tübingen, Tübinger Kapsel 255; Muhlenberg 2:636.

55. CO 5.141.1.195.

56. Muhlenberg 2:588. See Boltzius's letter of 4 July 1739 excusing the delay in teaching English (CO 5.640.2.330–31). See also entry for 14 May 1748.

57. Robbins, "John Tobler" 149; *AG* 317; Johannes Urlsperger 135. A list of the Ebenezer volumes survives (Winde 216–25).

58. *CR* 39:438.

59. De Vorsey, 144. The "Malabar" books may have been suggested to de Brahm's fertile imagination by the East Indian reports sent back to Halle by the Lutheran ministers in Malabar, copies of which were found in the Ebenezer library (*Der königlichen Dänischen Missionarien aus Ost-Indien eingesandte ausführliche Berichte* [Halle, 1735 ff.]). Ebenezer had twelve "Continuations," 986 pages (Winde 217).

60. Johannes Urlsperger 243.

61. Orlando B. Mayer, *The Dutch Fork*, ed. James E. Kibler (Columbia, S.C., 1982).

62. Ibid. 138.

63. "Gang uz, Nesso, mit niun nessinchilinon, uz fonna dem marge in deo adra, vonna den adrun in daz fleisk, fonna demu fleiske in daz fel, fonna demo velle in diz tulli." Wilhelm Braune, *Althochdeutsches Lesebuch* (Tübingen, 1979), 90.

64. *DR* 8:443, 470.

65. *Handbuch des Deutschen Aberglaubens*, ed. Hanns Bechtold-Stäubli (Berlin, 1935–36), 3, col. 1140.

66. Cecile Hulse Matschat, *Suwannee River, Strange Green Land* (New York, 1938; rpt., Athens, Ga., 1980), 79–80.

67. *DR* 6:309; Muhlenberg 2:646.

68. These hymns are listed and identified in the appendixes of *DR*, vols. 6–16, and in the notes of vols. 1–5.

69. Francis Harper and Delma E. Presley, *Okefinokee Album* (Athens, Ga., 1981), 141.

70. *AN* 3:416.

71. Urlsperger replaced the name of the city with an *N*. on this occasion but not in his edition of Boltzius's letter of 1 Feb. 1746 (*AN* 3:55).

72. On 1 Aug. 1750 Boltzius mentioned several other pictures hanging in the church.

73. *DR* 3:239. This portrait is possibly the one now hanging in the Chatham Club in Savannah.

74. See *Weald and Downland Open Air Museum*. Lansing, Sussex, ISBN 0/905/259/07/6.

75. *DR* 8:4.

76. Newman 406, 395.

77. *CR* 4Sup:128–29.

78. *CR* 4Sup:68, 87, 95, 97, 104, 107, 176–77.

79. *CR* 4Sup:58–59.

80. *CR* 4Sup:82.

81. Stephens 1:181.

82. Stephens 2:37.

83. See Bryan; Lafar; Georgia Dept. of Archives and History, Entry of Claims Book M.

84. *DR* 3:198.

85. Georgia Dept. of Archives and History, Inventory Book F, Record Group 49, ser. 6.

Summary 3: Indians, Slaves, and Soldiers

1. Typical is Gary B. Nash's textbook *Red, White and Black: The People of Early America* (Englewood Cliffs, N.J., 1974). While there are no absolute standards for judging cultures and all judgments must be subjective, it does appear that many third-world nations are willingly abandoning their ancestral values in favor of Western ones. Some are adopting not only medical and other technical advances but also music, literature, and even democracy and women's liberation.

2. *DR* 1:60–61.

3. Newman 514.

4. UA R.14 A 2, 3a.

5. Reck 24–25. See *DR* 1:142–48.

6. *DR* 1:135–48.

7. *DR* 1:67; 3:314.

8. *DR* 1:144. See also *DR* 2:2.

9. Von Reck says it was on 10 May (Reese, *Our First Visit* 53).

10. Jones, "Pastor Boltzius" 457–62; see also *DR* 7:228. Samuel Quincy, who had lived in New England and Georgia, expressed an entirely negative, yet convincing, view of the Indians (Newman 531–33).

11. UA R.14 A 6d.

12. *DR* 2:30. See also pp. 1, 85, 108, 126, 239. The following summer Spangenberg also wrote down some Indian words (UA R.14 7d, p. 130).
13. *DR* 8:436.
14. Universität Tübingen, Tübinger Kapsel 721. This was reported by Triebner.
15. The Indians thrust little pine splinters into their victims and set fire to them, thus causing prolonged excruciating pain. If the victim passed out from the pain, a bucket of cold water would revive him so that the torture could start again.
16. Johannes Urlsperger 111, 186.
17. Ibid. 115.
18. Ibid. 154.
19. CO 5.141.1.195v, 194.
20. Schad had arrived in 1737 with Hewitt, and Ubjer, using the name Upshaw, arrived in 1738 with Thomson. It is not possible to deduce what name lurked behind this distortion. Egmont asserts that Upshaw was a Palatine (Coulter and Saye 53).
21. Stephens 1:142–43. Indians from Florida also massacred two sick Scots on 13 Nov. 1739 (CO 5.654.2.236, 249–51, 257).
22. *DR* 8:339.
23. For an account of the Cherokee War, see Meriwether 213–40.
24. Johannes Urlsperger 132.
25. Ibid. 146.
26. Ibid. 121, 123, 136, 146.
27. *CR* 7:395.
28. CO 5.638.2.230, 232, 237.
29. Reese, *Our First Visit* 149.
30. CO 5.638.3.281.
31. Already in 1734 Boltzius had reported that, while the Creeks were honest, the Uchees were "much inclined to Robbing and Stealing" (Reck and Boltzius 37).
32. *DR* 8:378, 381, 388, 528; *CR* 24:362; *CR* 31:28.
33. *CR* 25:10; 31:281.
34. *CR* 25:10; 31:73–74, 81, 121.
35. *CR* 31:412.
36. *CR* 31:413. These may have been the long-awaited but never-heard-from people from Lucerne.
37. *CR* 31:412, 413; 26:115.
38. CO 5.643.1.21v.
39. Tübinger Kapsel 253–54. Samuel Dyssli of Purysburg also spoke well of the Indians (Schelbert 143).
40. Tübinger Kapsel 258.
41. This chapter was outlined before the appearance of Withuhn's article. The latter, in turn, had gone to press before my *Salzburger Saga* was published.

Nevertheless, our conclusions are very similar. Neither of us had yet seen Binder-Johnson's article.

42. See Wood.
43. *CR* 20:84.
44. Jones, "Commissary von Reck's Report" 102–3.
45. *DR* 1:104, 106; *CR* 20:169 (new).
46. *DR* 1:117, 76, 87, 96.
47. CO 5.641.2.519–26; *CR* 24:434–44.
48. *AN* 3:30–46.
49. CO 5.642, pp. 32–33.
50. *AN* 3:71.
51. CO 5.642, p. 83; *CR* 25:168.
52. CO 5.642, p. 104. See *CR* 24:40; 25:200, 205, 206, 213, 214.
53. CO 5.642, p. 106.
54. CO 5.642, p. 110. On 3 May 1748 Boltzius still contended that the introduction of slavery was "a most abominable thing not consistent with reason and Scripture which presages nothing else but God's punishment in his own time" (*CR* 25:289).
55. *CR* 25:285. These stipulations are itemized in Taylor 280–84. See *CR* 25:430–37.
56. MA D.24a, fol. 329–32.
57. Boltzius agreed with them that the Negroes were "lazy, thieving, and rebellious," which is not unusual among involuntary workers regardless of race. Nineteenth-century German-American scholars generally assumed that all eighteenth-century Germans in America were opposed to slavery, but Owen S. Ireland has convincingly proved that the Pennsylvania Germans, both Lutheran and Reformed, opposed the abolition of slavery. Ireland, "Germans Against Abolition: A Minority's View in Revolutionary Pennsylvania," *Journal of Interdisciplinary History* 3:4 (Spring 1973): 685–706.
58. *CR* 25:289.
59. MA 5.A.11, fol. 329–32.
60. *AG* 195, 254; Johannes Urlsperger 31.
61. Muhlenberg 2:637, 586.
62. *CR* 6:334, 374.
63. *CR* 12:10. See *CR* 6:229, 448.
64. Johannes Urlsperger 63.
65. *AG* 360–63. See *AG* 469, 488; Johannes Urlsperger 269.
66. Walker 30–31; *CR* 6:443; Georgia Dept. of Archives and History, Conveyance Book C–1, p. 159; *CR* 7:230, 791; *CR* 18:69, 88.
67. *CR* 12:56.

68. *CR* 10:777; *Die Mission der Brüdergemeinde in Surinam*, ed. F. Stähelin (Herrnhut/Paramaribo, n.d.), 113–14.

69. Fries 214; *CR* 15:456; *CR* 19, pt. 1, p. 417.

70. See E. G. Alderfer, *The Ephrata Commune* (Pittsburgh, 1985), 59–60, 71, 152–53. His wife was the widow Reinier who died at Ebenezer in 1777 (Jones and Exley). She had left money to Ebenezer and several of the inhabitants (Georgia Dept. of Archives and History, Colonial Wills, Book AA, pp. 292–94).

71. Jones, "Georgia's German" 24.

72. Jones, "Black Hessians."

73. Robert Davis 74; *CR* 19, pt. 1, p. 255.

74. *AN* 3:974–75. See also Johannes Urlsperger 250.

75. *AG* 252–54, 257, 268.

76. Johannes Urlsperger 249–50. See also Boltzius's entry for 7 May 1759.

77. Tresp, "Early Negro Baptisms"; Jones and Exley; Muhlenberg 2:645. See *AG* 406.

78. Johannes Urlsperger 2, 8.

79. Jones and Exley, 18, 21, 22, 31, 33, 34, 35.

80. *AG* 252–54, 257, 268.

81. Johannes Urlsperger 267.

82. Ibid. 62; Wood 140.

83. Lewis 431, 432.

84. Ivers, *Drums* 62, 100, 106, 107, 206.

85. CO 5.656, p. 72; Ivers, *Drums* 37.

86. Charles C. Jones, *The History of Georgia* (Boston, 1883), 1:242.

87. Fries 158, 173.

88. *DR* 1:35.

89. *CR* 2:189. See Rodney M. Baine and Mary E. Williams, "Oglethorpe's Missing Years," *GHQ* 49 (1985):193–210. Oglethorpe assumed the name John Tebey, perhaps suggested by Tybee Island.

90. *DR* 7:117; *CR* 4:572.

91. *CR* 4:638.

92. *DR* 8:148.

93. *CR* 27:464.

94. CGHS 7, pt. 3, pp. 52–60.

95. See Larry E. Ivers, "Rangers, Scouts, and Tythingmen," in Jackson and Spalding 152–62. See also index to Ivers, *Drums*.

96. Stephens 1:101. Since this muster was some nine days before the battle of Bloody Marsh, some of them may have served there. In any case, they stood by as a reserve.

97. Stephens 2:119.

98. Stephens 1:218. See also *CR* 2:104, 154.
99. *CR* 24:207.
100. *AG* 513.
101. Johannes Urlsperger 190, 207, 168. In 1751 the inhabitants of Goshen had to drill in Savannah, as they did on 11 June of that year.
102. *CR* 25:128–29.
103. *CR* 35:52.

Bibliography

Manuscripts

Archiv der Brüder-Unität (Moravian Archives), Herrnhut, Germany
  Universitätsarchiv Abteilung R.14 A. Voluminous reports from and correspondence with the Moravians during their sojourn in Savannh, 1735–1740.
British Public Record Office, Kew
  Colonial Office Papers. Class 5, vols. 636–712. Legislative and Council journals, laws, and personal correspondence for the entire colonial period. Much of this was published in *CR* and *RR*.
Franckesche Stiftungen (Universitäts- und Landesbibliothek Sachsen-Anhalt), Halle, Germany
  Missionsarchiv Abteilung 5.A.3. Major source of information on Salzburgers and other Germans in colonial Georgia. Contains reports from Ebenezer ministers and their correspondence with Halle, Augsburg, and London. Source of *AN* and *DR*.
Georgia Department of Archives and History, Atlanta
  Georgia Colonial Records
    Loose Wills, 1733–1777. RG 49–1–2
    Will Book A, 1754–1772. RG 49–1–5
    Will Book AA, 1772–1777. RG 49–1–5
    Entry of Claims Book M (U3), 1755–1757. RG 49–1–13
    Conveyance Book C–1, 1750–1761. RG 49–1–3
    Inventory Book F, 1754–1771. RG 49–1–6
    Marks and Brands Book K (Y3), 1755–1793. RG 49–1–12
Georgia Historical Society, Savannah
  Johann Christoph Bornemann, travelogue (photocopy). Journey from Göttingen via London to Port Royal, S.C., with family history.

Johann Christoph Bornemann, four letters to Albrecht von Haller (photocopy). Descriptions of flora and fauna of Georgia, 1752–1755.
Hessian State Archives, Marburg, Germany
Bestand 12. Kriegsministerium.
Library of Congress, Manuscript Division
Jerusalem Lutheran Church Records. Births, baptisms, and deaths in Ebenezer, 1754–1800.
Peter Force Papers. Series vii, E.3 to ix.
Murhardsche Bibliothek, Kassel
Handschriftenabteilung, Manuscripta Hassiaca 4 Ms. Hass. 205.
Royal Library of Denmark, Copenhagen
Von Reck archive, NKS 565,4. Sketchbook of drawings of flora, fauna, and Indians of Georgia collected in 1736. Some letters, and manuscript of von Reck's *Kurtz gefasste*.
Society for Promoting Christian Knowledge, London
Henry Newman Salzburger Letterbooks. Correspondence concerning expulsion of the Salzburgers and their establishment in Georgia, published in Newman.
Universität Tübingen
Tübinger Kapsel. Part of Halle Missionsarchiv stored in Tübingen during World War II.
University of Georgia, Athens
Phillips Collection. Egmont Papers. Correspondence and notes concerning establishment of Georgia and lists of settlers. Ships lists. Journal of William Stephens from October 1741 to September 1743. Insights into use and life of German indentured servants.
Keith Read Manuscript Collection. Sheftall Family Papers. Levi Sheftall Diary, 1733–1808. List of all Jews who came to, or were born in, colonial Georgia.
William L. Clements Library, University of Michigan, Ann Arbor
Von Jungkenn Papers. Includes official reports of Hessians serving in Georgia during the Revolution.

Published Materials

Works dealing primarily or substantially with the Georgia Dutch are preceded by an asterisk. For abbreviations, see the list at the beginning of the Notes section.

Aland, Kurt, ed. *Die Korrespondenz Heinrich Melchior Mühlenbergs*. Berlin, 1986–.
Arndt, C. Fr. *Die Vertreibung der Salzburger Protestanten und ihre Aufnahme bei den Glaubensgenossen*. Leipzig, 1900.

Atwood, Rodney. *The Hessians*. Cambridge, England, 1980.
Bailyn, Bernard. *The Peopling of North America*. New York, 1986.
Baine, Rodney M., and Phinizy Spalding. *Some Account of the Design of the Trustees for establishing Colonys in America*. Athens, Ga., 1990.
Beck, Hartmut. "Herrnhüter und Salzburger vor 250 Jahren." *Nürnberger Bibelaktion 1732. Unitas Fratrum* 12 (1982):45–73.
Beckemeyer, Frances Howell, ed. *Abstracts of Georgia Colonial Conveyance Book C–1, 1750–1761*. Atlanta, 1962.
*Binder-Johnson, Hildegard. "Die Haltung der Salzburger in Georgia zur Sklaverei (1734–1750)." *Mitteilungen der Gesellschaft für Salzburger Landeskunde* 78 (1938):183–96.
*Brantley, R. L. "The Salzburgers in Georgia." *GHQ* 14 (1930):214–22.
Bryan, Mary Givens, ed. *Abstracts of Colonial Wills of the State of Georgia, 1733–1777*. Atlanta, 1974. Rpt., Spartanburg, S.C., 1981.
Bryant, Pat, ed. *English Crown Grants for Islands in Georgia, 1755–1775*. Atlanta, 1972.
Bryant, Pat, ed. *English Crown Grants in St. Andrews Parish, 1733–1755*. Atlanta, 1972.
*Bryant, Pat, ed. *English Crown Grants in St. Matthews Parish in Georgia, 1733–1775*. Atlanta, 1974.
Bryant, Pat, ed. *English Crown Grants in St. Pauls Parish in Georgia, 1733–1775*. Atlanta, 1974.
Bryant, Pat, ed. *Entry Claims for Georgia Landholders, 1733–1755*. Atlanta, 1975.
Campbell, Archibald. *Journal of an Expedition against the Rebels of Georgia in North America*. Darien, Ga., 1981.
Candler, Allen D., ed. *The Colonial Records of the State of Georgia*. Vols. 1–19, 21–26. Atlanta, 1904–13. Vols. 20, 27–39, in typescript at Georgia Dept. of Archives and History, now being published by the University of Georgia Press, Athens. Already appeared, vols. 20 (1982); 27 (1978); 28, pt. 1 (1975); 28, pt. 2 (1979); 29 and 30 (1985); 31 (1986); 32 (1989). Vols. 20, 27–29, ed. Kenneth Coleman and Milton Ready. Vols. 30–32, ed. Kenneth Coleman.
Candler, Allen D., ed. *The Revolutionary Records of the State of Georgia*. 3 vols. Atlanta, 1903.
Clark, Murtie June. *Colonial Soldiers of the South, 1732–1774*. Baltimore, 1983.
Coleman, Kenneth. *The American Revolution in Georgia*. Athens, Ga., 1958.
Coleman, Kenneth. *Colonial Georgia: A History*. New York, 1976.
Coleman, Kenneth, and Charles Stephen Gurr, eds. *Dictionary of Georgia Biography*. Athens, Ga., 1983.
*Coulter, E. Merton, and Albert B. Saye. *A List of Early Settlers of Georgia*. Athens, Ga., 1949.
Cowen, David L. "The Folk Medicine of the Pennsylvania Dutch." In *Folklore and*

Folk Medicine, ed. by John Scarborough, 86–97. Madison, Wis., 1987.
*Crane, Verner W. "A Lost Utopia of the First American Frontier." *Sewanee Review* 27 (1919):48–61.
Davis, Harold E. *The Fledgling Province*. Chapel Hill, N.C., 1976.
Davis, Robert S., Jr. *Georgia Citizens and Soldiers of the American Revolution*. Easley, S.C., 1979.
Davis, William V., ed. *Georgie Whitefield's Journals, 1737–1741*. Gainesville, Fla., 1967.
De Vorsey, Louis, Jr., ed. *De Brahm's Report of the General Survey in the Southern District of North America*. Columbia, S.C., 1967.
Dürrenmatt, Peter. *Schweizer Geschichte*. 2 vols. Zurich, 1976.
Egmont, earl of (John Percival). *The Journal of the Earl of Egmont, 1732–38*. Ed. Robert G. McPherson. Athens, Ga., 1962. (Vols. 2–3 of Egmont's journal were published as *CR*, vol. 5.)
Elliott, Daniel T. *Ebenezer: An Alpine Village in the South Georgia Swamp*. Watkinsville, Ga., 1988.
Faust, Albert B. "Documents in Swiss Archives." *American Historical Review* 22 (1917):98–132.
Faust, Albert B. "Swiss Emigration to the American Colonies in the Eighteenth Century." *American Historical Review* 22 (1917):21–44.
Faust, Albert B. "Unpublished Documents on Emigration from the Archives of Switzerland." *Deutsch-Amerikanische Geschichtsblätter* 18/19 (1920):9–68.
Faust, Albert B., and G. M. Brumbaugh. *Lists of Swiss Emigrants in the Eighteenth Century*, 2 vols. Baltimore, 1976.
Florey, Gerhard. *Bischöfe, Ketzer, Emigranten*. Graz, 1967.
*Fries, Adelaide. *The Moravians in Georgia, 1735–1740*. Winston-Salem, N.C., 1967.
Gallay, Alan. *The Formation of a Planter Elite: Jonathan Bryan and the Southern Colonial Frontier*. Athens, Ga., 1989.
*Gnann, Pearl Rahn. *Georgia Salzburger and Allied Families*. Savannah, Ga., 1956. Rev. by Amy LeBey, Savannah, 1970.
Häberle, Daniel. *Auswanderung und Koloniebegründungen der Pfälzer im 18. Jahrhundert*. Kaiserslautern, 1909.
Hacker, Werner. "Auswanderer aus dem Territorium der Reichsstadt Ulm." *Ulm und Oberschwaben* 42/43 (1978):161–257.
Hacker, Werner. *Auswanderungen aus Oberschwaben*. Stuttgart, 1977.
Hacker, Werner. *Auswanderungen aus Baden und dem Breisgau*. Stuttgart, 1980.
Hacker, Werner. *Auswanderungen aus Rheinpfalz und Saarland im 18. Jahrhundert*. Stuttgart, 1987.
Hacker, Werner. *Kurpfälzische Auswanderer vom Unterem Neckar*. Stuttgart, 1983.
Hawes, Lilla Mills, ed. *The Journal of the Reverend John Joachim Zubly*. Savannah, Ga., 1989.

Hemperley, Marion R., ed. *English Crown Grants in Christ Church Parish in Georgia, 1755–1775*. Surveyor General Dept., State of Georgia, n.d.
Hemperley, Marion R. *Military Certificates of Georgia, 1776–1800*. Atlanta, 1983.
Hetrina. Hessische Truppen im amerikanischen Unabhängigkeitskrieg. Archivschule Marburg, 1976.
Hittel, Wolfgang von. *Auswanderung aus Südwestdeutschland*. Stuttgart, 1984.
*Hofer, J. M. "The Georgia Salzburgers." *GHQ* 18 (1934):99–117.
*Hollingsworth, Dixon. *The Bethany Colony*. Sylvania, Ga., 1974.
*Hollingsworth, Dixon. *The History of Screven County, Georgia*. Sylvania, Ga., 1989.
*Hurst, John F. "The Salzburghers in Georgia." *Harper's New Monthly Magazine* 85 (1898):392–99.
*Hvidt, Kristian. *Von Reck's Voyage*. Savannah, Ga., 1980.
Ivers, Larry E. *British Drums on the Southern Frontier*. Chapel Hill, N.C., 1974.
Jackson, Harvey H., and Phinizy Spalding, eds. *Forty Years of Diversity*. Athens, Ga., 1984.
*Jones, George Fenwick. "Baron von Reck's Travel Journal, 1734." *Bulletin of the Society for the History of the Germans in Maryland* 31 (1963):83–90.
Jones, George Fenwick. "The Black Hessians." *SCHM* 83 (1982):287–302.
*Jones, George Fenwick. "Cattle Raising on the Early Georgia Frontier: A Salzburger Contribution." In *Fide et Amore: A Festschrift for Hugo Bekker*, ed. William C. McDonald and Winder McConnell, pp. 173–84. Göppingen, 1990.
*Jones, George Fenwick. "Commissary von Reck's Report on Georgia." *GHQ* 47 (1963):94–110.
*Jones, George Fenwick, ed. *Detailed Reports on the Salzburger Emigrants Who Settled in America*. 16 vols. Athens, Ga., 1968– .
*Jones, George Fenwick. "The Fourth Transport of Georgia Salzburgers." *Concordia Historical Institute Quarterly* 56 (1983):3–26, 52–64.
*Jones, George Fenwick. "The Georgia Salzburgers and Slavery." *The Report: A Journal of German-American History* 41 (1990):55–63.
*Jones, George Fenwick. "Georgia's German-Language Proclamation." *The Report: A Journal of German-American History* 39 (1984):21–31.
*Jones, George Fenwick. "Georgia's Second Language." *The Georgia Review* 21 (1967):87–100.
*Jones, George Fenwick. "The German Element in Colonial Georgia." *Bulletin of the Society for the History of the Germans in Maryland* 31 (1963):71–78.
*Jones, George Fenwick. "German-Speaking Settlers in Georgia, 1733–1741." *The Report: A Journal of German-American History* 38 (1982):35–51.
*Jones, George Fenwick. "Hessian Deserters." *Journal of the Johannes Schwalm Historical Association* 4 (1990):54–58.
*Jones, George Fenwick. "Identifying Germans in Colonial Documents." In *Semper Idem et novus: Festschrift for Frank Banta*, ed. Francis C. Gentry, pp. 403–10. Göppingen, 1988.

*Jones, George Fenwick. "In Memoriam: John Martin Boltzius, 1703–1765, Patriarch of the Georgia Lutherans." *Lutheran Quarterly* 17 (1965):151–65.
*Jones, George Fenwick. "John Adam Treutlen's Origin and Rise to Prominence." In Jackson and Spalding, 217–32.
*Jones, George Fenwick. "John Martin Boltzius Reports on Georgia, 1739." *GHQ* 47 (1963):216–19.
*Jones, George Fenwick. "John Martin Boltzius' Trip to Charleston, October 1742." *SCHM* 83 (1981):87–110.
*Jones, George Fenwick. "Journal of a Trip from Georgia to South Carolina in 1734 by John Martin Boltzius." *Lutheran Quarterly* 16, no. 2 (1964):168–74.
*Jones, George Fenwick. "A Note on the Victor at Springhill Redoubt." *GHQ* 64 (1971):377–79.
*Jones, George Fenwick. "Pastor Boltzius' Letter of June 1737 to a Friend in Berlin." *The Georgia Review* 19 (1965):457–61.
Jones, George Fenwick. "Peter Gordon's (?) Plan of Savannah." *GHQ* 70 (1986):97–101.
Jones, George Fenwick. "Report of Mr. Ettwein's Journey to Georgia and South Carolina, 1765." *SCHM* 91 (1990):147–60.
*Jones, George Fenwick. *Salzburger Saga*. Athens, Ga., 1984.
*Jones, George Fenwick. "The Salzburger Mills." *Yearbook of German-American Studies* 23 (1988):105–17.
*Jones, George Fenwick. "The Secret Diary of Pastor Johann Martin Boltzius." *GHQ* 53 (1969):78–110.
*Jones, George Fenwick. "Sergeant Johann Wilhelm Jasper." *GHQ* 65 (1981):7–15.
*Jones, George Fenwick. "Two 'Salzburger' Letters from George Whitefield and Theobald Kieffer II." *GHQ* 62 (1978):50–57.
*Jones, George Fenwick. "Von Reck's Second Report from Georgia." *William and Mary Quarterly*, 3rd ser., 22 (1965):319–33.
*Jones, George Fenwick, and Sheryl Exley, eds. *Ebenezer Record Book*. Baltimore, 1991.
Jones, George Fenwick, and Terry W. Lipscomb. "A Hessian Map of the Stono Battlefield." *SCHM* 82 (1982):371–81.
Knittel, Walter Allen. *Early Eighteenth Century Palatine Emigration*. Philadelphia, 1937.
*Knox, Mellon, Jr. "Christian Prieber's Cherokee Kingdom of Paradise." *GHQ* 57 (1973):319–31.
Kocherthal, Josua. *Ausführlicher und Umständlicher Bericht von der Berühmten Landschaft Carolina in dem Engelländischen Gelegen*. 4th printing. Frankfurt am Main, 1709.
*Krämer, Johann Matthias. *Neueste und richtigste Nachricht von der Landschaft Georgia*. Göttingen, 1746.
Krön, Peter and Friederike Zaisberger. *Reformation Emigration: Protestanten in Salz-*

burg. Salzburg, 1981.

Lafar, Mabel Freeman, ed. *Abstracts of Wills, Chatham County, Ga*. Savannah, Ga., 1933.

Langen, August. *Der Wortschatz des deutschen Pietismus*. 2nd rev. ed. Tübingen, 1968.

*Lewis, Andrew W. "Henry Muhlenberg's Georgia Correspondence." *GHQ* 49 (1965):424–54.

*Loewald, Klaus G., Beverly Starika, and Paul S. Taylor. "Johann Martin Bolzius Answers a Questionnaire on Carolina and Georgia." *William and Mary Quarterly*, 3rd ser. Vols. 14 (part 1) 218–22 and 15 (part 2) 228–52.

Marsch, Angelika. *Die Salzburger Emigration in Bildern*. Weisshorn, Bayern, 1979.

*Martin, Roger A. "Zubly Comes to America." *GHQ* 61 (1977):125–39.

Meriwether, Robert L. *The Expansion of South Carolina, 1729–1765*. Kingsport, Tenn., 1940.

Meynen, Emil. *Bibliographie des Deutschtums der kolonialzeitlichen Einwandern in Nordamerika*. Leipzig, 1937.

Migliazzo, Arlin Charles. "Ethnic Diversity on the Southern Frontier: A Social History of Purrysburg, South Carolina, 1732–1792." Ph.D. diss., Washington State University, 1982.

*Miller, Randall M. *A Warm and Zealous Spirit*. Macon, Ga., 1982.

Mittelberger, Gottlieb. *Journey to Pennsylvania*. Ed. and trans. Oscar Handlin. Cambridge, Mass., 1960.

Moore, Francis. *A Voyage to Georgia Begun in the Year 1735*. London, 1744. Rpt., St. Simons, Ga., 1983. Also in Reese, *Our First Visit* 81–158.

Muhlenberg, Henry Melchior. *The Journals of Henry Melchior Muhlenberg*, 2 vols. Ed. Theodore Tappert and John W. Doberstein. Philadelphia, 1942–48.

*Newman, Henry. *Henry Newman's Salzburger Letterbooks*. Ed. George Fenwick Jones. Athens, Ga., 1966.

*Newton, Hester W. "The Industrial and Social Influence of the Salzburgers in Colonial Georgia." *GHQ* 18 (1934):335–53.

Ortner, Franz. *Reformation, Katholische Reform und Gegenreformation in Salzburg*. Salzburg, 1981.

*Pennington, Edgar Legare. "The Reverend Bartholomew Zouberbuhler." *GHQ* 18 (1934):354–63.

*Perkins, Eunice Ross. "John Joachim Zubli, Georgia's Conscientious Objector." *GHQ* 15 (1931):313–23.

Pfälzische Landeskunde: Beiträge zur Geographie, Biologie, Volkskunde und Geschichte. Ed. Michael Geiger. Landau, 1981–

Pfister, Hans Ulrich. "Zürcher Auswanderung nach Amerika 1734/1735 – Die Reisegruppe um Pfarrer Moritz Götschi." In *Zürcher Taschenbuch auf das Jahr 1986*, pp. 45–99.

*Prinzinger, A. "Die Ansiedlung der Salzburger im Staate Georgia." *Mitteilungen* der Gesellschaft für Salzburger Landskunde 22 (1882):1–36.

Purry, Peter. "A Description of the Province of South Carolina, 1731." Reprinted in *Historical Collections of South Carolina*, ed. B. R. Carroll, 2:121–40. New York, 1836.

Rattermann, Heinrich Armin. *Die Ursachen der Massenauswanderung aus Deutschland im 18. Jahrhundert.* Cincinnati, 1912. (Vol. 16 of *Ausgewählte Werke*.)

*Reck, Philip Georg Friedrich von. *Kurtzgefasste Nachricht von dem Etablissement derer Salzburger Emigranten zu Ebenezer.* Hamburg, 1777.

*Reck, Philip Georg Friedrich von, and Johann Martin Bolzius. *An Extract of the Journals of Mr. Commissary von Reck and the Reverend Mr. Bolzius.* London, 1734.

Reese, Trevor R., ed. *The Clamorous Malcontents.* Savannah, Ga., 1973.

Reese, Trevor R. *Colonial Georgia.* Athens, Ga., 1963.

Reese, Trevor. *The Most Delightful Country in the Universe: Promotional Literature in the Colony of Georgia, 1717–1734.* Savannah, Ga., 1972.

Reese, Trevor. *Our First Visit in America: Early Reports from the Colony of Georgia, 1732–1740.* Savannah, Ga., 1974.

Revill, Janie, ed. *A Compilation of the Original Lists of Protestant Immigrants to South Carolina, 1763–1773.* Rpt., Columbia, S.C., 1939.

Robbins, Walter L. "John Tobler's Description of South Carolina (1753)." *SCHM* 71 (1970):141–61.

Robbins, Walter L. "Swiss and German Immigrants to America in Rotterdam, 1736." *The Report: A Journal of German-American History* 35 (1972):46–51.

*Rubicam, Milton. "Historical Background of the Salzburger Emigration to Georgia." *GHQ* 35 (1951):99–115.

Rupp, I. Daniel. *A Collection of Upwards of Thirty Thousand Names.* Philadelphia, 1876.

Rush, Benjamin. *An Account of the Manners of the German Inhabitants of Pennsylvania*, ed. Wm. T. Parsons. Collegeville, Pa., 1974.

Salley, A. S. *The History of Orangeburg County.* Orangeburg, S.C., 1898.

Saunders, William L., ed. *The Colonial Records of North Carolina*, 2 vols. Raleigh, N.C., 1886ff.

Schelbert, Leo. *Einführung in die schweizerische Auswanderungsgeschichte der Neuzeit.* Zurich, 1976.

*Schmidt, Martin. "Die Anfänge der Kirchenbildung bei den Salzburgern in Georgia." *Lutherische Kirche in Bewegung*, ed. Gottfried Werner. Erlangen, 1937.

Smith, Abbot E. *Colonists in Bondage.* New York, 1971.

Smith, Henry A. M. "Purrysburgh." *SCHM* 10 (1909):189–219.

Smith, Warren B. *White Servitude in South Carolina.* Columbia, S.C., 1961.

South Carolina Synod. *A History of the Lutheran Church in South Carolina.* Columbia, S.C., 1971.

Spalding, Phinizy. *Oglethorpe in America.* Chicago, 1977.

Stearns, Raymond Phineas. *Science in the British Colonies of America*. Urbana, Ill., 1970.
Stephens, William. *The Journal of William Stephens, 1741–1745*. Ed. E. Merton Coulter. Athens, Ga., 1958–59.
Strassburger, Ralph R., and W. J. Hinke. *Pennsylvania German Pioneers*. Baltimore, 1980.
Strobel, Philip. *The Salzburgers and Their Descendants*. Baltimore, 1855.
Taylor, Paul S. *Georgia Plan: 1732–1752*. Berkeley, Calif., 1972.
Temple, Sarah G., and Kenneth Coleman. *Georgia Journeys*. Athens, Ga., 1961.
Trautz, Fritz. *Die Pfälzische Auswanderung nach Nordamerika im 18. Jahrhundert*. Heidelberg, 1959.
*Tresp, Lothar L., ed. "August 1748, in Georgia, from the Diary of John Martin Boltzius," and "September, 1748, in Georgia, from the Diary of John Martin Boltzius." *GHQ* 47 (1963):204–16, 320–32.
*Tresp, Lothar L. "Early Negro Baptisms in Colonial Georgia by the Salzburgers at Ebenezer." *Americana-Austriaca* 2 (1973):159–70.
*Tresp, Lothar L. "The Salzburger Orphanage at Ebenezer in Colonial Georgia." *Americana-Austriaca* 3 (1974):190–234.
Türler, Heinrich, ed. *Historisch-biographisches Lexikon der Schweiz*, 8 vols. Neuenburg, 1934.
Uhlendorf, Bernhard Alexander. *The Siege of Charleston*. Ann Arbor, Mich., 1938.
*Urlsperger, Johannes August, ed. *Americanisches Ackerwerck Gottes*. Augsburg, 1760, 1767. From 1 June 1759 to end of 1760, with pagination 45–286.
*Urlsperger, Samuel, ed. *Americanisches Ackerwerck Gottes*. Halle, 1751–1754. Vols. 1–3, pp. 1–525, and vol. 4, 1 Jan. to 31 May 1759, with pagination 1–57.
*Urlsperger, Samuel, ed. *Ausführliche Nachrichten von den Saltzburgischen Emigranten*. Halle, 1735–51, 3 vols., 17 continuations. Vol. IV, Jan.
*Urlsperger, Samuel. *Die Sammlung und Führung des IVten Transports Saltzburgischer Emigranten*. Halle, 1741.
*Urlsperger, Samuel. *Zuverlässiges Sendschreiben von den geist-und leiblichen Umständen der Saltzburgischen Emigranten*. Halle, 1736.
*Urlsperger, Samuel, ed. *Zwei Sendschreiben aus der Neuen Welt*. Augsburg, 1740.
van Ham, Herman. "Die Stellung der Staaten und der Regierungsbehörden im Rheinland zum Auswanderungsproblem im 18. und 19. Jahrhundert." *Deutsches Archiv für Landes- und Volksforschung* 6 (1942):261–309.
Ver Steeg, Clarence L., ed. *A True and Historical Narrative of the Colony of Georgia*. By Patrick Tailfer et al. Athens, Ga., 1960.
Voigt, Gilbert P. "The German and German-Swiss Element in South Carolina, 1732–1752." *Bulletin of the University of South Carolina* 113 (1922):4–20.
Voigt, Gilbert P. "Swiss Notes on South Carolina." *SCHM* 21 (1920):93–104.
Walker, George Fuller, comp. *Abstracts of Georgia Colonial Book J, 1755–1762*.

Atlanta, 1978.
Weir, Robert M., ed. "Muster Rolls of the South Carolina Granville and Colliton County Regiments of Militia, 1756." *SCHM* 70 (1969):226–39.
Weller, Karl, and Arnold Weller. *Württembergische Geschichte im süddeutschen Raum*. Stuttgart, 1975.
Wesley, John. *The Journal of John Wesley*. Ed. Nehemia Curnock. London, 1938.
Whitefield, George. *A Journal of a Voyage from London to Savannah in Georgia*. London, 1739.
Wiegandt, Otto. "Ulm als Stadt der Auswanderer." *Ulm und Oberschwaben* 31(1967):88–125.
*Wilson, Caroline Price, ed. *Annals of Georgia*. Vol. 2, *Effingham County Records*. Savannah, Ga., 1933.
Wilson, Renate. "Halle and Ebenezer: Pietism, Agriculture, and Commerce in Colonial Georgia." Ph.D. diss., University of Maryland, 1988.
Wilson, Renate. "Die Halleschen Waisenhausmedikamente und die 'Höchstnotige Erkenntnis' im amerikanischen Kolonialstaat Georgia." *Schriftenreihe Geschichte, Naturwissenschaft, Technik und Medizin*. Leipzig, 28 (1991):109–28.
Wilson, Renate, and H. J. Poeckern. "A Continental System of Medical Care in Colonial Georgia." In *Medizin, Gesellschaft und Geschichte. Jahrbuch des Institut für Geschichte der Medizin der Robert Bosch Stiftung*, forthcoming, 1992.
Wilson, Robert Cumming. *Drugs and Pharmacy in the Life of Georgia, 1733–1759*. Atlanta, 1959.
*Winde, Hermann. "Die Frühgeschichte der Lutherischen Kirche in Georgia." Ph.D. diss., Martin Luther University, Halle-Wittenberg, 1960.
*Withuhn, William L. "Salzburgers and Slavery: A Problem of Mentalité." *GHQ* 68 (1984):173–92.
Wood, Betty. *Slavery in Colonial Georgia, 1730–1775*. Athens, Ga., 1984.
Wust, Klaus. *Colonial America*. Baltimore, 1981.
Wust, Klaus. "The Emigration Season of 1738." *The Report: A Journal of German-American History* 40 (1986):21–56.
Wust, Klaus. "Feeding the Palatines: Shipboard Diet in the Eighteenth Century." *The Report: A Journal of German-American History* 39 (1984):32–42.
Wust, Klaus. "Palatines and Switzers for Virginia, 1705–1738: Costly Lessons for Promoters and Emigrants." *Yearbook of German-American Studies* 19 (1984):43–56.
Wust, Klaus. "William Byrd II and the Shipwreck of the 'Oliver.'" *Newsletter, Swiss-American Historical Society* 20 (1984):3–19.
Yoder, Don, ed. *Pennsylvania German Emigrants, 1709–1786*. Baltimore, 1980.
Yoder, Don, ed. *Rheinland Emigrants: Lists of German Settlers in Colonial America*. Baltimore, 1981.

Stearns, Raymond Phineas. *Science in the British Colonies of America*. Urbana, Ill., 1970.
Stephens, William. *The Journal of William Stephens, 1741–1745*. Ed. E. Merton Coulter. Athens, Ga., 1958–59.
Strassburger, Ralph R., and W. J. Hinke. *Pennsylvania German Pioneers*. Baltimore, 1980.
Strobel, Philip. *The Salzburgers and Their Descendants*. Baltimore, 1855.
Taylor, Paul S. *Georgia Plan: 1732–1752*. Berkeley, Calif., 1972.
Temple, Sarah G., and Kenneth Coleman. *Georgia Journeys*. Athens, Ga., 1961.
Trautz, Fritz. *Die Pfälzische Auswanderung nach Nordamerika im 18. Jahrhundert*. Heidelberg, 1959.
*Tresp, Lothar L., ed. "August 1748, in Georgia, from the Diary of John Martin Boltzius," and "September, 1748, in Georgia, from the Diary of John Martin Boltzius." *GHQ* 47 (1963):204–16, 320–32.
*Tresp, Lothar L. "Early Negro Baptisms in Colonial Georgia by the Salzburgers at Ebenezer." *Americana-Austriaca* 2 (1973):159–70.
*Tresp, Lothar L. "The Salzburger Orphanage at Ebenezer in Colonial Georgia." *Americana-Austriaca* 3 (1974):190–234.
Türler, Heinrich, ed. *Historisch-biographisches Lexikon der Schweiz*, 8 vols. Neuenburg, 1934.
Uhlendorf, Bernhard Alexander. *The Siege of Charleston*. Ann Arbor, Mich., 1938.
*Urlsperger, Johannes August, ed. *Americanisches Ackerwerck Gottes*. Augsburg, 1760, 1767. From 1 June 1759 to end of 1760, with pagination 45–286.
*Urlsperger, Samuel, ed. *Americanisches Ackerwerck Gottes*. Halle, 1751–1754. Vols. 1–3, pp. 1–525, and vol. 4, 1 Jan. to 31 May 1759, with pagination 1–57.
*Urlsperger, Samuel, ed. *Ausführliche Nachrichten von den Saltzburgischen Emigranten*. Halle, 1735–51, 3 vols., 17 continuations. Vol. IV, Jan.
*Urlsperger, Samuel. *Die Sammlung und Führung des IVten Transports Saltzburgischer Emigranten*. Halle, 1741.
*Urlsperger, Samuel. *Zuverlässiges Sendschreiben von den geist-und leiblichen Umständen der Saltzburgischen Emigranten*. Halle, 1736.
*Urlsperger, Samuel, ed. *Zwei Sendschreiben aus der Neuen Welt*. Augsburg, 1740.
van Ham, Herman. "Die Stellung der Staaten und der Regierungsbehörden im Rheinland zum Auswanderungsproblem im 18. und 19. Jahrhundert." *Deutsches Archiv für Landes- und Volksforschung* 6 (1942):261–309.
Ver Steeg, Clarence L., ed. *A True and Historical Narrative of the Colony of Georgia*. By Patrick Tailfer et al. Athens, Ga., 1960.
Voigt, Gilbert P. "The German and German-Swiss Element in South Carolina, 1732–1752." *Bulletin of the University of South Carolina* 113 (1922):4–20.
Voigt, Gilbert P. "Swiss Notes on South Carolina." *SCHM* 21 (1920):93–104.
Walker, George Fuller, comp. *Abstracts of Georgia Colonial Book J, 1755–1762*.

Atlanta, 1978.
Weir, Robert M., ed. "Muster Rolls of the South Carolina Granville and Colliton County Regiments of Militia, 1756." *SCHM* 70 (1969):226–39.
Weller, Karl, and Arnold Weller. *Württembergische Geschichte im süddeutschen Raum*. Stuttgart, 1975.
Wesley, John. *The Journal of John Wesley*. Ed. Nehemia Curnock. London, 1938.
Whitefield, George. *A Journal of a Voyage from London to Savannah in Georgia*. London, 1739.
Wiegandt, Otto. "Ulm als Stadt der Auswanderer." *Ulm und Oberschwaben* 31(1967):88–125.
*Wilson, Caroline Price, ed. *Annals of Georgia*. Vol. 2, *Effingham County Records*. Savannah, Ga., 1933.
Wilson, Renate. "Halle and Ebenezer: Pietism, Agriculture, and Commerce in Colonial Georgia." Ph.D. diss., University of Maryland, 1988.
Wilson, Renate. "Die Halleschen Waisenhausmedikamente und die 'Höchstnotige Erkenntnis' im amerikanischen Kolonialstaat Georgia." *Schriftenreihe Geschichte, Naturwissenschaft, Technik und Medizin*. Leipzig, 28 (1991):109–28.
Wilson, Renate, and H. J. Poeckern. "A Continental System of Medical Care in Colonial Georgia." In *Medizin, Gesellschaft und Geschichte. Jahrbuch des Institut für Geschichte der Medizin der Robert Bosch Stiftung*, forthcoming, 1992.
Wilson, Robert Cumming. *Drugs and Pharmacy in the Life of Georgia, 1733–1759*. Atlanta, 1959.
*Winde, Hermann. "Die Frühgeschichte der Lutherischen Kirche in Georgia." Ph.D. diss., Martin Luther University, Halle-Wittenberg, 1960.
*Withuhn, William L. "Salzburgers and Slavery: A Problem of Mentalité." *GHQ* 68 (1984):173–92.
Wood, Betty. *Slavery in Colonial Georgia, 1730–1775*. Athens, Ga., 1984.
Wust, Klaus. *Colonial America*. Baltimore, 1981.
Wust, Klaus. "The Emigration Season of 1738." *The Report: A Journal of German-American History* 40 (1986):21–56.
Wust, Klaus. "Feeding the Palatines: Shipboard Diet in the Eighteenth Century." *The Report: A Journal of German-American History* 39 (1984):32–42.
Wust, Klaus. "Palatines and Switzers for Virginia, 1705–1738: Costly Lessons for Promoters and Emigrants." *Yearbook of German-American Studies* 19 (1984):43–56.
Wust, Klaus. "William Byrd II and the Shipwreck of the 'Oliver.'" *Newsletter, Swiss-American Historical Society* 20 (1984):3–19.
Yoder, Don, ed. *Pennsylvania German Emigrants, 1709–1786*. Baltimore, 1980.
Yoder, Don, ed. *Rheinland Emigrants: Lists of German Settlers in Colonial America*. Baltimore, 1981.

Index

(Abbreviations: br = brother, d = daughter of, fr = from, m = marries, Pal = Palatine, s = son of, Salz = Salzburger, Sw = Swiss, Swab = Swabian, trans = transport, w = wife of, wid = widow)

Aarau, SW town, 78
Aare, Sw river, 21
Abercorn, settlement downstream from Ebenezer, 37, 38, 98, 104, 109, 111, 129, 134, 135, 169, 170, 205, 213, 218, 243, 268, 270
Abercorn Creek, former west channel of the Savannah River, 114, 134, 192, 205, 213, 214, 216, 218, 227, 243
Abercorn Island, flooded island bordered by Abercorn Creek, 114
Ackerwerck Gottes. See *Americanisches Ackerwerck*
Acton, "Dutch" village south of Savannah, 86–111, 169, 194, 278
Acton Church, 102
Ade (Adde), Hieronymus Salomo, Swab cobbler fr Tübingen, 32, 74, 75, 120
Ade (Adde), Johann, s Salomo, 74, 226
Ade (Adde), Margaretha, w Salomo, 74
Adventure, ship, 73
Agri Decumates, Roman frontier province, 2
Aingere, J. Michael, Pal at German Village, 8, 60
Albeck, town in Territory of Ulm, 150, 151; map, 141

Alemanni, Germanic tribe, 2, 22, 30
Alsace, former German province, 2, 167, 190, 203. *See also*, Strassburg
Altheim, town in Territory of Ulm, 151; map, 141
Alther(r), Johann, Sw butcher, 83, 100, 154, 229, 248; will of, 256
Alther, Josef, s Johann, 154
Americanisches Ackerwerck Gottes, Samuel Urlsperger's edition of the reports fr the Ebenezer ministers, ix, 56
Ample (am Buehl?), Johann, Sw, 87, 88, 91
Amsterdam, Dutch port, 126
Anabaptists, 128, 167
Andlau, Franz von, Alsatian officer, 182, 190
Anhalt regiment, 187
Anne, English queen, 10
Annoni, Hieronymus, SW minister, 27
Ansbach, German town, 164
Antilope, ship, 146
Anton, Paul, professor at Halle, 204
Appenzell, Sw canton, 105
Appenzell-ausser-Rhoden, division of Appenzell, 24, 108
Appenzellers, settlers at New Windsor, 128, 132
Architecture, 252

337

Index

Argyle. *See* Ft. Argyle
Arminius, Germanic chieftain, 2
Arndt, Johannes, author of *Wahres Christentum*, 203, 243
Arnsdorf, Catharina Dorothea, Pal wid, 207
Arnsdorf, Magdalena, Pal, 127
Arnsdorf, Peter, 235
Arnsdorf family in Savannah, 194
Art, 250–52
Asbury, Francis, Methodist bishop, 195
Ascension, Lutheran Church of the, 80–83
Aschbacher, Matthias, slave owner, 272
Ash. *See* Aschbacher
Associates of Dr. Bray, British missionary society, 51
A State of the Province, report on conditions in Georgia, 77
Augsburg, Swabian city, 8, 30, 38, 122, 123, 194, 225
Augspurger (Augsburger), Samuel, Sw surveyor, 59, 64, 65
Augusta, city on the Savannah River, 65, 75, 112, 166, 169, 170
Augustine, Walter, early English settler, 37
Augustine Creek, river east of Savannah, 154, 306 (n. 66)
Ausführliche Nachrichten (sometimes called *Urlsperger Nachrichten*), Samuel Urlsperger's edition of the reports of the Ebenezer ministers, vii, 39, 206, 240
Austin, George, Charleston merchant, 69
Austrians, religious exiles fr Carinthia and Upper Austria, 39
Avery, Joseph, English surveyor, 88, 91, 93–95, 97, 119, 197, 216, 245
Ayres, Jacob, master of the *King George*, 52
Azenheim, British resident at Frankfurt, 68

Bach, Gabriel, Swab, ranger, 56, 274, 276, 277
Bach, Margaretha. *See* Staude
Bacher, Balthasar, carpenter, 225
Bacher, Maria, midwife, 239
Bacher, Matthias, Salz, 124
Baden, German province, 2
Bader, Matthias, Swab returnee, 148
Bahner, Nikolaus, Hessian deserter, 191
Baine, Rodney M., 282 (n. 10)
Bakers, 229
Bandley. *See* Bentli
Barber, Jonathan, chaplain at Bethesda, 82, 127
Barker, manager at cowpen, 55
Barn in Salz style, 246, 253
Barriky (Barraquier), wid, silk producer fr Purysburg, 221, 317 (n. 93)
Basel, Sw city, 22
Bauer, Johann, Sw, 151
Baugh. *See* Gabriel Bach
Baumgarten, Sigmund Jacob, German scholar, 204
Bavaria, German province, 3
Bavarians, Germanic tribe, 3, 14; in Georgia, 38
Bears, 209, 211
Beaufain, Hector Bellinger de, S.C. planter, 223
Beaulieu. *See* Bewlie
Becu. *See* Beque
Beehives. *See* Honey
Beissel, Conrad, leader at Ephrata, Pa., 271
Bell, for Jerusalem Church, 122
Belligut, Johann, Pal, 8, 88
Bells on cattle, 211
Beltz, Sigismund, Sw planter, 99, 112; will of, 256
Beltz, (Hans) Ulrich, Sw planter, 86, 91
Benefactions. *See* Welfare
Bentli (Bandley) Agatha, Pal, 46, 93
Bentz, Karl, 170
Beque (Becu), Gile, French baker, 83, 295 (n. 83)
Bere, Christian, Pal, 59
Bere, Elisabetha, Pal, d Christian, 59
Bere, Maria, Pal, w Christian, 59
Berger (Berker), Johann, Pal, 83
Berghoffer (Berchoffer, Berhofter), Johann, Pal, 100

Index 339

Bergmann, Pastor Christoph Friedrich, son Johann Ernst, 195
Bergmann, Johann Ernst, minister at Ebenezer, 195
Bermaringen, town in Territory of Ulm, 151; map, 141
Bern, Sw city, 22, 54, 57, 65, 78, 79
Bernhardt, Pastor, Hessian deserter, 191
Bernstadt, town in Territory of Ulm, 151; map, 141
Berrier, Johann, Pal, 8, 88, 93
Bethany, Swab settlement on Blue Bluff, 135, 146, 148, 160, 161, 172, 263, 278; map of, 149
Bethany Church, 148
Bethany Company, military unit, 178, 182
Bethany school, 243
Bethesda, George Whitefield's orphanage, 71, 82, 118, 125, 128
Betz (Pett), passenger on *Judith*, 105
Betz, Johann Caspar, Pal, 155
Betz, Johann Michael, Pal, 155
Betz, Ulrich, Pal, 90
Bewlie (Beaulieu), Col. Stephens's estate, 72, 90, 97, 182, 186, 276
Biberach, Swab city, 122
Bichler, Maria, first w Thomas, 130
Bichler, Thomas, Salz, 55, 130, 131, 145, 166, 219, 227, 235, 277
Biddenbach, Matthäus, vestryman, 173, 182
Biel, Sw city, 38
Bilbao, Spanish port, 104
Biltz, Sigismund, tailor, 228
Bineke, Christina, d Johann, 59
Bineke, Johann Friedrich, Pal, 59, 60
Bineke, Johann Ulrich, Pal, s Joh Fr, 59
Bininger, Rudolf, militiaman, 166
Birmenstorff, Sw town, 34
Bischoff, Anna Maria, midwife, 239
Bishop, Henry, English servant to Boltzius, 62, 120, 130, 166, 168
Bishop, Sibilla Friederica, née Unselt, w Henry, 166
Black Creek, German settlement, 271

Black Forest, mountain range in Germany, 150, 186
Blacksmiths. *See* Smiths
Blackwelder (fr Schwarzwälder), Georgia family, 55, 194
Blasse (Plessi), Jacob, Pal, 112
Block Island, scene of shipwreck, 74
Blue Bluff, site of Bethany, 135, 143, 146–48, 182
Blume, Valentin, Pal, 88
Blunt, Stephan, patriot, 180
Bogg, Capt. Peter, master of *Charles Town Galley*, 136, 137, 138, 139, 145
Böhler, Peter, Moravian missionary, 51
Bohrmann, Johann Michael, passenger on *Judith*, 105, 135, 136, 155
Boltzius, Christina Elisabetha, d Martin, 171
Boltzius, Gertraut, w Martin, 125, 223, 239, 240
Boltzius, Gotthelf Israel, s Martin, 171, 172
Boltzius, Johann Martin, pastor of Georgia Salzburgers, viii, 11, 21, 29, 39–41, 43, 50–52, 54–56, 62, 69, 71, 73–85, 92, 94, 96, 98–105, 111, 114–22, 124–38, 142–47, 152–56, 159, 162–72, 175, 184, 197, 203–9, 212–56, 258, 259, 265–74, 276–78; picture, 251; will of, 256
Boltzius, Samuel Leberecht, s Martin, 171
Books, 132, 244–45
Boreman. See *Compendious Account*, 99, 131
Bormann. *See* Bohrmann
Bornemann, Benjamin Wilhelm, s JC, 162
Bornemann, Carolina Magdalena, née Greve, w JC, 152, 161, 162
Bornemann, Johann Christoph, fr Göttingen, 152, 161, 162, 208, 233, 263, 308 (n. 103); will of, 256
Bosomworth, Abraham, br of Thomas, 64
Bosomworth, Thomas, Anglican minister and Indian trader, 63, 102, 107
Botzenhardt, Barthel, Swab returnee, 148
Botzenhardt, Martin, Swab returnee, 148
Bourghalter. *See* Burckhalter

Bourquin, John, militia commander, 166, 209, 238
Bracke, Christoph, Hessian deserter, 189
Bradley, Wm, overseer of Trust servants, 47, 71, 229
Brahm, Johann Gerhard Wilhelm von, surveyor, 100, 146–48, 158–61, 182, 197, 226, 245, 275
Brahm, Wilhelmina von, w J.G.W., 159
Brakefield (Brachfeld?), Wendel, Pal, 104, 105
Braumberger (Braunberger), Matthias, Bavarian, 38
Brandenberger, Hans Cunrad, Sw, 45
Brandenburg, German province, 64, 165, 237
Brandner, Maria, d Matthias, 319 (n. 6)
Brandner, Matthias, Salz, 137, 212, 215, 268
Brandy, peach and plum, 215
Brauniger, Johann Abraham, Sw, 45
Breithaupt, Joachim Justus, professor at Halle, 204
Bretzel, Nikolaus, Sw 151
Breuer, Johann Friedrich, pastor in East Prussia, 123
Briar Creek, settlement up Savannah River, 146, 152, 156, 160
Brickmaking, 229
Brown, Capt., brought 3rd Swab trans, 150
Brunnholtz, Pastor, of Philadelphia, 219
Bryan, Hugh, S.C. planter, 210
Bryan, Jonathan, S.C. planter, br Hugh, 210
Buckhalter, 196, variant of Burckhalter
Bühler, Captain at Ebenezer, 182, 243, 311 (n. 44)
Bull, James, S.C. gentleman, 105
Bundy, Dr., Georgia Trustee, 19
Burck, Christian, will of, 256
Burckhalter, Michael, Sw, 54, 81, 83, 86, 95, 96, 98–100, 102, 105, 106, 112, 163, 224, 245; will of, 256
Burckhalter, Peter, observer, 178
Burckhalter, Rudolf, assessor, 111

Burckhalter (Burkhalter) family in Savannah, 194
Burgemeister, Christoph, Sw, 80, 86, 90, 91, 99
Burgholder, Burghalter. *See* Burckhalter
Burgi, Rudolf, Sw, 86, 90, 91
Burgstein, Sw town in Canton Bern, 57
Burgsteiner, Daniel, patriot, 180
Burgsteiner, Matthias, Salz, 237
Burgsteiner family in Savannah, 194
Burkhalter family in Savannah, 194
Burkhalter Road, 197
Burnemann. *See* Bornemann
Butchers, 129

Cadzant, province in Netherlands, 124, 233
Caledonia, immigrant ship, 148
Callenberg, Johann Heinrich, missionary to the Jews, 84
Calvin, John, 4
Calvinism, 4, 5, 8, 30, 48, 82, 83, 101, 107, 137
Campbell, Archibald, Col., British commander, 172, 178, 180, 188, 196, 306 (n. 52)
Camuse, Mary (Maria Camuso), Italian silk producer, 99, 221, 222
Cannstadt, Swab river port, 123
Carinthians, 48. *See also* Austrians
Carl Rudolf, imposter, 162, 163, 308 (n. 113)
Carpenter, Nicolas, English servant, 46
Carpenters, 225
Carver, John, English merchant, 104
Catesby, Mark, artist, 157
Catholic League, union of Catholic rulers, 4
Catholics (Catholicism), 8, 18, 39, 48, 49, 56, 84, 159, 195, 202, 271
Cattle: at Vernonburg, 98; at Ebenezer, 124, 210–12; destruction of wild cattle, 98, 212
Cattle Brand Book, register of brands, 211
Cattle disease, 96, 98, 212

Causton, Thomas, keeper of the stores, 37, 41, 42, 48, 50, 71, 95, 105, 119, 136, 154, 263; sketch of his boat, 42
Celts, early inhabitants of Western Europe, 1
Censorship, 38, 50, 53, 130–31, 247
Chad. *See* Schad
Charities. *See* Welfare
Charlemagne, Frankish emperor, 3, 22
Charleston, S.C. city, 12, 38, 46, 65, 69, 70, 101, 107, 124, 158, 160, 183, 188, 219, 223, 235, 267, 276, 277
Charles Town Galley, ship bringing Palatines, 136, 139
Charming Martha, passenger ship, 141, 164
Charms, 246–47
Cherokees. *See* Indians
Chiffelle (Chifelle), Henri François, Calvinist minister, 80, 82, 83, 145
Children, freed fr indenture, 94, 96
Christ, Gottfried, converted tailor, 227, 245, 248
Christ Church Parish, area containing Savannah, Acton, Hamptstead, and Vernonburg, 169; map of, 89
Christer, Franz Friedrich, Pal, 46
Christer, Maria Magdalena, w Franz, 46
Christianity, introduction of, 3
Christie, Thomas, recorder in Savannah, 53, 265
Churches. *See* Ascension Church, Bethany Church, Goshen Church, Jerusalem Church, Zion Church
Clarke, Col. Alured, British commander, 189, 190
Clay-eating. *See* Diseases
Clements, Wid, Pal, 59, 196
Clements, Andreas, Pal, 196; will of, 256
Clements, Josef, Pal, 59
Clemmands. *See* Clements
Clovis, Frankish king, 3
Cluer, Elisabetha, Pal, 59
Cockspur Island, at mouth of Savannah River, 141, 178

Colonial Records of the State of Georgia, ix, 45, 139
Compendious Account, treatise on silk culture by Boreman, 131
Congarees, German settlement in S.C., 167
Coram, Capt. Thomas, Georgia Trustee, 157, 232, 253
Cornberger, Christoph, patriot, 180
Corn-shilling, subsidy, 131, 213
Correspondence, 130
Costumes, 248
Cotton. *See* Crops
Cougar. *See* Mountain lions
Council, local Georgia government consisting of President and five Assistants, 53, 88, 103, 142, 212, 218, 269, 271
Counter Reformation, 4
Cow bells, 211
Cowes, English port of clearance, 70, 71
Cowpen (at Old Ebenezer), 55, 98, 135, 212
Crab grass, 213
Cramer. *See* Krämer
Crane in Savannah, 72, 218
Craus. *See* Krause
Creeks. *See* Indians
Croneberger, Heinrich, Pal fr Purysburg, 33
Crop reports, 86, 213
Crops: barley, 98, 213; beans, 213; corn, 213; cotton, 99–100, 215; flax, 215; fruit, 215; indigo, 214; oats, 213; rice, 213, 214; rye, 213; sweet potatoes, 213; wheat, 213. *See also* European grains
Cuius regio, eius religio, religious law, 3, 201
Cunradi, Heinrich, Sw, 87, 90, 91
Curraudi. *See* Cunradi
Curtius. *See* Kurtz, Jacob
Custobader, Catharina, Pal, 74
Customs, 246

Dagenfeld, General von, benefactor, 314 (n. 18)
Dancing, 250

Danner, Jacob, Sw, 87, 90, 91
Dansler (Danzler). *See* Densler
Danube River, 2
Danzig, free German city, 165
Darien, Scots settlement in Georgia, 60, 122, 146
Dasha Creek, 197
Dasha Landing, 197
Dasher, Christian, Sw, 134, 155, 180
Dasher, Johann Martin, Whig, 180, 192
Dasher, Martin, Sw, 55, 132, 178
Dasher Cemetery, 194
Dasher family in Savannah, 194
Daubuz, Capt., master of *Georgia Pink*, 47
Dauner, Michael, Swab, 151
Davis, Capt., brings Germans fr Frederica, 67
Davis, Jenking, doctor, 176, 179, 191
Davison, Samuel, quoted, 60
Decumates. *See* Agri
Deer, 208
Degmair, Matthäus Friedrich, chaplain, 194
De Gratia universali, religious treatise, 127
Deigler, Daniel, Pal, 88
Demaitre, Daniel, skipper, 110
Demere, Capt. Raymond, early English settler, 160
Dempsey, Charles, emissary, 275
Denny, Walther, Pal at German Village, 67, 60, 110, 112, 299 (n. 136)
Densler, Conrad, Pal, 80, 88, 93, 154
Densler, Heinrich, Pal planter, 98, 112, 155
Densler, Philip, Whig, 186
Densler family in Savannah, 194
Dependencies, 134. *See also* Abercorn; Bethany; Goshen
Depp, Valentin, Sw fr Orangeburg, 242
Derrick, Wid, Pal, 59
Derrick (Derick), Elisabetha, d Wid, 59
Derrick, Jacob, s Wid, 59
Derrick, Margaretha, d Wid, 59
Derrick, Melchior, s Wid, 59
Descriptions, 253–55
d'Estaing, Count Charles Henri, French commander, 182, 183, 186, 188
Dester (Textor ?), inhabitant of Hampstead, 54
Detailed Reports, translation of *Ausführliche Nachrichten* and *Ackerwerck Gottes*, ix, xiii, 101, 103, 139
Detzner, Ernst Ambrosius, Pal, 59
Detzner, Martha, w Ernst, 59
De Vorsey, Louis, geographer, 159
Diaspora, 193–98
Dice. *See* Theiss
Diehle, Peter, Pal planter, 88, 112; will of, 256
Dietzius, Andreas Gottfried, German settler, 158
Dippel, Johann Conrad, radical Pietist and spiritualist, 137, 205
Diseases, 231; bloody flux, 233; clay-eating (hookworm disease); 234–35; dysentery, 37, 233; epilepsy, 234; fever clot, 234; *Friesel* (military disease), 235; malaria, 231–34; Palatine fever, 11; pica, 234; purples (military disease, sometimes typhus), 236; scurvy, 41, 233; side-stitches, 235; smallpox, 235; typhus, 11; venereal disease, 236; whooping cough, 236; yellow fever, 235
Dobell, John, English schoolmaster, 81, 86, 94, 95, 111, 112, 142, 244, 263, 267
Domestic life, 245–53
Dover, English port, 21, 39, 131, 157
Drake, cartel ship, 104
Dresler (Dressler), Georg, Pal, 247
Dresler, Georgia town, 198
Driessler, Mrs., w Joh. Ul., letter fr, 67
Driessler, Johann Ulrich, pastor at Frederica, 62, 63, 65, 102, 126, 144
Dübendorfer, Heinrich, Sw, 45
Duchee, Andrew, potter, 74, 229
Dudweiler, Hans, Sw, 45
Dunbar, George, Scottish captain, 38, 136
Durlach, principality on Rhine, 76
Dürrenbergers, exiles fr Austria, 17, 233
Dusseign. *See* Tussing
Dutch, term for German-speaking people, vii, 34–35

Index

Dutch Fork, German area in S.C., 246
Dutch Island, southeast of Savannah, 154, 197
Dutch sea captain, 233
Dutchtown, hamlet near Vernonburg, 112
Dutchtown Road, 197
Dysentery. *See* Diseases

East Indies, Lutheran missions in, 206, 207
East Prussia, Salzburgers in, 14, 123, 206
Ebenezer, Salz settlement, 35 passim; sketch of founding of, 45; praise of, 121–22; map of, 160; decline of, 171–75
Ebenezer Church Records, records of Jerusalem Church, 56, 273
Ebenezer Creek, tributary of the Savannah, 35, 37, 39, 41, 264, 265
Ebenezer fortifications, map of, 180
Ebenezer Redoubt, 184
Eberhard, Anna, Swab, 151
Eberhard, Johann, Swab, 26, 151
Ebner, Johann Georg, fr Strassburg, 167
Eckhart, Martin, Swab, 151
Eckstein, Wilhelm, Hessian deserter, 189
Edict of Expulsion, decree expelling Salzburger Protestants, 14
Education, 243; adult education, 244
Eerhard. *See* Ehrhard
Effingham County, county containing Ebenezer, 193, 194, 197, 246
Egger, Margaretha, Salz, 120
Egmont, Earl of, Georgia Trustee, 17, 47, 48, 91, 95, 100, 123, 133
Ehrhard, Gabriel, planter, 170
Ehrhard, Johann, Swab, 151
Eigel, Johann, Whig, 180
Eischberger, David, miller, 217
Eisenmann, Philip, German in S.C., 269
Elba Island, in Savannah River, 154, 193
Elgg, Sw town in Canton Zurich, 29
Ellis, Henry, governor, 56, 155
Ellis, Thomas, constable, 133
Emigration, efforts to discourage, 24–30
Emigration, Palatine, 8–13
Emigration fr Georgia, 168–70

Enderli, Heinrich, Sw, 45, 93
Engelbrecht, Martin, engraver, 250
English language, 244
Engller, Zich Heinrich, Sw, 45
Enterprise. *See* Private enterprise
Eppinger, Johann, bricklayer, 229, 256
Erinxmann, Johann, Pal, 86–88, 90, 91
Ernst, Josef, Bavarian, ix, 129, 238, 254, 320 (n. 35)
Ettwein, Johann, Moravian, 53, 128, 167, 172, 309 (n. 1)
Europa, disease-ridden ship, 11, 33, 48, 78–80, 86, 90, 99, 220, 239
European grains (barley, oats, rye, wheat), 213–15, 248
Eveleigh, Samuel, Charleston merchant, 46
Ewen, William, neighbor of Salzburgers, 176, 277
Exley, town in Georgia, 197
Exley (fr Öchsele) family in Savannah, 194

Faber, Conrad, slave driver, 273
Fahan (?). *See* Fasan
Fahm, Friedrich, loyalist, 186, blacksmith, 228
Falck (Falk), Gabriel, Swedish preacher, 128
Fallowfield, John, constable, 73
Fasan (?), Benjamin Heinrich, Sw, 45
Faul, Georg, blacksmith, 228
Faust, Albert B., historian, 27
Fences, 92
Ferrier, family, 232
Ferrier, Conrad, Pal, 8, 88
Fetzer, Christian, carpenter, 225
Fink, Paul, Swab, 146
Firmian, Archbishop of Salzburg, 14
First Salz transport, 21
First Swabian transport, 139–42
Fischbeck, German town, 125, 126, 165
Fischer, Ambrosius, Swab fr Langenau, 151
Fischer, Catharina, Swab fr Langenau, 151
Fischer, David, planter, 98
Fischer, Georg, Swab fr Zähringen, 151

Fishing, 209–10; trout, 209; eels, 210; skittering, 210
Flax. *See* Crops
Fleinsheim, town in Württemberg, 152
Flerl, Anna Maria, née Höpflinger, w Johann, convert, 202
Flerl, Dorothea, née Kieffer, w Johann, 166
Flerl, Johann, Jun., Capt., 178
Flerl, Johann, Salz, 171, 173, 243
Flerl family graves, 194
Florida Indians. *See* Indians, Spanish
Foltz. *See* Voltz
Forst, town on the Elb, 165
Ft. Argyle, fort on Ogeechee, 55–57, 236, 270
Forts, service at, 57, 110, 279
Ft. St. George, 57, 275
Fourth Salz transport, 69, 122–24
Francke, August Hermann, head of Francke Foundation, 204
Francke, Gotthilf August, son and successor of A.H., 43, 62, 118, 119, 152, 171, 172, 237
Francke, Johann Paul, Pal, 260
Francke Foundation, charitable institution in Halle, 21, 118, 124, 125, 171, 237
Francis, Mrs., wife of W, 253
Francis, Lt. William, 253
Frankfurt am Main, German city, 20, 69
Frankfurt an der Oder, German city, 35
Franklin, Benjamin, 235
Franks, Germanic tribe, 2
Franks, Jacob, merchant in New York, 85
Frauenfeld, Sw town and canton, 79
Frederica, British settlement on Florida border, 39–41, 57, 65, 75, 80, 84, 101, 102, 105, 162, 205; map of, 58
Frederick William, Soldier King of Prussia, 14, 27
French, 18
French names among Georgia Germans, 8
Fretz, Georg, rower, 110
Fretz, Johann, rower, 110
Freudenstadt, town in Black Forest, 150

Frey, Abraham, Swab, 151
Freyermuth, Peter, Alsatian, 146
Freylinghausen's *Order of Salvation*, 243; songbook, 249
Friesel. See Diseases
Friesland, Georg, Hessian deserter, 189
Fritschi, Heinrich, Sw, 45, 112
Fritzler, Wid, Pal, 88
Fruit. *See* Peaches
Fry, Capt. Tobias, master of the *Purysburg*, 21, 131
Fulbright. *See* Vollbrecht

Gabel. *See* Gebel
Galliser, Hans Caspar, recruiter, 78
Gallus, Irish missionary, 22
Gampert (Gamphert), Christian, Pal, 59, 80, 112, 295 (n. 68), 314 (n. 23)
Gampert, Jeremias, s. Chr, 314 (n. 23)
Gampert (Gamphert), Margaretha, w Chr, 207
Garbet, Caspar, planter, 112
Garbut, Caspar, carpenter, 225, 226 (probably same as above)
Gardner, Alexander, Anglican commissary, 107
Gauls, early tribesmen, 1
Gebel, Abraham, carpenter, 182, 225
Gebel (Gable), Johann, 136; will of, 256
Gebhart (Gephard), Elisabetha, Pal, 59, 74
Gebhart, Hans Georg, s Phil, Sr., 59
Gebhart, Magdalena, Pal, 74, 294 (n. 47)
Gebhart, Maria Catharina, d Philip, Sr, 59
Gebhart, Martha, w Philip, Sr., 59
Gebhart, Philip, Jr., Pal, 59
Gebhart, Philip, Sr., Pal, 59, 76
Geiger, Lucas, schoolmaster, 243
Geiger family in Savannah, 194
George II, king of England, 20, 43, 156, 157
Georgia Packet, ship, 62
Georgia Pink, Capt. Daubuz's ship, 47, 237
Georgia Salzburger Society, 195, 313 (n. 6)
Gerber, Caspar. *See* Garbut

Gerber, Paul, Swab, 158
Gerdes (Guerdes), Walther, Lutheran minister in London, 102
Gering. *See* Goering
Germain, Widow, quoted, 60
Germania, area study by Tacitus, 2, 210
German Indian trader, benefactor, 206, 268
German place names in Georgia, 197
German schoolmaster in Savannah, 81, 126
Germans in Savannah, 80–85, 207
German slaveholders, 270–73
German Village, settlement on St. Simons, 49, 57–64, 67; map of, 58
Geywitz, Hans, Sw, 151
Giessendanner, Johann, nephew of above, 106
Giessendanner, Johann Ulrich, Sw engraver, 22, 29
Gimmel (Kümmel?), Balthasar, will of, 256
Giovanoli, Giovanni, Italian silkworker, 47
Giovanoli, Maria, Italian, w Giovanni, 47
Glaner, George, Salz, 142
Glocker, Elisabetha, Salz, w Bernhard, 124
Glöckler, wid and children, Sw, 151
Gnan Hammock, 197
Gnann, Mrs., the potter's wife, 229
Gnann, Jacob, vestryman, 192, 229
Gnann, Johann Georg, Swabian, 145
Gnann, Pearl Rahn, genealogist, 193
Gnann family in Savannah, 194
Göbel, Johann Otto, Hessian col., 180
Godfrey, John, Englishman at Southhampton, 70
Good Harmony, Boltzius' estate, 145
Gordon, Mr. George, leader of the Highlanders, 38
Göring, Simon, Pal, 91, 102
Goshen, settlement southeast of Ebenezer, 135; Goshen Church, 195, 219, 271; Goshen school, 243; military service, 263, 278
Gosport, English port, 104, 126, 164
Göttingen, German university town, 150, 161, 165

Graffenried, Christoph de, Sw promoter, 10
Graham, Dr. Patrick, neighbor of Salzburgers, 63
Granewetter, Catharina, 230
Great Embarkation (Salz, Moravians, Scots), 50
Great Ogeechee River, 50, 55, 57, 146, 167, 268
Green, Capt., 264
Greiner (Griner), Andreas, planter, 152
Greiner, Johann Caspar, Jr., captain, 162, 178
Greiner, Johann Caspar, Swab, 151, 162, 177
Greiner, Philip, Whig, 180
Grenier. *See* Greiner
Greve (Graeve), Johann Heinrich, fr Göttingen, 152, 161, 162
Greve (Graeve), Luisa Margaretha, w Johann Hr, 152, 161, 162
Grien, Johann, Jr., planter, 98
Grimmiger, Andreas, Austrian, 168
Griner (fr Greiner), family in Savannah, 194
Grisons, Sw canton, 3; immigrants fr, 45–47, 79
Groll, Johann, shoemaker, 226
Gronau, Catharina, w Is. Chr., 125, m Lemke, 126
Gronau, Friederica Maria, d Is. Chr., 125, 173
Gronau, Hanna Elisabeth, d Is. Chr., 125, 164, 173
Gronau, Israel Christian, second minister at Ebenezer, 21, 81, 82, 105, 111–17, 122, 124, 125, 134, 165, 171, 205, 206, 243, 253, 266
Gronau, Timotheaus, s Is. Chr., 239
Gröner, Barbara, Swab, 151
Groover (fr Gruber), family in Savannah, 194
Gross, Michel, Swab, 151
Grovenstine (fr Grabenstein or Graffenstein), family in Savannah, 194

346 Index

Grover (fr Gruber), family in Savannah, 194
Gruber, town in Georgia, 197
Gruber, Georg, Swab, 150
Gruber, Wilhelm (?), loyalist, 186
Gruber family in Savannah, 194
Grüning, Abraham, Sw laborer, 51, 52, 57, 80, 275
Gschwandl, Thomas, Salz, 268
Gugel, Matthias, Pal, 112; will of, 256
Gugel family in Savannah, 194
Gullah, 273
Gunther, David, Pal, 83
Günther, James, ranger, 111
Günther, Peter, ranger, 111
Guring. *See* Göring

Habersham, James, merchant, President of Council, 53, 127, 128, 135, 141–46, 153, 154, 159, 162, 164, 169, 174, 177, 218, 219, 264, 267, 269, 270; picture of, 144
Habersham, John, s James, 177, 178
Häckel, Jerg, Swab, 150
Häckel, Johann, Swab, 151
Hacker Werner, historian, 11, 150
Häfner, Wid Conrad, 88
Häfner, Conrad, Pal, 93
Häg, Mrs., w of schoolmaster, 172
Häg, schoolmaster at Bethany, 172, 243
Hagen, Josef, Moravian, 53
Haid, Georg, will of, 256
Haid, Johann Jacob, engraver, 250
Haisler, Georg, ranger, 111, loyalist, 186
Haisler, Johann, loyalist, 186
Häkel. *See* Häckel
Halifax, settlement on Savannah River, 150, 152, 162, 169, 183, 263
Halle, German university town, 54, 62, 125, 132, 171, 172; medicines fr, 239, 240; books fr, 244; clothes fr, 248
Haller, Albrecht von, Swiss scientist, 161
Haltz, Ulrich Johann, Sw, 86
Hamburg, German port, 165, 277
Hamilton, Henry, English wigmaker, schoolmaster at Ebenezer, 103, 129, 244
Hamilton, James, social scientist, 277

Hamilton, Regina Charlotte, Silesian, w Henry, 129, 165
Hamm, Hans Jacob, planter, 155, 156, 271
Hammer, Johann Daniel, loyalist, 186
Hammer, Maria Rosina, Saxon, 34
Hammer, Michael, Saxon planter, 169
Hammer, Samuel, planter, 112
Hampstead, German hamlet, 54, 86, 95, 107, 154, 276, 278
Handel, Friedrich, songs by, 250
Häner, Nikolaus, Jr., Sw, 86, 90, 91, 111
Häner, Nikolaus, Sr., Sw planter, 90, 91, 98, 111, 112, 186
Haner's Creek, 197
Hangleiter, Johannes, shoemaker, vestryman, 192, 227
Hangleiter, Joseph, church elder, 192
Hangleiter's Creek, 197
Hanner. *See* Häner
Hanover (Hannover), North German state, home of English kings, 21, 161
Harbeck. *See* Herbach
Harper, Simon, English boy, 51
Harrington, Lord, British secretary of state, 26, 69
Harris, Francis, English merchant, 87, 94, 143, 222, 276
Harris and Habersham, merchants, 143, 162, 223
Hart, Michael, Pal, 80
Harvie, Capt., master of the *Caledonia*, 148
Hasenlauer, Sebastian, Swab, 150, 151
Hauer. *See* Haefner
Hawk, warship, 39
Health, 231–36
Heck, Caspar, vestryman, 192
Heck's Branch, 197
Heid. *See* Haid
Heidelberg, German university town, 5, 126
Heidt family in Savannah, 194
Heinle, Jacob, Swab, s Joh., 142
Heinle, Johann, Jr., 142, 238
Heinle, Johann, Swab miller, 142
Heinrich, Catharina, d Peter, Pal, 74
Heinrich, Elisabeth, Pal, 112

Heinrich, Eva Barbara, d Peter, 74
Heinrich, Juliana, Pal, 74
Heinrich, Margaretha, d Peter, 74
Heinrich, Peter, Pal servant to Boltzius, 74, 75
Heinrich children, 75
Heintz, Johann Christoph, slave driver, 273
Heintzelmann, Israel, clerk, 167, 246
Heisler. *See* Haisler
Hek, Johann Peter, city scribe, 8
Held, Conrad, Pal, 74, 76
Held, Elisabetha, d Conrad, 74, 76
Held, Elisabetha, w Conrad, 74, 76
Held, Georg, Pal, s Conrad, 74, 230
Held, Hans Michael, Pal, s Conrad, 74, 76
Helfenstein, Dorothea, Pal, w J.J., 126
Helfenstein, Friederica, 237
Helfenstein, Johann Jacob, Sw tanner, 227
Helfenstein family, 232
Helme, Nikolaus, Swab, 142, 151
Helmy (fr Helme), Savannah family, 194
Hennery, Johann, Pal, 80
Herb, Friedrich, planter, 112
Herb River, 197
Herbach, Caspar, Pal, 86, 88, 90
Herbach, Jacob, Pal, 86–88, 90
Herbach, Maria Eva, w Jacob, 86
Herding, herdsmen, 211
Hermann, passenger on *Judith*, 105
Hermsdorf, Adolf von, German officer, 52, 57, 275
Hernberger, Anna Justina née Unselt, w Franz, 239
Hernberger, Franz Sigismund, tailor, 130, 166, 168, 227, 248
Heron, Col., commander at Frederica, 60
Herrnhut, estate in Saxony, 49, 50
Herrnhuter. *See* Moravians
Herson, Hergen (Hermann), 187; loyalist, 186
Hertzog, Martin, Salz, 118
Hessian deserters, 189–91
Hessians, 180, 182, 187–91, 271
Hewitt, Capt., master of *Three Sisters*, 70, 71–73

Highgate, French village, 54, 278
Highlanders, Scottish, 60
Hillmann, Sw., 151
Hinely (fr Heinle), family graves, 194; Savannah family, 194
Hinely, town in Georgia, 197
Hinke, William, historian, 184
Hinrichs, Capt. Johann, Hessian, 208
Hirnstein, Swab city, home of Rauners, 32
Hirsch, Dr., military doctor, 275
Hirsch, Barbara, w Johann, 273, 275
Hirsch, Johann Michael, Swab, 275
Hoffmann, Adelheit, 46
Hoffstätter, Caspar, boatbuilder, 154
Hohenstauffen, Swabian dynasty, 30
Holtstaller (?), inhabitant of Hampstead, probably same as Hoffstätter, 54
Holtzendorf, Friedrich, saddler (surgeon?), 227
Holtzendorf, Friedrich, surgeon, 64, 80, 236, 240; will of, 256
Holtzendorf, Johann, speaker of the house, 179, 180
Holtzendorf, William, Whig, 186
Holy Roman Empire, league of German states, 3, 22, 30
Holzkirch, town in Territory of Ulm, 150; map of, 141
Honey, 207, 208
Hookworm disease. *See* Diseases
Hope, Arnaud, Isaac, and Zachary, merchants, 60, 68–71, 74, 77, 78, 142
Hopkins, manager of Trustee's cowpen, 135
Horner, Capt. James, ship captain, 50
Horse Hoeing Husbandry, book by Tull, 131
Horses, 214; horse racing, 246
Horton, Maj. Wm, commander at Frederica, 62–64
Houlster (Holtzer?), inhabitant of Hampstead, 54
Houston, Sir Patrick, deserter, 190
Houston, William, botanist, 158
Hövelsingen, town in Territory of Ulm, 151; map, 141

Huber, town in Georgia, 197
Huber, Jacob, Swab, 150
Huber family, 232
Hubert, town in Georgia, 197
Huguenots, French Protestants, 8, 18, 26, 65
Hunting, 208–9; shooting cattle, 208
Huss, Jan, Bohemian reformer, 48
Hvidt, Kristian, archivist, 157, 252
Hymns, 249

Ichinger, Annalies, d Philip, Sr., 59
Ichinger, Catharina, w Jacob, 59
Ichinger, Hans Michael, 59
Ichinger, Jacob, Pal, 59
Ichinger, Philip, Pal, 59
Ichinger, Sophia, d Jacob, 59
Ihle, Jacob, Sr., lieutenant, 155, 178, 271, 306 (n. 59)
Ihle, Michael, passenger on *Judith*, 105, 155, 170
Immigration, individual, 155–56
India. *See* East Indies
Indian Hut, on Savannah River, 264
Indian lands, 264
Indians: 258–65; gather honey, 208; shoot cows, 211; scalp Bach, 56; cede lands, 264; patrol for British, 189; Cherokees, 65, 160, 260, 261, 262; Chickasaws, 260, Creeks, 56, 260, 265; Florida or Spanish Indians, 56, 253, 262; Uchees, 261, 264, 265, 323 (n. 31); Yamacraw Indians 50, 258
Indigo. *See* Crops
Indo-Europeans, early European tribes, 1
Inspirierten, religious sect, 126
Intzig, Valentin, Pal, 70
Inventories, 255
Irene, Indian settlement, site of Moravian mission, 50
Isaacs, Capt., master of the *Success*, 162
Isle of Hope, settlement south of Savannah, 99
Ivers, Larry E., 274

Jäckli, passenger on *Judith*, 105
James, Capt. Yoakley's ship, 46
Jasper, town in Georgia, 197
Jasper, Sgt. William, 152, 167, 183, 184; monument to, 185
Jenys, Paul, speaker of S.C. House, 37, 265
Jerusalem Church, mother church at Ebenezer, 153, 154, 195, 229; picture of, 153
Jews in Savannah, 35, 72, 84–85
Johannes, Heinrich, Sw, 54
Jones, Noble, surveyor and scoutboat captain, 37, 41, 43, 50, 57, 74, 95, 99, 110, 119, 129, 136, 142, 155, 156, 177, 276, 287 (n. 44)
Jones, Thomas, keeper of the stores, 41, 48, 62, 79, 94, 115, 122, 133, 205
Joseph II, Holy Roman Emperor, rescript, 30
Joseph's Town, settlement, 98, 135
Journal of the Johannes Schwalm Association, 190
Judith, Capt. Walter Quarme's ship, 11, 105
Juncker, Dr. Johann, professor at Halle, 119
Jung, Maria Barbel, Pal Wid, 88
Jüngbluth (Youngblood), Peter, Whig, 180
Junker. *See* Juncker

Kalcher, Margaretha, w Ruprecht, 118
Kalcher, Ruprecht, Salz, 118, 213
Kalcher, Ursula, d Ruprecht, 319 (n. 6)
Keebler. *See* Kübler
Keiffer Branch, 197
Keiffer Pond, 197
Keller, town in Georgia, 197
Keller, Johann Georg, Pal, 70
Kemp, Johann, Pal, 180, 196
Kensler, Agnes Christina, w Chris, 59
Kensler, Anna Margaretha, d Chris, 59
Kensler, Bastian, s Chris, 59
Kensler, Christoph, 59
Kessler, Adam, Swab, 152
Kessler family in Savannah, 194
Kieffer, David, s Theo II, 88, 111, 112

Kieffer, Dorothea, d Theo I, 166
Kieffer, Elisabetha Catharina, d Theo I, 127
Kieffer, Elisabetha Catharina, w Theo II, 166
Kieffer, Israel, inhabitant of Ebenezer, 182
Kieffer, Margaretha, d Theo I, 166
Kieffer, Maria, w Theo II, 241
Kieffer (Küffer), Theobald I (Master), 33, 34, 80, 134, 163, 166, 176; will of, 256, 269
Kieffer, Theobald II (Captain), s Th I, 166, 176, 171, 263, 272, 273
Kieffer, Theobald III, Pal, 80, 88, 93, 100, 112
Kieffer family, 232, 266, 272, 273; in Savannah, 194
Kikar, soldier, 228, 275, 277
King George, Capt. Ayres' ship, 51
King of Prussia, tavern, 229
Kirchner, Elisabetha, Pal, w Ri, 59
Kirchner, Ri(chard?), Pal, 59
Kirckel, town in Saarbrücken, 71
Klein, Johann Georg, Swab, 146
Kleinknecht, Conrad Daniel, Swab pastor, 141, 304 (n. 8)
Knippling, passenger on *Judith*, 105
Knoblauch Regiment, Hessian unit, 180, 188
Knox, William, English planter, 53, 170
Köcher, (Johann) Georg, Salz, 212, 230, 243
Kocherthal, Josua, German promoter, 10, 284 (n. 43)
Koel, Ludwig, Sw, 33
Kogler, Georg, Salz, 156, 205, 212, 216, 225, 226
Kogler's Creek, 197
Kohleisen, Maria, w Peter, 124
Kohleisen, Peter, cobbler, 124, 226
Koller, Engel, Sw, 120
Krämer, Christoph, Jr., 178
Krämer, Christoph, vestryman, locksmith, 173, 178, 192, 228
Krämer, Johann Matthias, secretary to Zinzendorf, 68–70, 292 (n. 4)

Kraft, Anna Barbara, née Brandt, w David, 146; m Rabenhorst, 152, 153
Kraft, David, Swab merchant, 146
Krause, Leonhard, Salz, 170
Krause, Samuel, vestryman, 173, 192
Krauss, Capt., artillery captain, 150, 171, 249
Krefeld, German city, 69
Kreusser, Christof, Sw, 151
Kröhr, Catharina. *See* Catharina Gronau
Kröhr, Gertraut. *See* Gertraut Boltzius
Kronstadt, Russian city, 165
Kroppenstedt, town in Sachsen-Anhalt, 165
Krüsy, Adrian, Sw, s Hans, 120
Krüsy, Hans, Sw, 120, 126, 225, 226
Kübler, Jacob, Pal, 136, 303 (n. 105)
Kübler, Johann, lieutenant, 178
Küffer, Sw. *See* Kieffer
Kugel. *See* Gugel
Kuhn, Balthasar, renegade, 129, absconds, 139
Künlin, Conrad, Salz, 123
Kuradi. *See* Cunradi
Kurtz, Jacob, Pal, 91, 92, 111
Kurtz, Jacob Friedrich, swindler, 158, 219–20
Kurtz, Matthias, Salz, 17, 124
Kusmaul, passenger on *Judith*, 105

Labhart (Laphart), merchant in St. Gall, 27, 113
Lackner, Mrs., midwife, 239
Lackner, Gertraut, Salz, 120
Lackner (Lechner), Magdalena. *See* Lechner
Lackner, Martin, Jr., teacher, 243
Lackner, Martin, Salz, blacksmith, 225
Lackner, Tobias, Salz, 37, 233
Lake Constance, 22, 30
Lamolliere, Stephen, philanthropist, 10
Lamprecht, Andreas, Pal, 196, 263
Landfelder, Veit, Salz, 130, 263
Lang, Catharina, Sw 151
Lang, Johann, planter, 112
Lange, Dr., theologian, 127

Langenaltheim, town in Territory of Ulm, 166
Langenau, town in Territory of Ulm, 148, 150, 151; map, 141
Langensee, town in Territory of Ulm, 151, map, 141
Lastinger, Johann, militiaman, 166
Lau(e), Samuel, pastor, 126
Lechner, Magdalena, 1st w Veit, 124
Lechner (Lackner), Veit, locksmith, 124
Leibnitz, Gottfried Wilhelm, philosopher, 204
Leimbacher, Christian, planter, 57, 170
Leimbacher, Georg, planter, 170, 186
Leimberger, Christian, Salz, 57, 236, 268, 270
Leinbacher (Leinebacher), Georg, passenger on *Judith*, 105, 235
Leipheim, town in Territory of Ulm, 141, map, 141
Leitner, Josef, Salz, 128
Leitner, Veit, s Josef, blacksmith, 228, 318 (n. 132)
Lemke, (Hanna) Catharina, née Kröhr, w. H.H., 126
Lemke, Hermann Heinrich, minister, 105, 125–26, 145–54, 165, 217, 236, 243, 265
Lemke, Johanna Christina, d H.H., 105, 126
Lemke, Salome, d H.H., 126, 179
Lemke, Timothaeus, s H.H., 126
Lemmenhofer, Mrs., 252
Lemmenhofer, Maria, 207
Lemon, Capt. John, master of the *Loyal Judith*, 123
Lesslie (Leslie), Capt. John, master of the *Charming Martha*, 141, 142
Leutkirch, town in Territory of Ulm, 38, map, 141
Leutzhausen (Liutzhausen), town in Territory of Ulm, 151; map, 141
Lewenberger, Christian, Sw, 34, 91, 93
Lewenberger, Margaretha, Sw, 34
Lichtenstaiger, Melchior, Sw, 108
Lichtenstein, Johann, planter, 169, loyalist, 186, 311 (n. 52)

Lincoln, Gen. Benjamin, Continental commander, 183, 188
Lindau, Swab city, 122, 130
Linder, captain and judge fr Purysburg, 106; planter (?), 93
Linder, Alexander, cadet, 279
Lion, Martin, Pal, will of, 256
Lion, Samuel, Pal, 86, 88, 90, 91, 155, 186
Lion family, Pal, 8
Litola, passenger on *Judith*, 105
Little, William, secretary, 224
Little Ogeechee River, stream near Ebenezer, 135
Little St. Simons, Augspurger's estate, 65
Lockner's Creek, 197
Locksmiths. *See* Ruprecht Schrempf; Christoph Krämer
Lohrmann, David, Swab, 151
London, England, 10, 17, 18, 26, 39, 43, 47, 50, 54, 55, 73, 84, 104, 139, 162, 237
London Merchant, Capt John Thomas's ship, 26, 27, 39, 50
Long lots, 91, 92, 246
Lords Commissioners for Trade and Plantations, successors to the Trustees, 29
Lots, casting of, 247
Lotter, Tobias Conrad, engraver, 316 (n. 63)
Louis XIV, king of France: wages peace against German states, 10
Lowther, James, Anglican minister, 157
Loyalists, 186–87
Loyal Judith, Capt. John Lemon's ship, 123
Lucerne (Luzern), Sw city and canton, 138
Lumber, 218
Luther, Martin: takes stand at Worms, 4; Bible translation, 24; *Small Catechism*, 243
Lutheran Church of the Ascension in Savannah, 80–83
Lutheran ministers. *See* Boltzius; Driessler; Gronau; Lemke; Rabenhorst; Triebener
Lützelflüh, town in Canton Bern, 54
Lyde, Mr. James, 122
Lyon, Lyons. *See* Lion

Index

Maajen Hoff, John van, 169
MacClellan, John, master of the *Antelope*, 69, 146
Macher, 112. See also Metzger, Johann Jacob
Mack, Wolfgang, Swab, 151
McKay, Charles, raider, 191
Madis, Wid, Pal, wid of Peter Pfitzel, 46
Magic, 247
Mail, burden of, 130; loss of, 131
Mainz, city on Rhine, 2
Malaria. See Diseases
Malcontents, disaffected group in Savannah, 57, 111, 112, 114, 132, 206, 267, 268
Mamour, Mr., English boatman, 37
Manigault, Gabriel, Huguenot planter, 65
Marold, Peter, Pal fr Saarbrücken, 168
Marsch, Angelika, 248
Martin Luther University, Halle, 237, 238
Martyn, Benjamin, Trustees' secretary, 20, 43, 55, 93, 98, 108, 109, 113–15, 136, 137, 142, 157, 158, 217, 221, 282 (n. 10)
Matschat, Cecile Hulse, 247
Maurer, Hans, Salz, 235
Maurer, Maria, Salz, 238, 255, 320 (n. 35)
Mayer, Adrian, militiaman, 166
Mayer (Meyer), (Johann) Georg, br (Johann) Ludwig, 145, 228, 243
Mayer, Georg, wheelwright, 226
Mayer, Johann, Swab, 151
Mayer (Meyer), (Johann) Ludwig, physician, 79, 131, 135, 143, 145, 163, 229, 238, 239, 241, 243, 267
Mayer, Orlando B., 246
Mayer, Paul, Swab, 151
Mayerhoffer, Heinrich, militiaman, 166
Mecklinburg, German Province, 165
Medical personnel. See Bourquin; Davis; Meissner; Ludwig Meyer; Thilo; Zwiffler
Medications, 240; brandy, 241; cardiobendicti, 240; chinchona (*china de china*), 240; *essentia amara*, 240; *essentia dulcis*, 240; ipecacuanha, 240; polychrest pills, 240; *pulvis vitalis*, 240; *pulvis anti spasmodicus*, 240; *pulvis bezoardicum*, 240; red powder (*rothes Pulver*), 240; Schauer's balm, 240; snake root, 242; theriac, 241;
Venetian theriac, 242
Meier, Caspar, Sw, 45
Meier, Hans Heinrich, Sw, 45
Meier, Jacob, Sw, 45
Meierhoffer, Heinrich, Sw, 45. See also Meyerhoffer
Meissner, Georg Friedrich, German doctor, 239, 240
Memmingen, Swab city, 122, 130
Mengersdorff. See Mingersdorf.
Mercantilism, 112–13, 147, 175, 176, 186, 230
Meriwether, Robert L., 27
Merklingen, town in Territory of Ulm, 151; map, 141
Metzger, Jacob, cobbler fr Purysburg, 165, 226
Metzger, Johann Jacob, 112
Metzger family, Pal, 165
Meyer, Anna, Pal, d Heinrich, 59
Meyer, Catharina, d Heinrich, 59
Meyer, Catharina, Pal, w Heinrich, 59
Meyer, Donald, Pal, s Heinrich, 59
Meyer, Heinrich, Pal, s of Thomas, 46
Meyer, Heinrich, Sw, worker at cowpen, 55
Meyer, Heinrich, planter at German Village, 47, 59, 60, 253
Meyer, Heinrich Friedrich, planter on Sea Islands, 155
Meyer, Johann, will of, 256
Meyer, Johann, Pal, s Heinrich, 59
Meyer, Johann Ludwig, will of, 296
Meyer, Magdalena, Sw, 55, 64
Meyer, Margaretha, Pal, d Heinrich, 59, 64
Meyer, Peter, Pal, s Heinrich, 59
Meyer, Thomas, s Heinrich, 59
Meyer, Thomas, Sw, 46, 55
Meyer, Ursula, w Th, 46, 55
Meyer family in Savannah, 194
Meyerhoffer, Heinrich, Sw, 45, 55, 59, 80
Michael's Creek, 197
Michel, Andreas, Pal, 46
Michel, Catharina, Swab, 150
Michel, Heinrich, planter at German village, 60, 253
Michel, Margaretha, w And, Pal, 46

Mick (Mueck?), passenger on *Judith*, 105
Midwives, 239. *See also* Maria Bacher; Maria Bischoff; Swiss midwife
Military, 274–79
Militia, 198, 277–78
Millar, Robert, botanist, 158
Mill District, 134
Milledge, John, early settler, 71
Millen, town in Georgia, 197
Millen, David, planter, 170
Millen, Stephan, neighbor of Ebenezer, 192
Millers, 217. *See also* Thomas Bichler; David Eischberger; Johann Heinle; Ruprecht Zimmerebner
Mill River. *See* Abercorn Creek
Mills, 213; gristmills, 96, 173, 214–17; stamping mill, 214, 216; millstones, 215–17; sawmills, 215–19
Minerva, ship, 184
Mingeldorf (fr Mingersdorf), family in Savannah, 194
Mingersdorf, Georg, Sw immigrant, 33, 166
Mingersdorf, Johann Georg, militiaman, 166
Minis, Abraham, 50, 84
Minis, Philip, Whig, 186
Ministers. *See* Bergmann; Boltzius; Chifelle; Driessler; Gronau; Lemke; Rabenhorst; Triebner; Zouberbuhler; Zubli
Minister's plantation, 172, 192, 195
Mittelberger, Gottlieb, visitor to Pennsylvania, 12, 13
Mohr, Jacob, Sw, 45
Moore, Francis, recorder, 114, 115, 121, 122, 129, 264
Moravians, religious sect, 37, 39, 46, 48–54, 57, 92, 124, 127, 129, 167, 170, 171, 208, 226, 227, 236, 238, 239, 241, 247, 259, 271, 275
Morel (Morelle), Pierre Rodolf, Sw inhabitant of Highgate, 54, 83, 278
Morgarten, site of Sw victory, 22
Moser, Regina, Sw, 151
Mountain lions, 209

Mount Pleasant, fort upstream fr Ebenezer in S.C., 203, 226, 262, 268
Mount Venture, fort on Altamaha River, 253, 262, 274
Muchler, Johannes, vestryman, 192
Mugg (Mück), Johann, Sw, 45
Muggitzer, Hans Michael, Salz, 128, 168, 273
Muhlenberg, Friedrich August Conrad, s Heinrich, 192
Muhlenberg, Heinrich Melchior, 109, 124, 135, 153, 162, 164, 167, 168, 173–75, 178, 193, 217, 232, 239, 243, 244, 249, 269, 273
Muhlenberg's Church in Philadelphia: collection for, 207
Mühler, Jacob, Capt., 192, 312 (n. 83)
Müller, Loyalist captain, 192, 312 (n. 83). Probably same as Bühler, Jacob
Müller, passenger on *Judith*, 105
Müller, Christian, painter, 252
Müller, Friedrich Wilhelm, clock maker fr Frankfurt, 215, 225, 318 (n. 116)
Müller, Ludwig, Moravian, 170
Müller, Paul, vestryman, 173, 241
Müllern, Johann Gottfried von, conductor of 4th Salz trans, 123, 233
Münch, Carl de, s Chr, 146
Münch, Chrétien de, banker, 139, 146, 147
Münch, Chrétien de, Jr., s Chr, 146
Münch, Thomas de, s Chr, 146
Musgrove, Mary, w Bosomworth, 63, 107, 128
Music, 249
Myerhoffer. *See* Meyerhoffer

Nassau-Saarbrücken, place in Palatinate, home of Schubdreins, 5, 138, 145
Naval stores, 208
Nease (fr Niess) family in Savannah, 194
Neckar, Swabian river, 30, 123
Nees, town in Georgia, 197
Neibling (Nübling), Bartholomäus, Swab, 151

Neidlinger, Johann, Swabian, 142, 145
Neidlinger, Johann Adam, sexton, 177, 256
Neidlinger, Johann Gottlieb, Whig, 180, 192
Neidlinger, Matthias, returnee, 249, 306 (n. 43)
Neidlinger, (Johann) Ulrich, vestryman, 173, 179
Neidlinger family in Savannah, 194
Neidlinger Lake, 197
Neisler, Johann Adam, lieutenant, 177, 178
Nerenstetten, town in Territory of Ulm, 158, map, 141
Nessler, Adam, (Same as Neisler?), Whig, 180
Ness River, stream east of Goshen, 136
Neuchâtel, Sw city, 26, 27
Neuss, city on Rhine, 27
New Bern, settlement in N.C., 10
Newcastle, Duke of, secretary of state, 70
New Ebenezer: picture of, 40, 44
New Goettingen, settlement near Halifax, 152, 162, 263
Newlanders (recruiters for Palatines), 24, 78
Newman, Henry, secretary of SPCK, 21, 84, 112, 146, 156, 157, 194, 237
Newton, William, Rebel soldier, 184
New Windsor, Sw town on the Savannah, 29, 106, 108, 127, 129, 132, 249
Neydlinger, Matthias, Swab returnee, 148
Niederstotzingen, town in Territory of Ulm, 151; map, 141
Niess, Mr., inhabitant of Ebenezer, 32, 194
Niess, Johann Georg, Swab, 152
Niess, Maria, Salz, 236
Nitschmann, David, Moravian, 49, 258
Nobellet, Johann, Pal, 8, 88
Norris, Wm, Anglican pastor, 54, 64, 253, 254
Nunes, Samuel, Sephardic Jew, 85
Nungasser, wid, 207
Nungasser, David, ranger, 111
Nungasser (Nongazzer), Heinrich, Pal, 88, 111

Nungasser, Jacob, Pal, 88, 112
Nungasser (Nongasser) family in Savannah, 194

Ochs, Johann Rudolf, German promoter, 29
Ockstead. *See* Oxted
Oechsele (Öchselin, Oechslin), Johann, Swab, 145
Oesler, Jacob, Sw, 45
Ogeechee River. *See* Great and Little Ogeechee
Oglethorpe, James, founder of Georgia, 17, 33, 35, 38–45, 50, 51, 53–57, 60–62, 66, 67, 70, 71, 75, 95, 106, 156, 159, 162, 205, 215, 216, 221, 231, 233, 253, 258–61, 263–65, 275, 276
Ohnfeld, Johannes, Sw, 45
Okefenokee Swamp, 173, 247–48
Old Ebenezer, temporary settlement, 40, 118, 174, 215, 232, 233, 243
Oldenburg, North German province, 165
Oliver, Palatine ship, 11, 148
Orangeburg, Sw settlement in S.C., 22, 29, 108, 154, 168, 202, 245
Ordentlich-Wöchentliche Anzeigs-Zettel, Ulm newspaper, 148
Ordner, Adam, Pal, 88, 111, 112
Ordner, Heinrich, ranger, 111, 112
Orphanage at Ebenezer, 213, 221
Orphanage at Halle, 118, 119
Orphanage at Savannah. *See* Bethesda
Ortmann, Christoph, Pal schoolmaster, 34, 52, 83, 90, 93, 102–04, 111, 117, 127, 133, 229, 243, 244
Ortmann, Juliana, w Christoph, 93, 102, 103, 127
Ortner. *See* Ordner
Orton, Christopher, Anglican minister, 80, 127
Ott, Sigmund, Salz, 245, 294 (n. 47)
Ottolenghe, Joseph, manager of the filature, 102, 223, 224
Overseers, 271, 273

354 Index

Owens, Wid, 282 (n. 6)
Oxted, Causton's estate, 73, 128, 154

Pagenköpp. *See* Poggenköpp
Palachocolas, fort on the Savannah, 106
Palatinate. *See* Rhenish Palatinate
Palatine, legendary name of *Princess Augusta*, 11, 74, 148
Palatine emigration, 10, 11, 166
Palatine fever, 11, 79, 105
Palatines (all German workers), 11, 33; recruitment of, 24, 68–76; at Ebenezer, 118, 119, 129, 136, 276; at Savannah, 82, 254, 276
Parker, Henry, magistrate, 134, 143
Parker's Mill, 135, 267
Parsonage at Ebenezer, 205
Pauli, Friedrich, Sw, 45
Paulitsch, Johann Martin, schoolmaster, 173, 243, 244
Paulitsch, Philip, Swab, schoolmaster, 142, 243
Paulus. *See* Paulitsch
Peaches, 214
Pedersheim, town in Palatinate, 8
Peltz. *See* Beltz
Penner, Elisabetha, Pal, 64, 254
Penniker, Christina, Pal at German Village, 64
Pennsylvania, 11–13, 28, 53, 69, 124, 128, 161, 167; immigrants fr, 166
Pensacola, 188
Percival, John. *See* Egmont
Petitions: for Calvinist minister, 83, 100; against introduction of slavery, 133; for introduction of slavery, 133; for fourth Salz transport, 122; for land to Ogeechee, 268
Pflüger, Hans, Swab, 151
Philadelphia, 46, 47, 54, 70, 81, 124, 130–32, 167, 172, 207, 219, 236, 243
Philips, Mr., of Old Ebenezer, 174
Phizzel, Wid, 46
Phizzel, Barbara, d Pet, Pal, 46
Phizzel, Margaretha, d Pet, Pal, 46

Phizzel, Peter, Pal, 46
Phyfer, Daniel, Sw, inhabitant of Hampstead, 54
Pica. *See* Diseases
Pietist terms, 203
Piltz, Andreas, Salz, 124, 225
Place names, 197
Plessi, Jacob, Pal, 88
Pletter, Johann, Austrian, 120, 230
Pletter, Maria Elisabetha, w Johann, 120
Plows: at Vernonburg, 111; at Ebenezer, 136, 213; attached to horns, 246; lacking, 315 (n. 51)
Poggenköpp (Pagenköpp), town in Hinterpommern, 152
Point Hope, place near Savannah, 154
Pongau, largely Protestant district in Salzburg, 14
Porbeck, Friedrich von, Hessian officer, 188–90, 271
Port Royal, small port in S.C., 12, 162, 165, 183
Portz, Georg Philip, passenger on *Judith*, 105, 136, 169; will of, 256
Pössneck, town in Thuringia, 165
Potters. *See* Duchee, Gnann
Pral, Hans, Sw, 45
Prefabricated houses, 218
Prevost, Augustine, British commander, 183, 188
Pricker (Prickel), Elisabetha, Salz, 235
Prieber, Christian Gottlieb, Saxon visionary, 63, 65–67, 165, 292 (nn. 170, 172)
Private enterprize, praise of, 76–78
Privateers, 45, 131
Proclamation of 1763, 167
Proclamation to deserters, 189
Protestant Union, league of Protestant princes, 4
Prussia. *See* East Prussia
Pryber. *See* Prieber
Pulaski, Count Casimir, 183, 187
Purcker. *See* Parker's mill
Pury, Charles, son of Jean-Pierre, 27

Pury (Purry), Jean-Pierre, founder of Purysburg, 26, 231, 238, 239, 284 (n. 52)
Purysburg, Capt. Tobias Fry's ship, 21
Purysburg, Sw township in S.C., 2, 6, 29, 33, 51, 64, 80–82, 93, 100, 106, 120, 152, 154, 163, 165, 221, 226, 228, 237–41, 245, 260, 276, 279
Pye, John, recorder in Savannah, 103, 105

Quarme, Walter, master of the *Judith*, 105
Quinche, Capt., of Neuchatel, 27
Quincy, Samuel, Anglican minister, 84, 322 (n. 10)
Quitman, town in Georgia, 197

Raag, passenger aboard *Judith*, 105
Rabenhorst, Anna Maria, wid Kraft, w Christian, 153, 171, 172, 179, 192, 214, 247, 274
Rabenhorst, Christian, pastor at Ebenezer, 152, 153, 160, 165–74, 179, 271, 273
Rabies Carolinae (South Carolina madness), 25, 26, 79
Radick, Michael, planter, 98, 154, 155
Radner, Leonhard, Pal, 88
Ragnous, Johann, Pal at German Village, 8, 60
Rahn, town in Georgia, 197
Rahn, Caspar, Swab, 166
Rahn, Matthias, captain at Bethany, 182
Rahn, Matthias, lieutenant, 178
Rahn family in Savannah, 194
Rangers, mounted scouts, 56, 110, 151, 277
Ranzau, town in Schleswig-Holstein, 158
Ratien, passenger on *Judith*, 105
Rau, Anna, spinner, 230
Rauner, Mrs., w Leonhard, 129, 276
Rauner, Leonhard, Swabian, 32, 128, 132
Ravensburg, Swabian city, 146
Reasons for Establishing the Colony of Georgia, 68
Reck, Ernst Ludwig, br of Baron, 43
Reck (Röck), Jacob, cobbler, 226, 276
Reck, Baron Philip Georg Friedrich von, 21, 28, 37, 39–42, 44, 59, 100, 114, 130, 156–58, 253, 259, 260, 266; his folio, 40, 42, 252, 261, 276
Recruitment in Germany, 28–70
Red Bluff, site of New Ebenezer, 39, 40, 43, 54, 114, 135, 147, 172, 213, 264; sketch of, 40
Redemptioners, 74
Reformation, 4, 202; in Salzburg 14; in Switzerland 22, 28
Reformed (Calvinists), 30, 54, 82–83, 100, 101, 126, 137; petition of, 101, 107
Regensburg, seat of German Diet, 39, 156
Regnier, Jean François, Sw physician, 51, 53, 236, 271
Rehm, Friedrich, surgeon fr Black Forest, 186
Reiter, Carl, Pal, 88
Reiter, Michael, planter on Sea Islands, 155
Reiter, Peter, Salz, 209
Reiter, Simon, Salz, 128, 129, 268
Reiter family in Savannah, 194
Religion, 201–6
Remigius, son-in-law of von Münch, 146
Remshart, Daniel, Swabian, 145
Renegades, 129
Rentz, town in Georgia, 197
Rentz, Georg, Swab, will of, 256
Rentz, Johann, Swab baker, 229
Rentz family in Savannah, 194
Rester, Friedrich, militiaman, 166, 178
Reuss, Sw river, 23
Reverend Fathers: benefactors of Salz, 43, 119
Revolution, 175–92
Reynolds, Gov. John, 151, 159, 171, 224
Rheinländer, Christian Colmann, s Friedrich, 165
Rheinländer, Friedrich, Pal, 165, 166, 168, 225
Rheinländer, Maria, née Kalcher, 236
Rheinländer, Maria Anna, w Fr, 84, 134, 165, 239, 255
Rheinländer, (Johann) Martin, s Fr, 165, 226, 319 (n. 6)
Rheinstettler, Adam, Pal, 88

Rheinstettler, David, planter, 112
Rhenish Palatinate, German province, 2, 5, 8, 10
Rhinegrave (Rheingraf), ruler of the Rhenish Palatinate, 5, 8
Rhinelanders (Rheinländer), inhabitants of Upper Rhine valley, 8
Rhine River, chief German river, 2, 8, 12, 22, 27, 30, 122
Rhylander, "correct" form of Rheinländer, 165
Rice. *See* Crops
Richard, Jacques, Sw commander fr Geneva, 275, 276
Richard (Ritschart?), Lorentz, passenger on the *Judith*, 105; absconds, 129
Richard, Michael, passenger on the *Judith*, 105; absconds, 129
Richard, Peter, passenger on the *Judith*, 105; absconds, 129
Richard, Thomas, passenger on the *Judith*, 105; grant to, 137
Richter, Christian Friedrich, physician, 119
Riedelsperger, butcher, 229
Riedelsperger, storekeeper, 229
Riedelsperger, Adam, will of, 256
Riedelsperger, Christian, Salz, 212, 255
Ridelsperger, Nikolaus, tanner, 227
Riedelsperger, Stephan, Salz, 128, 130, 168, 273
Riedheim, town in Territory of Ulm, 151; map, 141
Rieger (Riger), Nikolaus, Pal, 33
Riegler, Leonhard, Sw, 87, 90, 91, 93
Riemensperger, Hans Jacob, newlander, 78, 79, 136, 220
Rieser, Mrs., midwife, 239
Rieser, Magdalena, w Simon, 124
Rieser, Michael, Salz, 128, 129, 130, 133, 134, 254, 263
Rieser family in Savannah, 194
Ring (Rinck), Christoph, s Johann, 90, 170
Ring (Rinck), Johann, Pal, 90, 93
Ring, Johann, s Joh, 93

Ritter, Carl Johann Friedrich, Pal, 83, 98, 186
Robinson, John, Eng. indentured servant, 46
Robinson, Pickering, silk expert, 223
Roddenberry, Okefinokee inhabitant, 193, 243. *See also* Rottenberger
Roesberg. *See* Rösberg
Rohrmoser, Barbara, Salz, 125
Roman Empire, 1–3
Roman skills, 3
Romansh, Latin dialect in Switzerland, 22, 47
Rösberg, Georg, planter, 170
Rose, Peter, Moravian, 208
Ross (Rose), Hugh, surveyor, 43
Rote Friesel. See Diseases
Roth (Rott), Bartholomäus, Bavarian, 38, 56, 132
Roth, George Lewis, Catholic, 56; will of, 256
Roth, Maria Barbara, w Bart, 56
Rottenberger, Stephan, Salz, 212, 225, 226, 234
Rotterdam, city in Netherlands, 21, 25, 27, 68–70, 73, 83, 123, 126, 142, 145, 157, 168, 194, 243
Ruf, Jacob, Jr., Pal at German Village, 59, 64
Ruf, Jacob, Sr., Pal at German Village, 59, 291 (n. 161)
Ruf, Margaretha, Pal at German Village, 59
Ruf, William, 291 (n. 145)
Ruland, Barbara, Swab, 151
Rumpf, Christian, Pal at Cowpen, 55
Rush, Benjamin, physician, 92, 224, 233, 238, 246
Rüssel, Jacob, gunmaker, 312 (n. 76)
Russell, William, clerk at Trustees' store, 87, 94, 276

Saarbrücken, district in Palatinate, 168
Sabbatarians, 203

Index

Saddlers. *See* Thomas Bichler; Friedrich Holtzendorf
St. Andrews Parish, 169
St. Augustine, Spanish city in Florida, 56, 187, 191, 216, 226, 263, 275, 276
St. Gall, Sw city, 22, 28, 100
St. Gall, Zubly's plantation, 108, 109
St. George's Point, site of fort, 57
St. Matthews Parish, area of Ebenezer, 169; map of, 116
St. Paul, admonition of, 73
St. Pauls Parish, 170
St. Peter, admonition of, 73, 176
St. Simons, island on Georgia coast, 39, 40, 42, 59
Salfner, Matthias, ranger, 111, planter, 112
Salfner, Michael, ranger, 111
Salice (Salis), Anton, Grisons, 47, 48, 79
Salice, Anton, Jr., 48
Salice, Catharina, d Anton, 48
Salice, Catharina, w Anton, 47, 48
Saltzmann, Gregorius, Hessian officer, 180
Salzach, Austrian river, 13
Salzburg, archbishopric, 4, 13
Salzburger cottage, 252
Salzburgers, praise of, 38
Sanftleben, Elisabetha, Silesian, 120
Sanftleben, Georg, Silesian, 120, 127, 165, 207
Savannah, 51–55, 57, 67, 80, 82, 123, 129, 132, 148, 184, 205, 217, 218, 225; Lutherans at, 80–83; capture of, 180; siege of, 182–83
Savannah River, 26, 29, 35, 39, 41, 106, 114, 128, 141, 146, 150, 154, 159, 162, 167–69, 193, 216, 218, 269
Savannah Town, trading station near Augusta, 148, 206
Sawmill. *See* Mills
Saxe Gotha, German settlement in S.C., 78, 79, 91, 168, 245, 299 (n. 125)
Saxony, German state, 49, 165
Scarlet fever. *See* Diseases
Schaaf, passenger on *Judith*, 105

Schad, (Hans) Joachim, Sw, 86, 91, 93, 110, 163
Schad, Salomo, Sw, 154, 163, 193, 263, 275, 229; will of, 256
Schaffhausen, Sw city, 27
Schaitberger, Josef, 243
Schalkhauser & Co., mercantile house in Venice, benefactors, 206, 314 (n. 17)
Schantze (Shats), Peter, planter at German Village, 60
Scharnhausen, town in Territory of Ulm, 151
Schartner, Jacob, herdsman, 210
Schaub. *See* Schober
Schauer, Johann Caspar, apothecary of Augsburg, 240
Schauer's balm. *See* Medications
Scheffer, Johann Friedrich, renegade, 124, 129, 139
Scheffler, w Johann, 124
Schelhaas, Johannes, Hessian deserter, 189
Scheraus, Johann, planter, 112, 135
Schick, Friedrich, Whig, 186, 232
Schick, Johann, planter, 170, 226, 256
Schiefer, Christoph, Pal, 88
Schiele (Schüle), Georg, 191
Schiermeister, Amalia, Boltzius's servant, 229
Schlatter, Sw merchant, 131
Schlechtermann, Pal family, 57, 163
Schlechtermann, Jeremias, Pal, 57
Schlechtermann, Peter, Pal, 57, 270
Schlechtermann, Wilhelm; will of, 256
Schlumberger, Abraham, Swab, 150
Schlumberger, David, Swab, 150
Schlumberger, Jacob, Swab, 150
Schlumberger, Maria, née Groner, wid Jacob, 150
Schmidt, Hans, Austrian, 142, 262; will of, 256
Schneider, Andreas, Swab, 150
Schneider, Anna, Swab, 150
Schneider, Caspar, Pal, 70, 88, 112
Schneider, Elisabetha, d Andreas, 150

Schneider, Hans Michael, Pal herdsman, 74, 94, 120, 232
Schneider, Johann, s Hans Michael, 74
Schneider, Johann, Whig, 186
Schneider, Philip, loyalist, 186
Schober, Johann Michael, Moravian, 52
Schoepf (Schöpf), Johann, physician, 194
Schönbacher (Shanebacker), Wid, 59
Schönbacher, Hans Georg, s Wid, 59
Schönbacher, Hans Michael, s Wid, 59
Schönbacher, Magdalena, d Wid, 59
Schönmannsgruber, schoolmaster in Purysburg, 81
Schoolmasters. See also Education; Bühler; Johann Flerl; Lucas Geiger; Häg; Georg Köcher; Martin Lackner; Georg and Ludwig Meyer; Neidlinger; Ortmann; Georg and Philip Paulitsch; Schönmannsgruber; Ruprecht Steiner; Treutlen; Wertsch
Schrempff, Ruprecht, blacksmith, 168, 228; will of, 256
Schröder, Anna, Swab, 151
Schubdrein, Daniel, 138
Schubdrein, Johann Peter, Pal, 138, 145
Schubdrein, Josef, vestryman, 173
Schubdrein, Nikolaus, vestryman, 192, 311 (n. 45)
Schubdrein brothers, 137, 145, 225, 229
Schubdrine family in Savannah, 194
Schulius, Georg, Moravian missionary, 51
Schumacher, Angelica, Swab, 151
Schumacher, Caspar, Pal, 46, 48
Schumacher, Christiana, w Casp, Pal, 46, 48
Schumann, Archpriest in Prussia, 206
Schutz, Hans, vintner, 220
Schwarzwälder, family at cowpen, 55
Schweiger, Eva Regina, née Unselt, w Georg, 120, 127, 166
Schweiger, (Sibilla) Friederica, 120
Schweiger, Georg, Salz, 120, 166, 232, 235
Schweiger, Michael, will of, 256
Schweighofer, Ursula, Salz, 244
Schweikert, Christian, servant to von Reck, 157

Schweitzer, Michael, Pal, 83, 100, 307 (n. 74)
Schwyzerdütsch (Swiss German), 30
Scurvy. See Diseases
Sea Islands, 154–55
Seasoning, 231–34
Seckingdorf, Feldmarschall von, benefactor, 250
Seckinger, Andreas, Pal, 138
Seckinger family in Savannah, 194
Seckingheim, town in Palatinate, 68
Second Salzburger transport, 146
Second Swabian transport, 146
Seelmann (Soelmann), Dr., immigrant, 129, 137
Self-made men, 163–64. See also Treutlen, Wertsch
Sempach, site of Sw victory, 22
Setzingen, town in Territory of Ulm, 150; map, 141
Seuti, Hans, Sw, 45
Seward, William, 121, 197
Seybold, Georg, will of, 256
Shanbacker, corruption of Schönbacher, 32
Sheep, 212
Sheftall, Benjamin, fr Frankfurt an der Oder, 35, 84, 85, 169
Sheftall, Hanna, 2nd w Benj, 84
Sheftall, Levi, s Benj, 170, 182, 186, 311 (n. 41)
Sheftall, Mordecai, s Benj, 169, 170, 180, 186, 311 (n. 41)
Sheftall, Perla, 1st w Benj, 35, 84
Sheftall, Sheftall, Whig, 186
Sherouse (fr Scheraus) family in Savannah, 194
Shoemakers, 226. See also Salomo Adde; Johannes Groll; Johann Hangleiter; Jacob Kuhleisen; Jacob Metzger; Jacob Reck; Martin Rheinländer; Martin Strohacker; Ludwig Weidmann; Ulich; Zettler
Ships. See Adventure; Antilope; Caledonia; Charles; Charles Town Galley; Charming Martha; Charming Molly; Europa; Georgia Packet; Georgia Pink; James; Judith; King

George; London Merchant; Loyal Judith; Minerva; Prince of Wales; Purysburg; Simonds; Success; Three Sisters; Two Brothers; Two Sisters
Siegfried, Georg, Pal, 154
Siegler, David, Swab, 151
Siegler, Jerg, Swab, 151
Silesia, German province, 120, 165
Silk culture, 221–24; mulberry trees at Ebenezer, 118, 221; at Vernonburg, 99; filiature at Ebenezer, 222; silk reeling, 222, 223, 224; silkworm seed, 222
Simonds (Simon), Peter, London merchant, 26, 28
Skidaway Island, south of Savannah, 154
Slave drivers, 273
Slaves and slavery, 37, 173, 266, 265–74, 266, 267
Sledges, use of, 38
Small Catechism. See Luther, Martin
Smallpox. *See* Diseases
Smiths, 228. *See also* Friedrich Fahm; Georg Faul; Veit Lechner; Ruprecht Schrempf; Veit Lechner; Veit Leitner; Georg Streigel; Lucas Ziegler
Snakes and snakebite, 241, 242; house adders, 247–48
Snider. *See* Schneider
Snyder, Okefinokee inhabitant, 193, 248. *See also* Schneider
Snyder, Savannah family, 194
Social history, viii
Society. *See* SPCK
Soldiers. *See* Arnsdorf; Gruber; Kikar; Ortmann; Rauner
Songs, 249–50
South Carolina, 26, 45, 75, 211, 266, 267
South Carolina Gazette, 45
Spalding, Phinizy, 282
Spangenberg, August Gottlieb, Moravian bishop, 49, 50, 52, 57, 84, 231, 240, 302 (nn. 50, 66), 323 (n. 12)
Spaniards, 40, 277
SPCK (Society for Promoting Christian Knowledge), 18, 20, 21, 52, 126, 130, 152, 177, 179, 187, 194, 206, 210, 215, 236, 244
Spener, Jacob, Pietist, 203
Spielbiegler, Johann, Salz, 130, 133, 168, 229, 263
Spielbiegler, Rosina, Salz, 130, 168
Spinning, 230
Springhill Redoubt. *See* Ebenezer Redoubt
Spurrier, John, master of the *Minerva*, 184
Stagerisz, Ulrich, Sw, 45
Stäheli, Gottlieb; will of, 256
Stäheli, Johann, passenger on *Judith*, 105, 137
Staley, 196. *See* Stäheli
Starkey, Caspar, planter, 169
Staude, Johann, Pal fr Kirckel in Saarbrücken, father of Margaretha, 71
Staude (Stout), Margaretha, Pal, w Gabriel Bach, 56, 57, 236, 303 (n. 80)
Staudemeyer, Wid, Swab, 151
Staudemeyer, Johann, Swab, 151
Stedman (Steadman), Capt. Charles, master of the *Two Sisters*, 104
Steermann, Heinrich, tailor, will of, 256
Steheli. *See* Stäheli
Steiner, Christian, Jr., Lt., 178, 179
Steiner, Christian, vestryman, 173
Steiner, Ruprecht, Salz, 29, 212, 215, 241, 243, 268
Steiner, Simon, Salz, 212
Steinhebel, Heinrich, Pal, 80, 88
Steinhübel (Steinhebel, Steinhevel, Steinheavel), Christian, Pal, 75, 80, 83, 88, 93, 100
Stephens, Newdigate, s William, 97, 110
Stephens, Thomas, s William, 94, 103, 133
Stephens, William, Trustees' secretary, 51, 53, 54, 64, 71, 72, 75, 76, 78–82, 86, 87, 90, 92–99, 101–4, 109, 110–12, 127, 129, 137, 143, 175, 207, 209, 220, 221, 235, 239, 248, 253, 254, 264, 276–78
Stierle, Gregorius, Sw, 34
Stifter, Adalbert, Austrian author, viii
Stine (fr Stein) family in Savannah, 194
Stirk, Col. Samuel, Whig, 179

Stoll, Ezekiel, Sw, 86, 90, 91
Stout. *See* Staude
Strassburg, Alsatian city, 123, 167
Strassburger, Ralph, historian, 184
Streigel, Georg, blacksmith at Halifax, 228
Stricker, newlander, 27
Strohacker, Martin, shoemaker, 177, 227
Strohacker, Rudolf, Whig, 180, 186
Strohbart (Strobald), Mrs., 182
Strohbart, Georg, militiaman, 166
Strohbart, Nikolaus, militiaman, 166
Stumli, Hans, Sw, 45
Stuttgart, Swab city, 122, 273
Stutz, Hans, Sw, 86, 90, 91
Success, Capt. Isaacs's ship, 150, 162
Suitor (Sutor?, Seuter?), Elisabetha, Pal at German Village, 64, 291 (n. 157)
Sulamith, slave child, 270
Swabia, German territory, 30
Swabians, first transport, 145–46
Swabians, second transport, 146–47
Swabians, third transport, 150–52
Sweigoffer Creek, 197
Swiger (fr Schweiger) family in Savannah, 194
Swiss immigrants: to Rhenish Palatinate, 8; to America 20–29; at Ebenezer, 119–20, 126; at and near Savannah, 78–80, 87, 90, 106–108, 111; petition of, 26
Switzerland, description, 2, 21–22; map of, 23
Sybold. *See* Seybold
Symonds, ship in convoy with *London Merchant*, 39, 50

Tacitus, Cornelius, Roman historian, 2, 210, 247
Tailors, 227. *See* Sigmund Biltz; Gottfried Christ; Friedrich Helfenstein; Sigismund Hernberger; Kikar; Georg Mayer; Heinrich Steermann; Georg Uhland; Michael Weinkauf
Taissoux, Daniel, Germ, 8, 47
Tannenberger, David, Moravian shoemaker, 51, 226
Tanners. *See* Johann Jacob Helfenstein; Johann Neidlinger; Nikolaus Riedelsperger
Tar. *See* Naval stores
Teachers. *See* Schoolmasters
Tennent, John, Virginia physician, 131, 235
Terry (Thierry), John, recorder, 39, 63, 64, 67, 79, 286 (n. 25)
Teutoburg Forest, site of battle, 2
Theiss (Dice), Jacob, Pal, 83, 88, 102, 112, 186
Theology, 203–5
Theus, Christian, Reformed minister, 202
Theus, Jeremias, Sw painter, 202, 250
Thilo, Anna Maria Friederica, d Ernest, 237
Thilo, Ernst Christian, physician at Ebenezer, 73, 119, 126, 171, 137, 239, 240, 243, 249
Thilo, Hanna Elisabetha, d Ernest, 238
Third Salzburger transport, 39, 48
Third Swabian Transport, 150, 152
Thirty Years War (1618–1648), 5, 8
Thomas, Catholic slave, 271
Thomas, Capt. John, master of the *London Merchant*, 39
Thomson, Capt. William, master of *Two Brothers*, 26, 45, 57, 73–75, 81, 141, 162
Three Sisters, Capt. Hewitt's ship, 70, 71
Thunderbolt Bluff, 154
Tobler, Anna, d Johann, m J. J. Zubly, 108
Tobler, Johann, Sw mathematician, 24, 28, 29, 108, 120, 127, 132, 245, 249, 302 (n. 79)
Toggenburg, Sw valley, 29, 78
Töltschig, Johann, Moravian, 259
Tomochichi, Indian chief, 259
Torgler. *See* Torkler
Torig, Georg, Pal planter, 102
Torkler, Johann, Sw, 87, 90, 91
Trachsler, Hans Wernhard, detractor, 29
Trader, German, 206, 268
Trades, 224–30
Tresp, Lothar, 273
Treutlen, (Johann) Adam, Pal, 81, 105, 151,

163–64, 167–76, 178, 179, 184, 186, 229, 239, 243, 308 (n. 115)
Treutlen, Christian E., grandson Johann Adam, 312 (n. 60)
Treutlen, Friedrich, Pal, 105
Treutlen, Maria Clara, Pal, 105, 106
Treutlen, Rachel, d Adam, 167
Trevor, Robert, benefactor of Palatines, 69
Triebner, Anna Maria, 312 (n. 60)
Triebner, Christoph Friedrich, pastor, 165, 172–75, 177–80, 186, 187, 191, 204, 243, 311 (n. 59)
Triebner, Friederica Maria, née Gronau, w CF, 173
True Christianity. See *Wahres Christenthum*
Trümbach Regiment, Hessian unit, 180, 188
Trustees, founders of Georgia, 10, 17, 21, 33, 43, 45, 46, 48, 49, 52, 68–70, 74, 79, 80, 88, 95, 99, 101–8, 120, 122–23, 131, 135, 136, 155, 175, 214, 216, 219, 221–23, 230, 238, 239, 264–67, 276; resolutions of, 19–20
Trustees' Garden, experimental station, 48
Trustees' servants, 43–44
Tubear, David, German planter, 8, 112
Tübingen, university town in Wurttemberg, 32, 226
Turpentine. See Naval stores
Tussing, Jacob, Swab, 146, captain, 178
Two Brothers, Capt. Wm Thomson's ship, 45, 46, 49, 73, 75
Tybee Island, at mouth of the Savannah River, 39, 41, 48

Uchees. See Indians
Uhland, (Johann) Georg, Pal, 83, 100, 102, 112; will of, 256
Ulich, Johann Caspar, shoemaker, 120, 226
Ulm, Swabian city, 30, 122, 139, 148; council of, 148; picture of, 30
Ulm, Territory of, 30, 139, 145; maps of, 140, 141
Ulmann, passenger on *Judith*, 105
Unitas Fratrum, 48, 49. See also Moravians

Unitäts-Archiv, Moravian archives in Herrnhut, ix
Unselt, Anna Justina, Pal, 130, 166, 168
Unselt, David, Swab, 151, 167, 246
Unselt, Eva Regina, Pal, 120, 127, 166
Unselt, (Sibilla) Friederica, Pal, 120, 168
Unselt, Regula, Pal, 120
Upper Austria (Oberösterreich), immigrants from, 39
Upshaw (?) (Upjber ?), Pal, 59, 263, 275
Urlsperger, Johann August, s Sam, 139, 171, 304 (nn. 6, 7)
Urlsperger, Samuel, Senior of Lutheran Ministry at Augsburg, 8, 17, 20–21, 26, 28, 38, 43, 50, 53, 119, 122, 128, 130, 131, 132, 139, 152, 157, 175, 267, 268; picture of, 9
Urspring, town in Territory of Ulm, 151
Usenbenz, Johann Georg, Swab, 151

Valentin, Catherina, Pal, 168
Vat, Jean, conductor of second Salz trans, 38, 40–42, 114, 157
Verelst, Harman, Georgia Trustees' accountant, 41, 47, 48, 73, 218, 222, 292 (n. 1)
Verlii, Jacob, Sw, 45
Vernon, James, Georgia Trustee, 18, 33, 41, 43, 51, 71, 104, 264
Vernonburg, "Dutch" settlement, 88–113, 155, 194, 216, 244, 245, 278
Vernonburg church, 100
Vernon River, saltwater river, 87, 88, 90
Victor, Wid, Pal, 59
Victor, Anna, d Wid, 59
Victor, Annalies, d Wid, 59
Victor, Jacob, s Wid, 59
Victor, Peter, s Wid, 59
Victor, Sule, s Wid, 59
Vigera, Johannes, conductor of fourth Salz trans, 79, 123, 124, 162, 250, 301 (n. 29)
Virginians, lawless element in Georgia, 167
Volker, Josef, Sw, 45
Vollbrecht, Christian, planter, 165, 170
Volmar, Michael, Pal carpenter, 52

Voltz, passenger on *Judith*, 105, 129
Voltz, Johann Martin, renegade, probably same as above, 129

Wachovia, Moravian settlement in N.C., 53
Wachter (Wachster), Josef, Pal, 87, 90, 91, 93
Wadham, John, Capt., master of the *Europa*, 79
Wagner, Johann Georg, Moravian, 170
Wagner, Samuel, inhabitant of Hampstead, 54
Wahres Christenthum, Vier Bücher von, religious manual by Johann Arndt, 203
Waldburger, Jacob, planter, 112
Waldeck, German principality, 188
Waldhauer, Andreas, Pal, 59
Waldhauer, Andrew, Whig, 180
Waldhauer, Anna, w Andreas, 59
Waldhauer, Barbara, Pal, 74
Waldhauer, Christoph Conrad, passenger on the *Judith*, 105, renegade, 129
Waldhauer, Georg Jacob, passenger on *Judith*, 105
Waldhauer, Hans Georg, s Andreas, 59
Waldhauer, Jacob Caspar, vestryman, 191, 192, 270
Waldhauer, Tobias, s Andreas, 59
Waldmann, Hans, Sw dignitary, 24
Wallbaum, Counselor A. H., benefactor, 205, 240
Walliser, Michael, Swabian, 145
Walpole, Horace, British ambassador, 25, 69
Walser, Andreas, planter at German Village, 59, 60
Walser, Anna, Pal, d And, 59
Walser, Barbara, w And, 59
Walser, Johann, Pal, s And, 59, militiaman, 161
Walthauer, Walthour. *See* Waldhauer
Walthour (fr Waldhauer) family in Savannah, 194
Walthour Swamp, 197

Walthourville, town in Georgia, 197
Wannamaker (fr Wannemacher) family in Savannah, 155, 194, 271
Wannemacher, Johann Jacob, Pal, 155
Wassermann, Elisabeth, 120
Wassermann, Ursula, 120
Watson, Joseph, magistrate, 134
Waxter. *See* Wachter
Wayne, Gen. Anthony, 189, 191
Weatherly (Vetterli), Joseph, slave driver, 273
Weaving, 230
Weber, town in Georgia, 197
Weber, Jacob, religious fanatic, 313 (n. 2)
Weberites, followers of Jacob Weber, 203
Weems, Mason L., 184
Wegen, Carl, privy counselor, 240
Weidmann, Adam, Whig, 180
Weidmann, Ludwig, cobbler, 227
Weiher (Weyer), town in Alsace, 5, 145
Weinkauf, Michael, Swab, 145
Weissenbacher, passenger on *Judith*, 105
Weissenbacher, Christoph, 169; will of, 256
Weissengert ? (Wyssengert), passenger on *Judith*, 105
Weisshard, Caspar Schargold, carpenter, 225, 256
Weisshart, Thomas, will of, 256
Welder, 55. *See* Schwarzwälder
Welfare, 207
Weller, Arnold, 91, 97
Weller, Karl, 91
Wentz, Georg Ludwig, recruiter, 68
Werner, Creek Indian, 189
Wernigerode, East German city, 126
Wertsch, Hanna, d J. C., 187
Wertsch, (Hanna) Elisabeth, née Gronau, w J. C., 173
Wertsch, Johann Caspar, entrepreneur, 154, 163, 168, 173–75, 224, 229, 243
Wesley, Charles, br John, 50, 81
Wesley, John, Anglican minister, 27, 39, 41, 43, 50, 51, 101, 114, 127, 225
West Indies, market for lumber, 218

Westphalia, Treaty of, 3, 5, 14, 48
Wharf in Savannah, 218
Wheelwrights, 226. *See also* Hans Krüsy; Georg Mayer; Johann Schick
Whig Government, 177, 179
White, George, 197
White Bluff, site of Dutch settlement, 88, 96, 120, 148
Whitefield, George, evangelist, 81, 82, 114, 117, 118, 121, 127, 131, 134, 153, 159, 175, 205–7, 216, 244, 248, 254, 265, 267, 268
Whitehard. *See* Weisshard
Whitemarsh Island, east of Savannah, 154
Whooping cough. *See* Diseases
Wideman (fr Weidmann) family in Savannah, 194
Wiesenbacher. *See* Weissenbacher
Williamson, Robert, leader of Malcontents, 132
Wills, 255
Wilmington Island, east of Savannah, 154
Winckler, Andreas, Pal in Purysburg, 33
Winckler, Jacob, Sw, 33, 166
Winckler, Ludwig, militiaman, 166
Winckler, Nikolaus, militiaman, 166
Wine, 220–21
Winkel, Georg, Swab, 151
Winkler family in Savannah, 194
Wisenbaker (fr Weissenbacher), South Georgia family, 194; Savannah family, 194
Wissenbach Regiment, Hessian unit, 188
Wollf, Christian, 204
Wöllworth Regiment, Hessian unit, 188, 191
Wood, Betty, 273
Woodruff, taken by Spaniards, 131
Worms, city on Rhine, 4, 68
Wormsloe, Noble Jones's plantation, 155
Wragg, Samuel, Charleston merchant, 70, 113
Wright, Gov. James, 164, 176, 177, 179, 188, 189, 192, 230

Württemberg, German Duchy, 3, 13, 30, 138, 139, 141, 150, 152
Württemberg, Prince of. *See* Carl Rudolf
Württembergers, 30–32, 75, 82, 105. *See also* Swabians
Wüst, Matthias, Pal, 104, 105
Wüst, Matthias, Swab, 135

Yellow fever. *See* Diseases
Yemassee Indians. *See* Indians, Spanish
Yoakley, Capt. John, master of the *James*, 46, 47
Yodels, 250
Young. *See* Jung
Youngblood (fr Jungblüth), family in Savannah, 194
Yowel (Joel), German Jew in Savannah, 85

Zant, Bartholomäus, Sw, 119, 207
Zeagler (fr Ziegler) family in Savannah, 194
Zeigler, town in Georgia, 197
Zeisberger, David, Moravian, 51, 52
Zettler, Daniel, lieutenant, 179, 180, 310 (n. 34)
Zettler, Elisabetha Catharina, née Kieffer, w Matthias, 127
Zettler, Matthias, Salz, Whig, 166, 180, 226, 270, 276; will of, 256
Zettler, Nathaniel, Whig, 180
Zettler family in Savannah, 194
Ziegenhagen, Friedrich Michael, royal chaplain, 43, 179, 252, 267
Ziegler, Lucas, blacksmith, 228
Ziegler family in Savannah, 194
Zimmerebner, Ruprecht, Salz, miller, 217
Zinn, Jacob, Whig, 180
Zinzendorf, Nikolaus Ludwig von, leader of Moravians, 49, 51–53, 124
Zion Church, 205
Zipperer, Peter, Swab, will of, 256
Zipperer family in Savannah, 194
Zittrauer, Ernst, Whig, 179
Zittrauer, Margaretha, 232

Zittrauer, Paul, carpenter, 225
Zittrauer, Ruprecht, slave driver, 273, 279
Zittrauer family in Savannah, 194
Zoberbiller. *See* Zouberbuhler
Zoller, Balthasar, Pal, 129, 136, 139, 168
Zophi, Matthias, slave driver, 273
Zorn, Margaretha, passenger on *Judith*, 105
Zouberbuhler, Bartholomäus, Sw minister, 29, 105–9, 137, 145, 156, 256, 299 (n. 108)
Zouberbuhler, Sebastian, br of Bart, 29, 106, 108
Zuberbiller, Zuberbuhler. *See* Zouberbuhler
Zübli, Ambrosius, Sw, 101, 119, 129, 133
Zübli, David, Purysburg planter, 100, 101, 119

Zübli, Johann Jacob, Sw, 101, 119, 129, 133
Zubly (Zübli), Johann Joachim, Sw minister, s David, 12, 100–102, 106–9, 112, 119, 125, 145, 156, 164, 176, 198, 245, 272
Zubly's Ferry, 182
Zufrieden, misunderstood word, 45
Zurich, Sw city, mandates against emigration, 24–25, 150
Zwiffler, Andreas, Hungarian druggist, 119, 129, 169, 233, 236, 238
Zwingli, Ulrich (Huldrych), Sw reformer, 4, 22